The Cultural Life of the Early Polyphonic Mass

The "cyclic" polyphonic Mass has long been seen as the preeminent musical genre of the late Middle Ages, spawning some of the most impressive and engrossing musical edifices of the period. Modern study of these compositions has greatly enhanced our appreciation of their construction and aesthetic appeal. Yet close consideration of their meaning – cultural, social, spiritual, personal – for their composers and original users has begun only much more recently. This book considers the genre both as an expression of the needs of the society in which it arose and as a fulfillment of aesthetic priorities that arose in the wake of the Enlightenment. From this dual perspective, it aims to enhance both our appreciation of the genre for today's world, and our awareness of what it is that makes any cultural artefact endure: its susceptibility to fulfill the different evaluative criteria, and social needs, of different times.

ANDREW KIRKMAN is Associate Professor of Music at Mason Gross School of the Arts, Rutgers University, New Jersey, where he teaches on a broad range of historical topics. His research centers on sacred music of the fifteenth century, and he has published and lectured widely on English and Continental music of the period, including the music of Du Fay, Ockeghem, Walter Frye, and John Bedyngham. He is also very active as a violinist and conductor of vocal and instrumental ensembles, including the award-winning Binchois Consort, with which he has recorded eight CDs on the Hyperion label.

The Cultural Life of the Early Polyphonic Mass

Medieval Context to Modern Revival

ANDREW KIRKMAN

CAMBRIDGE
UNIVERSITY PRESS

CAMBRIDGE UNIVERSITY PRESS
Cambridge, New York, Melbourne, Madrid, Cape Town,
Singapore, São Paulo, Delhi, Tokyo, Mexico City

Cambridge University Press
32 Avenue of the Americas, New York NY 10013-2473, USA

Published in the United States of America by Cambridge University Press, New York

www.cambridge.org
Information on this title: www.cambridge.org/9780521114127

First published 2010

Printed in the United Kingdom at the University Press, Cambridge

A catalogue record for this publication is available from the British Library

Library of Congress Cataloguing in Publication Data
Kirkman, Andrew, 1961–
  The cultural life of the early polyphonic Mass : medieval context to modern
  revival / Andrew Kirkman.
      p. cm.
  Includes bibliographical references and index.
  ISBN 978-0-521-11412-7 (hardback) 1. Mass (Music)–15th century.
  2. Music–Social aspects–15th century. I. Title.
  ML3088.K56 2010
  782.32'31284–dc22
  2010000056
ISBN 978-0-521-11412-7 Hardback

#456170299

for Philip

Contents

Illustrations

Preface

The musical form of the Mass is the noblest fruit of the bond, rich with blessings, that, for nigh on two thousand years, has bound together liturgy and art. Musical interests and strivings alone could never have brought this about; outside the frame of the liturgy it would have occurred to no artist to link together texts like those of the Mass. The liturgy created this, but artists built, from the loosely juxtaposed pieces, an inwardly linked, cyclic form, the vessel for their most brilliant inspirations.[1]

Now approaching its centenary, Peter Wagner's *Geschichte der Messe* (billed as "Part 1") remains the only book to address the early history of the musical Mass in its entirety. The reason for this seems clear enough from the development of Mass scholarship since: as interest in the music, stimulated by scholars such as Wagner, has grown, the field has become too large, too ramified to be brought within the frame of any single monograph. That scholarship has grown out of a conviction, forged by musicology's pioneers, in the integral musical Mass setting as the forum for inspired inventions by original creative minds – "the vessel for their most brilliant inspirations."

Conviction in the message embodied in that phrase of the quotation above, from the foreword to Wagner's book, has borne spectacular fruit. Yet the implications of the larger context of his remark have begun to be addressed only much more recently. The past few years have seen the appearance of a range of studies associating pieces with individuals or occasions, or relating them to local liturgical practices on the basis of choice and application of chant.[2] Still others have offered more culturally grounded explanations of the forms of particular works on the basis of hidden symbolic or arcane programs, in terms of analogies with other cultural manifestations of the societies in question, as reflections of the specific career patterns of composers, and so on.[3] Yet for most of the modern history of interest in the polyphonic Mass, wonderment at the sheer fecundity of its musical invention has given the field such impetus and momentum that scholarship has seldom felt the need to enquire after the cultural circumstances that fostered the particular forms it took. It was enough, simply, that the music existed, that it could still, after half a millennium, provide aesthetic pleasure and the motivation, as a consequence, to investigate the material source of that pleasure.

The remarkable state of affairs, so particularly characteristic of Western civilization, whereby products of a distant culture can offer such aesthetic and intellectual fulfillment to modern perceptions (the motivation, in the end, behind this study) provides the focus of Part 1 of this book. Here I compare the evaluative criteria, beginning in the late eighteenth century, of modern scholarship (the subject of Chapter 1) with contemporary views of the polyphonic Mass – gleaned from the evidence of theory, music manuscripts and other written records (Chapter 2). My first question, then, is what drove people to revive this music for modern ears and eyes? What was it about it with which they identified, and what was the nature of their appreciation? What criteria, as a consequence, gave rise to the intellectual tools that allow us today to appreciate the repertory in the ways we do? By contrast, how, as far as we can determine, were fifteenth- and early sixteenth-century Mass compositions appreciated by their original users? Which among their features were particularly prized? Were certain kinds of constructions valued over others? As I will outline, the answers to these questions arise, as they must, from the particular needs and proclivities of the very different societies in which interest in the polyphonic Mass has been cultivated.

Part 2 of the book shifts the enquiry to the nature of the polyphonic music used in the Mass. In particular it addresses the function of the cantus firmus, a melody typically borrowed from outside the traditional chants of the Mass (and often from outside the whole repertory of liturgical chant) and laid out in the tenor – and increasingly in other voices as well – within each section of the new work. On both specific and general levels, construction on a cantus firmus offered, in the time of its most intense cultivation, signal advantages with regard to the function of the ritual of Mass: first, through the emblem of an individually chosen melody, it particularized the supplication to the Real Presence brought forth in the ritual within which it was embedded; and by imbuing, through its layout in each of the five sections of the Mass Ordinary, almost the entire course of the rite, it also afforded a uniquely specified expression of what had increasingly come to be seen as the unified message of Mass. But what gave rise to the specific choices of melody, and why, in particular, were secular pieces co-opted for use, in this manner, in the most sacred of settings? Chapter 3 introduces the issue, combining previous scholarship with new observations to enquire after the choices of particular songs as Mass cantus firmi: why did those who supported the composition and performance of polyphonic Masses, who were anxious for their posthumous welfare, foster works based on these particular melodies, and how were the new compositions shaped to give point to the supplications of earthly souls? Chapters 4 and 5 develop the resulting observations in two case studies in which, on account of the importance and sheer quantity of the works concerned, they emerge with particular prominence: the Masses on *Caput* and *L'homme armé*. Chapter 6 returns to a broader field of vision to consider the possible meanings, and surprising range, of incursions into the Mass by secular songs, not just as cantus firmi, but also in their naked, original forms.

The template of the cantus firmus Mass afforded a structure, combining local detail with unprecedented breadth, which gave rise to some of the most sophisticated musical edifices of its day. But however individual the composers of polyphonic Masses may have been, however gifted and celebrated in their own time, they could only have expressed that individuality within the confines of the worldview and practices in which they were steeped, and which were all they knew.[4] The polyphonic Mass had a function, and a powerful one, in the central and defining ritual of the church, and, by extension, of society generally.[5] Meaning arises from the circumstances in which a phenomenon is used and which give it life for its users, whether those users are from its own time and culture or another one.[6] But beyond even that, such meaning is always and essentially situated much more broadly within the larger profiles of society, its political and social realities and range of values, its intellectual and existential sense of itself.

The final part of the book places the polyphonic Mass in the context without which, as expressed by Wagner in the above quotation, it could never have assumed the form it did: that of the greater entity of Mass which it served and whose needs it articulated and enhanced. Chapter 7 outlines how, through a liturgical streamlining effected in the thirteenth century, to a large degree through the efforts of the Franciscans, the unchanging, "Ordinary" movements of the Mass ritual were thrown into the particular relief that allowed the polyphonic cyclic Mass to come into being. Broadening the lens, Chapter 8 examines the role of polyphonic music in the larger counterpoint, visual as well as sonic, of Mass. The most important component in that counterpoint, to which all others related and from which they derived their deepest meaning, was the transubstantiation of the host into the actual body of Christ, as revealed to the people in the elevation. This key moment of grace bestowed great spiritual power, and the potential for accelerated advancement, after death, to heaven. The particular structure and use of the polyphonic Mass were driven, I propose, by desire to particularize, and maximize, that advantage.

Of course contextual awareness too needs its sense of proportion: it is, after all, the particularity of a material phenomenon, its very physical morphology, that allows us to perceive in it a sense of intrinsic – and therefore inalienable – worth. To allow it to blend too much into the circumstances that permitted it to come into being might be to run the risk of losing sight of our reasons for caring about it, for wanting to appreciate it more deeply, in the first place. But to care about such a phenomenon is also, for us, to care about its creators, their reality, their hopes and fears, the world they inhabited and whose needs that phenomenon addressed. Appreciation of the cultural remnants of ages past was nurtured, after all, by conviction in the creative originality of those who fashioned them, seen as "ideal" representatives, and indeed embodiments, of their times. Thus connections – real or assumed – between composition, composer and composer's world were built into our modern models of appreciation from the start.

Yet such connections seem newly relevant today, as the experience of ever more cultures, ever more diverse musics, seems implicitly to call into question what once seemed to be the eternal cultural touchstones of the Western musical canon and its embodiments in the modern formal concert experience and its recorded progeny. The change of yesterday's eternal verities into today's cultural contingencies seems to invite us to seek new ways of experiencing musics not just from other cultures, but also from earlier phases of our own. To allow modern strategies of appreciation to become joined and modified by others is ultimately, then, greatly to enrich our wonderment at the polyphonic Mass. At the same time, it can sharpen our awareness of what it is that makes any cultural artifact endure: its susceptibility to fulfill the different evaluative criteria, and social needs, of different times.

This study has accrued numerous debts during its long gestation. I have benefited greatly from the opportunity to present parts of my research at conferences and at university colloquia in the United States and Great Britain, and from the comments those occasions engendered. I would like to acknowledge with gratitude those friends and colleagues who organized the latter. Parts of Chapters 3 and 6 were presented at the Eastman School of Music, the Ohio State University at Columbus, the University of North Carolina at Chapel Hill, Southampton University, King's College, London, Bangor University, All Souls College, Oxford and York University. I would like to thank Patrick Macey, Graeme Boone, James Haar and John Nadas, Mark Everist and Jeanice Brooks, Michael Fend and Daniel Leech-Wilkinson, Christian Leitmeir, Margaret Bent, and John Potter and

Jonathan Wainwright, respectively, for kindly arranging these events, for their feedback on the ideas presented, and for their generous hospitality. In addition to numerous conference outings, versions of Chapter 5 were presented at Princeton and Durham universities. Parts of Chapter 4 were presented at the Graduate Student Colloquia series at Oxford University.

It is hard to imagine this work without the generous assistance and advice I have received on its various chapters. First, thanks are due to the American Musicological Society for permission to reuse, in chapters 1 and 2, material from my article "The Invention of the Cyclic Mass" (*Journal of the American Musicological Society* 54/1 (Spring, 2001); many colleagues, named in that article, contributed to the growth and development of the ideas presented there. I would like to thank Graeme Boone for valuable comments on earlier versions of chapters 3 and 8, Christopher Reynolds for advice and suggestions regarding Chapter 3, and John Harper and Magnus Williamson for their readings of Chapter 4. For comments on various versions of Chapter 5 I am grateful to John Harper, Barbara Haggh Huglo, Patrick Macey, David Marsh and Joshua Rifkin. Chapters 7 and 8 benefited greatly from the expertise of John Caldwell, Barbara Haggh Huglo and Michel Huglo, and particularly John Harper, whose extraordinary generosity – at various stages – in close readings and suggestion (and provision) of materials has transformed earlier drafts beyond recognition. My friend Rob Wegman has been a source of valuable information used in Chapter 6 and of much-appreciated intellectual, and psychological, support. I am grateful to David Marsh for assistance with the translations in Appendix 3 and to Mary Lewis for the kind loan of her microfilm of RISM 1552. My wife Amy Brosius was a huge help in the task of compiling the index. Pat Harper proved a good-humored and unfailingly helpful copy-editor. I wish to proffer my grateful thanks to Rebecca Jones, Rosina Di Marzo and particularly Victoria Cooper of Cambridge University Press, who have been models of kindness, support, advice and collegiality, and to their anonymous readers, whose feedback generated substantial and valuable reworkings. But my greatest debt is to my friend and colleague Philip Weller: it is impossible for me to imagine what this book could have looked like without Philip's detailed comments on chapters (in numerous redactions), and without his endless fund of ideas and far-ranging discussion over many years. I dedicate the finished work to him in gratitude and friendship.

Abbreviated manuscript titles

Aosta Manuscript	Aosta, Biblioteca del Seminario Maggiore, MS A1 D 19
Bologna Q15	Bologna, Civico Museo Bibliografico Musicale, MS Q15
Bologna Q16	Bologna, Civico Museo Bibliografico Musicale, MS Q16
Cambrai 1328	Cambrai, Bibliothèque Municipale, MS B. 1328 (1176)
Cappella Sistina 14 etc.	Rome, Biblioteca Apostolica Vaticana, MSS 14, 22, 51, 63
Chigi Codex	Rome, Biblioteca Apostolica Vaticana, MS, Chigi VIII.234
Ivrea Codex	Ivrea, Biblioteca Capitolare, MS 115
Lucca Codex	Lucca, Archivio di Stato, MS 238
Naples Manuscript	Naples, Biblioteca Nazionale, MS VI. E. 40
Occo Codex	Brussels, Koninklijke Bibliotheek, MS IV. 922
Old Hall	London, British Library, Add. MS 57950
San Pietro B80	Rome, Biblioteca Apostolica Vaticana, MS San Pietro B80
Strahov Manuscript	Prague, Museum of Czech Literature, Strahov Library, D.G. IV. 47
Trémouïlle Manuscript	Paris, Bibliothèque Nationale, nouvelle acquisition française, MS 23190
Trent 88 etc.	Trento, Castello del Buon Consiglio, MSS 88, 89, 90, 92
Trent 93	Trento, Biblioteca Capitolaria/Museo Diocesano, MS BL
Verona 756 etc.	Verona, Biblioteca Capitolare, MSS 756, 761
Vienna 1783	Vienna, Österreichische Nationalbibliothek, MS 1783

PART I

The status of the early polyphonic Mass

1 | Enlightenment and beyond

> It takes a very bold and independent mind to conceive the idea that the invariable parts of the Mass should be composed not as separate items, but as a set of five musically coherent compositions. In the latter case the means of unification are provided by the composer, not the liturgy. This idea, which is the historical premise of the cyclic Ordinary, betrays the weakening of purely liturgical consideration and the strengthening of essentially aesthetic concepts. The "absolute" work of art begins to encroach on liturgical function. We discover here the typical Renaissance attitude – and it is indeed the Renaissance philosophy of art that furnishes the spiritual background to the cyclic Mass. The beginnings of the Mass cycle coincide with the beginnings of the musical Renaissance.
>
> It is therefore hardly surprising that the decisive turn in the development of the cyclic Mass occurred only in the early fifteenth century. At this time the first attempts are made to unify the movements of the Ordinary by means of the same musical material.[1]

Now more than half a century old, Bukofzer's statement remains the classic evaluation of the "cyclic" polyphonic Mass as masterwork. Located in one of the most influential articles in the history of the discipline, it has gained still broader currency in refractions through the standard textbooks which have shaped the image of the Mass for generations of students.

Its authority notwithstanding, aspects of this position have been challenged almost since it was articulated. Early challenges mostly grew out of attempts to situate the polyphonic Mass in its liturgical context. This began when, in the 1950s, scholars noticed the ordering of sections of the Ordinary into sets, a phenomenon hitherto thought to have originated in the context of polyphony, in fourteenth-century chant Kyriales.[2] This trend culminated in 1972 in Geoffrey Chew's observation that such groupings can be dated back at least as far as the publication of the Franciscan Gradual of 1251. Quoting the above passage directly, Chew noted that we need no longer necessarily seek, as Bukofzer had done, to explain the phenomenon of sets of Ordinary sections by appeal to artistic or aesthetic considerations: they had arisen in chant books about a century before the earliest

surviving polyphonic grouping.[3] More recent years have witnessed a proliferation of studies in which authors, rather than focusing on the "internal"
characteristics of the Mass *per se*, have sought instead to locate individual
Masses and other fifteenth-century works in the particular sets of "external"
circumstances that gave rise to their composition, structure and usage.[4]

Implicitly challenged on various fronts, however, the central message of
the Bukofzer quotation has never been subjected to a detailed critique. Part
of the reason for this is surely its very familiarity, particularly in the less
ideologically charged language through which its message has been filtered
into textbooks. But that familiarity and acceptability are rooted in an epistemological precondition that made Bukofzer's statement possible in the
first place: a conviction in the historical importance of the "cyclic" Mass
as an epoch-making development in Western music. To call into question
Bukofzer's position, the expression of an intellectual struggle that is inte-
grally bound up with the historiography of modern musicology itself, might
implicitly have been seen to question the historical status of the cyclic Mass,
and, implicitly, the scholarship that has taken that status as its premise.

My concern here is not with any perceived merits or otherwise of the
view summed up in the Bukofzer quotation. It is rather to enquire after its
origins and to consider how modern evaluations of the Mass might relate,
or not relate, to those of the period of its currency. Why, for example, has
the Mass based on a cantus firmus been singled out as historically and artistically superior not just to songs and motets, but to Masses not based on
recurring musical material? Why have we traditionally given it a higher
status than, say, freely composed Masses, Masses (including many Marian
Masses) based on series of chant antecedents, scribal Mass "compilations,"
plenary Masses, Proper cycles, and so on? On what basis do we view the
polyphonic Mass as a development of crucial historical importance? What
is the origin of our view of it as a watershed in the emergence of "unified" or
"cyclic" form? What alternatives might there be to this received view of its
historical status? And how, finally, might considerations thrown up by these
questions affect the way we construct the history of music in the fifteenth
and sixteenth centuries?

Enlightenment invention

The perspective encapsulated in the quotation from Bukofzer represents
the culmination of a long line of development.[5] This began not in the fifteenth century, however, but in the late eighteenth, in the cultural context

of the European Enlightenment, the environment in which – along with the notions of the aesthetic and the intrinsically valuable "work of art" – modern interest in early Western musical repertories was born. It culminated only in the early twentieth century, when, in what remains the only book-length study concerned solely with the history of the polyphonic Mass, Peter Wagner first applied to the Mass the notion of "cyclicity."[6]

The Enlightenment conviction in the value of collective cultural memory, seen as essential to civilization, gave historical enquiry in the late eighteenth century an unprecedented impetus. Driven as it was by a striving for self-discovery, though, that history was shaped directly in the Enlightenment's own image: thus the self-realization of the individual, from an Enlightenment perspective humanity's greatest goal, became the chief model for enquiries into the past. Based on an unshakable faith in the eternal durability of the human spirit, such enquiries as those of Burney and Forkel[7] focused on identifying great artists from the past as precursors of the geniuses identified in the present, in Bukofzer's words "bold and independent minds" capable of emancipating art from reliance on anything other than the unfettered imagination of the individual creator.[8] Since the mark of such genius had come to be seen to be the ability to produce works of art fashioned purely for the contemplation of beauty, the quest was on for similarly immutable objects to stand as embodiments of the achievements of the geniuses of the past. Thus the landmarks of the past became functions of those of the present, stages on the path of unending progress via which, in its turn, the present would also be superseded. As this model took shape in music history in the form of the achievements of a succession of generations each represented by an outstanding great man, so the rediscovery of increasingly early vestiges of the Western tradition gave the self-image of the post-Enlightenment West ever greater historical depth.

The early limits of the progress of rediscovery were defined by availability: of actual music, of the means to decipher it, and of information concerning it. As earlier repertories were recovered, so the aesthetic canonization of music was pushed back into ever earlier "phases" of music history. For our purposes the crucial point in this process was reached, as we will see, in the mid nineteenth century, with the incorporation into the canon of the generation of Du Fay, the first generation of composers to concern itself with the Mass based on a cantus firmus.

For Burney and Forkel, reliant as they were on Petrucci prints and available sixteenth-century theorists such as Glarean,[9] the earliest composer whose music was known in any depth was Josquin.[10] A representative, like his modern counterparts, of the eternal durability of human genius,

Josquin possessed, for the earliest music historians, a power of vision that allowed him to some extent to transcend the limitations perceived in the prevailing style of his times. Yet for all that, his music engendered little sympathy: unfamiliar and alien to late eighteenth-century ears, it was the target of more specific prejudice for its use of abstractly constructed compositional techniques, procedures antipathetic to the spirit of free expression so prized in the late eighteenth and early nineteenth centuries. Denigrated for the same reasons was the presence in cantus firmus Masses of externally borrowed tenors, the use of which – for these authors and still to some extent even, in the 1860s, for Ambros – was evidence of a "poverty of invention."[11] This was the original basis for the long-standing tendency, beginning with Burney and extending well into the twentieth century, to place higher value on Josquin's motets – composed as they frequently are without recourse to borrowed material – than his Masses, constructed on preexistent compositions. The new emphasis on pieces of music as self-contained, integrated "works" brought with it also the beginning of the tendency – first expressed by Forkel in 1801 and still familiar today – to criticize medieval theory for saying nothing about principles of large-scale musical construction.[12]

The next pioneer in the recovery of early repertories, Giuseppe Baini, was no more sympathetic to them than Burney and Forkel had been. Indeed, motivated as he was by the desire to demonstrate that Palestrina's achievement had been a huge advance over that of his forebears, Baini's judgment – in his celebrated *Memorie storico-critiche della vita e delle opere di Giovanni Pierluigi da Palestrina*[13] – of the precursors of his idol was even harsher than that of his predecessors. Giving vent to the same prejudice against overtly "constructivist" musical practices, Baini similarly inveighs against borrowed tenors, casting the cantus firmi of Masses by Du Fay and his generation as "boring tenors in the longest note values." He considers the Masses by Du Fay that he has seen – *Ecce ancilla domini*, *L'homme armé* and *Se la face ay pale* – to be fair achievements for their time, and superior to contemporary Masses, yet finds them sorely wanting by the standards of his own day. Misled by an erroneous interpretation of papal records that led him to conclude that Du Fay had been active in the late fourteenth century, Baini similarly misdated the Masses by Du Fay and others that he found in what are now the early Cappella Sistina manuscripts, thus bequeathing to music history a confusion that was to remain unresolved for more than fifty years.[14] Yet as the first modern commentary on Masses by Du Fay, Ockeghem and others, Baini's study stands as a watershed in the recovery of early cyclic Masses, and one that had considerable impact on his – particularly German-speaking – immediate successors. In perhaps his most signal contribution to the history of the music of this era, Baini was also the first modern music historian to construct the history of music before Palestrina in terms of a succession of progressively advancing "epochs" each headed by a representative "genius." But his future impact in this arena was channeled chiefly through his enormous influence on the *Geschichte*, published only six years later, of Raphael Georg Kiesewetter.[15]

Taking his cue from the rediscovery by Baini of the music – chiefly the Masses – of Du Fay, Ockeghem and their contemporaries, and following the same succession of musical "epochs" led by Du Fay, Ockeghem and Josquin, Kiesewetter is nonetheless considerably more positive than his predecessor in his musical judgments. In his hands, the boundaries of the Western musical canon are permitted to extend back beyond even the music of Josquin to embrace also that of Ockeghem. Even Du Fay, in a revolutionary judgment for its time, is cast as the architect of "a perfectly finished or cultivated art." Kiesewetter, like Baini, bases his conclusions on examples drawn from Masses in what are now the Cappella Sistina manuscripts, apparently the only music by Du Fay then known. Excerpts from his transcriptions of the Masses on *Ecce ancilla domini*, *L'homme armé* and *Se la face ay pale* – the first music by Du Fay to appear in print – occur, along with other pieces by Adam de la Halle, Machaut, Landini, Eloy d'Amerval, Ockeghem and Josquin, as an appendix to his history. Newly elevated as works that could be heard "without giving offence, but even communicating pleasure,"[16] Du Fay's Masses were, however, yet to be fully admitted into the canon. Notwithstanding his newly positive appraisal of Du Fay, it is to Ockeghem (distinguished by "great superiority over his celebrated predecessor") that Kiesewetter ascribes "the real foundation of that fame which the composers of the Netherlands enjoyed throughout the whole civilized world in the epochs that immediately follow." While Du Fay and his contemporaries were "illustrious as predecessors," it was Ockeghem who "must be regarded as the founder of all schools, from his own to the present age."[17]

Hegelian transformation

The exegetic force of the Enlightenment model of progress was revolutionized through assimilation, in the mid nineteenth century, into the totalizing system of Hegelian metaphysics. In a refinement of Enlightenment models, artworks became for Hegel – in common with all other manifestations of society – expressions of the prevailing *Zeitgeist*. At the same time they were also, like all other aspects of the particular *Zeitgeist* in which they were embedded, bound up in the ongoing process of historical dialectic whereby each age must logically constitute an advance over its predecessor. Individual styles and composers thus became part of the expression of the "spirit of the age," though that spirit was seen to achieve its optimal distillation in the work of particularly gifted individuals, figures who were able, through the advanced state of their art, to be at the same time perfect embodiments of their own time and, through their innovations, instrumental in the progress to the next stage. Thus the works of these individuals were caught up in the dialectical process which, for Hegel, bound both logic and history in all their manifestations. Such works were at one and the same time "thesis," through their optimal instantiation of the prevailing *Geist*, and "antithesis," through the creative irritancy of genius. They were therefore both perfect embodiments of the present and harbingers of things to come, pointing the way ultimately to a future synthesis to be crystalized by the representative figure of the next generation. The Hegelian historical model finds its most direct musical instantiation in the *Geschichte der Musik* of 1851 by Franz Brendel, the most widely promulgated and perhaps most influential music history of the mid nineteenth century.[18]

Brendel, like Baini before him, sees the "period of the Netherlanders" chiefly as a preparation for better things to come, a *Vorgeschichte* for the main historical eras that, as for Hegel, culminate in the "great movements" of the Reformation and Counter-Reformation. While for Hegel the fifteenth century had been "the dawn, the harbinger of a new fine day after the long, fateful and terrible night of the Middle Ages,"[19] for Brendel likewise it witnessed "the dawn of art music: daybreak is anticipated; it is perceptible in isolated appearances, but one has not yet emerged out of the dawn" (*Geschichte*, 29). Thus although his historical narrative borrows directly – sometimes almost word for word – from Kiesewetter, Brendel is considerably less charitable in his judgments of the music of the fifteenth century, motivated as he is to cast it as inferior to that of the "sublime" ("erhaben") and "beautiful" ("schön") phases that were to succeed it.

Yet in his characterization, again profoundly Hegelian, of music's interaction with the church, Brendel was an important harbinger of future perspectives on the cyclic Mass, as embodied, for instance, in the quotations from Bukofzer at the beginning of this chapter. From Brendel's perspective, the role of the church for music – as for art generally for Hegel – was in raising it from a bare and unsophisticated "natural" state to the more elevated realm of "the Spirit." Thus elevated by its interaction with the divine (Brendel's "sublime" phase), music was able to carry that divinity within it when it went out again into the secular world (his "beautiful" phase).[20] In a typically dramatic formulation, Brendel further describes how "scarcely matured, scarcely evolved to a higher, self-sufficient existence, [art] forsook the halls of the temple and rushed out into the world."[21] This departure from the church helps to explain why, in the end, music's "beautiful" phase is ranked above its "sublime" phase: the integrity of the ideal work of art, for Brendel, can only be weakened by a need to fulfill external functions, even those of the church.[22] Thus although raised to its proper status through its interaction with religion, art was ultimately destined to stand on its own, combining its divine and material elements in a self-contained and self-substantiating "organic" union. Here we can see the beginnings of the rationale through which such a development as the Mass based on an externally borrowed cantus firmus came to be seen as an expression of the composer as an individualist striking out from the confines of the church into the realm of free "artistic" expression.

Built on a model of forward dynamism, the notion of dialectical advancement gave a particular urgency to the rediscovery and reevaluation of earlier "phases" in musical history. Conviction that the achievements of each age were built incrementally on those which preceded them pushed the frame of aesthetic evaluation further and further back as historians strove to identify in the work of previous generations the qualities which had enabled the achievements they perceived in those already familiar. As increasingly early vestiges of Western musical history were rediscovered, so the phases already known acquired ever loftier status as advances on those being unearthed. At the same time, music's *Vorgeschichte* – that murky, unfamiliar period when, it was assumed, music was in its most rudimentary state – was pushed back further in time with the discoveries of each new generation of historians. For the perception of the cyclic Mass – and, more particularly, the cantus firmus Mass – this process reached a crucial point in the 1860s, with the publication of what is surely the greatest landmark in the rediscovery of late medieval music: the *Geschichte der Musik* of August Wilhelm Ambros.[23]

Ambros and the nineteenth-century invention of the cyclic Mass

Given the time and cultural milieu of its writing, the profoundly Hegelian stance of Ambros's history is probably its least surprising aspect.[24] Of special interest here, though, is the fact that its Hegelianism is filtered in a number of important respects through Jacob Burckhardt. The Hegelian frame of Burckhardt's *Die Kultur der Renaissance in Italien* – appearing, in 1860, just a few years before Ambros's *Geschichte* – has been well known at least since Gombrich's exposition of 1969.[25] In its central notion of a cultural and artistic Renaissance, Burckhardt's study was to have a powerful, if confusing, effect on Ambros's history, and, in turn, on the future perception of the cyclic Mass. While, as we shall see, Ambros himself never proposed that the "New Era" he saw as beginning in music in the fifteenth century constituted a "Renaissance," he was certainly construed to have done so by later writers. With the crystalization, in later historical writing, of the notion of a musical Renaissance beginning in the fifteenth century, the most characteristic expression of that era came to be seen to be the cyclic Mass, and, in particular, the Mass based on a cantus firmus, a perspective summed up in the quotation from Bukofzer cited above.

The high profile which accrued to the Mass from this time on was due to a particularly felicitous convergence of circumstances. The first of these concerned the point that had been reached in the process of the "discovery" of earlier phases in Western musical history. For Ambros the phase which separated music's "pre-history" from its "true" expression was that of the generation of Du Fay – significantly the earliest generation of Continental composers to concern itself with the cantus firmus Mass. It is easy to perceive how the Mass subsequently came to be seen as a particularly potent emblem of the "Renaissance" in music: first, its timing was impeccable, once, in the wake of Ambros's history, the beginning of the musical "Renaissance" had been fixed in the early–mid fifteenth century; second, its basis in a preexistent composition, chosen apparently by the composer rather than out of considerations of liturgical appropriateness, was cited repeatedly, beginning with Brendel, as early evidence of the "emancipation" of the artist from the "constraints" of his working environment; and, third, as the earliest large-scale multipartite form in Western musical history it was seen as the creative forum for the most sophisticated and ambitious structures and hence the greatest "works of art" of its era, an assessment which drew support, as we shall see in the next chapter, from Tinctoris's definition of the Mass as *cantus magnus*. Perhaps most important, though, is the way in which this form, subsequently to be cast as one of the chief expressions of the "Renaissance," was made to embrace another Hegelian notion which was applied to music for the first time by Ambros: that of organic unity.

Relentless in its linkage of general and particular, the unity which informed the various expressions of the prevailing historical *Geist* was seen, particularly at the hands of such Hegelian epigones as Brendel, to reveal itself at the level of microcosm in the organic unity of its individual instances.[26] While the progression of history was a manifestation of dialectic played out in time, artworks revealed its workings on a logical plane. From a Hegelian perspective, then, a "beautiful" work of art must not only be expressive of the spirit of its time; it must also be organically unified.[27] With its use of common borrowed material running through the parts of a multipiece composition that, when strung together, can last more than half an hour in performance, it is clear how the cyclic Mass came to be seen as a particularly sophisticated embodiment of this principle, in Bukofzer's words "a set of five musically coherent" and "unified" compositions. Here for Bukofzer was further evidence, moreover, of "bold and independent minds" providing the musical "means of unification" without recourse to the liturgy.

The same perceived tendency towards a self-conscious, "composerly" attitude to construction was further seen as distancing the cyclic Mass from its "medieval" musical antecedents. Knowledge which might have ascribed similarly elevated attributes to, say, the isorhythmic motet had simply not yet been acquired. Thus while the construction of the cantus firmus Mass accommodated it to the role of Renaissance masterwork with particular ease, the endowment upon it of the lofty historical importance summed up by Bukofzer was due more than anything to historical coincidence.[28] The convergence of the circumstances that enabled that coincidence was, as for so many received views on late medieval music, to a large extent the legacy of Ambros.

Following the advances of Kiesewetter, whose increased knowledge of early repertories had led to his enhanced appreciation of Du Fay and Ockeghem, Ambros's vastly expanded knowledge brought with it further retrograde progress of historical valuation, "recovering" the reputations and enhancing the status of early composers.[29] The most obvious beneficiary was Josquin, who at last acquired a canonic status equal, and in some respects even superior, to that of Palestrina. While his "genius" had never been in doubt, this was really the first time he had been allowed to rub shoulders on the aesthetic pedestal with Palestrina, to whose Apollonian status he was contrasted as a sort of Dionysian counterpart.[30]

Just as the allegedly free choice of Mass cantus firmus came to be seen as evidence of composers emancipating themselves from constraints imposed by the Church,[31] so for Ambros the Holy Rite (*kirchliche Ritus*) within which Josquin's times obliged him to work is seen as an obstacle which his heroism had to surmount in order to free himself, in true Romantic fashion, from reliance on anything other than his own uninhibited genius. In this Ambros echoes the Hegelian views of Brendel and Burckhardt, according to which the new Renaissance spirit of individualism transcended and thus conflicted with the expectations of the Church.[32]

Yet the deeper familiarity that had raised Josquin's status so dramatically also brought with it a much more positive assessment than hitherto of the music of the historical "phases" that preceded him. This again was an inevitable result, with the rediscovery of increasingly early music, of shifting the template of aesthetic evaluation back a historical notch, as Ambros himself was well aware.[33] The most obvious effect of this retrospective progress of evaluation was on the perception of the "First Netherlandish School,"[34] and especially Du Fay, whose activity Ambros – misled like most scholars of his day by the faulty chronology of Baini – dates to the late fourteenth and early fifteenth centuries. In spite of its perceived shortcomings, this, for Ambros, was the first phase of music history to produce a fully developed, written art music and real "artists" rather than simply scholars concerned with music.[35] Tentative and as yet only budding, the music nonetheless displays evidence of an undefined "idealism" that permitted it to produce works "which assume for all time the rank of valid works of art" (II, 453).

In discussing the music of Du Fay, Ambros draws on the Romantic rhetoric which infuses his evaluations of music of all ages and according to which, for the first time, this music was seen to speak directly to the emotions of the modern hearer.[36] He explains how – notwithstanding their perceived inferiority to the music of Palestrina – this art first revealed itself in Du Fay's late Masses:

> works of clarified, pure style, in which inner warmth of feeling and Du Fay's pure sense of beauty are expressed in the most attractive manner. The first Kyrie of the Mass *Se la face* already has something of the "seraphic" trait, like that which – albeit with far richer and much higher development of musical construction – Palestrina's compositions display. One could best characterize individual moments, like the end of the first Kyrie of the Mass *L'homme armé*, with the expression that they are [like] smiling through tears. (II, 496–7)

For Ambros, the quality of Du Fay's music, as of compositions by other composers and indeed of any music worthy of attention, rests to a large degree on its perceived "warmth" and its ability, from his perspective, to portray emotion.[37] As with earlier music historians it is Du Fay's settings of the Mass (in Ambros's words "the greatest and most important tasks for composers" of the era [III, 39]), rather than his (still little-known) works in other genres, which are chosen to receive such an accolade.

Of more lasting importance and of more specific interest here, however, is Ambros's judgment that these works are the first to possess not only "true style" but also "form," in the sense of Hegelian "organic construction."[38] While he does not elaborate on this statement, his more specific observation on Faugues's *Missa L'homme armé* gives at least a hint of the directions such ideas would take in the future. The transposition of the cantus firmus in the Kyrie of this work is, he says, "an indication that the master strove for musical architecture, and was already thinking further than just how to clothe a cantus firmus well or badly with counterpointing voices" (II, 500). For Ambros, such procedures are evidence of the mindset of the self-conscious, independently minded artist as opposed to the mere servant of the church. He thus aligns himself with the Hegelian/Burckhardtian conception of the artist as an individual shaking himself free of the constrictions of the church, a topos which was to become standard, as revealed for example by the above quotations from Bukofzer, in discussion of the music, and particularly the Masses, of fifteenth- and early sixteenth-century composers.

Broached in 1864 in volume II of Ambros's history, these notions were to be expanded on four years later in the introduction to his volume III. Here they become entwined with his complex approach to periodization, to which I will turn shortly. The introduction to this volume is important also for other reasons, however. Among these is its perspective on the "pre-Du Fay era" (albeit factually heavily dependent on Coussemaker),[39] and the general distinction it draws between the generation of Du Fay and those of his predecessors. This was a division which was to prove crucial to the growth of the notion of a musical "Renaissance" and, in turn, to the perception of the "cyclic" Mass.

For Ambros, the thirteenth and fourteenth centuries constituted the period during which music found its way back from the intellectualizing "science" (*Wissenschaft*) of the Middle Ages to the true "art" which for him begins with the "First Netherlandish School," significantly the first of the acknowledged "schools" to occupy itself with the "cyclic" Mass.[40] Revealing, as so frequently, his keen insight into the process whereby familiarity with ever earlier musics pushes aesthetic evaluation further and further back in time, he recognizes how the music of Du Fay's generation – for earlier historians music's "rough first attempts" – has become the "beginnings of true art" as still older repertories have emerged from the murky waters of history.

The change of perspective highlighted by Ambros was of course part of an ongoing process. Thus, some forty years later at the hands of Hugo Riemann, the repertory of the Squarcialupi Codex, which for Ambros had been the object only of historical curiosity, would in turn itself be assimilated into the aesthetic fold.[41] And it was this same process which also, in Ambros's history, extracted Josquin from the "childhood of music" and the role of flawed genius and endowed him with the status of canonic master: as new "discoveries" pushed ever older music up onto dry land, music which had already reached *terra firma* was in turn assimilated ever more securely into the canon.

But the dynamism of this model is anyway implicit in the Hegelian dialectical framework of Ambros's narrative: if history chooses to endow a particular repertory with eternal value, some quality must also be imputed to the antecedents from which it had progressed. This perspective emerges vividly in the exceptionally long view he takes of the progeny of the Tournai Mass:

The whole is still completely barbaric, though unmistakable throughout is the still early and crude formation of exactly the same style which – of course much more highly developed – we encounter again in the older, still black-notated chansons of Du Fay and Binchois, and which again in advancing cultivation led the way directly to the chansons of Ockeghem, Barbireau and further as far as Josquin, Compère and Willaert. (III, 27)

A similarly gradual process led, notwithstanding their remarkable step forward as the first "fully developed art," to the achievement of Du Fay's Masses; thus:

In their pure beauty, the Masses of Du Fay are and remain an endlessly astonishing apparition, even when one considers, as a preliminary development, the Mass of Tournai, which is at least a hundred years older; but to maintain that an ecclesiastical style of this grandeur and purity could develop overnight from the interplay of little song melodies would be nothing less than to affirm a miracle. (III, 27)

Embedded in this model at a deeper philosophical level is the Aristotelian notion, much invoked in Enlightenment theorizing, that all such developments have a natural telos which is predetermined by the particular nature of their content.[42] Drawing comparison with the "thinkers and poets" of the thirteenth and fourteenth centuries whose entire worldview, Ambros suggests, derived from and was permeated with "ecclesiastical doctrine" (*die Kirchenlehre*), he proposes that the "hidden and potential" meaning of plainsong was only truly worked out in its polyphonic "realization," a development he sees as culminating in the achievement of Palestrina. But in explaining the role of the "Netherlands composers" in this process he turns not to such layered and additive "medieval" constructs as commentary or "glossing" but to the Hegelian language of organicism.[43]

Taking issue with Glarean's condemnation of any chant-based composition that is more than the "decorative adjunct" (*schmückende Beigabe*) of a chant melody, preserving the chant in its original sequence and integrity, Ambros observes with approval that the true situation is very different. Far from being constrained by veneration for ancient holy chants, composers

rather manipulated [Gregorian chant] motifs with the most spirited freedom, and it is not difficult to recognize that their own contrapuntal inventions had an altogether different and higher meaning than that of an incidental, "into the bargain" decoration of the tenor, dispensable even in the best of cases ... The more richly and interestingly they formed their counterpoint, the more emphatically it emerges in its independent meaning. (III, 15)

To Ambros, then, the chant was no more than the handmaiden of the polyphonic construct formed around it. No longer just the foundation for the sort of mechanical gloss which he perceived in the music of the earlier "discantors" (*Discantoren*), for the Netherlands composers it served both to liberate the contrapuntal imagination and to guarantee its consistency. Indeed, the source of the preexisting melody, or even whether it was sacred or secular, was to that extent immaterial: what mattered was that it could endow (in the eyes of a German author writing in the middle of the nineteenth century) the finished product with the desired attributes of "organic perfection" and "inner unity":

The most serious and cerebral work of this most especially important epoch for the development of music is founded on this premise: to develop, on the given foundations of Gregorian chant and folksong, polyphony arising out of the most varied conditions, in [the form of] artworks encased in organic perfection and inner unity. (III, 9)

Thus we encounter, for the first time in music history, the notion of organic unity, the Hegelian principle whereby the individual artwork manifests at the level of the particular the systematic nature which at the general level is thought to embrace the universe in all its manifestations.[44] The particular power of the Hegelian system lies in the consistency with which it binds together history, metaphysics and logic under the common principle of dialectic. Thus the unified artwork is one in which contrasting subject matter has been resolved in an ultimate unifying synthesis. Continuing on the same Hegelian track, Ambros turns to the notion of dialectic to explain the process whereby, in his view, the adaptation of a monophonic melody to a polyphonic context can lend coherence to the finished piece:

The simple melody – as it breaks forth in monophonic song out of the innermost depth of the aroused spirit – now changes, in and through polyphony, to a new meaning, and here it places against itself now a second, now a third melody in counterpoint, so that out of the harmonic sounding together of these counterpoints a higher unity arises: thus may polyphony quite rightly be called a dialectical process. (III, 9)[45]

If such perceived characteristics were to receive such high approbation in music generally, how much more impressive would their workings be seen in drawing together the parts of a five-movement multipiece? Thus it is easy to perceive how the advent of complete Mass settings, with their perceived large-scale displays of "coherence," "organicism" and "unity" – attributes of such fundamental value in the post-Hegelian intellectual world to which Ambros belonged – came to be seen as a watershed of crucial importance to the advancement of Western music.

This perspective raises knotty epistemological issues to which I will return; for the moment, though, it will suffice to propose that we should be hesitant in ascribing the development of the composed Mass cycle solely or even principally to a self-conscious, "composerly" striving after new styles and techniques. In truth, the roots of the particular profile which music history has ascribed to the cyclic Mass are to be found less in developments in musical practice itself than in comparisons with the other arts, and, crucially, in the notion of a musical "Renaissance," as this came to be disseminated during Ambros's generation and subsequently.

Ambros and the question of a musical "Renaissance"

Appearing during the 1860s, only a few years after the publication of *Die Kultur der Renaissance in Italien* (1860), Ambros's music history was the first to feel the influence of Jacob Burckhardt, an influence that persists in cultural-historical thought to this day. An *éminence grise* in Ambros's history much as Hegel had been in Brendel's, Burckhardt, even when not mentioned by name, is almost constantly present in spirit.[46] Yet although Burckhardt is clearly the foreground influence on Ambros, behind him looms the unmistakable figure of Hegel. The Hegelian frame of Burckhardt's *Die Kultur der Renaissance in Italien* has already been mentioned, and although the term "Renaissance" had yet to be used in its Burckhardtian sense, the "new spirit" which for Hegel brought the Middle Ages to an end is a Renaissance in all but name.[47] In contrast to the omnipresent Hegel of Brendel's history,[48] though, the Hegel of Ambros's study has sunk more deeply into the epistemological fabric.[49] Oriented by a system in which the "fine" arts are embedded at a higher level in a consistently ordered universe, Burckhardt, Ambros and other cultural historians of the mid nineteenth century were encouraged to search for metaphors through which architecture, sculpture, painting, music and poetry could be seen to be governed by, and expressive of, an all-embracing *Zeitgeist*. Nonetheless, though Ambros's evaluation of the music of the "Netherlands composers" was strongly motivated by this aim, he never – contrary to popular opinion – proposed that it constituted a musical "Renaissance."

In one of the greatest ironies of music history, the deeply influential notion that a musical "Renaissance" began about 1450, though emanating from Ambros, is based on a misreading of him. While deeply concerned with the notion of a musical Renaissance, the only unequivocal "Renaissance" he postulates for music is dated not around 1450 but around 1600, with the rise of monody, for Ambros the most crucial turning point in the history of Western music.[50]

But the confusion is understandable, as can be most clearly seen by reference to the preface to volume II, the source of one of the many inconsistencies that led to the misconstruing of Ambros's "Renaissance" by subsequent writers. Having announced in the preface to volume II that volume IV would be concerned with "the musical Renaissance, the rise of monody, of opera, of the modern system of tonality," Ambros then proceeded to subtitle volume III, a history of the period c.1450–c.1600, "History of music in the age of the Renaissance up to Palestrina." ("Geschichte der Musik im Zeitalter der Renaissance bis zu Palestrina"). These words seem carefully chosen to sidestep the suggestion of a musical Renaissance at this time, alluding rather to the more palpably "Renaissance" currents flowing through other cultural manifestations. Yet this subtitle, dropped from subsequent editions of the volume, was undoubtedly the single most influential factor in the misapprehension of Ambros's view, a misapprehension which was to affirm the period 1450–1600, give or take a decade or two, as the musical "Renaissance" in musicological consciousness from this time forth.

In fact the inconsistency suggested by these titles is symptomatic of an anxiety which is deeply embedded in Ambros's narrative. Its source was the motivation, mentioned above, to integrate music into a Hegelian/ Burckhardtian scheme in which all the arts were temporally linked in the expression of a common cultural essence. The effect of this can be seen throughout Ambros's history, where analogies between music and the other arts, especially painting and sculpture, occur on almost every page. Searching for a music worthy to stand with the "Renaissance" achievements detailed by Burckhardt in literature and the plastic arts, Ambros found it in the music of the "Netherlanders": "Here music joined the ranks of the other arts on an equal footing and could claim to have found the same level of respect" (III, 13). Though more than a century later than what were viewed as the earliest manifestations of the Renaissance in literature and the visual arts, the music of the "Netherlands" composers was still chronologically much closer to them than was monody.[51]

But in any case, such analogizing tendencies could not be pushed much further back for the simple reason that music before Du Fay was still scarcely known. Ambros was certainly more aware of earlier repertories than his predecessors had been. Such repertories included the music of the hitherto unknown Squarcialupi Codex, a source of fourteenth-century Florentine repertory with more genuinely Renaissance pretensions than most. However, it was not until the first decade of the twentieth century that familiarity with Squarcialupi's music was sufficient to allow Hugo Riemann to propose moving the musical Renaissance back as far as 1300;[52] but by then, and in spite of a number of counterclaims since, the notion of a musical Renaissance beginning in the early–mid fifteenth century was too deeply engrained to be effectively challenged.

Pulled in two directions by the Italian background and genuinely "Renaissance" pretensions of monody on the one hand and his need for a Burckhardtian Renaissance "epoch" on the other, Ambros is forced into repeated circumlocutions as he attempts to characterize the music of the mid-fifteenth century as a watershed on a par with those perceived in the other "arts" while at the same time avoiding calling it a "Renaissance":

The fifteenth century, at [one and] the same time the end of the Middle Ages and beginning of the "new era" [*zugleich Abschluss des Mittelalters und Anfang der Neuzeit*], marks out intellectually a particularly exciting moment in history, and precisely in this century there also occurs a most noteworthy development in music. (III, 4)

Ambros's "new era" (*Neuzeit*), held together by an all-embracing Hegelian "Ideal," in fact goes no further than Hegel's "dawn of a new fine day after the ... night of the Middle Ages."[53] Echoing Hegel and foreshadowing count-less similar discussions since, Ambros's "Ideal" embodies a sense of discovery which drove people to seek to grasp the whole extent of the known universe, whether they be engaged in exploration as artists, sea explorers, scientists or in any other forum. Thus:

This entire century has something youthful, with its belief in that Ideal – sought after with endless enthusiasm – which the Renaissance believed to have found in the life and artefacts of the ancient world, [and] with its urge to grasp the whole breadth and content and depth of things. (III, 4)

By contrast, Ambros shows elsewhere a keenness to emphasize the histor-ical progress through which the new era was seen to transform "medieval" modes of expression in a newly relevant fashion. In a particularly virtu-oso narrative manoeuvre, procedures extolled in the laudatory passages quoted above as the instruments of "organic perfection" and "inner unity" are packaged as the revivification of the same structural principles which, only a page earlier, he had cast as directly analogous to elements of "Gothic" scholasticism:

There is indeed still something traceable here and there [in the music of the Netherlanders] which is analogous to the scholasticism – with its hair-splitting and circumlocutory methods [*spitzfindiger, wortkramender Methode*] – by now already superseded by a changed ideology [*Weltanschauung*]. Many large-scale musical sections are directly reminiscent of the intellectual edifices which the scholastic philosopher piled up over theses drawn from the dogmas of the church [*wie es der scholastische Philosoph über irgend eine den Dogmen der Kirche entnommene Thesis aufthürmte*] – [sections] built over a motif in the tenor consisting of a few notes drawn from Gregorian chant, constantly repeated or returning under changed mensurations, on which motif then in the counterpoints the most artful canonic imitations and all possible contrapuntal subtleties are constructed. (III, 8)

Ambros bolsters his claim, as ever, through comparison with the other arts, with which he is trying to bring music into communion. Thus he links this metamorphosis to what he sees as similar transformations in painting (at the hands of such figures as Verrocchio, Mantegna and Leonardo da Vinci) and architecture, drawing for corroboration, as elsewhere, on Burckhardt's *Cicerone*.[54] Similarly, complexities that in earlier repertories would be seen as "contrived" and "bizarre" Gothic excrescences are revamped for music after 1450 as evidence of the "fantastical tendency of the time" and as music's "bold attempts to seek out the limits of its realm," fully of a piece with the experimentation he sees going on in other artistic media.[55]

Transformations such as these, postulated in the interests of defining a new "spirit" which subsequent writers would characterize unambiguously as that of the "Renaissance," are so elegantly negotiated that their inconsistencies can go by virtually unnoticed. Yet it is precisely this bifurcated view of the use of borrowed material that has been used to draw a somewhat artificial distinction between a "medieval" tradition of "glossing" and "commentary" on the one hand and a "Renaissance" discovery of self-conscious, "purely musical" striving for coherence and unity on the other – a discovery which came to be identified most directly with the advent and development of the "cyclic" Mass. The notion that the latter were aims actively sought by "Renaissance-era" musicians was a logical outgrowth of two related nineteenth-century priorities: in the first place, "unity" seen as an essential attribute, from a post-Hegelian perspective, of artworks generally, while in the second, a "purely musical" unity seen as crucial to the hypostatizing of musical "works" tangible enough to stand comparison with those in the plastic arts. Thus fifteenth-century music, billed increasingly (and in any case by default, since it was the earliest polyphonic music then known) as the beginning of the "modern" musical era, had to demonstrate what in Ambros's words was its "obscure drive [*dunkle Drang*] towards that which was necessary for art itself" (III, 10). This notion of "necessity" is rooted in the dialectic principle whereby each stage of historical progress is necessary because it is inevitable. On an ethical level, furthermore, recognition of that necessity – from the Hegelian philosophical perspective in which Ambros and most other German historians of the mid nineteenth century were grounded – was a precondition of freedom.[56] What was necessary for art was in truth, then, what was necessary specifically from the perspective of Ambros's own time and philosophical milieu.

The successful combination of the tools through which this "necessity" began to make itself felt (namely borrowed melodies, imitation, and even the "Canon" and "Fuge" seen elsewhere as quintessentially "medieval") was, to Ambros, the great achievement of "Netherlandish" polyphony, "in its deepest essence the true – and thus for all later times legitimate – expression of a great cultural epoch" (III, 10). Thus it is not difficult to see how the "cyclic" Mass, as the most large-scale and obvious manifestation of the "unity" so highly prized, came to be seen as central to that achievement.

After Ambros

The general picture of fifteenth-century music history drawn by Ambros has proved remarkably durable. As future authors built on his achievements, the outlines of that picture became ever more strongly defined and increasingly assumed the status of historical "truth." The most significant change which took place involved Ambros's Renaissance of circa 1600 giving way to a fifteenth-century one, but most authors, not without some justification, simply assumed that the latter had been his view anyway. By 1949, Friedrich Blume could still claim that Ambros "organized the whole period substantially as it is still understood in our time, introducing a structural arrangement that is on the whole (despite certain alterations) maintained in present-day writings."[57] These alterations have only served to entrench the position of the cyclic Mass as the showpiece of the era, and even as the greatest musical achievement up to that time. Two changes have been particularly relevant. The first, concerning the discrediting of Baini's dating of Du Fay through the corrected chronology of Haberl, brought the generation of Du Fay into the "Renaissance" fold.[58] The second, partly a consequence of the same thing, concerned the rehabilitation as historical testimony of the theoretical writings of Johannes Tinctoris, his credibility restored by the discovery that aspects of his chronology contradicted by Baini had been right all along. Tinctoris's perceived value as a witness was further boosted by Ambros's own support (III, 454) – in the face of the contrary position of Kiesewetter – for Tinctoris's statements concerning the historical importance of English music. Thus Tinctoris's famous remarks in the *Liber de Arte Contrapuncti* of 1477 on the influence of English music on Du Fay and Binchois and the notion that only music written in the preceding forty years was worth listening to brought Dunstaple and everything else from about 1430 into the "Renaissance" frame. The effect of these changes on the already considerable status of the Mass is obvious, and could scarcely be better expressed than in the statement by Bukofzer quoted at the opening of this chapter.

In Bukofzer's words we see the distillation of the modern view of the history of fifteenth-century music as it had been pieced together from Burney to Ambros, an evolution which had expressed and run parallel with underlying epistemologies from the Enlightenment to Burckhardt. Thus Burckhardt's Renaissance spirit of individualism reveals itself in the "bold and independent mind" which conceived the linkage of the movements of the Mass. Similarly, the notion of the "emancipation" of that mind from beneath the yoke of the church echoes the Hegel/Brendel image of music, newly elevated to sublimity through its association with the church, discovering its independence and "rushing out into the world." Freeing himself from the "constraints" imposed by the demands of the church – for Ambros and others part of the struggle in which Josquin was engaged – the newly emancipated "artist" concentrated his attention instead on the instantiation of the values of the aesthetic in the "absolute" work of art, from a post-Kantian perspective the artwork's only true legitimation. Here again, then, the Mass could be portrayed as the apotheosis of the demands, articulated repeatedly by music historians from Forkel to Ambros, that music's concern should be first and foremost with its aesthetic content rather than with any "external" functions it had been constructed to fulfill.[59]

But the crux here is the confluence of the origins of the cyclic Mass and the supposed beginning of a musical "Renaissance." The location of this "Renaissance" in the early fifteenth century – really a historical accident arising out of the intersection of the influence of Burckhardt with the contemporary state of music-historical understanding[60] – was decisive for the future perception of the Mass. The reification of the Mass had already been effected by the integration, from the late eighteenth century, of music and its historical vestiges into a relativized system of "fine arts"; as one of the chief musical expressions of a Renaissance *Zeitgeist*, however, it was sundered even more decisively away from its antecedents and cast still further adrift from its cultural context. Reinvented as Renaissance icon, the Mass now attracted attention to its structure and internal workings. It is easy to perceive how certain components of the nineteenth-century formulation of a musical "Renaissance" (clear enough from Bukofzer's remarks) contributed to this iconic status. Searching, in Bukofzer's words, for an absolute musical work of art worthy to stand beside the more tangible Renaissance manifestations of the other "fine arts," historians found the perfect object in the Mass based on a cantus firmus. In its borrowing of external material and reuse of it from movement to movement – forming, in Bukofzer's words, a "set of five musically coherent compositions" in which "the means of unification are provided by the composer, not the liturgy" – the cantus firmus Mass offered a satisfying picture of "unity" and "coherence."[61] But the last piece in the puzzle came only in the twentieth century, when the Mass's reification was completed by the introduction of the ultimate spatializing metaphor of "cyclicity."[62]

The conception of the cyclic cantus firmus Mass encapsuled in Bukofzer's statement carries a great deal of weight: cogent and born of long tradition, it reveals a deep responsiveness to the historical–aesthetic priorities of the period of its currency. Part of that responsiveness lay in the ability of Bukofzer's conception not only to rationalize developments in fifteenth-century music but also to perceive in those developments ancestors for and analogues of procedures and structures valued in later, more immediately familiar, phases in Western musical history. It thus enabled newly relevant ways of hearing music from an alien and distant culture, stimulating interests and enquiries which continue to bear fruit in sound and word. The model for the understanding of the polyphonic Mass according to notions of structural "coherence," "unity" and "cyclicity" was thus hard won by pioneering scholarship, and it created a frame that enabled some of musicology's landmark achievements.

At the same time, however, it led to the viewing – and consequent evaluation – of the surviving repertory through a very particular lens: most obviously, while it provided a persuasive "internal," structural model for rationalizing those Masses built around a regularly repeating cantus firmus, this was at the expense of excluding those areas of the Mass repertory which display different kinds of construction. Thus were marginalized, for example, Masses that were apparently free of borrowed material, Masses that used borrowed material in ways which could not be construed as "structural" and – especially – Masses comprising movements (with or without external borrowings) that show little musical interconnection of any sort.[63]

Unsusceptible to modern models of overarching structure, cohesion and unity, powerfully validated by means of analytical models fashioned to address them in the form of transcriptions in score (in contradistinction to their original notational forms), such pieces seemed by comparison deficient, peripheral to the cutting edge of historical progress being forged by Masses unified by a consistently deployed cantus firmus. If many Masses that failed to fit the mold were still unfamiliar when such conceptual models were being formulated, others – such as Ockeghem's Masses *Au travail suis* and *Mi mi*, whose absence of obvious structural underpinning rendered them "irrational" according to traditional orthodoxy – were, on account of authorship if nothing else, very much part of the "central" repertory.[64]

Less monolithic than it once appeared, the cantus firmus Mass has itself increasingly emerged also as the result of a much less bold stylistic departure than that celebrated by the Bukofzer model. Radical though its structure was made to appear as an expression of the burgeoning "Renaissance" in music, it could in fact more easily be read as a continuation of what had gone before than a departure from it. Indeed, the cyclic Mass fits comfortably into the teleological development through which, in Ambros's model, the potential latent in chant was played out in a succession of contrapuntal "realizations" beginning with the earliest written polyphony and culminating in Palestrina. This is easier to see today than it was in the mid-nineteenth century, when such antecedents as the isorhythmic motet were still unfamiliar. Even so, the persistence – through the subsequent recovery of earlier repertories which might ostensibly have compromised it – of the characterization of the Mass as a watershed in the history of Western musical form has meant that its continuity with earlier trends has remained less clear than it would otherwise have been.[65]

One of the most powerful agents in obscuring that continuity has been terminology. This is revealed most obviously in the modern distinction between "isorhythm" (a term invented in the twentieth century) and "cantus firmus" (whose use to refer to a structural "backbone" for the Mass is similarly a product of modern scholarship). The rootedness of this distinction in the priorities of modern historical narrative rather than those of fifteenth-century practice can be highlighted via the example of what is universally acknowledged as one of the earliest "cantus firmus" Masses, the *Missa Alma redemptoris mater* of Leonel Power. The use of a borrowed melody in five movements rather than one is the only structural feature that distinguishes this Mass from some of the same composer's single "isorhythmic" Mass movements.[66] Though crucial from a modern historical perspective, this is a distinction that may have appeared arbitrary to the

Mass's original users: as we shall see in Chapter 2, there are good grounds to propose that at this early stage isorhythmic motets, single isorhythmic Mass movements and the individual movements of a "cantus firmus" Mass, for us distinct genres, were, to their users, all simply "motets."[67] Thus the distinction we perceive between Power's individual Mass movements and his complete Mass probably relates less to the views of his contemporaries than to our proclivity to see one as representative of "medieval" "isorhythm" and the other as the epoch-making innovation of the "cantus firmus." Here again we see the legacy of Ambros's bifurcated view, discussed above, of borrowed material in terms of a distinction between a "medieval" "glossing" on a borrowed melody and a "Renaissance" striving for "coherence" and "unity."[68]

The consistency of vision behind a strong conceptual frame such as that provided by the Bukofzer model has enormous advantages for the writing of history: it offers a purposeful narrative and a strong heuristic accessible to expansion and refinement by future scholars. Strongly redolent of Hegelian philosophy of history and aesthetics, the Bukofzer model has roots extending back to the Enlightenment, the cultural environment which stimulated and enabled the rediscovery of earlier musics in the first place; and if the Enlightenment provided the stimulus for the modern enquiry into dead musics, it is difficult to imagine even the possibility of cultural history without Hegel. Without such a strong theoretical framework, the present state of understanding would be inconceivable. As Terry Eagleton has put it, "If we can and must be severe critics of Enlightenment, it is Enlightenment which has empowered us to be so."[69] And as Gombrich observed of Burckhardt, the strength and influence of his perspective derive from the fact that his view of the Italian Renaissance is based on a theory, in his case that of Hegelian metaphysics. Thus "we should not reproach Burckhardt for having built his picture of the period on a 'preconceived idea.' Without such an idea history could never be written at all."[70]

But the vast increase in knowledge of the music of this era in the fifty years since Bukofzer's statements were published has inevitably given rise to new views of the early cyclic Mass, many of them, like those that form the substance of the central section of this book, driven by motivation to relate surviving pieces to the past cultures whose functions they were shaped to articulate. Coupled with an ever greater familiarity with the music in question and the extent of its diversity, this has in turn spawned a greater diversity of strategies for explaining the forms the music takes.

To attempt an understanding of the cyclic Mass during the period of its currency entails first of all, however, a consideration – as far as is possible – of its conceptualization during that time as a musical structure.

What evaluative models for the Mass can be detected in the writings of its composers, theorists and users more generally? Is there evidence of any common ground with the criteria summed up by Bukofzer? Was the cantus firmus Mass singled out then – as now – as the preeminent musical genre of its day, or as a historically significant development? What was the perception of Masses constructed according to different principles? Was there any sense of qualitative distinction between available compositional methods? What might the answers to these questions suggest to us about more general perceptions of the polyphonic Mass? Our first witnesses are the theorists, the closest analogue to modern-day scholars and the only group of individuals from the late Middle Ages whose writing was concerned, like our own, with the actual fabric of musical compositions. But further clues regarding the contemporary perception of the Mass are also to be found elsewhere, in copying records, in executors' accounts, in contemporary remarks, and, finally, in the music manuscripts themselves.

2 | Contemporary witnesses

Our first witness is inevitably Tinctoris. The most voluminous and meticulous theorist of his day, Tinctoris also presents the image of an individual with whom, of all late medieval theorists, we can most easily identify. Citing actual pieces of music to illustrate technical points, he strikes for us the classic pose of the musical connoisseur, and one whose bibliophilic cast of mind feels at once familiar to the modern scholar. Searching, as we might imagine, through volumes on the library shelves of the King of Naples in his efforts to illustrate this or that point, he offers in his work a clear analogy for our own as we, in our own libraries, reach for the volumes of our collected editions.

Tinctoris's practice of referring to individual pieces to illustrate particular points was far from new. Neither is it clear that he was the first to make reference to specific Masses: Hothby and Ramos draw briefly on particular Masses in theoretical tracts apparently dating from around the same time, the 1470s, that Tinctoris was writing. Tinctoris is exceptional, however, in the extent to which he underpins his technical observations with examples drawn from the works of named composers, acknowledged as masters. Thus his references form an overarching vindication of the achievements of the figures he isolates as the best representatives of their art, continually reaffirming and endorsing the praise bestowed upon them in his introductions. Here again he strikes a chord with the priorities of our own time, with its sense of the highest musical achievements of the fifteenth century based on an appreciation of the works of those same named individuals.

Tinctoris breaks entirely new ground, however, in the area of genre definition: while other genres, most notably the motet, had been defined by a wide range of earlier theorists, Tinctoris's two sets of remarks – in the *Terminorum musicae diffinitorium* and the *Liber de arte contrapuncti* – on the definition of and contents appropriate to the polyphonic Mass are without precedent. Here also modern perceptions have caught apparent resonances in his remarks: his description (in the *Diffinitorium*) of the Mass as "cantus magnus" – in contradistinction to the motet ("cantus mediocris") and song ("cantus parvus") – has been widely seen as a vindication of the position that the Mass, the "large" form of the triad, was considered the fifteenth century's preeminent demonstration of compositional prowess.[1] However, attention to context suggests that Tinctoris's definition is rooted in concerns not with artistic self-legitimation, but with appropriateness to function, as revealed in this case by his indebtedness to Cicero. The reliance on Cicero of Tinctoris, whose writings are soaked with references to, and borrowings from, the Latin master's oratorical treatises, would be hard to overstate. The use of "magnus," "mediocris" and "parvus" to refer respectively to Mass, motet and song is almost certainly a response, as Manuel Erviti has revealed, to passages from Cicero's *Orator*, where the same words are juxtaposed to refer not to degrees in dimension or prowess but rather to the "lofty," "tempered" and "commonplace" styles appropriate to the three *genera dicendi* of oratory. Central to these three *genera* for Cicero was the consideration of propriety or "decorum": the appropriate marriage of language and style to the subject being discussed, the occasion of the speech, and the character of both speaker and audience. Similar considerations of social appropriateness, this time in the context of the late medieval teachings of the church, are carried forth, Erviti proposes, into Tinctoris's definitions of Mass, motet and song, with musical settings of the Mass, functioning as they did within the central rite of medieval religious practice (and indeed of life at the time generally), standing supreme.[2]

If the definition of "Mass" as "cantus magnus" refers first to its primacy of social function, however, that function still needed a concrete musical response. Descriptions of the substance of that response are therefore the most obvious places to search for evidence of a contemporary estimation of the musical unity that has been so central to modern aesthetic criteria. In fact, however, contemporary evaluation, at least on the basis of surviving evidence, seems to have been oriented in quite the opposite direction. Tinctoris offers some indication of how a Mass might most appropriately, or "decorously," be put together in the third, and final, book of his *Liber de arte contrapuncti*.

Citing the authority of Horace, Cicero and Aristotle, the "eighth and last general rule" of this book famously advises "the most accurate seeking out of variety in all counterpoint." It proposes that:

> any composer or *concentor* of the greatest inventiveness may achieve this diversity if he either composes or "fits together" now by one quantity now by another, now by one perfection now by another, now by one proportion now by another, now by one conjunction now by another, now with syncopations now without syncopation, now with *fugae* [imitations] now without *fugae*, now with pauses now

without pauses, now diminished now plainly. Nevertheless, the highest reason must be adhered to in all these, although I may have kept silent about fitting together *super librum*, which may be diversified at the will of those doing the fitting together; neither do so many nor such varieties come together in a song as so many and such in a motet; neither do so many and such [varieties come together] in a motet as so many and such in a Mass.

Thus every *res facta* must be diversified in its quality and quantity, just as an infinite [number of] works teach ...[3]

If the influence of Ciceronian writings is implicit in the genre definitions of the *Diffinitorium*, it is explicit here: Tinctoris notes in the paragraph directly preceding the above quotation that "according to the opinion of Tullius [Cicero], as variety in the art of speaking most delights the hearer, so also in music a diversity of harmonies forcibly provokes the souls of the listeners into delight."[4] The widespread classical and medieval topos that all people and all senses are pleased by variety has its roots ultimately in Aristotle, to whom Tinctoris also refers in this context in the same chapter. For his specific definition of musical *varietas*, however, he draws on the *Rhetorica ad Herennium*, in Tinctoris's time still widely thought to be by Cicero.[5]

As with other terms used by Tinctoris, the word "varietas" acquires, in his hands, a range of meanings distinct from those both of classical times and of earlier in the Middle Ages. First, the application of the word to polyphonic music, rare in earlier music-theoretical writing, is the exclusive concern of the passage quoted above. Second, he emphasizes, typically for his time, the applications of *varietas* to music's technical aspects rather than, as in the *Rhetorica ad Herennium*, the effects of *varietas* on the souls of listeners. His comments do resonate with classical precepts, though, in his description of the relative degrees of variety desirable in Mass, motet and song. Here again, as in the *Diffinitorium*, his prescriptions for the three musical genres echo those for the three *genera dicendi*, their relative contents determined by propriety or "decorum." While they are linked to a rhetorical model, then, Tinctoris's definitions are in no way hidebound by it. There is no reason to believe that he used the term *varietas*, tailored as it was to his own particular purposes, any less precisely or pragmatically than any other. Indeed, the specificity of Tinctoris's terminology, without parallel in its time, has for modern scholarship been one of his chief virtues. In short, Tinctoris's testimony that diversity was, in his time, a primary attribute of music in general (and the Mass in particular) is the best guarantee we are likely to find that this was indeed the case. As it happens, though, his testimony gains further weight through being echoed in another tract written some thirty years later: the *De cardinalatu libri tres* of Paolo Cortese.[6]

Paolo Cortese

Cortese's remarks on music, forming a small part of a large treatise on the conduct appropriate to a cardinal, were published shortly after his death in 1510. A passionate humanist, Cortese imbues his treatise with a degree of Ciceronianism far more thoroughgoing even than that of Tinctoris. As for Tinctoris, though, his hierarchy of vocal music comprises the three tiers of Masses ("propitiatory songs"), motets ("precentorial songs") and (in this case improvised) songs ("carmina"). It seems clear that Cortese was not musically expert, and his very personal and imprecise use of terminology is motivated, as Pirrotta has noted, much more by its classical resonances than by real technical knowledge. Cortese does not specify the type or level of musical content appropriate to the latter two genres; neither does he apply the word *varietas* or any of its variants to his discussion of the three vocal genres. Yet it is clear from his description of the Mass that for him, as for Tinctoris, this was the forum for the greatest diversity, and indeed distinction, of musical expression:

> For sacrificial songs are those in which all kinds of modes [*pthongi*], tones [?] [*prosodiae*] and proportions [*analogicae mensiones*] are present, and in which the genus of musicians is accorded the greatest praise for devising the music [*laus cantus praeclare struendi*]. Wherefore not without cause does Cardinal Giovanni de' Medici, a man expert in the learned study of musical matters, maintain that no one is to be accounted amongst the leading musicians who is less skilled in the composing of the sacrificial [*litatorius*] genre. Thus it is for this one thing that they say Josquin the Frenchman stood out among many, because more learning was added by him to the sacrificial kinds of song than is wont to be added by the unskilled zeal [*ieiuna sedulitas*] of recent musicians.[7]

A similarity suggestive of a widespread topos, the parallel between Tinctoris and Cortese is not, however, repeated anywhere else known to me. Indeed, I know of no other definitions of the polyphonic Mass from their times or earlier. By contrast, in the case of the motet, a wide range of definitions extends back from a slightly earlier period to at least the beginning of the thirteenth century. Offering a context for late medieval perceptions of the Mass, these definitions, for reasons that will become clear, almost certainly also have a more direct bearing on conceptions of Mass polyphony at least until the early fifteenth century.

The motet

Comparison with earlier descriptions of the motet quickly throws the humanist-rhetorical frame of Tinctoris's and Cortese's descriptions into high relief. Earlier theoretical definitions invariably concentrate on one or both of two characteristics: first, the construction of the motet on the basis of a preexisting piece of chant heard in the tenor, and, second, its simultaneous use of different texts.[8] Either or both of these, the shared defining characteristics of the genre in its original form, were consistently invoked in definitions of the motet until the fifteenth century. Central to our concern is the prior existence of the tenor, the "cantus ... prius factus" in the words of Franco of Cologne, which separated at least the French motet from most other genres,[9] constructed as they were according to different principles.[10] Repeated formulas beginning with Franco around the middle of the thirteenth century emphasize the status of the tenor, its primacy assured by two considerations: first, its derivation from chant, which preconditioned in turn the choice of text for the *motetus* part, and second, its fundamental status in the contrapuntal edifice. In discussions of the latter the tenor was often likened to the foundations of a house, a notion which in the stipulations of Grocheio was applied specifically to the motet.[11]

Given that use of a preexistent tenor is the primary precondition also of the Mass based on a cantus firmus, it may reasonably be asked why such a definition, ready made in the context of descriptions of the motet, was not reapplied later to the Mass. The answer may be sought at least partly in disjunctions of timing and aim. By the time Tinctoris, in the 1470s, wrote his two prescriptions for the motet, such definitions as those alluded to above had long since fallen out of currency: by the early–mid fifteenth century they were the province solely of a handful of surviving treatises from Germany and Central Europe concerned with French music of Machaut's generation and the succeeding one, and thus bearing witness to the late transmission and currency of such music in those areas.[12] And, as Erviti has observed, Tinctoris's scholarly, humanist mode of expression, aimed at a select group of cognoscenti, is entirely distinct from the didactic and prosaic manner of those earlier definitions.[13] But in any case, by the time of Tinctoris a description of the motet as a work of middling length or significance most often set to words of a sacred nature was as close a definition as was feasible. Responding naturally to the demise of isorhythm and changing styles generally, application of the word "motet" had extended in range, even in circles formerly associated with "French" motet cultivation, to the point that neither multiple texts nor use of a *cantus prius factus* – in either the tenor or any other voice – was a precondition for its use.

Even during the time of the definitions alluded to above, though, the term "motet" apparently had a broader purchase than is customary today, and it is here that it bears directly on the present topic. It would appear that, at least until the mid fifteenth century, "motet" was a term that embraced also settings of individual – and also even musically linked – movements of the Mass. In the first place, this observation would make sense of the enormous disparity that exists between the large number of fourteenth- and early fifteenth-century discussions of "motet" compared with the almost total absence of similarly couched definitions of "Mass." But more direct evidence exists. An early instance is the surviving index of the so-called Trémouïlle Manuscript, a largely lost source copied, apparently in 1376, for a chapel of the French royal house, but bought in 1384 or later by the Burgundian Duke Philip the Bold. The forty-nine items listed under the heading "Motez – ordonez et escriz ci apres" include chaces and five Mass Ordinary movements.[14] In 1404 the court of Aragon paid for the compilation of a "libre appellat de cant d orgue de motets" for the chapel of Queen Margaret. The same book was listed in an inventory following the queen's death as a "libre scrit en pergamins appellat 'Libre de cant d orga,' ab Credos e ab Glorias e ab Sanctus e Agnus, e ab tenor e contratenor ab motets, e comensa 'Et in terra pax hominibus' e feneix 'Il est per.'"[15] In December, 1462 the chapter of Ferrara Cathedral gave over "for the use of the clerics" "unus liber in cantu figurato cum Mutetis Patrem, Et in terra et Gloria et Chirie, Sanctus et Agnus Dei, etc.," a wording suggestive of a lack of distinction from the viewpoint of the scribe between what for us would be unequivocally distinguished as "motets" and "Masses."[16]

Copying records add definition to this picture, with the following, dating from 1427, from the church fabric accounts of St. Donatian, Bruges, making the case with particular clarity:

Jacobo Couterman, pro quibusdam motetis, scilicet Patrem, Et in Terra, ac Sanctus scriptis in libro puerorum[17]

Copying records from the 1440s from Cambrai Cathedral, which refer to music for the Mass as "carmines" or "canti," also suggest that the separate status in the first half of the fifteenth century of polyphony for the Mass – presumably by now including linked Mass movements and "cycles" – was yet to be clearly defined.[18]

Even in the later years of the fifteenth century the notion of "the Mass" as a distinct polyphonic genre seems not to have been set in stone. Thus Du Fay's executors' account of 1474 itemizes "j livre en grant volume en parchemin contenant les messes de St. Anthoine de Pade aveuc pluiseurs aultres anthiennes en noire noté."[19] A document of 1480–1 from the parish church of St. Margaret's, Westminster details a payment for copying "a song called caput of iiii partys" in a context which makes it clear that the "song" in question was in fact a Mass, possibly, as Fiona Kisby has proposed, the anonymous English cycle on the *Caput* melisma.[20]

All this evidence would seem to point in the same direction: to a general lack, at least until around the mid fifteenth century, of a sense of "the Mass" as an integrated, composite work. To the extent that such questions of "genre" would have impinged on the scribes concerned at all, they seem most likely to have viewed complete Mass settings rather as aggregates of individual motets than as "cyclic" multipieces. Later copying records for major foundations leave a similar impression. The first fifteenth-century copying record for Cambrai Cathedral to refer specifically to a "Missa" occurs in 1457. Although the earliest of Simon Mellet's many copying assignments was fulfilled in 1446, the series of payments made to him specifying "missae" or "messes" began only in 1462.[21] Similarly, the first unequivocal record for the copying of a Mass at St. Donatian, Bruges occurs in 1455, although, as Reinhard Strohm has commented, much of the earlier, unspecified copying into books of "motets" at St. Donatian must actually have been of music for the Mass.[22] From 1463, records for the copying specifically of Masses at St. Donatian proliferate, and by 1479 they draw a distinction between "Masses" and motets. Records from other foundations reinforce the impression that the distinguishing of Mass music from settings of other liturgical texts began to become standard only in the 1450s and 1460s. The purchase by the Collegiate Church of St. Omer in 1462–3 of "ung grant livre … nottez en deschant contenant plusieurs messes …" was – on the evidence of the almost complete run of fabric accounts from that institution – the first made there for polyphonic Masses, or indeed for any polyphony at all.[23]

This growing sense in the later fifteenth century of "the Mass" as an integrated unit is surely linked to the great increase at that time in the number of polyphonic Mass settings. Given this situation one might expect terminology used in the musical sources to offer clues to changing perceptions of complete Mass settings. Headings, which could provide such information, are, however, generally scarce in sources of polyphonic music. In cases of borrowing from a *cantus prius factus*, Mass settings are typically distinguished by textual incipit beneath the borrowed melody in the tenor in each movement. Composer attributions at the head of the first movement of a "cycle," appearing increasingly from the mid fifteenth century, also serve to demarcate contiguously copied groupings from surrounding music. I know of only two groupings of Mass movements – both in their different ways highly exceptional – dating from before the mid fifteenth century that are designated as "Masses." The earliest and more celebrated of these is of course the copy of Machaut's Mass – the only copy to carry a heading – beginning with the rubric "Ci commence la messe de n[ost] re dame" (in US-NYw [MS "Vg"]).[24] The other is Du Fay's plenary Mass for St. James, probably composed in the late 1420s and headed in its only complete source, Bologna Q15, "Introitus misse sancti iacobi" (folio 121). The Ferrarese payment record of 1447 to "two Frenchmen who had given the Marquis a book containing six new Masses" testifies to the use of the term by that time in Ferrara to refer presumably to settings of the complete Ordinary.[25] The next instances are datable to the mid 1450s, when a number of Ordinary groupings among the later additions to Trent 90 are labelled "Missa," while Trent 88, copied apparently c.1456–62,[26] follows suit.

Precisely what sort of "belonging" such rubrics imply is not always clear, though: a number of sets of Ordinary movements in Trent 88 – including one on folios 54v–60r explicitly labeled as such – show no sign of compositional linkage. Such "composite" Masses in Trent 88 are thus part of a lineage of scribally initiated "cycles" extending back – via, most notably, Bologna Q15[27] – at least a century to such fourteenth-century "cycles" as the Mass of Tournai. If contiguity is no guarantee of compositional linkage, the reverse is also true: manuscript "dismemberment" of demonstrably compositional "cycles" is a feature of the transmission of Mass cycles from their beginnings until at least the 1460s.[28] Moreover, the handful of rubricated copies mentioned above makes no distinction between groupings of Ordinary movements, Proper movements and, in the case of the Sancti Jacobi Mass, both.

Such scraps of information do not constitute a large body of evidence; however, it is fair to state that, at least until the 1450s and 1460s, there is little to support the notion of a widespread or direct equation between the word "Missa" and contiguously grouped polyphonic settings of the Kyrie, Gloria, Credo, Sanctus and Agnus Dei. Further, such groupings, with or without headings, are no guarantee of compositional relationship, any more than compositional relationship is a guarantee of contiguous copying. Terminology was also, unsurprisingly, a good deal more fluid than in modern scholarship: "Missa" or "Officium" could refer to groupings of Ordinary or Proper settings, with or without compositional relationships between the movements, while the notion of a repertory designated "Mass" music, as distinct from the more blanket term for sacred polyphony of "motet," was slow to establish itself.

In theoretical writing, even by the 1470s, Tinctoris's meticulous terminological precision is not universally shared by his colleagues: for Hothby, whose *Dialogus in arte musica* was apparently written around the same time,[29] "carmen" and "cantilena" are entirely adequate terms for what Tinctoris, as we today, would refer to unequivocally as a "Mass."

Even Gaffurius, writing in the 1490s and very much under the shadow of Tinctoris, having discussed the signing of proportions in Du Fay's *Missa Sancti Antonii* and an "Et in terra" by Basiron, goes on to refer to the same pieces as "cantilenae," a term (like "carmen") restricted by Tinctoris exclusively to his discussion of songs.[30]

Terminological questions aside, though, even Tinctoris himself, notwithstanding his stated reverence for the composers whose music he discusses, draws on the specifics of the music of his time purely for the illustration of technical detail. On this general point his aims in the late fifteenth century are no different from those which prompted his fourteenth-century forebears to draw for illustration on the compositions current in their own time and milieus. Observations are concerned always with local features and specifics: there is no mention – beyond discussions of canons and the augmentation or diminution of tenor cantus firmi – of anything which could be construed as "structural," much less "unifying." And crucially, there is never any suggestion of a distinction, qualitative or otherwise, between those Masses based on a cantus firmus and those, such as Du Fay's *Mass for St. Anthony of Padua*, which are not, and certainly no hint that the cantus firmus Mass in Tinctoris's day, as for twentieth-century scholarship, was privileged as a watershed in large-scale musical construction.

Johannes Ott

One, rather later, source that does discuss cantus firmus layout is, intriguingly, also a landmark in the discussion of *varietas*: this is the preface to the *Missae tredecim quatuor vocibus* (Nuremberg: Hieronymus Graphaeus, 1539) by Johannes Ott. In Ott's case the notion of *varietas*, though clearly emanating ultimately from the same Ciceronian sources as the discussion of Tinctoris, gains a more specifically sixteenth-century humanist tint from its relationship to the poetical theory of Pietro Bembo.[31] Ott, in contrast to Tinctoris, addresses his concerns directly to the cantus firmus repetitions that link the movements of the Mass. Yet far from emphasizing the "unifying" effect of the cantus firmus on a grouping of five separate movements – for modern scholarship the Mass's signal historical achievement – he, like Tinctoris, sees the skill of the composer as oriented in exactly the opposite direction. For him, such skill is to be seen not in emphasis on the "unity" that is already inherent in the repeated statements of a borrowed melody, but rather in the avoidance of the potential monotony of cantus firmus repetitions through the clothing of the melody in the most infinite variety:

First, then, the nature of such a piece of music [*ratio carminis*] – of which the form [*forma*] must needs be consistent throughout all its parts, of which there are a great many – requires great wealth of invention [*ingentem copiam requirit*]. In some cases the melody of the whole Mass is over in four breves, in other cases fewer. Who indeed can fail to see how great – but also how scrupulous and painstaking – must be this richness [of ideas], so that the same melodic contour may be repeated throughout the whole composition, not only without stiffness, but rather with sweetness and winning applause for its inventiveness? And this is the reason why musical crafts-men have displayed so much artistry in their Masses. For it is the purpose of art so to embellish this richness [of invention] that it shall not engender boredom and appear to be excessive. Hence there is observed in Masses what is extremely rare in other [types of] compositions – such variety of signatures [*signa*], so wonderful a disposition of rhythms. Great is the error of those who think that these things have been invented by vain and idle minds for the sake of showing off. It was necessity that prompted composers to seek out these conjuring tricks, as it were, by means of which they might both disguise the sameness of the melody, and present the same sounds in ever different forms, like so many actors on stage in different guises.[32]

Ott's comments provide evidence, then, of at least a mid-sixteenth-century interest in the Mass as an overarching entity. To the extent that his com-ments are essentially historicizing remarks made from a *post facto* stance, his position has something in common with our own: the single-voice can-tus firmus had, by the time of his writing, long been superseded by poly-phonic models as the standard compositional basis for Masses. Introducing a collection of Masses by Josquin and his contemporaries, Ott reveals his allegiance to the particular humanistic perspective in the Germany of the 1530s and 1540s according to which Josquin was viewed, in lieu of any surviving music from classical times, as a model for the composers of his generation.[33] And in seeing the achievement of the Masses of Josquin and his contemporaries as an expression of principles not of "unity" but of *vari-etas*, Ott reveals the nature and degree according to which his sense of that achievement differs from that of our own times.[34]

Contemporary sources offer few grounds for ascribing demand for poly-phonic Masses to the kind of "internally" driven stylistic motivation that has traditionally been assumed in modern evaluations. And far from priv-ileging the Mass as a landmark in the development of musical unity, the testimonies of Tinctoris and Ott – their rootedness in rhetorical models notwithstanding – emphasize instead its scope and need for diversity. What, then, were the forces that gave rise to and sustained this genre, its unprece-dented scope and musical ingenuity, and its celebrated structural unity? The scale of its cultivation and its stimulation of some of the most sophisticated music from the finest musical minds of the era make it obvious enough that the early "cyclic" Mass in general, and the cantus firmus Mass in particular, was a compositional forum of special significance during the period of its currency. And its pre-eminent status in its own time, as the loftiest available genre produced by composers worthy of the highest praise, receives strong confirmation from the comments of Tinctoris and Cortese. Musical achievements notwithstanding, though, it has become increasingly clear from more recent scholarship that that loftiness, the driving force behind its creation and propagation, derived rather from concerns that were personal, cultural and, ultimately, eschatological. The last section of this book will explore some ways in which the cyclic Mass offered, in the context of the central rite of the church, a unique kind of access – and supplication – to the Real Presence of Christ. That access was forged by the deployment of cantus firmi that allowed it to be particularized and personalized with unusual precision.

How, though, was such particularization effected? What devices and images were adopted, which achieved greatest popularity, and why? What procedures might have been chosen for private, personal intercessory pleas, and which, on the other hand, may have been more suitable for grander, more public statement? These are the kinds of questions addressed in the next, central, section of this study.

PART II

The ritual world of the early polyphonic Mass

3 | "Faisant regretz pour ma dolente vie": piety, polyphony and musical borrowing

> Regarde cy, homme mondain
> Plein d'orgueil et de vanité
> Laisse ton hault vouloir soubdain
> N'ayes de peché voulenté;
> Tu mourras, c'est ta seureté
> Ayes en ton cueur ce remort
> Et si saches de verité
> Qu'il n'est riens plus seur que la mort.[1]

Whatever their mutual bonds or differences, fifteenth-century men and women shared one important motivation: the desire to shorten the time in purgatory that, short of sainthood and immediate passage to paradise, would follow earthly life.[2] Preparation for death therefore had serious implications for conduct throughout life, particularly for those with the money and leisure to prepare in an appropriate manner. Acts of philanthropy, in the form of distributions of bread to the poor, money to hospitals and prisons, and so on were good works that would weigh in favor of the posthumous soul. But the most prominent expression of concern for one's ultimate fate, standing as the culmination of a late medieval trend, was the endowment of personal devotions.

For those with adequate means, the clearest manifestation of the desire to shorten purgatory was – as revealed in countless wills and executors' accounts – the payment for regular offerings in the form of performance of sacred rites, chiefly Masses. The individual made bequests to pay priests to celebrate Mass on specified days of the year, or – funds permitting – on specified days every week or even every day. Every medieval will reminds us that "nothing is more certain than death, nor less certain than the hour of the same." Yet preparations for the afterlife would accelerate markedly as old age encroached, reaching a point of particular intensity in the immediate aftermath of death.[3] Very large proportions of personal wealth, as witnessed by the surviving executors' accounts of the well-to-do, would typically be channeled into the celebration of Masses, through which, it was hoped, effective pleading would be articulated for the welfare of the soul. Funeral services and obits could be provided for in a variety of churches, monasteries and convents, while in some cases a veritable army of priests would be paid to celebrate Masses for the soul of the departed at specified times and places. Favored altars in the mother church and in other churches of particular importance to the deceased would become sites of intense activity on behalf of his soul. Often this would take the form of sets of thirty Masses – the so-called "trentaine" of St. Gregory, performed on the day of the funeral or on successive days thereafter – or in some cases an "annuel" of Masses: one each day for a year beginning with the funeral. Death would also, for those with the wherewithal to provide for them, activate more permanent foundations: Masses or other devotions to be performed on specified days in perpetuity.

Such practices are revealing of more than merely selfish concern: spiritual advantages accrued not only to the endower of devotions but also to those performing and participating in them. This collective emphasis served actively to reinforce the social bond that linked endowed devotions with the giving of alms, offering clear expression of the maxim that there is no such thing as a truly "private" Mass in the later Middle Ages.[4] At the same time the reciprocal benefit of the giving of such gifts – whether spiritual in the form of devotions or material in the form of alms – came in the prayers of their beneficiaries for the soul of the individual who had paid for them.[5] And such prayers – it was believed – carried particular efficacy when they were uttered by those drawn, like the disciples of Christ, from the ranks of the poor. Besides their posthumous benefits, then, such endowments also contributed to social cohesion and solidarity across boundaries of wealth and entitlement.

While conventions and practices naturally varied from place to place, the general pattern is clear: the endowment of personal votive observances gathered enormous momentum over the course of the fifteenth century, reaching its peak in the later years of that century. Since this same period is also that of the early growth and proliferation of polyphonic Mass composition, it has been plausibly inferred that the two phenomena are interrelated, an assumption that lies at the foundation of this book. A problem with this equation has always been the nature of the surviving evidence: while payment records for endowments are frequently very specific in defining the materials and forces required for their enactment, they almost never specify particular musical works.[6] Yet such cases as the matching – via parallels between endowments and cantus firmi in the works concerned – by Reinhard Strohm of Obrecht's Masses for St. Martin and St. Donatian with particular endowments in Bruges suggest that such relationships must have been much more common than surviving documentation allows us to demonstrate.[7] Unusually and serendipitously, moreover, the link between endowments and musical works finds direct expression in a case that is well known to musicology: that of Guillaume Du Fay.

The polyphonic endowments of Guillaume Du Fay

Like countless others of similar station, Du Fay left money in his will to churches, convents, prisons and the poor, all with the same goal: that the beneficiaries would pray for his soul and that his good works would be looked on favorably by those members of the celestial company whose advocacy, after death, was what concerned him above all else.[8] Typically again, Du Fay's provisions for his soul range from the transitory through the perennial to – at least in intention – the perpetual. Thus the image, on his grave slab, of the dead composer being presented by St. Waudru to a scene of the resurrection is echoed in innumerable similar funerary reliefs of canons being ushered by their saintly sponsors before the nativity, the Trinity, the Virgin and child or the *pietà*. Masses to be celebrated for favored saints and on the second day of each month of the year provided, along with his annual obit service, forms of human intercession for Du Fay's soul in perpetuity. Like so many of his station a member of a confraternity, Du Fay also provided for a Mass "which it is the custom to celebrate after the death of each confrère" in front of the icon of Notre Dame de Grâce which was the focus of his particular confraternity. Here we see one of a number of expressions of Du Fay's concern, universally shared, to be looked on favorably by the Virgin, the prime *mediatrix* for the souls of earthly sinners with Christ.

More unusually, one of the gifts itemized in his will and executors' account is of what was evidently a painted diptych of the Virgin facing the image of Du Fay's fellow singer and canon of Cambrai, Symon le Breton, who had predeceased him by a year. Du Fay instructs that this is to be given to the "grans vicaires" of the cathedral in order that they should place it on the altar of their chapel of St. Stephen, where both he and Symon were buried, during the observances "on feast days" and on the days of his own and Symon's obits. Here we see one of many instances in which the potential power of a permanent prayer in the form of a fixed image could be activated through its use in ritual: in this way different methods of devotion could be combined to yield a correspondingly heightened sense of invocatory power.[9] That same interaction of the fixed and permanent with the temporary and evanescent emerges again in his request for four candles to be burnt (one each before his epitaph and three other "images" including that of St. Anthony of Padua) at every Mass endowed by him and during every performance of the *Salve regina*. Here, in a ritualized and intensified form, is something akin to the imploration of the deceased found on almost every epitaph of this period for passers-by to "priez dieu pour son ame," or to say ritual numbers of Pater nosters or Ave Marias in return for a specified period of remission of sins.

In his devotion to his divine and saintly sponsors Du Fay was entirely typical of his time: fifteenth-century wills and executors' accounts attest again and again to the endowment, by those with means to afford them, of Masses and commemorations for saints who would typically have been similarly venerated in life. Frequently, as in Du Fay's case, such devotions would have taken place in the chapel in which the testator was to be laid to rest. To read the wills of such men and to be made aware of their poignant witness to final days on earth is to be left in no doubt of the sincerity of their authors in their veneration of their chosen sponsors, of Christ and the Virgin. For a man of his station, the sheer number of Masses endowed by Du Fay is comparatively modest: Masses endowed by canons of similar standing frequently ran into the hundreds. And while the specification of polyphony – for his Requiem and the annual Masses dedicated to saints Waudru, William and Anthony of Padua – is unusual, it is not unheard of. Even the technical details relating to performance practice, though rare, are not unique: the instructions that the funeral service was to be sung "well and slowly" ("bien et a tret") and that the hymn *Magno salutis gaudio* was to be performed quietly ("en fausset" or "submissa voce") have parallels elsewhere.[10]

Other aspects of Du Fay's case, though, are indeed exceptional: first, the precision of the instructions, but most of all the fact that two of the polyphonic Masses to be performed, the Requiem Mass and the Mass for St. Anthony of Padua, are specified; and not only specified, but composed by the dying man himself. We read of the numbers of singers required to perform these items, the fact that the composer's copies of both settings (and of his Mass for St. Anthony of Vienne) were to be donated to the Chapel of St. Stephen, and even that a dinner was paid for at Du Fay's expense following the first performance after his death of the Mass for St. Anthony of Padua. In harnessing his skills as a polyphonist to his most important and expensive endowments, Du Fay demonstrated a clear belief that those skills were capable of bestowing the utmost decorum on the rite that, with its focus on the appearance on the altar of his redeemer, was without rival in earthly significance. By the same token, the prestige of that rite would have been seen to validate and ennoble his musical skill.

That he chose also to endow that skill on what, from the point of view of his personal salvation, were the most important enactments of Mass that he could envisage drives home the efficacy that he believed to inhere in the embellishment, by means of his earthly craft, of sacred ritual. The surviving plenary Mass for St. Anthony of Padua provides powerful testimony to that belief in its sensitive dialectic between preexisting chant melodies (heard in the proper sections) and the composer's own polyphony, as an example adduced later in this chapter will demonstrate with particular eloquence.[11] Thus it was Du Fay's consummating act to yoke his human art to the highest of sacred observances, and thereby to ensure, via endlessly self-perpetuating repetition, a spiritually potent legacy for his posthumous soul.

Secular music in the Mass

It is this lofty significance of Mass that appeared, to nineteenth- and early twentieth-century commentators such as Huizinga,[12] to make such a jarring dissonance of the use by a composer such as Du Fay of secular tunes as Mass cantus firmi. What on earth could the Mass, the central and most solemn focus of Christian belief, have to do with songs of courtly love, such as *Se la face ay pale* or *La belle se siet*, or one with military connotations such as *L'homme armé*, still less with songs set to such scurrilous texts as "Tu m'as asoté / monté su[s] la pance et riens n'a[s] fait"?[13] A consideration of these questions, and some possible answers, constitutes the remainder of this chapter.

As is now widely recognized, many of these songs were clearly chosen for their potential to give voice to veneration of the Virgin.[14] Since this application of song texts and melodies within the Mass has received considerable attention recently it will be sufficient here to offer a synthesized picture, and to present only such observations as are necessary to provide a platform for the next phase of the argument, concerned with the borrowing of preexistent melodies for Christological purposes. Combining received scholarship with a series of new observations and perspectives, this will form the conceptual foundation for the following two chapters, which address Christological meanings of the early polyphonic Mass in two of its best-known repertories. Our first concern, though, is with the broader epistemology of this use of preexistent melodies, the processes and patterns of thought that allowed it to arise in the first place, to develop as it did, and to embody new – and newly important – meanings.

Recastings of melodies for at least the more ribald secular songs (the example last cited being a case in point) could most easily be rationalized as marginal or incidental decorations to the Mass.[15] From this perspective they would have been devised after the manner of the irreverent, grotesque, parodistic, and sometimes obscene images found on the misericords, choir screens, stained glass and corbels of the churches in which such works were sung, and indeed in the borders of many of the manuscripts in which those same works were copied, not to mention countless books of hours and copies of sundry other religious texts. Such are the visual elements and motifs that have been characterized by Michael Camille as images "on the edge."[16]

Yet the close scholarly attention given in recent years to details and presuppositions of cultural context has revealed that the choice of Mass cantus firmi arose frequently out of concern for liturgical appropriateness, in some form or other, to their new settings. Indeed it would be surprising if this were not the case. As Michael Long, quoting Huizinga, has commented: "Late medieval culture was so thoroughly permeated by Christian symbolism that there could be neither 'an object nor an action, however trivial, that [was] not constantly correlated with Christ or salvation.'"[17] Such symbolism was nowhere more strongly focused than on the Mass, the prime locus of heavenly grace on earth. Long himself made a seminal musical case for this perspective via the eloquent example of Josquin's *Missa Di Dadi*: while the Mass up to the first part of the Sanctus draws only on the music that sets the first line of the tenor of Robert Morton's song *N'aray je jamais mieux que j'ay* ("Shall I never have better than I have"), the plea articulated in those words is answered, in theological terms, only beginning at the first Osanna, with the introduction of the remainder of the song tenor.[18] Here, the spiritual "gain" of the appearance of the risen Christ in the elevated host (which was clearly intended to coincide with this moment) is greeted by the devout and attentive soul, affirming, in the words of the song, "I am yours and will remain so … My love and all my delight."[19]

From the perspective of a late medieval worldview permeated by patterns of religious allegory, such interpretation of a secular Mass model in sacred terms was clearly more than an abstract intellectual exercise: potentially spiritual content inhered already in the secular entity, awaiting, as it were, the appropriate context or mindset to activate its higher, spiritual meaning.[20] This procedure offers a musical analogue to the imbuing, in devotional panel paintings of the same period, of everyday objects with spiritual significance, a viewing of them as metaphors for things beyond the direct perception of the human intellect. Art history, of course, has long recognized this equation, as revealed, for example, in Long's illustrative quotation from Thomas Aquinas, drawn from Panofsky. Although such practices remained for many years unexplored by musical scholarship, evidence is steadily emerging that music, as might be expected, engaged with this same conceptual world in which the sacred could be seen to penetrate the secular at every level.

A clear access to such an allegorical plane of thought can be seen in the broader context of the passage from Aquinas adduced by Panofsky and Long, and it is fruitful to investigate and expand on that context in the present connection. The passage encapsulates a view that surely had an important bearing on the way in which such secular borrowing would have been rationalized.[21] It comes from Part 1 of the *Summa theologiae* (Q. 1, art. 9), where Aquinas considers "Whether Holy Scripture should use metaphors." His (affirmative) conclusion states that:

It is befitting Holy Writ to put forward divine and spiritual truths by means of comparisons with material things. For God provides for everything according to the capacity of its nature. Now it is natural to man to attain to intellectual truths through sensible objects, because all our knowledge originates from sense. Hence in Holy Writ, spiritual truths are fittingly taught under the likeness of material things. This is what Dionysius [the Pseudo-Areopagite] says (*De coelesti hierarchia* i): "We cannot be enlightened by the divine rays except they be hidden within the covering of many sacred veils."[22] It is also befitting Holy Writ, which is proposed to all without distinction of persons – "To the wise and to the unwise I am a debtor" (Romans 1: 14) – that spiritual truths be expounded by means of figures taken from corporeal things, in order that thereby even the simple who are unable by themselves to grasp intellectual things may be able to understand it.[23]

In other words the revelation of divine and spiritual truth was possible only via the laws of the created order, and was made accessible to human perception through allegory (*sub metaphoris, sub similitudine corporalium*, and so on, in the language of scholastic discourse). This is the first reason for the allegorical reading of nature and the natural environment. The laws of divine grace then demand that such truth be made available to all without prejudice of education or learning, thereby further confirming, as Aquinas points out, the metaphorical principle. Indeed he pursues this path still further, to the extent of advocating lower forms of metaphor in the interests of avoiding error, of emphasizing the distance of God from earthly things, and of concealing the highest things from lowly minds. "Objection 3" to the use in scripture of metaphor suggests that "the higher creatures are, the nearer they approach to the divine likeness. If therefore any creature be taken to represent God, this representation ought chiefly to be taken from the higher creatures, and not from the lower; yet this is often found in Scriptures." To this Aquinas answers as follows:

As Dionysius says (*De caelesti hierarchia* i), it is more fitting that divine truths should be expounded under the figure of less noble than of nobler bodies,[24] and this for three reasons. Firstly, because thereby men's minds are the better preserved from error. For then it is clear that these things are not literal descriptions of divine truths, which might have been open to doubt had they been expressed under the figure of nobler bodies, especially for those who could think of nothing nobler than bodies. Secondly, because this is more befitting the knowledge of God that we have in this life. For what He is not is clearer to us than what He is. Therefore similitudes drawn from things farthest away from God form within us a truer estimate that God is above whatsoever we may say or think of Him. Thirdly, because thereby divine truths are the better hidden from the unworthy.[25]

In this formulation Aquinas was articulating a position, inherited from Pseudo-Dionysius especially via John Scotus Eriugena, expressed in various contemporary fora. A particularly obvious arena for its application is in the cultivation, from the mid thirteenth century, of *ad status* sermons. Here, as Jacqueline Jung has expressed it, "biblical passages and exempla were carefully selected for their ability to prompt quick identification and subsequent self-reflection on the part of the given audience."[26] Thus in the words of Jacques de Vitry,

for the edification of uncultured people and the instruction of rustic folks, you should often present things that seem corporeal and palpable and similar to what they are familiar with through experience; for they are moved more deeply by outward exempla than by [the words of] authorities or profound proclamations.[27]

Spiritual allegory yields further examples. Thus, for example, Anne Walters Robertson quotes a similar statement from Heinrich Suso's *Horologium Sapientiae*. On asking Wisdom/Christ why she proposes metaphors for herself based on "fleshly things," the latter replies, "The human intellect cannot understand simple truths about matters that are most sublime, and therefore it is necessary to convey them through images and accepted comparisons."[28] Christopher Reynolds draws attention to the same view as expressed by ecclesiastical humanists, a position he sees as deriving from a desire to relate their intellectual perspective to that of scholastic theologians, as well to the principles of rhetoric as expounded by Cicero and Quintilian. Thus the Neapolitan humanist Giovanni Pontano holds that "We must discuss divine matters with the same words we employ in talking and reasoning about human affairs."[29] The same symbolic mode is also famously discussed in Huizinga's chapter "The Decline of Symbolism" in *The Autumn of the Middle Ages*.[30]

Writing a full century and a half after Aquinas, Jean Gerson, as Jennifer Bloxam has noted, explained how human experience provides the model through which higher things can be contemplated, if not fully grasped. Thus, as Bloxam points out, the absorbing and even obsessive nature of worldly love becomes for him a paradigm for the ecstatic devotion of spiritual love, "in which the lover forgets the world in her all-consuming love of God. Thus it is the movement to a state of rapturous transport, in which all but the beloved is forgotten, that is the same in both carnal and spiritual love ..." Bloxam goes on to quote Gerson in illustration of his use, to depict the love of Christ, of the linguistic conventions of courtly love, with Christ's beckoning voice likened to the music of "chansonnettes amoureuses."[31]

Commentaries such as these seem amply to support the notion of a general familiarity, as least among the reasonably educated, of such allegorical parallels between the earthly and the divine. Such indeed, one might surmise, was the familiarity required to pierce the workaday surface of the household objects in contemporary Flemish devotional paintings and to perceive their higher, spiritual import. Only through such a mode of awareness can, say, the basin, ewer, lilies, guttered candle and so on of contemporary Annunciation scenes reveal their deeper meanings, and their inherent promise of a better world to come. Art historians have postulated the cultivation, in various fora beginning in the thirteenth century, of simple styles involving everyday imagery, aimed specifically at lay comprehension. The classic case is surely that represented by the fresco cycle of the life of St. Francis in the upper basilica at Assisi, part of a trend, beginning apparently in the 1330s, towards a new "vernacular" imagery that, in the words of James H. Stubblebine, "partook of the same life experiences as those of the spectators themselves." In the frescoes' images the profound message of Francis's ministry is given expression, in Stubblebine's words, "in a popular vein, purposefully employing a vernacular language of gesture, expression, costume, and architectural ambience."[32] Similar trends may be detected in the stained-glass windows of the great cathedrals, including the thirteenth-century windows of Chartres, in whose simple narrative idiom and naturalistic detail Wolfgang Kemp has detected parallels with the vernacular poetry of the jongleurs.[33] Jacqueline Jung relates these examples from Assisi and Chartres to the "visual vernacular" of the naturalistic images and subject matter presented on the west faces of some thirteenth-century choir screens. She sets this imagery, directed at the laity in their customary position in the nave, against the more formalized, hieratic schemes on the east fronts of the same screens, directed at the clergy in the choir. Presenting, like contemporary *ad status* sermons, images of humanity to the laity that resonated with their personal experience, such sculpture aimed, she suggests, "to stimulate positive behavioral changes in viewers through a process of recognition, identification, and empathy."[34]

That same distinction, drawn by the screen, between lay and clerical, naturalistic and symbolic is reinforced, Jung notes, by the screen's various functions and, crucially, by language. Thus the screen could be the site of delivery, to the public in the nave, of the Gospel and Epistle (in Latin), or of sermons and public proclamations (most typically in the vernacular). In a particularly telling instance, she relates how, at the end of processions in the Sarum Use, the priest, on reaching the screen before proceeding into the world of sacred mystery defined by the choir, was instructed to turn to the people and, departing from the otherwise customary Latin, address them in their mother tongue.[35] Yet there was one important respect in which the barrier, articulated by the screen, between vernacular and Latin, worldly and divine, could be breached, and the public voice could, at least in a proxy sense, proceed into the choir: this involves vernacular music, and in particular, by the fifteenth century, the secular cantus firmus.

The unattainable lady

The clearest manifestation of that mingling of voices, the realization of direct dialog between sacred and secular, is the outpouring, from the mid fifteenth century on, of Masses constructed on material borrowed from courtly love songs.[36] Here composers built on a musical and textual tradition extending back to the thirteenth-century motet in which the expression, in the poems of *fin amour*, of love for an unattainable lady could also be understood as directed, on a spiritual plane, towards the Virgin.[37] In other words a fully engaged love for a remote yet courteous lady could take as its object either the secular or the sacred ideal; both are embraced – or embraceable – by the late medieval model of devotion. Such a parallel is made explicit in a wide range of texts from the thirteenth to the fifteenth century. For the context of the early polyphonic Mass, though, it comes into particularly sharp focus in the lyric works of Jean Molinet. As chronicler of the court of Burgundy in the later fifteenth century and a composer himself, Molinet worked alongside and in the same cultural milieu as the composers of many of the songs and Masses in question.[38] The link is especially striking in his *Oraison a nostre dame*, the first and last lines of each verse of which quote the first lines of secular songs. To illustrate the – for us vast – conceptual distance that secular songs could travel in the process of such sacralization Bloxam cites the example of *Allegiez moy, doulce plaisant brunette* ("Sooth me, sweet pleasing brunette"), which in the original proceeds "dessoubt la boudinette" ("beneath the navel"). This dubious origin does nothing to deter a Marian reinterpretation, nor its segue, in the Molinet poem, directly into the unambiguously sacred "Ou Jesus Crist volt prendre char humaine" ("through whom Jesus Christ assumes human form").[39]

Bloxam draws attention to a similar parallel in another Molinet poem, *Dame sans per*, in the words of its rubric a "Dictier que se poeult adreschier soit a la vierge Marie ou pour un amant a sa dame" ("Poem that may be addressed either to the Virgin Mary or by a lover to his lady"). Here again the poet alludes to secular song, in this case a rondeau also cited in the *Oraison* and composed by a fellow employee of the Burgundian court: Hayne van Ghizeghem's widely circulated *De tous biens plaine*. Bloxam notes the allusion to the first line of the song ("De tous biens plaine est ma maistresse") in the first line of verse 8 of the poem ("De tous biens plaine et de beaulté l'exemple"). Yet there are other allusions, too, not least in the body of the first verse: here, as in the song's "chascun luy doit tribut d'honneur" ("everyone owes her the tribute of honour"), the lady/Virgin is one "A qui chascun doit tribut et homaige" ("to whom everyone owes tribute and homage"). More fleeting allusions such as this reveal the unforced commonality in language and imagery between the realms of poem and song, and the ease with which the one could drift into the other.

A similarly parallel model of devotion for both earthly and celestial ladies functions at the level of musical settings, most obviously in motets in which a close resonance is established between a sacred text and that of a secular model. Here too a number of instances involve *De tous biens plaine*. The best known is Compère's great "musicians' motet" in praise of the Virgin, *Omnium bonorum plena*, its first line a direct translation of the first line of the song whose tenor forms the basis of the new work.[40] An almost equally literal marriage of Latin and vernacular sense is embodied in Josquin's setting of the *Stabat mater*, with its cantus firmus drawn from Binchois's *Comme femme desconfortée*.[41] Here the disconsolate woman of the song becomes transformed into the lamenting Virgin at the foot of the cross.

Clearly the nature of the courtly love lyric, with its focus on a female object of admiration, offered innumerable possibilities for such conceptualization, possibilities that were exploited widely at a time of urgently felt need for Marian intervention on behalf of mortal souls. In such a situation, it is not difficult to envisage that a model having particular significance to an individual or body (such as a confraternity) could have been chosen to particularize a setting paid for, and thus "sponsored" as a votive offering, by that same individual or body. Such an act of sponsorship would have given the ritual celebration a special meaning and – it would surely have been hoped – a correspondingly special level of advocacy.[42] But whether selected to put a personal stamp on a votive work or simply out of a desire to intensify Marian devotion more generally, the songs chosen for such purposes are typically very clearly and easily susceptible to Marian resonance.

This basic fact must account for the repeated appearance in sacred settings of such songs as *De tous biens plaine*, *Comme femme desconfortée*, *Je ne vis oncques la pareille* and *Le serviteur*; and it is unsurprising that a number of settings of the *Salve regina* and other standard devotional texts likewise draw together the sacred and the profane, with borrowed songs often quoted intact and prominently highlighted in the superius voices of the new works.[43]

Yet such a practice assumes another dimension in the context of the Mass. If the commissioning, or – as in the case of Du Fay's four-voice *Ave regina caelorum* – the composing of a personal plea in the form of an antiphon setting was felt to have particular efficacy, how much more powerful would be the similar particularization of a complete Mass setting. Here the personal plea could be imprinted across almost the entire expanse of the central rite of the church, and, most crucially, drawn into communion with Christ himself, his appearance in the elevated host enveloped, as I shall discuss in detail in Chapter 8, in the sound of the polyphonic Sanctus. In this context the plea to the *alma mater* and prime *mediatrix* – directly via a Marian chant or in the *ersatz* form of a courtly love song – would, it must have been hoped, activate her desired grace at the one moment on earth when her son, the judge of earthly souls, would become physically present. It is this powerful sense of advocacy that surely explains the advent and sudden spread of chanson-based Masses in the later fifteenth century.

Secular song and the image of Christ

In light of this, the congruence between the poetic register and forms of the courtly love lyric, on the one hand, and the rhetoric of Marian devotion, on the other, was a highly propitious one. By contrast, the typically male gendering of the narrator of the love lyric would seem, at first sight, to have precluded in many cases the reuse of secular material to carry Christological significance. As we shall see in Chapter 6, in a consideration of the modes of identification and allusion raised in Anne Walters Robertson's study of the Machaut motets, this situation may at least on occasion be only apparent; yet it seems clear in any case that the ungendered status of the narrator in a few songs led to their widespread application in settings fashioned – more or less explicitly – to express devotion to Christ.

The most conspicuous example – probably one of the reasons behind its uniquely wide and long-lasting currency as a Mass cantus firmus – is *L'homme armé*, the subject of Chapter 5. The same possibility can be seen, though, in a number of other cases. A rare example in which application to Christ is unambiguous is provided by the cluster of works – motets, Masses, a Sanctus, and one other song – based on Ockeghem's *D'ung aultre amer*.[44] Thomas Noblitt noted that the use of the superius of this song both in the superius of part 1 of Josquin's setting of the Easter sequence *Victimae paschali laudes* and in an individual Sanctus by the same composer presumably resulted from his "desire to symbolize his devotion to the 'Paschal Victim' and to the One 'who comes in the name of the Lord.' "[45] Maria Rika Maniates pointed out the Marian impetus behind the analogous quotation of *De tous biens plaine* that follows in part 2 of the same motet.[46] More recently, David Rothenberg has discussed the same relation between Christological application of *D'ung aultre amer* in part 1 of the motet, addressed directly to Christ, and the (at least functionally) Marian part 2.[47]

Noblitt points out the even clearer symbolism of the use of the same song in the third part of Josquin's elevation motet *Tu solus qui facis mirabilia*: here the opening of the song in the superius, significantly juxtaposed with the original French words "D'ung aultre amer" ("To love another") in superius and bassus, is answered directly in the tenor and contratenor by "nobis esset fallacia" ("would be deceitful"). A repeat of the same procedure then follows on directly, the same chanson quotation (both text and music) being answered by "magna esset stultitia et peccatum" (hence "To love another would be a great folly and sin").[48] Since this is the same motet whose first two parts take the places of the Benedictus and Osanna II of Josquin's *Missa D'ung aultre amer*, the decision to quote the same song in the motet's third part, the only section of the motet not transmitted as part of the Mass, is clearly a reflection of the perceived link between song, motet, Mass and the figure of Christ. No fully persuasive explanation has been adduced for this curious state of affairs;[49] whatever the chronology of Mass and motet, though, the text of this elevation motet makes it particularly apt as a substitute for the Benedictus in its parent Mass and hence as the musical accompaniment to the elevation with which it would have coincided.[50] The link between song and imploration to Christ seems even more clearly flagged at the opening of the "Christe" section of the same Mass's Kyrie, the only place in the cycle to present an extended quotation of the entire polyphonic complex of the song.

A similarly Christological sense lies, as Rothenberg notes, behind the use of *D'ung aultre amer* in the anonymous setting in Rome, Cappella Sistina MS 63 of the Marian antiphon *Regina celi*. The ostensibly curious interjection, via this secular song, of Christ into a Marian work is explained by the location of its occurrence: it is quoted at the beginning of the secunda pars in tandem with the words "Resurrexit sicut dixit," thus invoking the one who "is risen, as he said,"[51] in music as well as text. There is a final, hitherto unnoticed piece of this puzzle, however, one that adds another dimension to the equation between this song and the figure of Christ: this is the double chanson by Basiron in which *D'ung aultre amer* is intertwined with none other than *L'homme armé*. Craig Wright has already identified Christ as the principal "armed man" of the song in its use as a Mass cantus firmus, an identification for which Chapter 5 will present substantial new evidence. With this intertwining of the armed man with a pledge of unwavering love, two ostensibly secular songs are harnessed, through an appeal to familiarity that Aquinas would surely have recognized, in raising the mind to devotion to Christ.

The gender-unspecific text of the popular anonymous song *J'ay pris amours* could, one might suppose, have engendered Christological applications; yet the context of its use in sacred works seems nonetheless to have been exclusively Marian. This orientation is clear from the appearance of its superius as one of a series of song antecedents used as the bases of successive verses of a *Salve Regina* ascribed to "Ar. Fer." in Munich, Bayerische Staatsbibliothek MS 34. More ambiguous, though, is the quotation of the same voice of the song in the contratenor of the invocation to Christ, *Christe, fili dei*, from the *Vultum tuum* motet cycle by Josquin.[52] Taken in isolation, the text of this motet, a conventional prayer to Christ as savior to have mercy on earthly sinners, would seem clearly to imply a Christological application for the song. Its context suggests differently, however: first, it is one of a series of seven motets that are otherwise exclusively Marian; further, while its six companions set intercessory prayers directed to the Virgin, this one, addressed to her son, implores him to "aid us through the prayers of your most holy mother."[53] Its circumstance here strongly suggests, therefore, that – in a reversal of the situation of the anonymous *Regina celi* setting mentioned above – the song quotation in *Christe, fili dei* functions as an emblem for the *alma mater* herself, bringing her into direct communion, through the proxy presence of the song, with the prayers she utters to her son.[54]

An essentially non-liturgical genre with a certain fluidity of potential application, the motet presented in some respects the most obvious musical forum for pleas for the intercession of saints, and particularly the Virgin. The same potential is clearly exploited in the Mass based on borrowed material; yet here the role of polyphony was fixed and subject to liturgical function. Built into the ritual re-enactment of the defining, salvific moment of Christian truth, the polyphonic Mass was susceptible to various means of presenting that moment with particularized and personalized nuance. That potential, and some of its specific manifestations, form the substance of the next, final section of this chapter.

A dialogue between model and Mass?

To build a Mass setting around a borrowed melody is to unlock the potential of that melody for symbolic and emblematic significance. With its presence in each section of the Ordinary it weaves a continuous metaphorical thread through the entire musical setting, and hence also through the ritual enactment of which it is part. Yet any more detailed and specific semantic correlation between model and Mass is generally much more difficult to make. Certainly no such argument is available when, as in the majority of cases, the borrowed melody is simply presented consecutively, from first note to last, once or twice in the course of each movement of its parent Mass: in such circumstances any closer interaction between Mass and borrowed melody is likely to be fortuitous.[55]

Where borrowing is more fragmented or sporadic, though, the question of a closer dialogue becomes, if susceptible to the danger of overinterpretation, at least more viable, and in some cases rich with possibility. Long's exegesis of Josquin's *Missa Di dadi* presents a classic case, its musical gearchange at the first Osanna forming – with or without consideration of the symbolic significance of its eponymous dice game – a clearly eucharistic telos. Since that same telos at Osanna I or Benedictus was a feature – as we shall see in Chapter 8 – of every enactment of Mass involving polyphony, this would seem to constitute the most likely locus for musical articulations in the borrowing patterns of other Masses. On the most general level, the textual and musical markers that, as in various other Masses that will be discussed in Chapter 8, signal the point of the elevation would likewise, *in situ*, have imbued those settings with a sense of the climactic nature of the focal point of the rite. But borrowing procedures offer the potential for more individualized articulation of the spiritual climax of Mass. A thorough search would likely yield a range of examples; for present purposes, though, it will suffice to present a few representative cases.

A particularly striking instance is presented by Obrecht's *Missa Ave regina caelorum*. While mostly concerned only with the tenor of Frye's famous motet of the same name, two sections of the Mass exceptionally feature its superius, in both cases in the superius also of the new work and set apart from the surrounding voices by a contrasting mensuration. There seems no reason to doubt that the choice of *loci* for this sudden shift – the passage in the Credo setting "Qui propter nos homines et propter nostram salutem descendit de caelis" ("Who for us men and for our salvation descended from heaven") and the Benedictus – were motivated by a heightened desire for the intercession of the Virgin – invoked in the model motet – at these crucial moments.[56]

A sudden change in borrowing procedure in the Sanctus of the *Missa La mort de Saint Gothard* attributed at various times to Du Fay and Martini seems strongly suggestive of some now lost symbolic meaning.[57] Following consistent quotation of the same (unknown) cantus firmus in the Mass's first three movements, the Sanctus first presents the same melody in inversion before, from the "Pleni" onwards, abandoning it entirely. While the two reduced-voice sections – setting, respectively, the Pleni-Osanna I and Benedictus – are apparently free of borrowed material, the Osanna II and Agnus Dei, falling after the healing apparition of Christ in the elevation, introduce a new melody that smacks strongly of popular origins. Since, however, the identity of this tune, like that of the main cantus firmus, is unknown, any more specific speculation on the meaning of this pattern of borrowing is impossible.

The popularity as a Mass cantus firmus of Du Fay's rondeau *Le serviteur* is surely due to the devotional cast of its text. In the context of Mass, I suggest, its "well-placed word" becomes the word that, in the incarnational sense of St. John's Gospel, "was made flesh and dwelt among us":[58]

> The well-rewarded servant,
> satisfied and fortunate,
> first among France's happy men
> I find myself, because of
> a single word well placed.
> I feel as though I am new-born,
> for, after unbounded grief, now
> I am become, by a new bond,
> the well-rewarded servant …
> I was as a man lost
> and the unfortunate lamenter
> when your humble good will
> served to confirm my hope,
> and that fair word was given to me.
> The well-rewarded servant …[59]

Three of the four Masses based on the song present its tenor consecutively in each movement. While thus, I propose, imbuing each setting with the sense of renewed faith activated through the gift of the word, this method obviously precludes closer correlation between the present words of the Mass and implicit words of the model. On the other hand the anonymous Mass on ff. 153v–60r of Trent 89 belongs with a group of early song-based Masses that treat their models with the greatest freedom.[60] Only the Kyrie presents the song tenor complete, and even here its original sequence is altered. Elsewhere the composer picks and chooses, sometimes eschewing the borrowed melody altogether, a practice that correspondingly serves to highlight the song when it is quoted. Noteworthy for present purposes is the Benedictus, one of only two duos in the Mass to introduce song quotation, a practice highly unusual in duo writing in Masses of this period generally. Still more intriguing, though, is the choice of the passage highlighted in Example 1a: following a partial statement of the song tenor in the fully scored sections of the Sanctus up to this point, the tenor in the Benedictus enters directly with the phrase set in the song to the words "D'ung tout seul mot bien ordonné," which, following the song, is imitated in the superius. With this choice, which seems unlikely to be fortuitous, the well-placed word of the song is thus made to coincide with the presence of the ultimate well-placed word – that being simultaneously made flesh in the elevation. As if to crown this pregnant moment, the duo (from bar 98) proceeds to build an imitative descending sequence out of a variant of the imitative figure that, at bar 29 of the song, had ushered in the conclusion of that phrase-setting and indeed of the entire work (Examples 1a and 1b).

A somewhat similar case involves the anonymous Mass in Trent 89 which, on account of its unusual mensural usage, Louis Gottlieb dubbed the *Missa O2*.[61] Robert Mitchell identified quotations from Du Fay's rondeau *Adieu m'amour* in the first part of the Sanctus, noting polyphonic similarities between song and Mass at the beginning and end of that section.[62] Elsewhere, and in a different context, I expanded on Mitchell's observation, pointing out that the tenor of the entire first part of the Sanctus in fact comprises an almost note-for-note statement of the tenor of the song.[63] As I also noted, though, the song is conspicuous, in most of the remainder of the Mass, by its absence. Why then, I wondered, did the composer of this cycle quote from *Adieu m'amour* at all? It now seems clear that the answer is to be found in the text of the borrowed song. The opening two stanzas carry what seems a fairly generic message of farewell to a loved one:

> Farewell my love, farewell my joy,
> Farewell the solace that I had,
> Farewell my loyal mistress!

Example 1a Du Fay, *Le serviteur*, bars 24–33

> To say farewell wounds me so much
> That it seems I must die.
>
> With sorrow I lament mightily.
> There is no comfort that I see
> When I depart from you, my princess.
> Farewell my love, farewell my joy …

The third stanza, though, gets to what, from the perspective of the Mass, is the heart of the matter:

> I pray to God that he may attend on me
> And grant that I may soon see you again,
> My wealth, my love and my goddess!
> For well I know what I leave, and
> That after my sorrow I shall have joy.[64]

Example 1b Anon., *Missa Le serviteur*, Trent 89, ff. 153v–60r, Benedictus

What is surely, in the context of this Mass setting, a Marian supplication is thus – as in the Obrecht example cited above – given a charged location in the musical section that, in its ritual setting, will frame the arrival of Christ in the form of the consecrated host. Viewed from this perspective, therefore, the supplicant asks for God to attend on his arrival when, following post-mortem cleansing ("after my sorrow"), his soul will finally attain the company of heaven and he will again be brought before the face of his love, the Virgin herself. What would appear to be general hints at the material of the song occur intermittently in other parts of the Mass; yet the only other direct quotations may well have been positioned to underscore the point of the Sanctus, occurring as they do at moments of direct supplication to Christ, in the Christe eleison and, in the Gloria, at "Quoniam tu solus sanctus, tu solus altissimus, Jesu Christe, Cum sancto spiritu in gloria Dei Patris,

Amen." Heard at these points such references to the song may have been envisaged to amplify the prevailing Mass text and thereby to draw Christ's attention before the fuller supplication to come, in preparation for his physical transubstantiation, in the Sanctus.

The absence of *Adieu m'amour* from the opening of the cycle that encases its quotation is clearly what obscured it from view for so long, and it seems likely that similar internal quotations remain hidden elsewhere within the Mass repertory. But cases such as this serve also to suggest a new perspective on a different, more fleeting kind of borrowing, one that has been examined in a pair of studies by Christopher Reynolds.[65] Extending his view beyond the relative clarity of cantus firmus statement, Reynolds details a wide range of apparent interquotations between various mid-to-late fifteenth-century Mass settings and contemporary songs, often in textual contexts strongly suggestive of mutual commentary. In the light of the above discussion it comes as no surprise to find that many of these associations involve settings of the Sanctus/Benedictus.

An example that would appear to relate particularly well to the one just described involves the twin case of the *Missa Pour lamour dune* assigned by Reynolds to Faugues and the song *Pour tant se mon voloir s'est mis* variously ascribed to Caron and Busnoys. Reynolds proposes quotation of the song at the opening of the Benedictus, prefigured, as in the case just examined, by similar quotation in the Christe.[66] While only one stanza of the poem has survived,[67] this is more than adequate to add depth and real plausibility to Reynolds's suggestion. The original text and a proposed translation follow:

> Pour tant se mon voloir s'est mis
> Et a servir me suis submis
> En lieu que bien m'a voulu plaire,
> Me souvient il,[68] pour cest affaire,
> Des biens d'amours estre desmis?
>
> If therefore my will has set itself,
> And I have committed myself to serve
> In a manner that has pleased me greatly,
> Does it befit me, in such a case,
> To be deprived of the fruits of love?

The stanza presents the words of a protagonist who has given himself to devotion with such commitment that he cannot imagine being denied its fruits. The sentiment seems particularly germane to the moment when, with

its singing during the Benedictus of this Mass, the proxy presence of whoever instigated its quotation – and implicit supplication – would have been
ushered before the redeemer at the moment of his transubstantiation.

That supplication was likely redoubled by the lost song, *Pour l'amour
d'une*, that formed the cantus firmus of the same Mass, and whose presumed
quotation, mostly in long notes, is heard simultaneously, in both Christe
and Benedictus, with the brief allusions discussed by Reynolds. Whether
or not this was the song of the same name known today only from its text
in the *Jardin de Plaisance* anthology, the "une" for whom, in the context of
Mass, it expressed love must, as in so many analogous cases, have been the
Virgin.[69] Here as elsewhere she would have appeared as the prime *mediatrix*, addressed in the customary supplicatory fashion. In fact, though, the
very nature and message of the *Jardin de Plaisance* lyric can only strengthen
the likelihood that it was indeed the text of the lost song that provided the
cantus firmus for this Mass. The Marian resonances of the poem, which
mesh closely with those of *Pour tant se mon voloir s'est mis*, would have been
barely escapable even in its original state: the poem sings of an admirer of
surpassing loyalty, free of envy towards the lady, even envy of "her love" –
the latter surely an allusion, from the sacred perspective, to Christ himself.
His devotion renders him free from care, and ready to oppose those who
speak evil, even to the point of leading them ultimately to mercy. Finally,
the fact that the speaker announces himself as a musician, one who proposes to sing "a new song" to the lady, would surely have given the poem a
special appeal to a composer planning, in his turn, to envelop it in the "new
song" of a cantus firmus Mass. It would seem reasonable to surmise, then,
that this combined nexus of quotation was intended by the composer, or
whoever willed or paid for his composition, to strike an attitude of humble
supplication both to the Virgin as *mediatrix* and, at the moment of his physical appearance, to the son with whom she was to intercede.

Yet such apparent references are not restricted to settings of the Sanctus/
Benedictus. The following examples will suffice to illustrate the range of
possible intertextual reference proposed by Reynolds. The "Cum sancto"
of a Du Fay Gloria in Trent 92, seems, he notes, to allude to the same composer's song *Adieu, quitte le demeurant de ma vie*. Such a reference would
make perfect sense in this instance, since, as he says, "The combined
imagery of the chanson (leaving 'the abode' of one's life) and the Mass ('with
the Holy Spirit in the Glory of God the Father') suggests a vision of life
after death, whether for Christ or a recently deceased relative of Du Fay."[70]
The likelihood of intentionality in this case is enhanced by the clear cases
(discussed below) of mutual reference elsewhere in Du Fay's work, and by

his demonstrable propensity, revisited at the beginning of this chapter, to co-opt his own music for his posthumous benefit. In similar fashion, the seeming allusion in the Kyrie II of Cornago's *Missa Ayo visto lo mappamundo* to the same composer's song "Moro perché non day fede" suggests, Reynolds posits, reinforcement through the song text – "I die because you will not give faith / To the pain that grieves me. / I beg your mercy" – of the more generic plea for mercy being simultaneously enunciated in the Mass. The point, he notes, gains further specificity from the fact that the setting in this instance is a Marian Mass, and the poet of the song is seeking mercy from his lady.[71] A further, and particularly suggestive, example involves the two-voice quotation, at the "Et incarnatus" of the anonymous *L'homme armé* Mass in Bologna, Civico Museo Bibliografico Musicale MS Q16, from Busnoys's *Ma très souveraine princesse*. Here the sovereign princess of the song, without whom its singer "cannot live," becomes identified with the Queen of Heaven, simultaneously invoked in the coincident Mass text, of whom Christ was born.[72] The apparent reference in the Agnus Dei II of Caron's *L'homme armé* Mass to two songs – themselves interrelated – set to texts begging for mercy (part of a much wider complex of interquotation proposed by Reynolds) likewise seems apposite in the context of a Mass text supplicating for mercy for sins committed.[73]

Reynolds's cases are not confined to allusions to individual songs in particular Masses: many of his examples propose mutual references between songs used as cantus firmi and those apparently quoted only fleetingly and across broader networks of songs and Masses. Neither need such putative quotation proceed in only one direction: source traditions suggest that in some instances the song constituted the response rather than the model. Thus, for example, Reynolds proposes textually meaningful interquotation between three passages from different Masses – the Benedictus of the three-voice *Sine nomine* Mass ascribed to Ockeghem,[74] the "Crucifixus" of the Credo of the second of the anonymous Naples *L'homme armé* Masses, and the "Qui tollis" of the Gloria of Caron's *Missa Jesus autem transiens* – and the second part of Agricola's apparently later song *Je n'ay dueil*. Credence is given to such a hypothesis by the text of the corresponding song passage: "For God desired to make you so perfect / that nothing can please me / except to praise your great virtues." Plausible textual relationships could be posited between any of the above Mass passages and the song fragment, which may conceivably have been devised in response to any or all of them. A comment by Howard Mayer Brown, quoted in this connection by Reynolds, sums up the latter's case as neatly as he could have wished: remarking solely on his encounter with this piece of text-setting in the song, Brown observed that "it is impossible not to think of the human soul worshipping Christ."[75]

Reynolds acknowledges that it may sometimes be impossible to separate, in a context of such motivic commonality as prevailed in this repertory, intended quotation from accidental resemblances which may or may not have struck performers as meaningful during the time of the music's currency.[76] But he is surely correct that "For composers who were schooled and employed by the church, allusions in chansons to Mass or motet texts must have been unavoidable."[77] Thus, he concludes, "Textual correspondences and contemporary rhetorical practices make it unlikely that all of these similarities are purely melodic coincidences."[78] To extrapolate a little, it is less important whether this or that case of interquotation can be demonstrated beyond a shadow of a doubt than that such interquotation went on, and that clear and potent motivation existed that would have given ample impetus for its operation. Moreover, at the root of any proposed exegesis of this kind must be the inference that such quotation surely did not need to be patent: its perceptibility to mortal beings, save to the supplicant whose needs brought it into existence, was likely superfluous and perhaps even undesirable. If awareness of the identity of the patron, or endower, of a particular polyphonic Mass was requisite for the prayers it would elicit, such familiarity had no reason to extend to whatever allusions and symbolism lay beneath its surface. Such an apparent dichotomy between awareness of general purpose and concealment of specific program held, for the late medieval psyche, no inherent contradiction, here any more than in the experience of Mass generally.

Real or illusory, fleeting or extended, all the above cases rely, nonetheless, on the idea of quotation, with all the semantic richness of association that this entails. In the absence of that idea, any notion of the musical/textual deepening of liturgically significant moments loses its moorings, and becomes much more elusive. Yet the final group of examples in this chapter suggests that distinctive shifts in musical surface, whether or not coupled with inter-piece musical reference, may in the right circumstances appear highly suggestive.

One of the most striking cases of abrupt change in borrowing procedure in a Sanctus setting occurs in a Mass that, in terms of construction, probably stands closer to the *Missa Di dadi* than any other: Josquin's also apparently early *Missa Faisant regretz*. As in the case of the *Missa Di dadi*, the greater part of this cycle is based on the repetition of a short fragment of an antecedent song, in this instance Frye's widely circulated rondeau *Tout*

Example 2 Josquin, *Missa Faisant regretz*, Sanctus, opening

a par moy. The reason behind the choice of fragment – a motif of only four notes – in this case is not hard to deduce: associated with the opening text, "Faisant regretz [pour ma dolente vie"] ("Feeling regrets [for my wretched life]"), of the second part of the song, the motif strikes the apposite pose for the penitent worshipper, imbuing the resulting Mass setting with a near-constant reiteration of the repentance demanded of the supplicant for Christ's mercy. As in the *Missa Di dadi*, though in this case not until the final Agnus Dei, the Mass culminates in quotation of an entire voice of the antecedent song, setting the superius of the model in the superius of the Mass.

But the addition of distinctive musical gestures in both Sanctus and Agnus points to links with other works by Josquin that, although their precise meaning seems destined to remain obscure, suggest some kind of eschatological significance. The first of these occurs at the opening of the Sanctus, where the four-note ostinato, in long notes in the tenor, is combined with a repeated motif comprising a falling third in dotted rhythm followed by a repeated note (Example 2).

Having saturated the three other voices for the greater part of the section, however, the motif then disappears. Following a reduced-voice "Pleni"

Example 3 Josquin, *Missa Faisant regretz*, Osanna I, opening

constructed from a new ostinato motif, the opening of the first Osanna combines the "Faisant regretz" figure, now presented in the bass as well as the tenor, with another repeated motif (Example 3). The upper neighbor-note figure from the beginning of this gesture becomes, in the final Agnus, the sole melodic material of the altus voice, where it is presented in long notes in a contrapuntal context that in most cases demands, or at least permits, that the interval in question be a minor rather than a major second (Example 4).

This motif might be seen to refer (as Jennifer Bloxam has noted)[79] to the first notes of the tenor of the antecedent song, which outline the same interval. However, a possible broader context that links together all these motifs is suggested by Long's close comparison between the *Missa Di dadi* and what is by common consent one of Josquin's latest Masses, the *Missa Pange lingua*.[80] Long observed the shared use in the two Masses of two musical motifs which, though simple in themselves, are presented in contrapuntal contexts so similar as to suggest with real musical insistence that their use in the later work constitutes a deliberate reference back to the earlier work. Having demonstrated that *Di dadi* is constructed on a

Example 4 Josquin, *Missa Faisant regretz*, Agnus Dei III

climactic trajectory designed to highlight the moment of the elevation, Long speculated that the common material used in the later work, a Mass *de venerabili sacramento* based on the Corpus Christi hymn, was inserted to forge a deliberate link between two Masses focused on adoration of the holy sacrament. Focus on the elevation – and hence on the sacrament – is a feature of every Mass in the later Middle Ages, whether polyphonic or otherwise; thus the telos in the moment of the elevation of the *Missa Di dadi* need not in itself imply an association with Corpus Christi, or indeed with any other specifically sacramental observance, though the quotation

Example 5a Josquin, *Missa Di dadi*, Benedictus, bars 1–29

of its material in a Corpus Christi Mass might. Yet the prominent focus in all three of these Masses on the Phrygian semitone of the *Pange lingua* hymn may plausibly support the notion of a more specifically sacramental link between them.

Whatever the grounds for these apparent musical cross-references, however, the point here (as examples 5a–d make clear) is that both the motifs in question – the dotted falling third with repeated note, and the upper

Example 5b Josquin, *Missa Pange lingua*, Agnus II, bars 41–60

Example 5c Josquin, *Missa Di dadi*, Gloria, bars 179–87

auxiliary figure – are the same as those featured in the last two movements of the *Missa Faisant regretz*.

If the upper auxiliary figure may perhaps constitute a shared reference to the Corpus Christi hymn, no obvious explanation presents itself for such concentrated and repeated use of the falling dotted figure. Yet other works by Josquin offer depth to the picture already presented. The most prominent of these is his famous lamenting chanson *Nimphes, nappés*. There are good reasons to believe that this song, which enjoyed great popularity in the sixteenth century, may have held some particular eschatological significance for its composer. Commonly assumed to date from his later years,[81] its mood of lamenting and (canonic) construction on the chant "Circumdederunt me gemitus mortis" ("the groans of death surround me"), a responsory following the Mass for the Dead, would certainly seem apt for a composer contemplating the end of his earthly existence. Possible support for that view may be seen in the use, likewise in canon, of the same chant melody in Richafort's Requiem, where it is enveloped, as John Milsom has pointed out,[82] in closely similar counterpoint. Here the possibility of a link to Josquin, which has been frequently remarked on, is strengthened by the likewise canonic quotation of the setting of the words "c'est douleur non pareille" ("it is a grief without equal") from the composer's chanson *Faulte d'argent*.[83] With these things in mind, it is interesting to note the prominence in this work of the same falling dotted figure. In fact the figure frames the entire piece, featuring strongly in its opening imitative point, where it also forms part of the pattern of interlocking thirds familiar from the *Missa Di dadi*, and, in a thrice-repeated ostinato in the superius, at its conclusion (Examples 6a and 6b).

The same figure turns up prominently in another song by Josquin that combines a mood of lamentation with canon in two of its parts: *Incessement livré suis a martire*. Here it figures prominently, in all five voices, in the opening imitative point and in the next one, set to the phrase "triste et pensif" ("gloomy and pensive") (Example 7). In itself this figure is of course entirely formulaic. Yet its consistent presence in these five pieces ascribed to Josquin suggests that it carried some particular significance: its textual contexts are either directly concerned with repentance or with lamenting, or linked to the moment in Mass that offered the one hope on earth of deliverance from their cause.[84] And its combination, in the three Masses, with other similarly repeated figures adds further to the tissue of possible meaning.

Of course no composer of the fifteenth or early sixteenth century has left direct verbal testimony concerning the intended meaning of such apparent

Example 5d Josquin, *Missa Pange lingua*, Benedictus, bars 1–13

motivic interquotation, and none is likely to turn up. But at least one group of pieces offers something very close. To consider these takes us back to the Masses of the composer whose posthumous prescriptions formed the introduction to this discussion: Guillaume Du Fay.

There can be no more directly personal or pathos-laden motivic usage in a polyphonic Mass than that which occurs in the Agnus Dei II of Du Fay's late and summatory *Missa Ave regina caelorum*. Students of Western music are universally familiar with the sudden and poignant tonal shift that, on the words "[Qui tollis peccata mundi] miserere nobis" ("[Who takest away the sins of the world,] have mercy upon us"), recalls the same musical passage from the composer's four-voice motet setting of the *Ave regina*, there personalized by the trope "miserere tui labentis Du Fay" ("Have mercy on your sinning Du Fay"). Thus Du Fay puts his personal stamp, via his proxy presence in the form of a quotation from his own motet, on the plea for mercy in a Mass from that phase in his life when the impending certainty of death would have been most prominent in his mind (Example 8a).[85]

Less familiar, though, is the fact that this striking passage, set off abruptly from the surrounding musical fabric in the "major" by its shift to "minor" sonorities and emphasis on (in modern parlance) diminished fourths, is a late echo of a number of similar text/music combinations from earlier phases of Du Fay's Mass writing. One of these, taking us back to the beginning of this chapter, is none other than his Mass for St. Anthony of Padua. Here, a similarly abrupt shift to minor sonorities and emphasis on the diminished fourth marks the extraordinary passage that in the Gloria sets the similarly imploring "Qui tollis peccata mundi suscipe deprecationem

Example 6a *Nimphes, nappés*, bars 1–15

nostram" ("Who takest away the sins of the world, receive our prayer").[86]
As in the Agnus Dei of the *Missa Ave regina caelorum*, the musical language
of the statement, once articulated, disappears as suddenly as it had arrived
(Example 8b). An earlier adumbration of the same gesture emerges in what
by common consent is its composer's earliest complete Mass cycle: the
Missa La belle se siet. Here again the "Qui tollis" of the Gloria is marked by

Example 6b *Nimphes, nappés*, bars 50–66

the same diminished fourth, F♯–B♭ in a "G minor" context, with accidentals notated in the superius in all early sources of the work precisely on the word "miserere" (Example 8c).[87] Finally, a notated B♭ in the music of the second Agnus Dei of a Sanctus-Agnus pair by Du Fay in Bologna Q15 and Trent 92 pulls the music to the flat side for the setting of the phrase "peccata

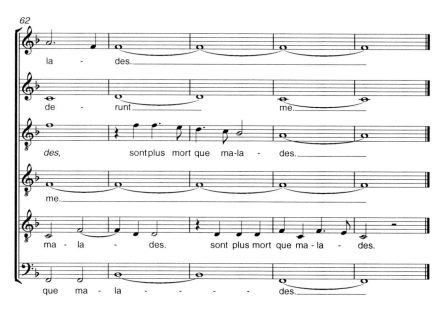

Example 6b (*cont.*)

mundi," a musical darkening that, as in the other examples cited, dissipates
as quickly as it had arisen (Example 8d).[88]

   While the two late applications of this remarkable musical idea provide
inescapable evidence of its eschatological significance for its composer in
his old age, its foreshadowings suggest that that significance was of long
standing, and had accumulated, over the course of a long and productive
life, from early in his career. For Du Fay's sense of himself, then – both per-
sonally and as a composer – these earlier statements lend to the valedictory
later ones a deeper and even summatory significance.

What are we to learn from the examples in this chapter in terms of musical
behavior more generally? Might we be able to glean from them any point-
ers to broader patterns of mediation between musical and cultural practice?
Could they help us to begin to map possible interactions of significance and
affective meaning, on the one hand, and musical articulation and patterning,
on the other? More particularly, are further such cases embedded in the Mass
repertory, and – finally – to what extent are we likely to be able to decipher
them? As acquaintance deepens not just with the repertory, but with its motivations and the needs it expressed, more probable cases of interquotation and
mutual commentary are likely to emerge. Yet the answer to this last question
seems likely, in most instances, to be at best ambivalent. The extent to which

Example 7 *Incessement livré suis a martire*, bars 1–22

individual circumstances and their associated networks of significance, which will typically be highly specific and localized, can be reconstructed with any degree of confidence is likely to remain limited. As Anmon Linder has observed in another context, "dedicated Masses are specific by definition; their relevance to particular circumstances is their only rationale, the real reason for their creation and performance." Although "they certainly responded to concrete circumstances when they were minted … as a general rule their relevance to that particular situation obviously stood in inverse proportion to the distance – spatial as well as temporal – that separated them from that

Example 7 (*cont.*)

particular original situation." While the material results of such specific vol-
ition may survive, and be observable, in what he has described as "fossilised"
form, their original relevance and meaning, so closely tied to their original
circumstances, will generally be transparent, or at best opaque, to subsequent
users.[89] As in the instances discussed above, we may in some cases be able to
surmise possible meanings of specific quotations or motivic usages by a process of inference sensitive to contextual, usually implicit, values. But in most
instances the mode of their survival is likely to remain limited to their material traces, mute as to the specific forces that shaped them.

Example 8a Du Fay, *Missa Ave regina caelorum*, Agnus Dei II, bars 72–82

Leads to the uncovering of such specific information are probably in
most cases, as in many of the instances discussed, most fruitfully to be
found in the circumstances surrounding and enabling the particular forms
of the pieces themselves. A contemporary understanding of the meaning
of local utterances can only be approached via awareness of the larger conceptual world whose expression they were shaped to articulate in particular ways. Yet here also we are likely often to find ourselves at a loss. To
quote Linder again, "contemporary performers had no difficulty in perceiving topicality through generic rubrics and contents; they could grasp
the link between the sign and the signified easily and almost unconsciously,
because these links formed part of their common intellectual heritage. But
no modern historian is equipped with these sensitive, almost congenital,
antennae …"[90]

Yet music, by its particular nature, offers at least some grounds for opti-
mism: its inherent potential for allusiveness, combined with the various
semantic strategies opened up by its interaction with text, offers the possibility, as we have seen, for a richer and more ramified body of potential
meaning. And in investigating the history of the polyphonic Mass we have
a more particular advantage: the widespread reuse of preexisting pieces,
most obviously in the wholesale form of the cantus firmus. For the use of a
particular preexistent melody in particular circumstances of itself suggests

Example 8b Du Fay, Mass for St. Anthony of Padua, Gloria, bars 151–64

Example 8c Du Fay, *Missa La belle se siet*, Gloria, bars 42–6

Example 8d Du Fay, Agnus Dei II [Besseler no. 6b], bars 18–27

avenues of exploration that may yield fruit, and may lead on to further, more localized insights into the workings of the pieces concerned. The next two chapters constitute interpretative explorations of just this nature into two of the most important and intriguing cantus firmi in the early history of the polyphonic Mass: *Caput* and *L'homme armé*.

4 | "Head of the church that is his body": Christological imagery and the *Caput* Masses

With seven surviving sources (unique for a Mass before about 1480) as well as a string of apparent emulations – not least of them the Masses by Ockeghem and Obrecht based on the earlier Mass's rhythmic layout of the same chant – the English *Missa Caput* has assumed unrivaled historical significance in the early history of the cantus firmus Mass.[1] Manfred Bukofzer's discovery of the antecedent chant solved a major puzzle, but in the process, as he noted, created new ones. While not alone in using a portion of chant other than its beginning (Bukofzer himself identified a series of other such cases),[2] the *Caput* Masses presented, in their quotation of the melismatic setting of a single word, a very particular problem of interpretation: why just this one word? What, or whose, head was being alluded to, and with what particular import? Should we assume that the word carried the same signification for all three cycles, and in all times and places of their currency?

Through investigation of the liturgical and biblical sources of the *Caput* melisma's parent antiphon, Bukofzer was able to put forward some plausible hypotheses. As is now – thanks to his work – well known to scholarship, the melisma constitutes the final passage from an antiphon, *Venit ad Petrum*, found in various French and English uses in the so-called *pedilavium* (foot-washing) ceremony held, generally after Vespers, on Maundy Thursday. The fact that Bukofzer's closest musical antecedent was found not in a Continental chant source but in a Sarum processional was the first element in a gradual process of realization that the Mass was not, as indicated in Trent 88, by Du Fay, but was rather the work of an anonymous English composer.[3] Other significant details of Bukofzer's discussion concerned the biblical source of the parent antiphon and its context in its liturgical setting. The source of *Venit ad Petrum*, and of the antiphon *Ante diem festum*, which always precedes it in the liturgical settings identified by Bukofzer, is John 13, a passage describing Christ's washing of the disciples' feet at the Last Supper:

[*Ante diem festum*:]
(1) Now before the festival of the Passover, Jesus knew that his hour had come to depart from this world and go to the Father. Having loved his own who were in this world, he loved them to the end. (2) The devil had already put it into the heart of

Judas son of Simon Iscariot to betray him. And during supper (3) Jesus, knowing that the Father had given all things into his hands, and that he had come from God and was going to God, (4) got up from the table, took off his outer robe, and tied a towel around himself. (5) Then he poured water into a basin and began to wash the disciples' feet and to wipe them with the towel that was tied around him.

[*Venit ad Petrum*:]
(6) He came to Simon Peter, who said to him, "Lord, are you going to wash my feet?" (7) Jesus answered, "You do not know now what I am doing, but later you will understand." (8) Peter said to him, "You will never wash my feet." Jesus answered, "Unless I wash you, you have no share with me." (9) Simon Peter said to him, "Lord, not my feet only but also my hands and my head!"[4]

Bukofzer noted that such long melismas as that on "caput" are rare in antiphons, which tend to observe the neumatic text/music relationship that characterizes the remainder of *Venit ad Petrum*. However, a similarly long and wide-ranging melisma also concludes *Ante diem festum*, where it falls on the word "discipulorum." Two elaborate melismas concluding paired antiphon settings of adjacent biblical passages would seem to reflect some specific design and intention: as Bukofzer observed, "Since in plainchant melismas are not inserted haphazardly but usually lend emphasis, the two words must be of special significance."[5] Why, though, the emphasis on these two words, and why indeed on "caput" rather than, in a foot-washing ceremony, the more obvious "pedes"?

Bukofzer's proposed explanation points to the connection in many non-Roman rites between the washing of the feet, symbolizing the baptism of the apostles, and the anointing of the head with water, as in the sacrament of baptism. This is not, as Bukofzer noted, necessarily to imply that this same putative interpretation had also motivated the choice of cantus firmus for the *Caput* Masses; neither, as he also observed, is such a choice bound to presuppose composition for Maundy Thursday or indeed for any other particular feast, though either is of course possible. A number of alternative fora for the Masses have been put forward: Bukofzer himself, for obvious reasons, suggested composition in veneration of St. Peter, a proposal that has been seconded by Reinhard Strohm, who mentions Peter's status as "head" of Christendom.[6] Geoffrey Chew surmised that the English Mass might have been composed for a king, and perhaps more specifically, given its basis on a cantus firmus associated with anointing, for a coronation.[7] As an alternative, he put forward possible association of the Mass with the papacy, its cantus firmus putatively chosen in reference to the pope as head of the universal church, and more specifically, perhaps, to the 1439 decree, delivered at the Council of Florence, of union between the Eastern and Western churches.[8] A very different view has recently been proposed by Anne Walters Robertson, who sees the cantus firmus as a reference to the devil, corresponding to the incipit "Caput draconis," written in the tenor of the anonymous Mass as it appears in the Lucca Codex, and the depiction of dragons on the first opening of the copy of Ockeghem's Mass in the Chigi Codex.[9]

Whatever the merits of these various proposals (some of which will be reviewed below), the setting of a chant quotation in a new polyphonic context need not presuppose a direct link to its original context: as Bukofzer himself pointed out, "cantus firmi of Mass cycles do not necessarily indicate the liturgical season." Neither need a meaning, once invoked, necessarily be maintained through subsequent uses of the work in question. In short the possibility must be entertained, as Bukofzer noted, "that the antiphon had no influence whatsoever on the liturgical destination of the Mass."[10]

This point is widely corroborated in the motet repertory. A classic instance, and one that offers a close analogy to the case under discussion, is provided by Du Fay's *Ecclesie militantis*, a work based on two unrelated chant fragments chosen for the emblematic significance that their associated texts could be made to assume in their new context. As in the case of the "Caput" melisma, one of these fragments was associated with just a single word, "Gabriel," drawn from an original context referring to the Archangel and reused on account of the common nomenclature of the pope, Gabriele Condulmer (Eugenius IV) in whose honor the motet was composed.[11] David Rothenberg has made the same point more generally. He emphasizes the important caveat that, while it is often possible to adduce plausible symbolic reasons for musical borrowing and methods of borrowing, it is usually much more difficult to pinpoint specific occasions – or even kinds of occasions – for performance. As he notes, a tradition extends back to the thirteenth century of choosing preexistent melodies "solely for their textual content," which may often imply a variety of possible performance occasions. All that was required was a conceptual or emblematic link to the text of the borrowed melody. Still more germanely in the present context, he points out that "numerous motet tenors of the later thirteenth and fourteenth centuries remain unidentified precisely because they were chosen from obscure chants that happened to contain a convenient word that relates to the subject matter of the motet."[12] He underscores the point via reference to the fourteenth-century treatise by Egidius de Murino on the method of composing the tenors of motets: Egidius advises "First choose a tenor from an antiphon or responsory or some other song in the antiphoner, and the words should agree with the matter ['concordare cum materia'] from which you wish to make the motet."[13]

None of this is necessarily to discount any particular hypothesis regarding the use as a cantus firmus of the "Caput" melisma; but neither, *prima facie*, should the reason for that use be assumed to lie in any one particular direction, whether liturgical or otherwise. Nor need we presuppose that the specific meaning – or range of meanings – carried by a cantus firmus in a particular polyphonic context is bound to have remained fixed and immutable throughout the history of the use of the piece in which it is embedded, much less for any subsequent pieces modeled on the same tune. Indeed, in explaining the continued life of pieces beyond their originating circumstances, there may be considerable merit in the idea of more generally applicable, "exemplary" meanings which had the potential to be enriched and deepened by additional meanings in a broader range of contexts.[14] Clarity of primary meaning, in other words, plus potential for adaptability to changing circumstances, would seem to be prerequisites for the extended currency of a cantus firmus and its polyphonic progeny. Such considerations may carry particular weight in the case of the *Caput* Masses, a series of works spanning as much as half a century and copied in a wide variety of sources. With these things in mind I propose here a further possible meaning for the "Caput" melisma, one that has the capacity to embrace both earlier and new potential hypotheses while also having the advantage of more direct and widely applicable relevance to the sacramental meaning of Mass.

Christ as head

A search for a plausible "caput" in the Bible quickly yields a clear favorite: the word is allied repeatedly and exclusively in the Pauline epistles with none other than Christ himself. Ephesians 1 articulates what was to become the commonplace juxtaposition of Christ, as head, in relation to the church, which is his body:

(20) God put this power to work in Christ when he raised him from the dead and seated him at his right hand in the heavenly places, (21) far above all rule and authority and power and dominion, and above every name that is named, not only in this age but also in the age to come. (22) And he has put all things under his feet and has made him the head over all things for the church, (23) which is his body, the fullness of him who fills all in all.[15]

The inextricable nature of this link between the head and body, to become such a powerful symbol in late antiquity and the Middle Ages of the unity of the church with and in Christ, receives further clarity in Ephesians 4:

(15) But speaking the truth in love, we must grow up in every way into him who is the head, into Christ, (16) from whom the whole body, joined and knit together by every ligament with which it is equipped, as each part is working properly, promotes the body's growth in building itself up in love.[16]

Colossians 2 foreshadows the late medieval emphasis on the indivisibility of the Christian "body" as a guard against heresy and superstitions:

(17) … but the substance belongs to Christ. (18) Do not let anyone disqualify you, insisting on self-abasement and worship of angels, dwelling on visions, puffed up without cause by a human way of thinking, (19) and not holding fast to the head, from whom the whole body, nourished and held together by its ligaments and sinews, grows with a growth that is from God.[17]

Like so much else in the Pauline epistles, the head/body analogy for Christ and his church became a focus of debate and commentary from the church fathers onwards. For Augustine, in whose writings the analogy is invoked repeatedly, the indivisibility of head and body bore with it the guarantee of salvation:

For the Resurrection we Christians know already hath come to pass in our Head, and in the members it is to be. The Head of the Church is Christ, the members of Christ are the Church. That which hath preceded in the Head, will follow in the Body. This is our hope.[18]

Ambrose debates the degree to which the sharing in flesh of the head and the body permits the assertion that man is placed at God's right hand:

It is written, thou sayest, that "when we were dead in sins, He hath quickened us in Christ, by Whose grace ye are saved, and hath raised us up together, and made us sit together in heavenly places in Christ Jesus." [Ephesians 2: 5–6]. I acknowledge that it is so written; but it is not written that God suffers men to sit on His right hand, but only to sit there in the Person of Christ. For He is the foundation of all, and is the head of the Church [Ephesians 5: 23] in Whom our common nature according to the flesh has merited the right to the heavenly throne. For the flesh is honored as having a share in Christ Who is God, and the nature of the whole human race is honored as having a share in the flesh.[19]

In the first of his *Two Books Concerning Repentance*, Ambrose draws on Colossians 2: 18–19 (quoted above) in inveighing against the Novatians for refusing communion to sinners; in so doing, he asserts, they decline – in refusing to some members of the church the mercy bought by Christ's sacrifice – to "hold the head" and as a result diminish the whole body:

But you say: "Touch me not." You who wish to justify yourselves say, "He is not our neighbor," being more proud than that lawyer who wished to tempt Christ, for he said "Who is my neighbor?" He asked, you deny, going on like that priest, like that Levite passing by him whom you ought to have taken and tended, and not receiving them into the inn for whom Christ paid the two pence, whose neighbor Christ bids you to become that you might show mercy to him. For he is our neighbor whom not only a similar condition has joined, but whom mercy has bound to us. You make yourself strange to him through pride, in vain puffing up yourself in your carnal mind, and not holding the Head. For if you held the Head you would consider that you must not forsake him for whom Christ died. If you held the Head you would consider that the whole body, by joining together rather than by separating, grows unto the increase of God by the bond of charity and the rescue of a sinner.[20]

A similar mode of discourse is widespread also in a later literature whose ethos is fundamental to fifteenth-century conceptions of the Mass: the corpus of late-medieval Mass commentary.[21] A pivotal source in this regard was the late-twelfth-century *De sacro altaris mysterio libri sex* by Lotario de' Conti di Segno, the future Pope Innocent III. In the last of the six books of this work Innocent expounds on the promise of posthumous salvation inherent in the unified Christian body of Christ and his church:

This mystery can be otherwise explained. For the body of Christ is the universal Church, that is to say head with members, according to which the Apostle [Paul] says: we many are one bread and one body [1 Corinthians 10]. And in this body are found, as it were, three parts, out of which the whole body is constituted. One part is the actual head, that is to say Christ, who is both head and part of the body. The other parts are those of which the bodies rest in their tombs, even as their souls reign with Christ.[22]

Innocent's contemporary Sicard of Cremona uses the same corporal analogy in expounding on the spiritual battles on the one hand of the head, and on the other of his "members" here on earth:

[The battle] is fashioned "in the head" because Christ, battling with the devil, overcame him and despoiled hell; it is fashioned "in the members," because we are assailed not only by the world, but by flesh and by the devil.[23]

Like Augustine and Innocent, Sicard sees in the head/body symbolism the promise of salvation; for him, though, that promise is rendered still more emphatic through being located in the very physical indivisibility of head and body:

"… no one has ascended into heaven except the Son of Man" (John 3), from which, just as the members of the body are joined to the head, all who in the faith of this sacrament are made the sons of God, and thus one body, head with members, ascend into heaven.[24]

For Sicard as for Augustine, the resurrection of the head (Christ) is the precursor and guarantor of that of the body (his disciples, the faithful). Yet that resurrection is possible only via the perpetual spiritual battle of Mass, a battle in which the celebrant, taking Christ's part, should have in mind the prior and more complete victory of the head:

Therefore let the priest celebrating Mass, from these things he does, and which are done about him, briefly and swiftly have in mind the symbolic things that happened before, which symbols are realized in the head, and which are to be fulfilled by us in our conduct.[25]

The later characterization of Peter as *caput ecclesiae* (and proto-pope) derives precisely from his assumption of that role from Christ, the first and supreme head,[26] a status he was seen subsequently to bequeath to the See of Rome and to his successors as its occupiers. That legacy is clarified in the following passage from Innocent III:

For Peter succeeded Christ, not only in his form of martyrdom, but also in the sequence of spiritual authority. The which Christ showed, when he said: "you shall be called Cephas" (John 1). Although in one tongue "Cephas" may be translated as "Peter," according to another, however, it is rendered as "head." For just as the head has an abundance of senses, and the remaining members receive but part of that abundance, so the other priests are called to part of the burden, but the pope is taken up in the fullness of power.[27]

The role – and power – emanating from the partaking by any priest of part of that role as "head" was never more strongly drawn than in his act of receiving communion on behalf of his "body," the assembled populace. Thus, as Charles Caspers has noted, "when the 'mouth' received the sacramental communion, the other 'members' could communicate along with him spiritually."[28] Like Innocent, though, Durandus, in discussing the communication of priests, draws an authoritative distinction between the pope, as head, and the rest of the priesthood. He emphasizes the different procedure typically appropriate for the supreme pontiff, accounted for by the fact that "in the Church militant the pope, as vicar of Christ and head of all prelates, more perfectly resembles Christ." Other priests are thus separated from the pope "because they do not so rightly represent Christ as head of the Church."[29] Writing around 1320, Augustinus Triumphus of Ancona adds an additional Christological, as well as dynamic, aspect to this superior status when he claims, paraphrasing Ephesians 1: 22–3, "The Pope is elected head of the whole Church … It is for the head, however, to flow life to all members."[30]

Such elevated perspectives on the status of the pope reveal a hint of the process, which we will explore below, whereby his assumption of the role of "caput" could be manipulated for political ends. Whatever its earthly ramifications, though, the overwhelming emphasis, in the writings of the late Middle Ages as in those of the early church, in identifying a *caput ecclesiae* lies in the clear association of that term directly with Christ, the first and supreme head. It is to this association that all other applications of the term are ultimately to be traced. Aquinas, whose discourses on the theme of Christ as Head address the topic in its various aspects, clarifies the point:

… Christ is the Head of all who pertain to the Church in every place and time and state; but all other men are called heads with reference to certain special places, as bishops of their Churches. Or with reference to a determined time as the Pope is the head of the whole Church, viz. during the time of his Pontificate, and with reference to a determined state, inasmuch as they are in the state of wayfarers.[31]

Indeed the power and potency of this image of Christ seems, if anything, to have intensified in the later Middle Ages, and perhaps especially in the writings of such commentators on the Mass as Innocent, Sicard, and particularly Durandus, an exegete who, in the words of Joseph Sauer,

forgets in almost no situation (like his predecessor Innocent III) to search for connections with Christ, the head of the church. Since we encounter this spiritual realm physically embodied in the house of God, this will further afford us the opportunity to see what a rich and life-enhancing unfolding, what a magnificent perception of this medieval perspective is given us by the [physical presence of the] church. Ficker described Christ and the church as the central idea of Sicard's symbolic system. And yet we believe that this idea can be still more precisely grasped, for Sicard as for Durandus, if we recognize the conception of the church as the body of Christ as the most profound concept of medieval symbolism, as of the entire contemporary worldview generally. [For] Christ appears to these authors only in his connection with and in his continuing life and deeds within the [life of the] church.[32]

To return to Bukofzer's essay, it might reasonably now be proposed that the placement of elaborate melismas, in the antiphon *Venit ad Petrum* and its preceding companion in *pedilavium* liturgies, only on the words "caput" and "discipulorum" was intended precisely to highlight the connection between the head and body in their prototypical historical and symbolic relation: namely that between Christ and his apostles. Further, while conclusive proof is unlikely to emerge, it seems probable in such a context that the eponymous figure of the *Caput* Masses, whatever its subsequent history, was first and foremost Christ himself, head of the universal church that is his body.

Where and for whom?

If this explanation is accepted as the likely ultimate source of meaning of the *Caput* Masses, the question that remains is what kinds of settings might have been considered appropriate for their performance? More specifically, who might have ordered their composition and performances and with what intended ends? As in the case – as we shall see in Chapter 5 – of *L'homme armé*, the application of such a potent image, fashioned for the ultimate model of all Christian leaders, would have been unlikely to remain restricted solely to its primary embodiment. Before considering the candidature of further possible "heads," however, we should first of all address some more general circumstances for which Masses on the *Caput* melisma might have been deemed fitting.

As already noted, the original location of the antecedent chant need not necessarily presuppose that the Masses were intended for that same occasion; but in any case a Maundy Thursday setting, at least of the anonymous English cycle, may be unlikely for other reasons. At least in the Sarum rite, the Kyrie prescribed for that occasion is "Conditor Kyrie" without its prosula verses, not the "Deus creator" prosula, assigned for principal and major doubles, found in the Kyrie of the anonymous progenitor of the *Caput* series.[33]

One possible locus for the performance of *Caput* Masses might seem to be suggested by the tradition of Masses on the Holy Name of Jesus that were celebrated widely, sometimes with polyphonic provision, in dedicated chapels during the later Middle Ages. But while the history of the Jesus Mass in England extends back at least to the late fourteenth century, evidence of choral Masses is lacking until the second half of the fifteenth century. Moreover, the Feast of the Holy Name acquired canonical status in England only at the end of that century; before that, Jesus Masses would have been celebrated solely as votive observances, for which large-scale Kyries, designed – as in the case of the anonymous *Caput* Mass – to carry prosula texts would have been permissible only "sine versibus."[34] It would thus appear that such polyphonic developments of the Jesus Mass occurred too late to have inspired the anonymous *Caput* cycle. But thematic and symbolic focus on the head and body of the church suggests another scenario, for which occasions would have been both abundant and propitious: the feast of Corpus Christi.

Composition – or at least performance – of a *Caput* Mass for Corpus Christi would have constituted a particularly eloquent expression of the corporate notion of Christ as head of an earthly body. A likely scenario, since such gilds had both the occasion and, frequently, more than adequate funds, is provided by the Masses celebrated by gilds of Corpus Christi.[35] Such a setting would have expressed with particular clarity Paul's formulation, in the Epistle to the Romans, that "as in one body we have many members, and not all the members have the same function, so we, who are many, are one body in Christ, and individually we are members one of another."[36] Suggestive in this regard are the ordnances, from 1408, of the York gild of Corpus Christi, for whose Mass it is instructed "as Christ unites the members to the Head by means of his precious Passion, so we shall be united in faith, hope and charity by the daily celebration of this sacrament of remembrance." Advocating for the efficacy of the gild, the text goes on: "In this fraternal unity, likewise, all the brethren will become members of Christ … For, just as all the natural members of man have an innate compassion with the head, so will all the brethren have a reciprocal love for Christ."[37] As Eamon Duffy notes, "The Mass is the sign of unity, the bond of love: whoever desires to live, must be 'incorporated' by this food and drink [of the sacrament]. Thus the unity and fellowship of the Corpus Christi gild is just one aspect of the 'mystical body of Christ,' a unity rooted in charity and expressed in the works of mercy."[38]

But the idea of Corpus Christi, via its eucharistic symbolism, came to embrace a much broader sense of unity: that of late medieval society as a whole, a society that, as Mervyn James has expressed it, was one "seen in terms of the body."[39] A hierarchy of "members" held in check by the magistrature, this "social body" of a late medieval town found perhaps its clearest physical embodiment and expression in the festal event that followed the Mass of the day: the Corpus Christi procession. While the Mass – for which performance of a Mass on *Caput* would have been especially fitting – was fixed in its particulars, the nature of the procession and its route were at the discretion of the ecclesiastical and civic leaders of the town.[40] We know for example that antiphons and motets were often sung *en route*, in addition to the traditional hymns, perhaps embodying a thematic and/or sonic link to music that had been heard in the preceding Mass.[41] In the procession, as James notes, the host, consecrated in the mother church before setting out on its peregrination, "becomes the point of reference in relation to which the structure of precedence and authority in the town is made visually present on Corpus Christi Day." The gilds processed in order of seniority, culminating with the town magistracy and, last of all, along with the highest-ranking clerics, the mayor, his place next to the host itself symbolizing a status rooted in an authority not merely human, but divine. Here was the ultimate source of his authority over his civic subjects: in James's words, "he was the head, and they the members." Likewise the carrying by priests – representing individual parishes or other ecclesiastical foundations – of their saintly relics emphasized both institutional pride in their power and, implicitly, their subsidiary and dependent positions in relation to the body of Christ.[42]

A similar sense of precedence and tradition informs the assigning of the pageants, or "Corpus Christi plays," presented traditionally by the individual gilds on wagons positioned along the processional route. That route gave a sense of the larger, spatial aspect of this civic sense of embodiment – and authority – with Christ, creating as it did a symbolic link between the marking of civic space and the *via crucis* itself, and casting the people not as mere onlookers, however pious, but as the populace of Jerusalem. It was also the forum for assertion of a higher, divinely endowed secular authority in cases where, as for example in York and Coventry in England and Lérida and Barcelona in Spain, the same route was also followed by royal entries.[43] Indeed, as for the Corpus Christi procession, a function of the process of the royal entry was the symbolic transformation of the city in question into a celestial Jerusalem,[44] and, by the same token (as we shall explore below), the casting of the entering monarch as a type of Christ.[45] The possibility of an association between *Caput* and Corpus Christi gains a more specific focus from the presence in Coventry, a city with a powerful Corpus Christi gild and a particularly strong tradition of processions and Corpus Christi plays (two of which have survived), of a fragment of none other than the anonymous *Caput* Mass itself.[46] The fact that this sheet was found in the binding of the Coventry Leet book – a series of records of the mayoral court dealing chiefly with local by-laws and ordinances and containing considerable detail on the events surrounding Corpus Christi – adds a further tantalizing twist to this already highly suggestive conjunction.

Yet the message embodied in Corpus Christi and its various devotions, both within the church and out into the secular world, was really only an extension and intensification of the symbolism of Mass, and, most particularly, of the idea of communion.[47] As the sermon of St. John Chrysostom, read at Matins in the season of Corpus Christi, affirms: "Christ hath mingled himself with us, and infused his Body into our bodies, that we may be one together, as limbs of one body."[48] Thus it seems reasonable to speculate that the Masses may at least on certain occasions have been performed, and perhaps even composed, for celebrations at which the people communicated. Given that for most this event occurred only annually on Easter Day, this may constitute the most likely occasion. Such a putative performance would also set up a close resonance with the parent antiphon of the

Caput melisma itself, situated as it was in the Holy Thursday literature that memorialized Christ's institution, at the Last Supper, of the New Covenant. Performance at Easter would conform most easily to the dual nature of the Christian sacrifice and its promise of eternal life: the sacrifice of Christ himself, celebrated with particular intensity at Easter, and that offered, in the form of bread and wine, by the people through the agency of the celebrating priest. The sacrificial gifts of bread and wine, instances of the food and drink that sustain earthly life, are at the same time symbols of community here and, through their sacramental properties, in the life to come. They are also, in their ritual role as sacrifice, blended with the sacrifice of Christ, so that the offerings both of redeemer and of future redeemed become together the sacrifice of one Church. The bodily consuming of the sacrifice – "Christ in us" – enacts the communion of "head" and "members," uniting the whole body of the church and embodying the promise of salvation of the members through the prior resurrection of the head.[49] The prayer "Salve salutaris hostia," printed in England in various early sixteenth-century primers to be uttered by worshippers about to receive communion, expresses this spirit and intention as well as anything:

Make me, O Lord … that I may be worthy to be incorporated into Your body, which is the Church. May I be one of Your members, and may You be my head, that I may remain in You, and You in me, so that in the resurrection my lowly body may be conformed to Your glorious body, according to the promise of [St. Paul] the Apostle, and so that I may rejoice in You and your glory eternally.[50]

It was to this ultimate communion of the body with the head that, as countless prayers remind us, the mind was to turn at the moment of the earthly reception of communion at Mass. And it is in this sense of incorporation that the deeply integrated structure of the Christian sacraments comes full circle: for it is this same notion of bodily belonging with Christ that links the first sacrament, that of baptism, with its biblical precursor in Christ's washing of his disciples' feet. With the act of communicating at Mass this acknowledgment of belonging, this shared coinherence in the body of the universal church, was linked all the way back to its origins in the baptismal rite of initiation. As Christ reminds Peter in the passage in John from which the antiphon carrying the *caput* melisma was drawn, "Unless I wash you, you have no share with me." The concept of the union of the body with the head was, in the beginning and the end, what focused and gave meaning to the constitution of the earthly church. Perhaps, on certain occasions, it was also what linked the enactment of Mass with performance of one or other of the *Caput* Masses, in an eloquent symbolic, as well as sonic, whole.

It is this union of the symbolic and the societal sense of such belonging, I propose, that underlies the cultural significance of the texts and music addressed in this chapter. According to this model the tradition of the *Caput* Masses elaborates, in assuming and highlighting the concept of the head, the primary and unifying bond for the church – in both its earthly and transcendental forms – of Christ. At the same time, though, this primary meaning opens up the possibility for a range of references to further, earthly figures seeking to affirm an authority, grounded in that of Christ, as "head" of his body here on earth.

Earthly heads

Not surprisingly, the most characteristic and frequent claims to a partaking of Christ's status as head are made on behalf of those acting explicitly as his spiritual vicars, namely the clergy. Only ordained priests had control over the sacraments, and, most crucially, the God-given power to bring forth Christ's physical presence in the transubstantiated host. Ordination, like the eucharist, was one of the Seven Sacraments, and a man could be admitted into priestly orders only by another "head," the presiding bishop. Thus in discussing the bishop's vestments, Innocent III speaks of "the bishop in the office of the altar representing the person of his head, Christ, of whom he is a member."[51] As noted above (page 83) in quotations from Innocent III and Durandus, however, that privilege resided in particular measure with the pope, inheritor of the role of Peter, bestowed by Christ himself, as head of the Church. With the struggle for temporal power between pope and emperor – in which Innocent was himself such a defining figure[52] – emphasis on priestly, and especially papal, power assumed a powerful, and distinctly political, magnitude.

Nowhere, at least by the twelfth century, was this distinction more clearly wrought than in the act of the anointing of kings. "Kings," Innocent wrote, "are anointed by priests, not priests by kings. Lower thus is he who is anointed, than he who anoints, and more dignified the anointer than the anointed."[53] With similar import Durandus, drawing on Ephesians 5: 23, notes that, in contrast to the procedure applied to princes, who are anointed on the arm or shoulder, "in the case of a bishop the sacramental anointing is applied to the head, because in his episcopal office he represents the head of the church, that is Christ."[54] For Innocent, however, not only was the pope head of the church: he was without earthly peer, "set between God and man, below God but above man, less than God but more than man, who judges all men but is judged by no one."[55]

Not surprisingly, emphasis on the role of the pope as head seems to have been proportional to the degree to which, particularly from the early fourteenth century on,[56] that office increasingly asserted itself as a terrestrial and political power. Kantorowicz adduces numerous witnesses to testify that by the fourteenth century the view of the pope as a princely "head" ruling a political entity was commonplace. Thus the Neapolitan jurist Lucas de Penna affirmed, paraphrasing Aquinas, that "the Church compares with a political congregation of men, and the pope is like to a king in his realm on account of his plenitude of power." Just how easily the Pauline characterization of Christ as head could by now be transferred also to the pope is illustrated in the statement by the fourteenth-century Bavarian Hermann of Schilditz that "Just as all the limbs in the body natural refer to the head, so do all the faithful in the mystical body of the Church refer to the head of the Church, the Roman pontiff."[57]

As we shall see again in Chapter 5, the development in the sacred realm of such metaphors for the justification of secular power has its counterpart – typically for the interactions of late medieval power structures – in the sacred conceits of secular courts. One way into a view of how such authority was asserted takes us back to an earthly corporate ritual already alluded to, but from the opposite, civic perspective: the practice of royal entries.

When Richard III entered York via the Corpus Christi route in 1483 he was making a statement of both dynastic and personal significance: in the first place this was the principal seat of the royal house to which he belonged; in the second the king and queen were members of the York Corpus Christi gild and were attended by representatives of churches situated on the route of the procession.[58] But in choosing this path he was demonstrating far more than secular regal status and solidarity with the members of a gild in which he held membership (though that in itself constituted a telling expression of regal civic authority). In proceeding thus – and especially in choosing to do so on the symbolically significant feast day of the Decollation of St. John the Baptist – he was coming among the citizens of York, in the words of Pamela Tudor-Craig, "as the incarnate and temporal representative of divine order."[59] More profoundly even than this, though, in following this processional route, a symbolic *via crucis*, the king was affirming his status as a type of Christ, triumphally entering Jerusalem on Palm Sunday. Concomitantly, as Tudor-Craig notes, the populace of York were transformed "into the citizens of Jerusalem, and their city into a type of the two Jerusalems, earthly and heavenly."[60]

The parallel of king with Christ was still more vividly drawn when, during the entry into Paris, in 1431, of the boy king Henry VI, the king's head was surmounted by a large canopy painted with an azure sky, "in the form and manner that one does for Our Lord on Corpus Christi."[61] The link with Corpus Christi, and its attendant physical conflation of king with Christ, was more directly expressed even than this chronicle suggests however: the canopy in question, used for royal entries from 1360 until the sixteenth century, was one actually used for Corpus Christi processions, borrowed for this regal purpose from the priory of St. Catherine.[62] Here again, timing was of the essence, though the day in question was not that of Corpus Christi: the entry was staged on the first Sunday in Advent, the day traditionally chosen, for its Christological significance, for processions to the cathedral by French kings. As was customary in such entries, the parallel was underscored by the chanting of "Nowell."[63] Likewise in common with royal entries generally, biblical episodes enacted in plays along the route underscored the divine resonances of the occasion.[64] A repeated representation in late-fifteenth-century Parisian royal entries was the image of the "king-child," the implied parallel being that linking the king's advent to the throne, as a symbolic "new-born infant," with the birth of Christ in Bethlehem.[65] Similarly, one of the pageants greeting the entry of Prince Edward (the future Edward V) into Coventry in 1474 involved a speech in which a "patriarch" drew a parallel between the arrival of the prince and the Advent of Christ, while elsewhere "children of Israel" sang and threw white wafers and flowers.[66]

Indeed, as Gordon Kipling has encapsulated it, the royal entry, in its depiction of the entering monarch as a type of Christ, drew on not one, but a whole series of Christian advents: that of Christ's coming to humankind, his entry into the individual hearts of believers, his entry into Jerusalem on Palm Sunday, his ascension into heaven and – finally and crucially – his Second Coming to judge mortal souls. Song, with its implications of combined celestial and political harmony, was a distinctive feature of most such entries, with the singing of angels, and especially of the "Benedictus qui venit" which greeted Christ as he entered Jerusalem on Palm Sunday, figuring prominently. Thus at his entry into Bruges in 1477 Maximilian I was hailed at the city gate by a painted depiction of himself as Christ entering Jerusalem with the children of Israel singing the Benedictus.[67] The same custom marked the French King Francis I's entry, in 1532, into Caen.[68] Still more vivid in its parallel between earthly and celestial "heads" was the entry, on 14 April 1485, of Charles VIII into Rouen: here, at the conclusion of the first tableau, "shepherds" sang a rondeau "faicte a quatre partz, donc le subget de l'ung costé est *Benedictus qui venit in nomine domini. Et à lautre costé, pour subget: O Francorum rex.*" The song ended with a paean to the regal "head," Charles himself: "Longuement vive le chef du corps mistique."[69] In similar fashion the tableaux that greeted the Parisian entry in 1437 of Charles VII and the

Bruges entry in 1440 of Duke Philip the Good of Burgundy invoked, in the singing by angels to shepherds of the *Gloria in excelsis*, the angelic annunciation of the birth of Christ.[70] The English King Henry VII's Household Ordinances of 1494 stipulate that on the next reception of a queen into London "at the Condit in Conylle ther must be ordained *a sight with angelles singinge*, and freshe balettes theron in latene, englishe, and ffrench, mad by the wyseste doctours of this realme; and the condyt in Chepe in the same wyse." Similarly the double triumph in 1522 of Henry VIII and the Emperor Charles V was marked by a "pageant representyng hevyn ... w^t ... angellys knelyng and dyuers tymes sensyng w^t sensers and w^t voyces off yonge queretters [choristers] syngyng psalmys and ympnys [hymns]."[71] The climactic moment of the 1486 entry of Henry VII into York was marked, as he was about to enter the Minster, by "our lady comyng frome hevin," who thereafter "ascend ayene into heven wit angell sang ..."[72] There is no question but that this grandiose scene, like the series of magnificent tableaux of which it formed a part, was fashioned to make a particular impact on those who had witnessed, only a few years earlier, the entry into the same city of Henry's now-vanquished Yorkist predecessor Richard III.[73]

A similar message is evocatively inscribed in the records of a much more famous entry: that with which, in 1415, Henry V processed into London after his victory at Agincourt. Here the king was greeted by music including a Benedictus sung by "a lyon and a antlope [*sic*] with many angeles."[74] Margaret Bent has proposed actual music that may have accompanied this great event in the form of motets by Damett, Cooke and Sturgeon in the Old Hall Manuscript.[75] All three composers were members of Henry V's chapel – all appearing in the records for the first time in the first year of his reign – and the texts they set either relate closely to music that, according to the contemporary accounts she quotes, was sung on that occasion, or at least express directly appropriate sentiments. Thus the middle voice of Cooke's motet invokes the aid of the Virgin and St. George (patron and protector of England and addressed, like the king himself in the chronicles, as "knight of Christ") for victory and peace while its tenor quotes the chant of the rogation litany for peace; similarly the middle voice of Damett's motet sings a patriotic text addressed to St. George, while its top voice is set to a Marian sequence adapted to request eternal life for the king. It is clear at any rate that the motets by Damett and Sturgeon (the latter a votive Marian piece without topical texts) were composed as a linked pair: their tenors are based on contiguous sections of a Sarum Benedictus chant incorporating the common trope "Mariae filius."[76] Equally intriguing, though, is the position – and likely status – of these pieces in their source: their insertion within the first-layer Sanctus section of Old Hall suggests that, as Bukofzer surmised,[77] they were viewed as elaborately troped Sanctus settings. With this in mind their copying, probably (Bent has suggested) by the composers themselves, into a source from which they themselves sang in the Chapel Royal, becomes highly suggestive. In a scenario that, as we shall see in Chapter 6, now appears far more plausible than hitherto, it thus seems highly likely that performance of these pieces was envisaged (in addition, perhaps, to that by the menagerie mentioned above) in the liturgical context of the Benedictus, with the plea on behalf of the king thus coinciding directly with the moment of the transubstantiation.[78]

Such musical juxtaposition, at the focal point of Mass, of the presence of Christ with the musical embodiment of the king in his role as head of state and *miles Christi* raises tantalizing possibilities. From this perspective the joint Damett–Sturgeon Benedictus might be viewed as an isolated, one-movement precursor – dating from a time before the advent of the cyclic cantus firmus Mass could have allowed for something analogous on a grander scale – of the anonymous English *Missa Caput*.

It seems clear that, as Kipling has observed, such royal entries as this of Henry V are informed less by scripture directly than via its function in liturgy. Thus Henry VI's London triumph of 1432, for Kipling the high-water mark of this tendency,

dramatizes Henry's entry into the city as a liturgical event – almost an act of worship – designed to mark the first manifestation of the Christ-king. More explicitly than in any previous British civic triumph, this show conceives of the people of the city more as a congregation of worshippers than as an audience. They play their part not merely by witnessing, but also by acclaiming and celebrating Henry's manifestations.[79]

Another detail, one whose implications will be explored in depth in Chapter 5, added a significant further liturgical *tinta* to this event. In an echo of Isaiah's prophecy of the sevenfold spiritual gift that will identify the Messiah, the last of a series of three tableaux designed to endow Henry's entry with a messianic import sees him presented with seven pieces of spiritual armor. With language deriving from Ephesians 6 and, as we shall see, a succession of late medieval texts including the vesting prayers of priests, he is advised, by seven angelic virgins, to "Accept the crown of glory, the sceptre of clemency, the sword of justice, the cloak of prudence, the shield of faith, the helmet of salvation, and the girdle of peace." Kipling notes that "on the one hand, the virgins offer him Pauline spiritual armour proper to a Christian knight, a *miles Christi*; on the other, they present him with spiritual regalia specifically appropriate to a Christian king, a *rex christus*."[80]

Although such records suggest numerous possible royally motivated scenarios for the composition – or at least performance – of Masses based on *Caput*, however, few explicitly identify the king, in something akin to the original, Pauline sense, as head. Any such perceived lack is easily made up, however, by the plentiful and diverse application of such analogies throughout late medieval political writing.

For the citation of a particularly elegant example we will return to 1483, and the first year of the reign of Richard III. The sermon at the opening of Parliament in that year, of which an excerpt reads as follows, was given by John Russell, Bishop of Lincoln and Chancellor of England:

> In thys politike body of Englonde there be iij. estates as principalle membres vndir oone hede, – thestate of the lordys spiritualle, thestate of the lordes temperalle, and thestate of the cominallete. The hede ys owre souuverayne lord the kynge here presente. What due proporcion and armonye ought to be yn thys body, amonges alle the membres, grett and smalle, Synt Paule, takynge hys similitude from the naturalle body of man, declareth at large j Cor [1 Corinthians 12: 12] ...[81]

In his treatise on the tempered role – in the British political model – of the king, the great Lancastrian lawyer Sir John Fortescue writes as follows:

> Saint Augustine, in the 19th book of the De Civitate Dei, chapter 23, said that *A people is a body of men united by consent of law and by community of interest.* But such a people does not deserve to be called a body whilst it is acephalous, i.e. without a head. Because, just as in natural bodies, what is left over after decapitation is not a body, but is what we call a trunk, so in bodies politic a community without a head is not by any means a body. Hence Aristotle in the first book of the *Politics* said that *Whensoever one body is constituted out of many, one will rule, and the others be ruled.* So a people wishing to erect itself into a kingdom or any other body politic must always set up one man for the government of all that body. Who, by analogy with a kingdom, is, from "regendo," usually called a king. As in this way the physical body grows out of the embryo, regulated by one head, so the kingdom issues from the people, and exists as a body mystical, governed by one man as head.[82]

Kantorowicz observes the exceptional degree to which rule in England by the whole body politic – with the king as head and the "body" of parliament ideally playing reciprocal roles – encouraged sacred analogies, including that whereby, in 1401, the Speaker of the House of Commons compared parliamentary procedures with the celebration of Mass.[83] The corporate model of rule through a process of interaction between head and body had a considerable lifespan. Thus it is no surprise to find it similarly invoked (albeit with a certain historical irony), on addressing his council in 1542, by Henry VIII:

We be informed by our judges that we at no time stand so highly in our estate royal as in the time of Parliament, wherein we as head and you as members are conjoined and knit together in one body politic.[84]

Yet however frequent and diverse may have been its application there, use of the corporational metaphor in such secular fora was far from restricted to England. Indeed the sense of luster perceived to flow from its biblical roots and history of sacred application ensured that its adoption was widespread. In this connection Kantorowicz again quotes from Lucas de Penna's commentary, concerning the relations between the prince and the state, on the final three books of Justinian's *Corpus juris civilis*. Drawing his analogy from Paul's dictum, from Ephesians 5, that "The man is the head of the wife, and the wife the body of the man," Lucas notes that

just as men are joined together spiritually in the spiritual body, the head of which is Christ ... so are men joined together morally and politically in the *respublica*, which is a body the head of which is the Prince.

Written in fourteenth-century Naples, Lucas's treatise found an attentive audience in the absolutist climate of sixteenth-century France, where it gained wide currency in explications of the laws governing the relation between king and state.[85] Yet its French cultivation was itself rooted in a long-existing tradition whereby the king, acting through divine grace, was characterized as head of a body conceived variously as political, civil or – as in the case involving Charles VIII cited above – mystical.[86] Thus Gerson's 1405 sermon "Vivat Rex" casts the king as "ordonnée pour le salut de tout le commun, ainsi comme du chef descent et s'espand la vie par tout le corps."[87] The report on the États Généraux de France, held at Tours in 1484, relating the departure of the sick king (Charles VIII) from the proceedings, notes that on his health depends the health of his entire realm: "Quel est le corps sans la tête? Un cadavre gisant à terre, privé de sentiment, de mouvement et d'âme." Here, as for Gerson,

le roi est la première portion et la tête du corps politique, il est le principe du sentiment et de la vie ... il puisât comme un souffle de vie, et ... le fit circuler depuis la tête jusqu'aux pieds ...[88]

For the same king's reception at Paris in the same year, a figure of the king, as mystical head of state, dispensed from a scaffold appropriate succor "by means of a subtle and quaint engine" to the three estates (nobility, clergy and common people) that constituted his body. Kipling notes that "The pageant not only demonstrates the moral nature of the King's marriage to his state, but also demonstrates that the body politic depends for its welfare upon the virtues of its head."[89]

In the third tract of his defense, of 1418/19, of the Dauphin's case for the French throne against the opposing claim of John the Fearless, Duke of Burgundy, the royal advocate Jean de Terre Rouge assumes a more absolutist stance. Thus for him the body can exist only under the aegis of one will, located in the head, which in this case is the king:

[Fidelity consists in that] every political or mystical member is held to adhere to, and to follow the will of the lord or mystical head, totally molding himself to it.

Echoing the pronouncement, quoted above, of Augustinus Triumphus concerning the dynamic role in the church of the pope, Terre Rouge notes that "The mystical head flows its being into all of its members." The fundamental aim here, Ralph Giesey notes, is no less than to

transfer to the state that powerful force of spiritual unity which the Christian religion had developed in the sacrament of the Eucharist and in the institution of the Church. Ultimately, Terre Rouge conceives of the union of the subjects as exactly the same as the union of the faithful in the body of Christ sacramentally, or in the church metaphysically.[90]

Further corroborative examples are surely surplus to the needs of the argument being advanced here. The force, as an explanatory model for the *Caput* tradition, of the bodily, Pauline image of Christ and his church lies in its fundamental exemplarity. Moored to this concept of the "head," the *Caput* tradition would thus be defined in terms of the primary and defining basis of the church: its corporate unity in Christ. Implicit in the model's exemplarity is a remarkable fecundity, embracing applications formulated – depending on priorities and circumstance – from the perspective either of the "body" or of the "head." In the former case it gave access to a potent sense of belonging in Christ, whether at the level of confraternity, or of civic, court or ecclesiastical body politic; in the latter it admitted of the assertion of the role of "head" by earthly leaders – whether in the sacred or the secular sphere – seeking to ground their authority in that of Christ. Thus in its scriptural basis and venerable lineage, it offers, for example, deep potential foundations for the proposals, first made by Geoffrey Chew, that the anonymous Mass may have been composed for a pope, or for a royal coronation, where its powerful original association with the act of anointing could have added an important further layer of significance.

But beyond any putative specific application, the Pauline model may also, I suggest, offer an explanation for the exceptionally broad transmission and emulation of the anonymous founder of the *Caput* tradition. In a discursive climate in which the notion of Christ as head was universally familiar and widely adapted to a variety of contexts and arguments, it is not hard to imagine any number of potential appropriations of *Caput* to raise the perceived status of earthly heads, asserting their authority via reference to the first, transcendent head. Such potential, indeed, is implicit in the quotation from Aquinas given above (page 84), and still more so in the following passage from the same article:

As Augustine says (Tract. xlvi in Joan.): "If the rulers of the Church are Shepherds, how is there one Shepherd, except that all these are members of one Shepherd?" So likewise others may be called foundations and heads, inasmuch as they are members of the one Head and Foundation.[91]

Desire for corporate association with – or rule through the authority of – Christ as head was a constant throughout the later Middle Ages, and certainly across the half century or so that separated the composition of the first *Caput* Mass from that of the last.

In its exemplarity as initiated in and defined by the figure of Christ, the use as a cantus firmus of the *Caput* melisma has much in common, I propose, with that of *L'homme armé*, the subject of the next chapter. Like that melody, it carried the potential for repeated, yet distinct, instantiations by a succession of mortal powers who sought, through access to its sacred authority, to present themselves as earthly "types" of Christ. And, as was surely the case with *Caput*, the symbolic weight of the image of *L'homme armé* increased as it was appropriated by a succession of princely magnates, each seeking – as perhaps reflected in the patterns of musical interquotation that characterize that tradition – to outdo the others in the assertion of heavenly authority.

Yet the melody of *L'homme armé* added an extra dimension to the Christological imagery encountered thus far: that of Christ as military champion. It thus bolstered the assertion of a further layer of secular authority: that of military might. In an age characterized by almost constant civil strife and its attendant military and therefore also ceremonial/chivalric posturings, it is surely this that explains the uniqueness of the melody's diffusion and longevity. For all the scrutiny that has been addressed to the question of *L'homme armé*, however, no direct link has yet been demonstrated between the role of Christ as armed man and the rite of Mass itself. That link is provided, along with much further potential elucidation of questions surrounding *L'homme armé*, by the same body of writings just addressed in relation to *Caput*: the corpus of late medieval Mass commentary. This association, and the rich tapestry woven by its many threads, forms the material of Chapter 5.

Embracing some forty Masses spanning more than a century, the musical family of *L'homme armé* has, not surprisingly, engendered more exegetical effort than any other. Contexts have been proposed for individual Masses and groups of Masses, and the eponymous armed man has been identified with a variety of figures, most prominently the Dukes of Burgundy Charles the Bold and Philip the Good.[1] Yet however persuasive such hypotheses may have appeared on a local level, their explanatory power was limited to the piece, or pieces, to which they were addressed. A fundamental question remained: what was it about this melody that extended its sway beyond the confines of any court, however magnificent, embracing the work of most composers of note from the 1450s to the 1520s and a number, albeit a diminishing one, thereafter? Whatever further resonances it may have carried, the primary identification with the figure hailed in its cantus firmus, and thus placed at the center of the ritual embodiment of the defining mystery of the Christian church, seemed unlikely to be of this world.

Such was the conclusion reached recently by Craig Wright. Wright concluded that the first and foremost "armed man" was Christ himself, the *bonus miles* who had redeemed humanity through his victory over evil on the cross, doing daily battle for the souls of the faithful through his reappearance in the elevated host.[2] This primary identification strongly encouraged further associations with the central figure of the cantus firmus: for a princely magnate paying for the production and performance of such a Mass, a metaphorical link with a martial cantus firmus could only add luster to his self-image as a soldier of Christ. Thus the identification of the armed man as Christ would have given powerful encouragement to other potential warriors, staking their claim as leaders of the church militant here on earth, *milites christiani* in the spiritual battle for the souls of their subjects, and – perhaps still more important – in physical warfare with heathens abroad. The claims of a secular lord to the status of Christian soldier could find no more compelling forum than through being entwined in the Mass with the musical embodiment of Christ himself.

Citing late antique and medieval sources, Wright demonstrates the persistence of the notion of the holy armor of the redeemer and of all who would follow him into spiritual combat. He proposes a more specific musical image of Christ in the casting, in the Agnus Dei settings of *L'homme armé* Masses by Du Fay and Josquin, of the tune in retrograde, interpreting this as an embodiment of Christ's victorious return from his harrowing in hell. This, as he explains, is the journey symbolized in the Eastertide ritual of the priest's entering and (backward) exiting of the inlaid mazes that were a feature of many of the larger churches of medieval France.[3]

Yet no one prior to the hypothesis advanced here had demonstrated a tangible link between this martial allegory – and its putative expression in the *L'homme armé* melody – and the rite of Mass itself. Such a link is powerfully forged, however, in a body of writing that is here addressed from this perspective for the first time: the corpus of late medieval Mass commentary. Such commentary reveals that martial allegories of the Mass, and Christ's central role within them, were both more widespread and more fundamentally expressive of the late medieval understanding of Mass than has hitherto been suspected. But to begin to understand the functioning of such allegory in the Mass we must turn first of all, as did Wright and as must anyone addressing military Christian allegory, to its fundamental text, Paul's letter to the Ephesians. This reads as follows:

Put on the whole armor of God, so that you may be able to stand against the wiles of the devil. For our struggle is not against enemies of blood and flesh, but against the rulers, against the authorities, against the cosmic powers of this present darkness, against the spiritual forces of evil in the heavenly places. Therefore take up the whole armor of God, so that you may be able to withstand on that evil day, and having done everything, to stand firm. Stand therefore, and fasten the belt of truth around your waist, and put on the breastplate of righteousness. As shoes for your feet put on whatever will make you ready to proclaim the Gospel of peace. With all of these, take the shield of faith, with which you will be able to quench all the flaming arrows of the evil one. Take the helmet of salvation, and the sword of the spirit, which is the word of God.[4]

Paul's exhortation must have found a special resonance in the late medieval mind. Traditionally a rallying call to the battle for the defense and spread of Christianity,[5] it sounded – in the context of Mass – a much more personal note. A wide range of late medieval literature – from Mass commentaries to sermons – suggests that for the individual worshipper, the battlefield was not some distant heathen land, but one's own soul. From that perspective the conflict with the forces of evil, waged on one's behalf at Mass by the celebrant at the altar, must have assumed a particular vividness: for the late medieval worshipper, the appearance of Christ in the elevated host was a prefiguration – if that moment could be adequately anticipated – of the last communion immediately before death, and a reminder of the judgment that would follow. It was thus a cause as much of foreboding as of hope, the ultimate reminder that "the beginning of wisdom is fear of the Lord."[6] In this fertile soil, from the late twelfth century on, Mass allegory concerned with the battle against evil proliferated. For such allegory, the role of Christ as warrior was embedded directly – as we shall see – in the fabric of Mass itself, in the person of his spiritual stand-in, the celebrating priest, and his allegorical armor, the priestly vestments. But it was not until the later fifteenth century, when the early maturity of the cyclic Mass coincided with the high-water mark in public fear of purgatory, that such allegory saw the emergence of what – I suggest – was its chief expression in polyphonic music, in the form of Masses based on *L'homme armé*.

The warrior priest

This model finds perhaps its most straightforward exposition in the commentary that was apparently most widely familiar to fifteenth-century clerics themselves: the late thirteenth-century *Rationale divinorum officiorum* of Guillelmus Durandus. (See Appendix 1, text 1 for the original text.) The relevant passages are in Book III, devoted to the Mass:

[3.] The bishop, then, looking towards the north, or towards the east, or the altar, if it may be more fitting, just as an advocate and warrior about to do battle with an old enemy, is dressed in the sacred vestments as with arms, just as the Apostle [says], as I shall presently set forth.

4. First, he has the sandals for the greaves [of war], lest any worldly blemish or dust may cleave to him. Second, the amice, for a helmet, shields his head. Third, the alb, as a breastplate [cuirass], envelops his body. Fourth, he takes to himself the girdle as a bow, and the undergirdle as a quiver … Fifth, the stole surrounds his neck, like a spear brandished against the foe. Sixth, the maniple he wields as a mace. Seventh, with the chasuble as with a shield he is protected; and his hand with the book as with a sword is armed. Of these separate things I will speak otherwise below. These, therefore, are the arms with which the bishop or priest should be armed, prepared to do battle against spiritual wickedness. For, as says the Apostle [Paul]: "the weapons of our warfare are not carnal; but mighty to the pulling down of strongholds" [2 Corinthians 10: 4]. And in another Epistle, that to the Ephesians, in the sixth chapter [vv. 13–17]: "Put ye on," he says, "the armor of God, that ye may be able to stand against the wiles of the devil. Stand therefore having your loins girt about with truth, and having on the breastplate of righteousness, and your feet shod with the preparation of the Gospel of peace; above all, taking the shield of faith, wherewith ye shall be able to quench all the fiery darts of the wicked: and take the

helmet of salvation, and the sword of the spirit, which is the word of God." Which armor is the aforesaid sevenfold priestly vesture, signifying the sevenfold virtue of the priest; and representing the vesture of Christ, with which he was dressed in the time of the Passion, as shall be said below.

This allegory relates closely to the characterization of Christ's Passion as a battle against the devil, and to the view of the Mass, and particularly the Canon of the Mass, as its re-enactment. Just as Christ, in his self-sacrifice, was a warrior against the forces of evil, so his representative on earth was similarly cast as humanity's champion, symbolically reenacting in the Mass the victory of the Passion. But the allegory does not end with the person and actions of the priest himself: Chapter 6 of the same book extends it more generally into the action and participants of Mass, the battle in which the sacred weapons will be wielded (see Appendix 1, text 1 for the original text):

Thus fortified, therefore, for the battle against celestial wickedness, and for the calming of the judge's wrath towards his subjects, he [the bishop] proceeds to the altar; and by confession he renounces the dominion of the devil, and accuses himself. And on ferial days, the people, as though about to pray for their champion, prostrate themselves on the ground. When, moreover, he recites the collects and other things, it is as though he fights for all men against the devil. When, before the Gospel on fast days, the deacon folds back his chasuble over his shoulder, he brandishes as it were a sword against the foe. When the epistle is read, the edicts of the emperor are proclaimed by the voice of the herald. The chants are the trumpeters, the precentors ruling the choir are the commanders marshalling the army for battle, to the which, becoming weary, others come to aid. Moreover the song of the sequence constitutes the plaudits, or the praise, of victory. When the Gospel is read, the foe is as it were wounded with the sword; or the dispersed army after victory is gathered into line. The bishop preaching is the emperor lauding the victors. The oblations are the spoils that are divided among the victors. The song of the offertory is the triumph due to the emperor. The pax at the end is given to bring quiet to the people now that the foe is overthrown. And thereafter the people, leave having been granted them by the *Ite missa est*, return to their own with gladness, that victory and peace be won.

As for most martial commentaries on the Mass from late Antiquity on, the seed of Durandus's remarks is Paul's Epistle to the Ephesians. But the identification of the vestments as arms is closely bound up with the identity of the priest with Christ, and particularly the suffering Christ of the Passion.

Previously seen to represent aspects of Christ's character and the virtues expected of a priest, from the late thirteenth century the vestments came, most influentially through the words of Durandus himself, to symbolize also the garments and "instruments" of the Passion. Thus, for Durandus, the amice represents the veil with which the Jews covered Christ's face, the alb is the garment in which Herod had him clothed, the girdle is the lash with which he was scourged, the stole and maniple are the ropes with which he was bound to the column and with which his hands were bound on the Mount of Olives; and lastly the chasuble is the purple robe.[7] These accoutrements, along with the other instruments of the Passion, were the "arma Christi" venerated with particular fervor in the fifteenth century, especially in such favored devotional images as the Man of Sorrows and the Mass of St. Gregory (Plate 1). They were the "arms" that marked the stages of the battle of Christ, the good soldier, for humankind's redemption through the process of the Passion. Thus the celebrating priest, in the words of the early-sixteenth-century *Tractatus de misteriis missae* of Balthasar de Porta, is "armed with the arms of Christ" ("christi armis armatus"), and, so accoutered, must put himself in mind of the suffering Christ as he enacts the mystery of Mass.[8]

Durandus draws directly on earlier Mass commentaries, including those commonly available at the time of his writing.[9] His acknowledged primary source is the most widely circulating and widely quoted Mass commentary of his time, the late-twelfth-century *De sacro altaris mysterio libri sex* by Lotario de' Conti di Segni, soon to be elected as Pope Innocent III. The above-quoted passage embracing the citations from Corinthians and Ephesians, along with the immediately following chapter concerning the virtuous state of mind appropriate for the priest while wearing the sacred vestments, comprises an almost direct quotation of Chapter LXIV of Innocent's first book (see Appendix 1, text 2). Similarly, the passage directly preceding Durandus's quotations from Paul, and Durundus's sixth chapter, quoted above, expand only slightly on what are otherwise virtually direct quotations of two passages in chapters XXXII and XXXIII of the mid-twelfth-century *Summa de ecclesiasticis officiis* of Johannes Beleth (see Appendix 1, text 3).

But Durandus's most important precursor, and one that adds further and – for the purposes of this chapter – more extensively relevant detail, is the early-twelfth-century *Gemma animae* of Honorius Augustodunensis (see Appendix 1, text 4). Martial allegory familiar already from Durandus finds its place also here. Thus chapters 74 and, particularly, 82 of Honorius's book embody material, including a paraphrase of the passage from Ephesians, found also in the two quoted chapters from Durandus: the priest, the people's champion about to face the enemy, is protected by the arms of the spirit in preparation to do battle against spiritual wickedness. But Honorius develops this imagery far beyond anything in the work of his successor. He does

Plate 1 Mass of St. Gregory, Simon Bening, Bruges, 1531

this by means of traditional Old Testament parallels: as the Mass repeatedly reenacts the victory of Christ over the devil, so the historical momentousness of that victory, like everything else in the New Testament from a medieval perspective, is deepened by a series of Old Testament archetypes (see Appendix 1, text 4).

The warrior Christ

The parallels begin with Honorius's characterizations of the procession that opens Mass. Just as the defeat by the returning Israelites of the army of Amalek (Exodus 17: 8–13) opened up the way back to the promised land, so that procession leads to victory over evil and the passage of the faithful back to the Father (Chapter 68). The link is tightened in Chapter 72 (see Appendix 1) by conflation not only of the two battles but, following a traditional parallel, of Joshua, the commander of the Israelites, and his Greek namesake, Jesus, who is thus directly credited with opening up the way back to the promised land.[10] Likewise the delivery of the Israelites from captivity under Pharaoh by Moses – along with David the most frequently cited Old Testament archetype of Christ – finds its perpetual reenactment in Mass in Christ's redemption of the Christian people from the clutches of the devil (Chapter 69):

The tablets of the commandments were brought down from a mountain, as the Gospel books are taken up and carried from the altar; the Israelites went forth armed, while the Christian people advance marked by faith and baptism. Standards were borne forth before their troops; and before us crosses and a banner are carried. A column of fire went before them, and the light of candles precedes us. That people was purged by blood; this one is sprinkled by holy water; the Levites bore the tabernacle of faith, and here the sacred books and caskets are borne by the deacon and subdeacon. The ark of the covenant was carried by priests; and [among us] are carried the reliquary or bier with relics of the church fathers. The king, if present, ruler of the people with his scepter, signifies Moses, leader of the people, with his staff. If the king is not there, then the bishop represents both Moses, carrying the staff, and Aaron, in covering his head with the miter. The blast of trumpets is expressed by the sounds of bells.

The siege of Jericho by the Israelites, again credited to "Jesus" (= Joshua), offers a further model for the procession that opens Mass (Chapter 68), and a more detailed model for processions to, and around, another church (Chapter 70). The allusion here is to Joshua 6, where the people were instructed by God, through Joshua, to encircle the city on seven consecutive days, with the armed men leading seven priests blowing trumpets of rams' horns followed by the ark of the covenant, and with the remainder of the people bringing up the rear. Finally on the seventh day, following heavenly instructions, the people brought down the walls of the city with a loud shout. In like manner, Honorius proposes, "we [that is the clergy at Mass] carry forth the reliquary with relics against demons, just as the children of Israel carried forth the ark of God against the Philistine enemy" (Chapter 73). The fall of Jericho was a particularly potent model for the Mass, since the complete devastation of that city by the Israelites stood as the end of the old Canaanite society and the beginning of the new Israelite one,[11] just as the victory of Christ on the cross, reenacted in the Mass, signaled the end of the old order and the beginning of the new.

But Honorius's most extended Old Testament parallel is with David's victory over Goliath, as recounted in 1 Samuel 17 (see his chapters 78, 79, 81).[12]

David's victory offers the most obvious bellicose Old Testament precursor of Christ's victory over evil: thus Goliath is the devil, while David is Christ; likewise Christ's penetration of the hearts and minds of the people is the stone that pierced the giant's head. As David's victory rescued the Israelites from Philistine tyranny, that of Christ freed the populace from its subjection by the devil; David was sent forth to fight by his father, and Christ was sent into the world to do battle by his father; David grazed sheep, and Christ gathered together the innocent on the pasture of life; David overcame the bear and the lion (as he recounts in 1 Samuel 17: 34–6), and Christ overcame the temptations of the devil; David, abandoning his sheep, encamped on the battleground, and Christ, abandoned by his disciples, came to the assembly of the enemy; at David's arrival a loud shout rose up in the camp, while at Christ's arrival among the Jews the cry "guilty of death" sprang up.

As for Durandus, the Mass vestments and altar paraphernalia have their allegorical roots in the "arma Christi," the robes and accoutrements of Christ's Passion (Chapter 79). But at the hands of Honorius, the story of David adds an additional, Old Testament, dimension. Thus David was clothed by Saul in armor which he soon discarded; likewise Christ soon laid aside the battle dress in which he was clothed by Pilate. David carried a staff against the Philistine, as Christ bore a cross against the devil; David carried a milk pail, while Christ received a vessel filled with vinegar; Goliath was overthrown by sling and stone, while the devil was vanquished by Christ with flesh. The sling is Christ's flesh, the stone his soul, David his deity. The stone flung from the sling penetrated the forehead of the enemy, as Christ's soul, cast out by torment of the flesh, entered and despoiled the infernal realm; the defeated enemy had his throat cut by his own sword, as Christ, through his own passing, conquered death; the returning David was greeted by the rejoicing populace, while Christ, returned from Hell, was greeted with joy by the faithful; David, entering Jerusalem, was received with song, while Christ was taken up from Jerusalem to heaven by angels praising him with hymns.

For each aspect of David's story Honorius offers a parallel in the Mass (see chapters 72, 73, 79, 82): the subdeacon and others make preparation for the sacrifice, just as David was armed by Saul and the Israelites; when the bishop proceeds to the altar, it is as if David is proceeding against the Philistines; the chalice is David's milk pail, the corporass which covers it is the sling, the host is the stone, the bowing of the priest is the rotating of the sling, while, with the elevation, the stone is hurled at the enemy; the priest's second bow signifies that the foe has been vanquished; the sung Preface is the clamor with which David was roused to battle against the giant; the deacon's approach to the priest to lay down the elevated chalice signifies

David rushing to the giant and beheading him with his drawn sword; peace having been achieved, the people take communion, just as, peace having been won by David, the Israelites partook in sacrifice to God; the singing in the communion is the praise of the people for the exultation of victory; the prayer and benediction that follow stand for the trophy with which David, entering Jerusalem, was welcomed by the people. Finally, these things having been accomplished, the people return, refreshed, to their own, just as the Israelites, after the victory, returned to their own with gladness.

Foreshadowing an important resonance of the *L'homme armé* melody which will be addressed later, Honorius, like Durandus, makes considerable metaphorical play on the notion of trumpets: thus the ringing of bells and singing symbolize the trumpets and war cries of the crowd inciting the army to battle (chapters 73, 75). Similarly for Durandus, in addition to other effects, bells are rung "that the hostile armies and all snares of the enemy may be banished." For these as for other late medieval commentators, the bells correspond to the trumpets of the old order: thus in Durandus's words, they "signify the silver trumpets by which under the old law the populace was summoned to the sacrifice … For just as the watchmen in a camp rouse themselves with trumpets, so do the ministers of the church with the sound of bells, that they may keep watch through the night against the wiles of the Devil." Likewise, "bells are rung during processions, that fearful demons may be put to flight … For they fear when the trumpets of the Church Militant, that is the bells, are heard, just as a tyrant fears on hearing the trumpets of a powerful enemy king on his own land."[13]

For Honorius (Chapter 74), the cantor is the trumpeter who gives the signal for the onset of battle. The bearer of the banner before the archbishop is the standard-bearer who carries the flag before the emperor in battle. The two sides of the choir are the battle lines laid out for the conflict, and they are directed on each side by the precentors, the commanders who draw up the army for battle. The singers cover their heads with caps, and bear staffs or portable altars, just as warriors cover their heads with helmets and protect themselves with the arms of war. Invoking, to express the nature of spiritual combat, the one sentence from Ephesians 6: 11–17 omitted by Durandus and Innocent III, Honorius explains how the singers in the Mass "battle vigorously like warriors, as they sing from both sides for all men. They repel the fiery darts of concupiscence hurled by the wicked enemy with the shield of faith, and strike down the enemy, fiercely persevering with sin, with the sword of the word of God" (Chapter 75). Further, "the singers, with hand and voice, inspire the others to harmony, because they lead them in the fighting with their hands and with the urging of their voices incite them to combat"

(Chapter 76). Thus singing, for Honorius, has a particular efficacy in the spiritual battle. Underscoring the point, he goes on: "the better voices are selected for the singing of the gradual and alleluia, just as those stronger in hand are brought to the fore in the fighting. For the others come to the aid of those who are deficient in singing. Likewise those constant in heart come to aid the common people laboring in the battle." Reinforcements having thus arrived, the sequence is sung out joyfully by voices and organs (Chapter 77).

As for Durandus and others, the reading of the Gospel is a turning point in the spiritual battle: "The deacon who, on high, reads the gospel, is the herald who calls together the dispersed army, driven about by battle, with the trumpet." The bishop addressing the people is the emperor praising the victors; the sacraments are the spoils of victory, divided in the imperial presence; and with the singing of the offertory the victors in turn offer their praise to the emperor.

The influence of Honorius's battle allegories on later Mass commentries was considerable. The most striking instance is the "Brevis recapitulatio Missae," Chapter IX of the early thirteenth-century *Mitrale, sive Summa de officiis ecclesiasticis* by Sicard of Cremona (see Appendix 1, text 5). In this brief tract Honorius's Old Testament pugilistic models, plus others, troop by at a breathless pace, along with the familiar summary of Ephesians 6 and a generic battle scenario. Sicard distinguishes between combats by recourse to the *caput/membra* dichotomy we discussed in Chapter 4, with Christ – "the head" – enacting the principal combat with the devil and despoiling Hell, while we – "the limbs" – conduct our own campaign against the devil and pleasures of the flesh. The priest is instructed briefly to consider, while celebrating Mass, its foregoing models, "prefigurations that are completed in the head [= Christ] and fulfilled by our customs."

Related allegories are scattered through other late medieval Mass commentaries. Thus for Innocent III, the extending of the celebrant's arms during prayer in the Mass recalls the outstretched arms not only of the crucified Christ but also of Moses, which, while held aloft in prayer, guaranteed that Joshua and the Israelite army would prevail against the army of Amalek. Since, however, when Moses let his arms sink down only a little, the balance began to shift in favor of Amalek, Aaron and Hur held up Moses' arms from either side until, with the setting of the sun, Joshua emerged victorious. Likewise in the Mass the celebrant's hands are held aloft by his ministers, guaranteeing a similarly victorious outcome. Innocent explains:

For Christ, when he stretched out his arms on the cross, prayed for his persecutors, and said: "Father, forgive them, for they know not what they do" (Luke 23), morally instructing that Christ is always ready to receive sinners, as he promised: "All who come unto me, I shall not cast out" (John 6). When, moreover, the true Moses – that is Christ – raises his hands – that is, expends aid and comfort – Israel – that is the Church – triumphs. For "if God is for us, who [can be] against us?" (Romans 8). If, however, he relaxes his hands even a little – that is if, while driving out sin, he with-draws aid and comfort – Amalek – that is the Devil – wins. "For it depends not on [human] will or exertion, but on God's mercy" (Romans 9). Because Christ in truth promised the Church: "Behold, I am with you all of your days unto the end of time" (Matthew 28), on account of this Aaron – that is the mountain of steadfastness – and Hur – that is the fire of charity – sustain his hands, that in steadfastness they may bring forth aid, and from charity comfort; neither do his hands tire until the setting of the sun, that is until the end of the world. And thus through Joshua the commander, that is Christ the leader, Israel puts Amalek and his people to flight, that is the Church vanquishes the devil and the troop of demons with the edge of the sword, that is through the virtue of prayer. For the sword is the word of God (Ephesians 6). If, therefore, anyone wishes through the virtue of prayer to defeat the Devil, he must raise his hands – that is his deeds – to God, that his way shall be in heaven (Philippians 3).[14]

The sounds of battle

However broadly martial allegories were applied in Mass commentaries of the late Middle Ages, the question that remains is how wide was their currency more generally? Or, put another way, how likely is it that authors, and hearers, of *L'homme armé* Masses might have been aware of them? Here again Durandus provides the obvious starting point: his *Rationale* was unquestionably the most widespread manual of Christian worship in the later Middle Ages. From the time of its writing in the late thirteenth century, it circulated widely in manuscript copies;[15] but it was in the later fifteenth century, with the early spread of printing – the same period that saw the inception and early flowering of the *L'homme armé* Mass tradition – that its circulation really took off. In 1459, it became only the fifth book in history to be printed, preceded only by the Bible, a missal, a psalter and a Latin grammar of Donatus. Still more remarkable was the sheer number of early printings: by 1501 it had run to no fewer than 44 editions, making it one of the most frequently printed books of the fifteenth century.[16] Editions petered out in the second decade of the sixteenth century, to experience a modest revival in the post-Tridentine period, when the *Rationale* was invariably coupled with Beleth's *Summa de ecclesiasticis officiis*, sometimes also called the *Rationale divinorum officiorum*.

Ubiquitous though it was, however, the *Rationale* offered little that was new: on the contrary, it is by its nature a compendium of earlier writings that its author deemed to be of value concerning the meanings embedded in the ceremonies of Mass.[17] Its great value was that it accumulated in one place perceived meanings of the Mass that were otherwise scattered through various volumes: that it laid out, clearly and comprehensibly, what was already received wisdom. It seems clear that its popularity derived from the perception that its contents were of vital relevance not just to theologians, but to everyone. That broad appeal is nowhere more vividly exemplified than in its allegorical treatment of the vestments. The significance of this model, in Durandus and elsewhere, derives from the focus on the person and actions of the officiating priest, and especially his identification with the figure of the suffering Christ. The primary instrument of that identification was typological allegory: the drawing of parallels to events in Christ's earthly life, and especially his Passion. By this means the message – basic to the Mass – of Christ's victory over death and the promise that it embodied for the salvation of earthly souls was conveyed, via sermons and through prayers to be uttered at key points in the ritual, to the worshipping laity. The characterization of the vestments as pieces of armor is a corollary of their association with the Passion garments, items of the "arma Christi." This emphasis in Mass commentaries served not only to focus attention appropriately, but also to compensate for the inaudibility of most of the rite, and particularly the canon, access to whose words was closed to all but the celebrant himself. For Joseph Braun, the rise in popularity of this easily comprehensible model was part of a marked intensification in the late thirteenth century – the time when the *Rationale* appeared – in efforts to draw the populace more deeply into the meaning of the Mass.[18] Actually, though, the roots of that development extend back at least into the previous century: as Franz noted, Honorius's commentaries – including his modeling of the proper worship and ethics of the laity on Old Testament devotional practices – seem to have been shaped with a similar aim in view.[19]

The particular appeal of allegory concerning the sacred vestments resided, then, in its directness and simplicity, a feature that extended its reach far beyond the confines of scholarly volumes such as those of Honorius, Innocent III and Durandus and into the basic ministry of the clergy.[20] The extraordinary early printed history of Durandus's manual would seem to reflect a peak in awareness of this model in the fifteenth century. But the *Rationale*'s message was extended far beyond the confines even of its own pages. For example, Johann Ulrich Surgant, in his widely circulating *Manuale curatorum* (Guide for Preachers) lists it as one of only six books, all of which would have been widely available in monastic libraries, that he considers indispensable to writers of sermons.[21] A similar message is conveyed by Jean Le Munerat's *Compendium divinorum officiorum sive Tabula sine quo esse nolo* (Paris, 1496), an alphabetical index to the contents of the *Rationale* which, its author states in his subtitle, "I do not wish to be without."[22]

The fifteenth century saw many new extended Mass commentaries added to those already available; yet the spread of such simple teachings as those concerning the vestments can be accounted less to these volumes directly than to their progeny: the trickle of simpler and more popular guides to the Mass that in the fifteenth century, as Franz has amply documented, became a river.[23] Not least among these are the abridged versions of the *Rationale* itself, most prominently the widely circulated *Collectorium libri qui dicitur Rationale diuinorum officiorum* of the fourteenth-century canon of Münster Hermann Galigaen.[24] Supply fed demand, and with these more cursory treatments, aimed at the less sophisticated end of the priesthood, emphasis fell particularly on explanatory models which, like the vestment allegories, were most easily graspable not only by the laity but also by the simpler clergy who had care of their souls.[25] It is not hard to imagine that for worshippers in general, mostly illiterate and fearful for their posthumous fate, such access to the mystery of the canon as was afforded by models such as this could have been a source of great comfort.

In fact the equation, rooted in Ephesians, of the vestments with armor and the book with the sword had a much longer currency than that of the Mass commentaries examined here: it surfaces already in the ninth century in the prayers to be said by the priest while vesting. Thus in the Sacramentary of Tours, Pontifical of Troyes, and other early sources the priest, on donning the amice, which is first to be placed on the head, is instructed to recite "Pone, Domine, galeam salutis in capite meo ad expugnandas diabolicas fraudes …" ("Place, O Lord, the helmet of salvation upon my head, that I may overcome the deceits of the devil …"). Similarly, among many other examples, the Pontifical of Troyes instructs the vesting priest to pray "Indue me, Domine, lorica fidei et galea salutis et gladio Spiritus Sancti" ("Provide me, O Lord, with the breastplate of faith and the helmet of salvation and the sword of the Holy Spirit").[26] A variant of the prayer while donning the amice, "Impone Domine, capiti meo galeam salutis, ad expungnandos diabolicos incursus" ("Place, O Lord, the helmet of salvation on my head, that I may overcome the assaults of the devil") is familiar to older Catholics even today: it persisted until the 1960s, losing its currency only in the wake of Vatican II.[27]

The development of metaphors for the vestments and accoutrements of Mass traces a path of increasing literalism, from representations of priestly virtues to the "arma Christi" to metaphorical items of armor. That path had one logical further stage, however: the symbolic armor and sword were augmented, on some occasions, by their actual physical counterparts. It is to such displays, and their metaphorical and political significance, that we will now turn.

Arms and religious ceremony

A number of ceremonies involving the wearing of armor and drawing of swords in direct proximity to the altar have been described in detail by Flynn Warmington. Warmington draws attention to various Mass rituals apparently dating back at least to the fourteenth century in which the priest wears actual armor, sometimes in combination with sacred vestments,[28] and the related custom whereby arms are displayed on or in direct proximity to the altar during Mass.[29]

More widespread, though, are the many ceremonies that she and others describe that involve the drawing, and sometimes brandishing, of the sword during the Gospel or a related reading. Many of these involve secular magnates or those holding combined sacred and secular power: prince-bishops, kings, and, first and foremost, emperors. Numerous documents describe ceremonies involving the emperor dressed as a deacon, or attired in a combination of ecclesiastical and military garments, giving a reading at Christmas Day Matins while holding up a drawn sword. Quoting as it does the Gospel incipit "An edict went out from Caesar Augustus, through all the world,"[30] the implication of the reading in this context is clearly to cast the emperor as a soldier of Christ ready to take up arms in defense of the faith.

A number of related customs did in fact involve the drawing of a sword during the reading of the Gospel: Giovanni Rucellai describes a procedure whereby, when the King of France was at Mass, his page would draw a sword during the Gospel, returning it to its sheath once the reading had ended. A similar convention was observed by Henry VIII of England, who, following the endowment upon him by Leo X of the title Defender of the Faith, apparently cultivated the practice of drawing his own sword during the Gospel whenever he was at Mass.[31]

Coronation ceremonies involved similar procedures. Bestowal on the emperor of a sword by the pope was apparently a feature of imperial coronations at least as early as 1014.[32] The emperor pledged, in the presence of God and St. Peter, to defend the Holy Roman Church, as he may be aided

by God and by the holy Gospel on which he swore. After having been conducted to St. Peter's, he was anointed at the altar of the warrior St. Maurice,
on the right arm and between the shoulder blades. But – significantly – it
was at the high altar of St. Peter where he was presented by the pope with
a sword endowed with the papal blessing with which to defend the church
and the faithful. Having received the sword he would put it on and, as in
a number of ceremonies discussed by Warmington, draw and brandish it
three times before returning it to its sheath. Only after having thus committed himself to defense of the church and, implicitly, deference to the papacy,
would he be ready for the coronation itself, where he would be crowned
first with a miter, which would itself then be surmounted by the crown.
Emphasizing this investiture of sacred as well as spiritual authority, he subsequently assumed the role of the subdeacon in passing the pope the chalice
and wine in preparation for the reception of communion (see Appendix 1,
text 8, from the Roman Court pontifical of the thirteenth century).

Appendices to the Pontifical of Durandus, which became accepted as the
standard Roman pontifical in the fourteenth century, include a similar rite
for the anointing and coronation of the King of Sicily. Composed for the
crowning by Clement V of Robert the Wise in 1309, it was later reused by
Clement VII for the coronation, in 1382, of Louis, Duke of Anjou. This ritual took place as part of a pontifical Mass in which the monarch received
communion from the pope. Like the imperial coronation ceremony, it
involved anointing of the right arm and between the shoulder blades, as
well as between the Gradual and Alleluia, a threefold brandishing of the
sword presented by the pope before the crowning itself.[33]

Yet one did not need to be a ruler to partake in religious ceremonies
using weapons to invoke the defense of Christendom. Orders of religious
knights apparently observed the custom whereby a knight would lay a hand
on the hilt of his sword, or indeed draw it and hold it aloft, during the
Gospel reading.[34] In a related practice, records attest to the assignment in a
number of French cathedrals of soldiers to chant, in celebration of the victorious Christian army, the martial *laudes regiae* "Christus vincit, Christus
regnat, Christus imperat."[35] And pontificals spanning at least eight centuries
detail standardized ceremonies for the blessing by bishops of knights and
their swords, armor and other weapons, frequently on or in proximity to the
altar. The earliest such example that I have been able to trace is the series of
prayers for the blessing of a new sword in the so-called Romano-Germanic
Pontifical, the standard pontifical throughout Western Christendom from
the late tenth century on.[36] This presents three versions of a formula asking
God for his blessing of the sword of the knight in question, that it may be

used in defense of the Church and its servants against pagan threats. This is followed by a "prayer for the army" which, like the Mass commentary of Honorius, invokes God's aid to the people of Israel fleeing persecution in Egypt in pleading for divine guidance in battle and victory in Christ (see Appendix 1, text 9 for the original).

Likewise the Pontifical of Durandus includes rites for the blessing of a new knight and for the blessing of arms (texts and reference are given as Appendix 1, text 10). While the prayers of the former rite closely echo prayers of the Romano-Germanic Pontifical, Durandus adds considerable detail on the ceremony in which they are embedded. Before reading the Gospel the bishop blesses the knight's sword with one of the prayers already encountered. Having put on the sword, the knight prays for God's help in giving him strength and justice in defense of the faith, invoking, again like Honorius, biblical precursors including David and Judas Maccabaeus. The ritual from this point proceeds similarly to the coronation ceremonies. The bishop takes the sword from the altar and presents it to the knight, instructing him to use it in defense of the church and – this being a text of French origin – the kings of France; then the knight dons the sword, and, having drawn it, brandishes it thrice before wiping it on his arm and replacing it in its scabbard. The closing rituals include the spectacle of the bishop lightly striking the knight and ordering him to rouse himself from the sleep of wickedness, to be vigilant in the faith of Christ and of worthy reputation. Following on from this the soldiers present vest the new knight in spurs and sing an antiphon comprising two quotations from (Vulgate) Psalm 44: "You are the most handsome of men ... Gird your sword on your thigh, O mighty one." Since this antiphon, the closing prayer that follows it and the two prayers prescribed at the beginning were all present also in the Romano-Germanic Pontifical, it seems clear that the ritual as a whole was already at least three centuries old by the time when, at the end of the thirteenth century, it was outlined by Durandus.

Four new prayers were added in the fifteenth century by Conrad of Nebbio,[37] but even in the new pontifical ordered by Clement VIII and published in 1595 the ceremonies for the blessing of new knights and for the blessing of weapons differed only in detail from the format of Durandus, and from this time forth remained virtually unchanged.[38] This pontifical does however add a few new details, including the note that the arms to be blessed can either be held by other ministers present or placed on the altar, the latter an arrangement that is illustrated in the first and subsequent editions (see Plate 2). The illustrations of the printed pontificals are of particular interest in showing the precise configurations of these rituals, including

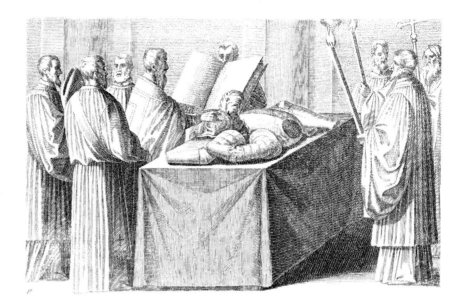

Plate 2 The blessing of arms, Pontifical of Clement VIII (1595)

the holding of the drawn sword in front of the open book whose truth it is to defend (Plate 3).

The conceptual roots of all these practices should by now be clear: they extend ultimately to the equation, deriving from Ephesians and a common-place in medieval religious commentary, between "the word of God and the sword of the spirit."[39] More directly, though, they are active counter-parts of the martial allegories of late-medieval Mass commentary. Thus, as Durandus expounds, not only is the priest's hand armed with the book as with a sword, but, in preparation for his reading of the Gospel, the dea-con folds back his chasuble over his shoulder and "brandishes, as it were, a sword against the foe." Similarly when the deacon reads the Gospel, "the foe is as it were wounded with the sword, or the dispersed army is gathered into line."

Such rituals affirmed a twofold commitment: to defend the word of the Lord and to follow and represent the first and foremost Christian soldier, Christ himself. In accepting this charge the emperor, magnate or knight asserted himself as an earthly leader of an army that embraced the whole of Christendom. With cohorts both terrestrial – the church militant – and heavenly – the church triumphant – this army had as its supreme com-mander the Redeemer himself, a role reaffirmed daily by his miraculous physical transubstantiation at Mass. This complex of ideas could scarcely

Plate 3 The blessing of a new knight, Pontifical of Clement VIII (1595)

be better encapsulated than in the words of an anonymous late fourteenth-century sermon in which Christ's role in rallying his troops is numbered among the reasons for the elevation itself: thus the act of raising the transubstantiated host encourages and rouses the warriors in his army, who rejoice at the appearance of their leader and his banner.[40]

As visible assertions of both spiritual and temporal authority, then, these various ceremonies are expressive of the close reciprocation – entirely characteristic of medieval power structures – between ecclesiastical and secular power. As such they are embedded in broader soldierly assertions of combined sacred and secular might which, though rooted ultimately in the ideas and practices of imperial Rome, first crystalized in the West in the Gallo-Frankish court culture of the eighth century. In asserting this nexus of power, the Franks, unsurprisingly, constructed their regal self-image in terms of familiar Old Testament archetypes – including the return of the Israelites from Egyptian bondage, and, particularly, David's victory over Goliath – in an attempt to cast themselves as the inheritors from God of the mantle of divine vocation and providence. [41] Perhaps the most widespread and multivalent ritual manifestation to emerge from this was the triad of acclamations to Christ's victory and rule known as the *laudes regiae* – "Christus vincit, Christus regnat, Christus imperat" – that occurs in myriad physical and ceremonial assertions of combined sacred/secular power. In his classic study, Ernst H. Kantorowicz notes the ubiquity of the motto on devotional and other objects, including "the blades of swords that they might gain victory and on church bells that they might announce it."[42]

Linked in its beginnings with Charlemagne, and with his particular appreciation of the value, for the assertion of temporal power, of the stamp of ecclesiastical authority, the motto receives a telling adaptation on the script of a groschen from Aachen: XC : VINCIT : XC : REGNAT + KAROLUS MAGNUS IMPERAT.[43] Yet such literalism was not necessary to express the desired linkage of emperor, church, and indeed Christ himself as defenders of the faith, which was an accepted and ubiquitous part of the panoply of leadership. Nowhere was the potency of the *laudes regiae* so powerfully expressed as in coronation rituals, a context in which Kantorowicz is worth quoting at length:

> the [coronation] Orders continually emphasize the parallelism between Christ and King. Even formulae so insignificant as the finales concluding the prayers occasionally would display a singular elaboration by placing Christ, the anointed and ever victorious, in parallel with his royal vicar on earth. When finally the laudes, inserted as a special festal song in the High Mass which followed the consecration, were voiced, the chant inevitably elicited the vision that not only the visible Church acclaimed, confirmed, and recognized the new ruler, but also that the Church and the Heavens consented to the new *a Deo coronatus*. The chant implied that the new king was acclaimed also by the choirs of angels and saints, as well as by Christ himself, who, in his quality as Victor, King, and Commander, recognized the new *christus* of the Church as his fellow ruler and, at the same time, reacknowledged, along with the new king, all the other powers ruling on earth … Much of the passionate emotion of the "Royal Chant" [*laudes regiae*] results from … the haziness of the horizontal line where the two spheres, divine and human, still could dissolve into one, just as they did in the pre-Christian past.[44]

The chanting of the *laudes regiae* was, then, part of a much larger assertion of regal power in Christ. Fundamental to that assertion was the ritual of coronation, with its symbolically crucial act of anointment. Following the literal meaning of the Greek *christos* (= Hebrew "Messiah") as "anointed one," the emperor became, through anointment with chrism, a new "Christ," empowered as Christ's vicar and champion here on earth. This endowment of sacred status and direct symbolic parallelism with Christ was powerfully underscored by the enactment of imperial, and later – in what would become widespread subsequent emulations – royal and other coronations in the context of Mass, with the *laudes regiae* typically being chanted between the first Collect and the Epistle. With this combined ritual act the physical presence of Christ and his newly anointed earthly representative were yoked together into a combined spiritual/temporal force for the championing and defense of Christendom. From here the chanting of the *laudes regiae* and associated rituals, with all their accumulated richness of meaning, became broadly traditional in situations that demanded the sanctioning of earthly might by heavenly authority: crown-wearings at Masses celebrating the principal liturgical feasts,[45] civic entries (themselves frequently timed, as we saw in Chapter 4, to coincide with one of the great church festivals),[46] and so on. Concurrently, episcopal and regal ritual became mutually assimilated as kings sought to enhance their self-image as champions of Christ, while conversely popes and bishops, for whom various similar acclamations developed, accrued the trappings of temporal power.[47]

For the papacy this process was closely bound up with the Investiture Controversy of the eleventh and twelfth centuries and its responses to it, expressed in newly explicit and emphatic assertions of temporal authority. Thus, from the late eleventh century on, the papacy came to assume and – through the inauguration of coronations (as compared to its earlier episcopal consecrations), crown-wearings and the carrying of military regalia – to assert imperial status in public affirmations of not merely ecclesiastical, but also temporal preeminence. From the papal perspective, such divinely sanctioned power as resided in the office of emperor was now bestowed not directly by God but through the aegis of the pope, for whom, in the words of Innocent III – in whose reign the process of the erosion of priestly imperial status came to a head – the emperor was now no more than the "fighting arm of the church." Thus the imperial coronation ritual, hitherto conducted in the context of Mass in acknowledgment of the emperor's role as a new *christus*, was now separated from it, taking place before the eucharistic celebration in which it was endowed with sacred sanction by the pope. Similarly the earlier practice of anointment on the head with holy chrism was now supplanted by anointing with unconsecrated oil, and only (as noted earlier) between the shoulders and on the arm which – from the papal altar and in accordance with its ultimately papal control – would take up the sword.[48]

Such conflict, however, seems to have done little to diminish the desire of kings to claim holy sanction for their power, or for the anointment that bestowed it – a privilege that was eagerly sought by royal houses from the papacy.[49] Neither did it discourage, at least in England and France, the persistence of coronation anointments – with holy chrism – on the royal head and hands.[50] In the case of France, moreover, such ritual, and the power it expressed, was maintained independently of both pope and emperor: the coronation unction of the kings of France with a balm claimed to have been received directly from heaven for the anointment of Clovis was a key constituent of the French royal claim to an authority answerable only to God.[51] It was, furthermore, only the most prominent sacred trapping of a procedure designed to confer on the king a status both secular and ecclesiastical. Besides the anointment, the coronation ritual, which took place in the context of Mass, embraced prayers, divesting and revesting of garments, and communication in both species, actions all characteristic of episcopal consecrations. Still more potently, it embraced aspects of all seven holy sacraments.[52] These various acts, on the other hand, were interleaved with others asserting the new king's willingness to defend the faith with arms, most prominently involving a ceremonial sword reputedly inherited from Charlemagne. This the king received from the Archbishop of Rheims, who took it from the altar and blessed it, while thereafter it was held aloft by his seneschal throughout the remainder of the coronation and subsequent rituals.[53]

Such acts, and the tension between papal and regal power of which, ultimately, they were expressions, articulate a cultural and ritual space particularly rich with potential for the cultivation of *L'homme armé* Masses. Anointment, as (in the French context) Carra Ferguson O'Meara has expressed it,

> endowed the ruler with the grace of the Holy Spirit, transmitting the wisdom and power to rule over God's people and transforming the ruler physically into a *Christus domini*. Anointed, the ruler became a *christos*, an *imago Christi*, and his rule, an *imitatio Christi*. In theory this transmission of power was not from ruler to ruler, nor from consecrator to ruler, but from God to ruler, who consequently became a *rex Dei gratia* and *vicarius Dei* whose power originated with God.[54]

The symbolic force of performing a *L'homme armé* Mass in such a context would have been twofold: it would have resonated strongly with the struggle of the celebrating bishop, Christ's champion in the concurrent spiritual battle of Mass, while at the same time powerfully underscoring the claim of the monarch to status as a terrestrial type of Christ and captain of his army here on earth.

But possible fora for the performance of *L'homme armé* Masses are not limited to the greatest and most powerful royal houses, nor indeed to coronations: for if performance of a *L'homme armé* Mass could have added definition and luster to the coronation even of the French *rex christianissimus*, how much more powerfully might it have impacted the coronations of less prominent rulers? In contexts where, for example, the right of anointment had been harder won, or where the sense of spiritual status was less firmly established, the potency of such an aural presence would surely have been that much more keenly felt. Thus coronations and their perpetual adumbrations in such rituals as royal entries offer, I suggest, myriad possibilities for the symbolically meaningful performance of *L'homme armé* Masses. At the same time, their wide applicability, coupled with the prestige accruing from their association with such opulent courts as that of the Dukes of Burgundy, surely proved stimulants both to their wider composition and to the breadth of their transmission.

Coronation and other ritual enactments of status provided, however, only one type of forum for the assertion of divinely ordained power. Elsewhere the "grace of spiritual gifts" bestowed, in the words of William of Occam,[55] on the kings of England and France by anointment was also the basis for the socially powerful claim, current in both realms, of the royal ability to heal the inflammations and lesions known as scrofula.[56] This was achieved, following attendance at Mass or at least intense prayer, simply by the touch of the royal fingers, or – in an even more telling assumption of sacerdotal power – by making the sign of the cross.[57] In England, the practice became embedded in a ceremony that had all the trappings of a liturgical office, with the king, supported by his personal chaplain, assuming the role of *quasi*-celebrant.[58] Likewise the chanting of the *laudes regiae*, founded on the assertion of that same state of grace, continued in English coronations until the late fourteenth century, with English monarchs to this day laying claim to possession of their office "by the grace of God."

Whatever their geographical and historical fluctuations, all such rituals are united by acute awareness of the mutually enhancing power of the assertion of terrestrial and heavenly authority, and of the centrality of public display in affirming them. There can surely be little doubt that such assertion lay at the root, as a number of earlier theories have suggested, of the *L'homme armé* tradition: just as the armed man could be identified with the celebrant representing Christ in the spiritual struggle of Mass, so that same role could be assumed by secular rulers asserting, via claims to heavenly authority, defense of the faith through physical might.

Indeed, a rare piece of contemporary evidence reveals a direct connection between the conceit linking Christ's battle for souls with earthly combat and the *L'homme armé* song itself. This is provided by none other than the poet, composer and long-time associate and official chronicler of the court of Burgundy Jean Molinet. The first line of each verse of Molinet's *Le debat du viel gendarme et du viel amoureux*, couched as a debate between the lover ("l'amoureux") and the man of arms ("L'homme armé,"), famously presents the first line of a polyphonic song, including, in the following verse concerned – at least ostensibly – with jousting, *L'homme armé*:

L'homme armé doibt on redoubter
Il n'est riens qui tant plaise aux dames
Que le behourt et le jouster,
Et qui voeult en gloire monter,
C'est l'eschielle a sauver les ames;
Rompre bois et quasser hëalmes
Est ung cler bruyt qui tousjours dure.[59]

In a juxtaposition surely more jarring to modern than to contemporary readers, then, the armed man, in addition to pleasing the ladies and breaking wood and helmets, is, for those who would ascend to glory, the stairway to the saving of souls, an *exemplum* applicable only to the principal armed man himself.

Yet the parallel between earthly and heavenly armed men was clearly far more than a political or poetic conceit, however powerful in its ritual functioning: it stood also as a legitimation for earthly warfare in defense, real or imagined, of the cross. And in the late Middle Ages such warfare found its grandest and symbolically most profound expression in the crusades to liberate the Holy Land. It is in this context, one that frequently echoed to the acclamations of the *laudes regiae*,[60] that the *L'homme armé* Masses find their closest temporal resonance.

L'homme armé and the Crusades

The first *L'homme armé* Masses appeared against a historical backdrop of liturgical responses to assaults on Christendom that was already almost three centuries old. That this is now apparent is due to the pioneering work of Anmon Linder.[61] Linder's work traces the history of liturgical responses to Islamic assaults on the Holy Land beginning with the defeat, in 1187, of Hattin and the fall of Jerusalem to the Ayyubids under Saladin. The liturgical response of the papacy to this calamity was the promulgation of the so-called "Holy Land clamor," a collection of pleas – in the form of psalms, versicles and prayers – for liberation of the Holy Land to be inserted into Mass and Office.[62] While the clamor became a fixed part of Mass and Office for three centuries, more extended contributions were to follow. The next step comprised the institution of Masses dedicated to the liberation of the Holy Land. Beginning in the fourteenth century, these centered most typically on "triple sets" of dedicated collect, secret and post-communion.[63] But these developments reached their logical conclusion in the complete "war Mass," in which texts chosen or adapted for their applicability to the Holy Land were incorporated in the Mass in all its variable sections. With this move, the self-sacrifice of crusading knights became another sacrificial layer added to the fundamental sacrifice of the first Christian soldier as reenacted in the eucharist.

Yet while that message of sacrifice involved, as Linder notes, a convergence of both Proper and Ordinary parts of the rite, only the Proper parts were susceptible to verbal specifics, the Ordinary, as he puts it, being "practically immune to change."[64] Such specificity could have been admitted, though, via the insertion of Ordinary cycles based on a cantus firmus, especially if that cantus firmus was *L'homme armé*. This assumes a particular likelihood in the context of the later fifteenth-century history of the war Mass, and the events to which it responded. War Masses were widely instituted across Europe in the fifteenth century in response to the newly urgent threat of the Ottoman Turks and the key events involved. This already suggests links to earlier theories – that will be reconsidered shortly – concerning *L'homme armé*, particularly those involving the anonymous Naples Masses and the Court of Burgundy. But the pattern of war Masses opens up the possibility of associations with the *L'homme armé* tradition that are at once broader and more specific.

Not surprisingly, a number of war Masses were instituted in response to the fall of Constantinople in 1453. The key text here is the *Missa contra Turcos* promulgated in 1456 by Calixtus III.[65] This was widely copied in German-speaking areas over the next five decades, though its absence from French sources would seem to preclude links with putative *L'homme armé* Mass performances at the Burgundian or royal French courts. Many other Masses against the Turks did circulate in non-German lands, including France, however, and form likely contexts for performances of *L'homme armé* Masses.[66] Among the most significant of these is the *Missa contra Turcum* (*Omnia que fecisti*), promulgated by Sixtus IV in response to the Turkish occupation of Otranto between 1480 and 1481 and known today from a large number of French sources and in many adaptations.[67] It may be significant in this regard that a series of *L'homme armé* Masses, those by Du Fay, Busnoys, Regis, Caron and Faugues, are bound consecutively in Rome, Biblioteca Apostolica Vaticana, Cappella Sistina MS 14, a choirbook apparently acquired during the pontificate of Sixtus, the most lavish and proactive musical patron among later fifteenth-century popes.[68] While this source seems not to have been compiled directly for the Sistine Chapel, but rather was apparently acquired later for its use, it seems likely that its *L'homme armé* Masses could have been used there in the context of Masses *contra Turcos*.[69] This possibility serves as another reminder that, for polyphonic music as for the liturgy it adorned, the original circumstances of composition need not remain directly relevant to uses in later, changed, situations. Such durability is clear enough from the mere presence in Cappella Sistina 14 of Masses such as these *L'homme armé* cycles, some of which were probably twenty-five or more years old by the time these copies were made.[70]

It is worth remembering in this context that the Regis Mass on *L'homme armé* is dedicated, via a series of specific chants, to the archangel warrior St. Michael, the patron saint of soldiers of Christ and a figure frequently invoked in the crusading context.[71] Elsewhere in the Holy Land Mass tradition we see further reference to the Old Testament archetypes discussed above in the context of Mass commentaries. Thus Sixtus's *Missa contra Turcum*, in imploring God for protection of the crusading forces in their quest to repel the infidel, invokes the sacrificial prayer of the Maccabees for the deliverance of Israel.[72] Similarly the epistle (Jeremiah 22:3–5) of a war Mass preserved in two late-fifteenth-century French missals draws comparison between the benefits to follow from crusading deeds and God's promised reward of Davidic rule to a righteous Israel delivering the people from oppression.[73] Most telling is the comparison, like that already cited by Innocent III, between the spiritual and temporal roles of Moses and Joshua in the victory over the Amalekites. While both are deemed essential, here, as for Innocent, the spiritual role of Moses, compared implicitly with the prayers and supplications of Christendom, is primary.[74] Ultimately, though, this emphasis on the Spiritual is an expression of the extent of belief in the power of the eucharist, and its susceptibility to being "harnessed," as Linder puts it, to specific goals.[75]

This recourse to Old Testament archetypes to add historical depth to the message of eucharistic redemption is of course one that is shared with most manifestations of late medieval religiosity: sermons, liturgical books, stained glass, and so on. But increasingly in the later Middle Ages and Renaissance, the syncretism that joined the old and new laws was extended to embrace also pagan antiquity (as, at least notionally, in the case of the Sibylline prophecies). Thus Christianity – and, by extension, its defenders – became the apotheosis of a providential scheme that embraced the whole of history. By a marvelous accident of survival, the whole spectrum of Christian symbolism – complete with Old Testament, pagan, and modern ecclesiastical and temporal shades – finds eloquent evocation in a collection of *L'homme armé* Masses, a group of works that have long been seen as key to the tradition more generally: the six anonymous *L'homme armé* Masses in the manuscript Naples, Biblioteca Nazionale MS VI. E. 40.

The sacralizing of secular power

The Naples Masses have been subjected to intense scrutiny, not just on account of their cyclic underpinning by a series of related canons and tropes, but because of their use and likely origin in the circle of Charles the Bold, one of the most frequently, and plausibly, hypothesized "armed men." Craig Wright has discussed their Christological significance and embrace of Old Testament and antique models. However, the martial allegorical perspective outlined above now allows us to situate their meaning directly in terms of the celebration of Mass, whether in the context of dedicated war Masses or in any number of other settings. Indeed from this perspective the Masses appear as an astonishingly fortuitous survival of martial Mass allegory in polyphonic form. Much in the narrative that they articulate would seem to speak directly to Christ's spiritual stand-in at Mass, doing battle with the forces of wickedness on behalf of the souls under his care. But here that narrative is taken in a very particular direction, weaving the allegorical strands into a fabric crafted to bring maximum glory to the institutions and aspirations of the magnate for whom they were apparently created.

As Wright noted, a distinction both of language and subject matter separates the canons, which instruct the performer on the proper performance of the cantus firmus of each Mass, from the tropes that occur in each of the Kyrie settings: while the former use the language of classical Latin and allude to Vergil's *Aeneid*, the latter, which focus on Christ's victory and its Old Testament prefigurations, are expressed in the Latin of the medieval church. (See Appendix 1, text 11 for texts and translations.)

In light of the martial allegories of late medieval Mass commentary, the language and imagery of the Kyrie tropes acquire resonances that now appear instantly familiar. Following the general redemptive message of the Kyrie trope of Mass 1,[76] the arms in Mass 2, given by God that man might do battle with the obstinate enemy, lend themselves to easy parallel with the arms of Christ and actual items of armor symbolized by the vestments worn by the officiating priest. Further, as in Durandus, who characterizes these "arms" as the "sevenfold priestly vesture," the "arms" that are given in this case – the "sevenfold gift" – are brought into parallel with the seven gifts of God. The Kyrie trope of Mass 3 introduces one of the Mass metaphors used by Honorius: that involving the victory, through God's intervention, of the Israelites over Pharaoh's army on their return from exile in Egypt. Mass 4, with its focus on the trumpet, gives rise to a broader range of interpretations that will be addressed shortly.

But it is Mass 5, with its cantus firmus "un haubregon de fer," that focuses with particular clarity on the topics addressed in this chapter. The text of Kyrie 1 invokes Honorius's other great Old Testament archetype of the spiritual conflict of Mass, imploring God to arm Christians with a breastplate (or cuirass) and helmet, just as David vanquished Goliath and Israel her enemy. The text of the Christe, on the other hand, leaves little doubt that it was composed in reference to vesting prayers such as those discussed earlier: Christ is asked to "clothe us with the helmet of hope, with the shield of faith in salvation from the penitent shadows and with the armor of light." Similarly Kyrie 2 prays for the breastplate of sweet love to withstand the javelins of the impure enemy. Lastly, the texts of Mass 6 round off the cycle with an elegant return to a direct invocation, as in Mass 1, to Christ.

Actions of the celebrating priest are also suggested by the texts of the canons, which instruct the tenor on the proper construction of the cantus firmus for each Mass. Only Mass 6 quotes the whole tune, while each of the others is based on only one of its constitutive fragments, with the corresponding text clearly indicated. Thus the "armed man" who goes forth with his face turned away in Mass 2 has his parallel in the priest processing to perform Mass, whose business is indeed largely conducted with his face turned away from the people, in the direction of the altar. However, in a series of steps which also have a rich history of biblical interpretation, the ritual involves him in moves, as in the canon, to the right and left, the "Epistle" and "Gospel" sides of the altar from which the two readings are respectively given. The end of Mass is marked, as in the canon, by the priest stepping back down to resume his status – following his charged, mystical actions as the representative of Christ – as just another man; the end, as the canon says, "corresponds to the beginning."

It seems clear that, as Wright has observed, the principal "man" and "arms" being addressed in the famous quotation from Vergil's *Aeneid* in the canon to Mass 6 are Christ and his spiritual armor.[77] Particularly suggestive is the verbal conceit whereby the quotation from the *Aeneid*, "I sing of arms and a man," is turned around in the words newly composed: "and I am conquered by arms and a man." The parallel emerges still more clearly at the end of the canon: the man being addressed is the God who *became* man, fashioned, as the text says, "out of my own entrails," or, rather, out of my "flesh" or "innermost part," the "flesh and blood" ("plasma") and "Word incarnate" addressed in the same Mass's Kyrie trope. But the quotation from Vergil points far beyond itself, alluding to one of the most durable of narrative traditions used to draw pagan antiquity into the Christian providential scheme: that which cast Aeneas as a precursor of Christ.[78] Quoting from the very first words of the *Aeneid*, the allusion to Aeneas functions, Laurenz Lütteken has proposed, after the manner of a catchword, standing *pars pro toto* for the figure of the Trojan hero. That suggestion gains depth from other apparent allusions to the *Aeneid* that Lütteken identifies elsewhere in the canons of the Naples Masses.[79] The opening sentence of the canon of Mass 6 seems clearly, with its verbal reversal, to draw the figure of Aeneas to that of Christ, who, in Craig Wright's words, "is now equated with Aeneas: a man of arms who conquers by means of spiritual armor."[80]

The Christianization of the *Aeneid* began in the late fourth century, as part of the apologism that sought to reinvent the history of the newly converted Roman state from a Christian perspective. Beginning with the *Psychomachia* of Prudentius (348–c.405), Aeneas was cast as a precursor of Christ, and his foundation of Rome as the building of the New Jerusalem. This model was sustained by the notion, first propagated by Origen (born c.180), according to which Christian legitimation for the Roman Empire, and particularly the rule of Augustus, was seen in the proposition that they had been sanctified by God through being chosen for the enactment of his redemptive plan. Providing a model for later imperial apologists including Dante,[81] this notion derived its attractiveness, from an imperial standpoint, from the peace that was seen to flow from subsuming the entire world under the rule of one man. Not surprisingly, then, this notion was co-opted to legitimize not only the existence of imperial rule but also its perpetuation: it was the emperor's role, emulating Christ's victory over sin and echoing the wars chronicled in Vergil's *Aeneid* and *Fourth Eclogue*, to do battle for the faith and ultimately to bring about a return of the Golden Age that would usher in Christ's second coming. Thus the Christianizing of the *Aeneid* imbued it with a providential import that was imperial as well as divine.

In exploiting the potential of the *Aeneid* for imperial legitimation, future commentators were cultivating a seed that was present in it from the beginning. Fashioned by Vergil to honor Augustus's victory at Actium in 31 BC, an event that marked the end of civil war and the unification by Rome of the eastern and western parts of the empire, the emperor was cast in the *Aeneid* in emulation of the Trojan hero and as the fulfilment of his prophesies.[82] Most propitious of all, though, was the succession that was claimed to link Augustus to Aeneas through blood descent, a notion that inspired the cultivation of the ever more elaborate mythic genealogies that were to sustain claims to imperial status through the fifteenth century and beyond. Thus on various levels the *Aeneid* formed the basis for future models of imperial legitimation, and its role in sustaining and even enhancing the potency of the Trojan myths over the centuries offers the most likely explanation for its application in the Naples *L'homme armé* Masses.

A dedicatory poem in the manuscript containing the Masses offering them as a gift to Beatrice of Aragon, daughter of King Ferdinand I (Ferrante) of Naples and wife of Matthias Corvinus, King of Hungary, famously claims that a "Charolus princeps" had formerly been wont to enjoy them. This prince has traditionally been identified with Charles the Bold, last Valois Duke of Burgundy, and the Burgundian court has been proposed as the most likely place of origin of the Masses themselves. The combined notion of the emperor's mythic ancestry and God's perpetual endowment of the rule of the Roman Empire on the successor of Aeneas had lost none of its power in the course of the more than millennial history that separated its inception from the composition, almost certainly in the 1460s or 1470s, of the Naples Masses. Indeed the genealogical claims of actual and would-be (now Holy Roman) Emperors had grown exponentially over the intervening centuries. Thus the claims of Charles's father Duke Philip the Good for imperial status, resting on his descent from the imperial line via Charlemagne, were bolstered, through genealogical accretions devised by earlier emperors, by notional descent from the pagan gods Saturn and Jupiter and, through biblical lineage, from Noah, Adam and the houses of Levi and Judah which had allegedly converged in Christ.[83] But Philip's claim to Trojan and biblical ancestry was expressed also in a more purposive and public forum than had been the case with his forebears, one that embodied, crucially, a particular conviction to defend the Christian faith with arms: the Order of the Golden Fleece.

In naming his chivalric order for the Golden Fleece, Philip combined his dynastic and military pretensions in a symbol of great concentration and potency. In the first place it reflected and amplified his claim to Trojan ancestry through the link it forged with Aeneas's forebear, Jason.[84] But it was also imbued with Christian significance, being identified with the Lamb of God, and more specifically with the Apocalyptic Lamb of the Revelation to St. John whose appearance would herald Christ's second coming and the return of the Golden Age.[85] Finally, it offered the perfect talisman for the cause that had inspired the founding of the Order: the call for the uniting of European chivalry in a crusade to free the Holy Land from the rule of the Turks. Along with the destruction of Troy, the capture of the Golden Fleece from the temple of Colchis by the Argonauts had signaled the collapse of the power of Asia, an occurrence that preceded the events, culminating in the founding of Rome, narrated in the *Aeneid*.[86]

Whether or not, as has been claimed,[87] the six Naples Masses were fashioned for the celebration of Mass on the consecutive days of chapter meetings of the Order of the Golden Fleece, there is much in their canons and tropes to support the notion that they were composed with the Order, and its avowed purpose, in mind. Most obviously, the military implications of the cantus firmus are amplified by allusions to a series of victories that may be viewed, as Lütteken has suggested, as precursors of Philip the Good's planned victory over the Turks. First among these is Aeneas's victory over Turnus which, while not directly mentioned, is, as Lütteken notes, strongly implied by the juxtaposition of the *L'homme armé* melody and the quotation from the *Aeneid*. This proto-duel, which enabled the founding of Rome, can thereby, he observes, be seen to stand for the princely duel generally, and forms the ultimate model for the personal challenge to a duel issued against Sultan Mehmed II by Philip the Good at the Feast of the Pheasant in 1454. As Lütteken comments, however, the notion of the duel also has a prominent biblical model, and it is here that we return to the battle allegory of late medieval Mass commentary. That model is of course the duel between David and Goliath, developed in particular detail by Honorius, who also, as mentioned, draws on the archetype, shared with the Kyrie trope of Mass 3, of the victory of the homecoming Israelites over the Egyptian army. As Lütteken notes, the canons, tenor excerpts from the *L'homme armé* song, and tropes combine in a multi-layered semantic field.[88]

But each of these victories is, ultimately, no more than an adumbration of another, whose linchpin significance in this context has not hitherto been recognized. That victory, from a Christian perspective the greatest triumph in the history of the world, the one that provides the link between the others and, in the context of Mass, gives them their singular force, is Christ's victory – reenacted daily in the ritual of Mass – over death for the salvation of humankind. It is only in the context of this triumph that the other conflicts embraced by the schema of the Naples Masses acquire their true logic and their most profound meaning. With the introduction of the Trojan myth, pagan antiquity is drawn, via the imagined forebears of the Burgundian dukes – to the late medieval imagination the preeminent embodiment of courtly chivalry – into the series of prefigurations for the greatest victory of all. That victory is also the rallying cry and ultimate model for the intended victory invoked by the Burgundian call to a crusade, and on which, as models, the other conflicts alluded to by the Naples Masses may be seen to converge. The "armed man" of the Naples Masses, then, is again Christ, who, in what now appears as a grandly eucharistic scheme, becomes fully present, "made flesh," only in the summatory Mass 6, where the hitherto fragmented cantus firmus is at last presented complete.[89] The same conceit of a Trojan antecedent for the ultimate, Christian, victory forms another link with the ceremonies of the Order of the Golden Fleece: this was made visibly manifest, as we learn from the eyewitness account of the Mantuan ambassador Niccolò Frigio, in the tapestries hung in the Church of Notre Dame des Carmes in Brussels for the 1501 meeting of the Order. Here hangings in the nave of the church depicting the destruction of Troy (the prelude to the founding of Rome, the New Jerusalem) were juxtaposed, forming a direct exegetical link, with Passion scenes in the choir, the location of the enactment of the victory of Mass.[90]

This great confluence of meaning gives added force to the speculation that the Naples Masses were fashioned not simply for the use of the Burgundian court but more specifically, as Lütteken has surmised, as an expression of the intensification in the call to arms that followed the fall to the Turks of Constantinople in 1453, a call that found its most evocative expression the following year in the Feast of the Pheasant. Thus the loss of Constantinople was a strike, by a new Antichrist, the Sultan Mehmed II, not only against Christendom, but against the descendants of the Trojans in the West.[91] Certainly it would be hard to imagine a more concentrated and powerful expression of such a call to arms than the Naples Masses: the cycle would have given eloquent voice to the Duke's declaration of himself as Christ's champion and worthy inheritor to an ancient tradition of the greatest Christian and proto-Christian knights, with Christ himself standing at the center. The grandiosity of such a claim is reflected in the epic scale of the cycle, the ritual of Mass itself becoming almost a eucharist within a eucharist, with the armed man, in the form of the complete *L'homme armé* melody, appearing fully before us only in Mass 6.

While Mass 6 forms the climax of the grand design of the Naples Masses, though, it is Mass 4, focused on the Last Judgment, which most directly addresses late medieval Christendom's principal concern. This is also the only Mass, its cantus firmus fashioned from the music set in the song to the phrase "On a fait partout crier," whose trope and canon seem to comment directly on the *L'homme armé* tune: both are concerned with the trumpet. Scholars have variously remarked on the trumpet-like repetitions and falling fifth figures of the *L'homme armé* melody, features appropriate to a song that presumably arose in a military – or at least pseudo-military – context. Such associations are endorsed by no less a contemporary authority than Tinctoris, who allows for repeated pitches and motifs in counterpoint only in imitation of bells and trumpets.[92] It seems likely that its associations with the sounds of the trumpet contributed to the popularity of *L'homme armé* as a cantus firmus for use in the great spiritual battle of Mass; certainly the actions of the ritual gave rise, at the hands of contemporary commentators, to a number of trumpet-inspired parallels. Some of these have already been encountered: most obvious is the equation, made by Durandus, Honorius and others, of trumpets with the chants and singing in the Mass, which function, according to military allegory, to marshal the army for battle and signal battle's onset.[93] The same authors link the functions of military trumpets with those of the sounding of bells during Mass, the aim in both cases being to incite battle, to instill fear in the enemy and to put demons to flight, and finally to call together the dispersed army, driven about by the conflict. The sixteenth of Tinctoris's twenty effects of music – to spur men's spirits to battle – is similarly, following Isidore and other antecedents, assigned to the trumpet, and here, as in the Naples Masses, a parallel is found in the *Aeneid*:

Thus it is said of Misenus that, with Hector at the siege of Troy, he surpassed all in setting battle ablaze with the trumpet … Vergil speaks thus of him in the *Aeneid* (Bk. VI) "… Misenus of Aeolus's race, whom none surpassed in rousing men with brass, with tune setting warfare ablaze …" Thus one reads that Alexander the Great's piper Timotheus frequently summoned him from feasting to fighting. Quintilian agrees with this in *Institutio oratoria* (Bk. 1): "It is recorded … that the Spartans' armies were set ablaze by musical tunes." Such melodies, however, tend to arouse anger, as the philosopher [Aristotle] asserts in *Politics* (Bk. 8). The louder they are, the more they embolden the combatants' spirits, as Isidore says in his *Etymologiae* (Bk. 3: 17), so that in the end they win a glorious victory. Hence Quintilian says in *Institutio oratoria* (Bk. 1): "But what else is the purpose of the horns and trumpets in our legions? The louder their combined sound, the more does Roman martial glory surpass any other nation's."[94]

This latter association of the trumpet with splendor provides a link to another of its functions, in the late Middle Ages as today: to herald the arrival of an important personage.[95] There could be no more important personage than Christ himself; thus the Kyrie trope of Naples Mass 4 exhorts – with double relevance in a text from a polyphonic Mass – "May every trumpet sing/sound [*canat*] to you."[96] This function of the trumpet received its general metaphorical realization in the use at Mass of the bell to announce the elevation.[97] But Christ's arrival in the form of the transubstantiated host was clearly the trigger for the further practice, which seems to have been quite widespread, whereby the elevation of the host was signaled also by the trumpet itself.[98] This was standard, for example, at the outdoor chapel on the Campo in Siena, and probably also in Siena Cathedral, in the fifteenth century and beyond.[99] A similar use of trumpets was probably envisaged in the foundation in 1479, by the Ghent gild of *carilloneurs*, of two annual Masses "with deacon and subdeacon, discant, organs, and trumpets, and also including carillon playing," and for the monthly Mass with singers and trumpeters endowed by the same city's gild of traders in secondhand goods.[100] At least some of the sundry records elsewhere of payments to trumpeters for performing at Mass and for providing less clearly specified services to churches, chapels and confraternities surely point in the same direction.[101] More direct evidence comes from the late fourteenth-century *Songe du vieil pelerin* by the French Chancellor of Cyprus, Philippe de Mézières. In exhorting the prince to moderation, Reine Verité, a central character in the *Songe*, nonetheless advises him as follows:

"Que se dira, Beau Filz," dist la royne, "des dons mal employez des hesraulx et des menestriers et des faiseurs de bourdes, qui n'ont pas oublie la brochete grivelee, c'est assavoir flaterie, pour prendre a leur chasse une tresgrosse beste? Je ne dy pas, Beau Filz, que tu ne puisses bien avoir des menestriers a l'onneur et reverence de Dieu et de ta royalle mageste, comme grosses trompes et clerons, sicomme avoit le grand Moyse pour assembler au tabernacle le people d'Israel, et pour sonner et tromper en l'ost, et a leur son fere cheoir les murs de la cite de Hay; lesquelles grosses trompes, Beau Filz, es grans solennites tu feras sonner doulcement a l'elevacion du corps Jesucrist, et en ton ost et par tout es solennitez royals, et les trompetes aussi, qui seront tousjours devant toy et en ton ost et ailleurs, pour assembler ta vaillant chevalerie et anoncier les commandemens royaulx …".[102]

Royne Verité's advice may well imply that this practice was followed at the French royal court of Charles VI, to whom the words of the *Songe* were directed.[103] That such musical heralding of the elevation need not always have been "douce" is suggested by Gianozzo Manetti's famous description of the Mass commemorating the Dedication of Florence Cathedral on 25 March 1436 (the occasion of the first performance of Du Fay's *Nuper rosarum flores*):

Indeed at the elevation of the consecrated Host all the places of the Temple resounded with the sounds of harmonious symphonies [of voices] as well as the concords of diverse instruments, so that it seemed not without reason that the angels and the sounds and singing of divine paradise had been sent from heaven to us on earth to insinuate in our ears a certain incredible divine sweetness.[104]

A similarly grand Mass in the presence of the pope and the assembled dignitaries of the Eastern and Western churches at the Council of Florence in 1439 climaxed in the same sonorous fashion: "lorsque vint l'élévation, ils se mirent tous à jouer des chalmies et des orgues et des tambours et de tous les instruments."[105] Likewise at a ceremonial Mass at the Council of Constance in 1416 "tubae et fistulae altis vocibus" played "ad ampliorem expressionem gaudii" from the Sanctus to the Pater noster.[106]

In this context Durandus again provides a valuable symbolic reference, comparing the sounding of the bell at the elevation and on other occasions involving carrying of the host and saintly relics to the use by the Levites in the Old Testament of trumpets to incite prayer at the time of the sacrifice:

In elevatione autem utriusque squilla pulsatur. Nam et in veteri testamento levite tempore sacrificii tubas clangebant argenteas, ut earum sonitu populus premunitus foret ad orandum Dominum preparatus. Et propter eandem causam squilla pulsatur, cum corpus domini ad infirmum portatur. Mula etiam capellam domini pape baiulans squillam fert ob reverentiam reliquiarum, quas portat.[107]

A corollary to the notion of Christ as military captain is the characterization of the faithful as his army, as in the anonymous late fourteenth-century sermon, discussed by Franz, mentioned above (page 115). Yet the sight of the elevated host was associated as much with foreboding as with cheer, calling to mind, as noted at the beginning of this chapter, the final vision of the host just before death, turning thoughts as much to fear of Christ's judgment as to hope in his mercy. The role of the trumpet in the Last Judgment can seldom have been far from the minds of those who heard its sounds at the moment of the elevation, and it is this, its primary biblical association, that forms the principal focus of the trope of Naples Mass 4. Thus the words of the trope beg Christ to "comfort us at the end when the final trumpet shall sound." The supplication "At the sound of the trumpet be merciful to your awakening people," may suggest that, as in the instances described above, the sounding of the trumpet at the elevation was a practice followed in the original performances of the Naples Masses.

The apocalyptic imagery of Naples Mass 4 links it to another *L'homme armé* Mass: that of Johannes Regis.[108] With this Mass we encounter a heavenly soldier second in prominence only to Christ himself, one whose name in Hebrew is in fact a rhetorical question meaning "Who is like God?": the Archangel Michael. Given Michael's status and the nature of his role, deriving from passages in Revelation and Daniel, as celestial champion, it is perhaps surprising that this is the only *L'homme armé* Mass to invoke him.[109] His twin function in medieval theology as helper of Christian armies against the heathen and – particularly – as advocate of individual souls against the devil, especially at the moment of death, was the source of his widespread veneration by a late medieval public preoccupied with purgatory and ultimate reckoning. Michael was conflated in medieval consciousness with the apocalyptic trumpet players of the Revelation, as in the text that carries his most extended presence in Regis's Mass. This is the Magnificat antiphon, stripped of its original music and set to the *L'homme armé* melody itself, for first Vespers of the Feast of St. Michael: "Dum sacrum mysterium cerneret Johannes, archangelus Michael tuba cecinit" ("When John saw the sacred mystery, the archangel Michael blew the trumpet"). Drawing on this and other chant references throughout the Mass, Regis, in Wright's words, "saturates the air with symbolic references"; crucially, though, he also, as Wright notes, brings Michael's victory over the dragon into close dialogue with the ultimate triumph for which, in the medieval exegetical mode, it stands as an allegory: Christ's victory on the cross.[110] Thus "In the Gloria ... Christ the Mystical Lamb opens the book of the seven seals while Michael leads the angelic host. In the Sanctus John sees the Apocalypse, Michael plays the trumpet of the Last Judgment, and Christ enters Jerusalem" (the latter a reference to Regis's allusion to the Palm Sunday antiphon "Pueri Hebreorum portantes").

While arguments based on something as potentially fluid as text underlay need to be handled with care, the dialogue in certain particularly charged places in the Mass becomes too suggestive to be coincidental. This degree of textual interaction can be illustrated, for example, by the point in the Gloria when the standard plea to the "Domine Deus, Agnus Dei," sung by the outer voices, coincides directly with the tenor's "Domine Deus meus, accipere librum." This is a clear reference to the allusion, in the continuation of the antiphon text quoted above, to the apocalyptic book containing the names of those to be judged. The texting of the Sanctus strongly suggests that the original performance context of the Regis Mass entailed coincidence between the elevation and Osanna I:[111] the outer parts, carrying the text of the Osanna (which follows on from the "Pleni" without a break) are set against "Laudamus Christum quem laudant Osanna in excelsis" in the contra altus, while the tenor sings "Audita est vox milia milium dicentium salus Deo nostro." Perhaps the most obvious intertextual moment comes, as might be expected, in the Credo at "Et iterum venturus est cum gloria judicare vivos et mortuos" (a passage which, unusually, instigates a new musical section). Here Michael's role in executing Christ's judgment is vividly announced by his entry in the middle voices in a passage conflated from two texts used at Matins on his feast day: after the voices proclaim "Michael archangelus, millia millium ministrabant ei" the contra altus proceeds: "Michaeli, et decies milia assistebant ei," while the tenor takes up with "Michaeli, quem honorificant cives angelorum."[112] The immediately following "Et expecto resurrectionem mortuorum" articulates the hoped-for outcome of Mass and the ultimate reason for its existence.

In a powerful resonance with one of the main themes of this chapter, Michael's role as intermediary between God and man – the "praepositus paradisi" named in the liturgical texts of Regis's Mass[113] – also suggests another reference to the ceremony of Mass and its earthly intermediary, the celebrating priest, a link underscored by the iconographic tradition that presents Michael in priestly vestments.[114] Thus the image of Michael stood to draw believers still further into the experience of Mass not just through his embodiment of the notions of advocacy and intercession, but through the link he forged with their own, human intercessor at the altar. Indeed such concentration on the figure of Michael and on the Last Judgment, both here and in Naples Mass 4, serves to remind us that, to whatever great patrons such Masses owed their existence,[115] the ultimate significance – and surely the extent and durability – of the *L'homme armé* tradition derives from the perceived relevance of its message to everyone.

This is not to suggest that lay public attendees at Mass need always have been cognizant of the allegorical model discussed in this chapter. Nor indeed need composers engaging in that tradition and in its well-documented patterns of musical borrowing necessarily always have seen it as their primary motivating force, though it is unlikely, as we have seen, that they can have been unaware of it. What I am proposing, though, is that it was this pattern of meaning that allowed the *L'homme armé* melody to be meaningful in a sacred context, and that opened up the cultural space for its use as a cantus firmus. It is also, I suggest, the force behind the great breadth and duration of its success. Even more than for the Masses based on *Caput*, the *L'homme armé* tradition carried the seed, in the context of its time, of almost limitless development: on the one hand it was grounded in a fundamental contemporary conceptualization of Christ's role in the redemption of humanity, while on the other it admitted of repeated – yet repeatedly particularized – affirmations of the earthly role, crucial to late-medieval princely image creation, of champion of Christ.

It is this, the putative generating force of the tradition, that provides what is surely its most fundamental strength: from this perspective *L'homme armé* Masses profited not just the magnates who paid for individual settings: they carried a charged significance that promised benefit also to their subjects and to all else who were present, reminding us again that there was no such thing in the Middle Ages as a truly private Mass. That awareness of the function of Mass lay behind not just the profusion and brilliance of its polyphonic expressions: it gave it the social purpose that, as the center of an all-encompassing belief system, also lent its weight to social cohesion. Attendance at a *L'homme armé* Mass, for whoever was present, could provide a catalyst for the same fears of the impending horrors of purgatory, the same awareness of the need to lead a life that might minimize them as far as possible, and the same hope for ultimate salvation.

Whatever its origins, however humble and however distinct from those of the lavish settings it received in polyphony, the presence of the *L'homme armé* tune in the Mass was ultimately an expression of the unity and shared purpose of the whole earthly army of Christ. It thus drew the mundane world of the church militant into the service of the heavenly church triumphant, and, with it – ideally – the hearts and minds of the members of the society within which it functioned. Yet as the next chapter will demonstrate, such outside borrowings did not necessarily need the context of sacred words to carry their new spiritual import; nor indeed did they need sacred musical restructuring at all.

6 | The profane made sacred: outside texts and music in the Mass

It is clear by now that the use of borrowed melodies in polyphonic Mass settings was driven – at least in a large number of instances – by emblematic and/or symbolic associations perceived in their original texts. Yet this practice did not provide the only avenue by which "outside" music entered the celebration of Mass in the fifteenth century. This chapter will show that musical borrowing in cantus firmi was part of a much wider range of musical incursions – secular as well as sacred – into the rite, incursions that in turn prompt a range of inferences concerning the origin and proliferation of the cantus firmus Mass itself. But to address this issue demands first of all a consideration of the role played in the polyphonic Mass by the original texts of the melodies used as cantus firmi: the words whose meanings brought such melodies into the celebration of Mass in the first place.

As long ago as 1965, Maria Rika Maniates invoked the concept of "melos" in support of the notion that a melody is intimately and inextricably bound to its originally associated text, and that the same textual associations are carried forward when the melody is used in another verbal or intellectual context.[1] Michael Long noted that the use of a borrowed song in a Mass setting would have called to mind the words to which it had first been set and their semantic association with the sacred Latin words being simultaneously sung.[2] Christopher Reynolds has similarly suggested that quotation of secular melodies in sacred contexts carries with it the notional presence of the original texts, and hence their implicit commentary on the new texts to which they are set.[3] What remains unclear, though, is the extent to which, when melodies were transplanted to new settings, their original words were carried with them and, further, what force of meaning such integral quotation might have exerted. The easiest way into this question is via a body of works in which, in at least some respects, the view is reasonably clear: those Masses that quote the texts as well as the music of sacred cantus firmi.

Outside sacred texts in the Mass

It has been suggested that, since the original text of a quoted melody is implied already by the very use of that melody, the presence or absence in such circumstances of the original words may be immaterial.[4] Yet there is a clear distinction between motets, in which cantus firmi are typically accompanied by their original words, and Mass settings, in which the same is true only rarely. This imbalance begs questions concerning those Masses that do quote outside texts, questions regarding both the semantic and symbolic content of the texts themselves and the range of possible reasons for their quotation.[5]

Most of the Masses in this group quote texts of plainsong cantus firmi that seem likely for the most part to have been chosen in connection with specific endowments. Such choices would thus have reflected the desire to associate the resulting cycles as closely as possible with Christ or the particular saints whose intercession was desired by their donors. A special case is represented by those Masses that borrow from multiple chant antecedents, frequently in ways that seem calculated to imply dialogue both between the borrowed chants themselves and with the words of the Mass.[6] Perhaps not surprisingly, the presence of underlaid chant texts is particularly common among copies of works in this category: such underlay seems likely to have been more crucial to locally and specifically cited quotations than to single cantus firmi laid out repeatedly from movement to movement without apparent regard for the specifics of the prevailing Mass text.[7] The possible interpretative value of underlay in such cases is highlighted by the handful of works in which quotation of texts transcends in importance, and may even supplant, that of their associated melodies, as for example in the striking cases of Regis's Masses on *Ecce ancilla domini* and *L'homme armé*.[8]

Further Masses open up additional perspectives on this issue, however.[9] A number of examples survive in which underlay of the original words of a tenor cantus firmus in the Kyrie is discarded in subsequent movements in favor of the standard Mass texts.[10] Various reasons for this tactic seem plausible. Such partial underlay may have served not merely to identify the antecedent melody but also, through reinforcing the integrity of its words and music, to emphasize its emblematic function for the entire piece. Stamped clearly on the identity of the Mass at its beginning, the words of the cantus firmus would thus have been rendered superfluous for the remaining movements.[11] On the other hand the same pattern could perhaps have had performance implications: thus underlay of the original words of a cantus firmus in the Kyrie could have served as a template for performance,

enabling the same procedure to be replicated in the subsequent movements. Certainly such an approach would have been easy enough to follow, especially in the many cases in which the cantus firmus was widely
familiar. Alternatively such hybrid presentation may imply availability of a
choice to sing the borrowed melody either to its original words or to those
of the Mass. Precisely that choice seems to be presented in the case of the
Regis *Missa Ecce ancilla domini*, for which both sources provide both sets of
words in a two-line underlay throughout much of the duration of the two
lower voices.[12] Demonstrable loss in transmission of cantus firmus texting
in some instances makes it clear that the practice of texted quotation was
broader than the surviving source tradition suggests.[13] On the other hand
the divergent perspectives offered by the sources may also indicate the perception, at least in some circumstances, of a material distinction in cantus firmus usage between implicit and explicit reference to the antecedent
words.

Secular texts in the Mass

If patterns of textual quotation are hard to discern among Masses struc-
tured on sacred cantus firmi, the picture looks a great deal more confused
in the case of secular models. Quotation of secular words in sacred works
generally, while rare, is not unknown. Perhaps the most striking case is that,
discussed in Chapter 3, concerning Josquin's elevation motet *Tu solus qui
facis mirabilia*, its Latin text combined semantically with the French incipit
of Ockeghem's song *D'ung aultre amer*. David Rothenberg has pointed to
what may be a similar, though less clear-cut, example in the case of the
five-voice motet *Missus est Gabriel angelus* variously ascribed to Josquin
and Mouton. Setting up a direct parallel between the vow to an earthly lady
in the borrowed song and that to the heavenly lady of the motet, the tenor
quotes the tenor of Busnoys's song *A une dame j'ay fait veu*.[14] But the two
seem to be drawn more closely together by the text underlay of the tenor.
In the copy in the Medici Codex, the song incipit, more extended than in
the other sources (and slightly varied textually), proceeds directly from "A
une dame j'ay promis" to "Missus est Gabriel angelus ....," perhaps implying, as Rothenberg suggests, that the song's promise to the earthly woman
has become, in the new context of the motet, explicitly tied to the angel's
sacred promise to the Virgin at the Annunciation. Rothenberg extends the
argument to suggest that the widespread presence of secular incipits, hitherto viewed only as indications of the sources of the borrowed tenors, could

be taken to imply an alternative performance possibility, akin to that considered above in connection with sacred cantus firmi. According to this view the relevant song texts, doubtless familiar to many of the likely singers, might well, like those of the sacred cantus firmi discussed above, have been sung in their entirety.[15]

A few Mass sources offer some, albeit limited, support for this idea. Some of that support comes from copies, like those discussed above, in which underlay of original cantus firmus text in the Kyrie could be taken to imply continuation of the same practice through the remainder of the work. A possible remnant of that procedure has been detected in the copy, in Cappella Sistina MS 14, of Du Fay's *Missa Se la face ay pale*. Following the song incipit at the beginning of the tenor in Kyrie I of this Mass, Kyrie II carries the words "Tant je me deduis," presumably a corruption, as Alejandro Planchart has noted, of the text of the portion of the song quoted at that point, "La belle a qui suis."[16] A much more controversial case concerns the copy, in Verona, Biblioteca Capitolare 761, of Josquin's *Missa L'ami Baudichon*. Here the scurrilous words of the popular song (with one apparently notorious exception) are supplied throughout the Kyrie tenor, only to disappear, save for a brief incipit at the opening of the Gloria, from the rest of the Mass.[17] Consciousness of the vulgarity of the antecedent text and an apparently personifying identification of the tenor with the model song may conceivably have lain behind a written canon found in the Verona copy. Here, at the "Et incarnatus," one of the most profound moments in the Mass from the viewpoint of its sacramental message, that voice is rendered tacit with the instruction to be "like a mute, not opening his mouth" ("sicut mutus non aperiens os suum").

Most promising, perhaps, is the case of the complete copy, in Trent 88, of Cornago's *Missa Ayo visto lo mappa mundi*. Here the *integer valor* tenor statements that underpin the final sections of the Gloria and Credo carry the complete text of what was presumably the refrain of the lost antecedent song (apparently a *barzelletta*).[18] Other details in the Gloria, moreover, may suggest that the Trent copy is a descendant of one in which the tenor was more comprehensively accompanied by its original text.[19] The reason behind the quotation of this song, a paean to the island of Sicily, in a Mass cycle remains obscure, a situation that, in the absence of any immediate context for this sole surviving Mass by a Spaniard working at the Aragonese court of Naples, seems unlikely to change.

The quotation, in the second Kyrie of Obrecht's *Missa de Sancto Donatiano*, of the words and music of the Dutch devotional song *Gefft den armen gefangen* provides more solid evidence of the integration at least of vernacular words into a Mass cycle. Here, in a seemingly unique case, the meaning of the song is demonstrably bound up with that of other preexistent material in the cycle, and the whole complex of borrowings is connected with details relating to the individual for whom it was composed.[20]

A rare example of unambiguous quotation of the words of a borrowed secular song occurs in the Gradual and Offertory of Richafort's Requiem. Like the example in Josquin's *Tu solus, qui facis mirabilia*, this was clearly motivated by a very specific resonance between the text of the borrowed work and that of its new setting. Here the outside borrowing involves canonic quotation of the music and text of the passage "c'est douleur non pareille" ("it is a pain without equal") from Josquin's song *Faulte d'argent*. This follows, in these two movements, directly on from the similarly canonic setting in two tenor voices – heard also in all the other movements of the Mass – of a responsory following the Mass for the Dead, "Circumdederunt me gemitus mortis, dolores inferni circumdederunt me" ("the groans of death have encircled me, the pains of hell have encircled me").[21] Thus the borrowings in these two movements considerably sharpen the plangency of the prevailing texts, begging for deliverance from infernal suffering, of the two movements into which they are inserted.[22] These two closely entwined references may, it has been proposed, also point to a third: the combination of a song involving canon by Josquin with the likewise canonic setting of "Circumdederunt me," as found in no fewer than three of Josquin's own works, two of them similarly addressing the theme of redemption through Christ, may indicate that the Requiem was composed in memory of none other than Josquin himself.[23]

A different case entirely is presented by the curious example of the paired Gloria and Credo by Du Fay whose extended Amens quote respectively from a French and an Italian popular song of decidedly earthy nature. Here the settings carry the secular words themselves alongside a pair of liturgical Easter texts that surely reveal the season of their intended performance.[24] Even ears unfamiliar with the borrowed songs would surely have noticed the rustic quality of their closely related melodic and rhythmic profiles, spanning in both cases the fifth from F to C in alternations of simple rhythmic patterns. Here is a graphic instance, to return to the words of Aquinas quoted in Chapter 3, of "spiritual truths ... expounded by means of figures taken from corporeal things." The figures in this case could hardly have failed to guide the ear to the spiritual truths embodied in the Easter texts that they vividly enunciate, one voice at a time, in each line of the polyphonic fabric. Whatever the reason for citing the secular words in these instances, the quotation of the melodies would appear to constitute an expression of the characteristic

late-medieval linkage of Easter with the season of spring, nature's counterpart to the season of spiritual rebirth triggered by Christ's resurrection, and
the occasion for revelry with joyous songs and dances such as those apparently alluded to in this case.[25] In this respect Du Fay's Mass pair relates to
a polyphonic tradition extending back to the thirteenth-century motet in
which sacred and secular were drawn together in a festive celebration of resurrection.[26] The lively rhythms interjected by the secular quotations succeed
in infusing the accompanying Easter tropes, and their polyphonic settings,
with a mood of celebration almost unrestrained in its exuberance.[27]

A loftier tradition of secular texting can be seen in a series of sixteenth-century Masses devoted to princely magnates. In each of these cases the Mass text
is combined with an emblematic textual/musical rebus highlighting or praising
the name of the ruler in question and implicitly, one might suggest, embodying claims for combined spiritual/secular leadership of the kinds outlined in
Chapters 4 and 5. Typically such Masses are built around a tenor cantus firmus
derived from solmization syllables drawn from the component vowels of the
name of the ruler concerned. Singing of the syllables themselves is not explicitly indicated in sources for the first such Mass (and clearly the progenitor of
the others), Josquin's *Missa Hercules dux Ferrarie*.[28] However, the currency of
exactly that procedure in the later cycles and the absence of any other obvious
means of texting the brief, repeating tenor motif on which the Mass is based
encouraged Lewis Lockwood to propose that that voice should repeatedly sing
the text from which its *soggetto* was derived: "Hercules dux Ferrariae."[29]

Secular songs in the Mass

While evidence for the singing of secular cantus firmi to their original words
is at best scattered and diffuse, other indications suggest that the interpene-
tration of sacred and secular in the Mass was more complete than has been
suspected. That this has not been properly recognized before has surely been
due to the tendency of musicology at least since Ambros to sidestep the
question of the contemporary meaning and significance of the use of secular music in the Mass.[30] Yet a considerable body of evidence extending over
a long period provides ample evidence that secular songs were heard in the
Mass not only as musical quotations, but in their original, unaltered forms.

As might be expected, a good deal of the evidence for this claim is negative: in other words, it comprises proscriptions of various kinds against precisely this practice. The most obvious place to start, and the locus of the most
prominent and – to musicology – best-known cluster of rulings against the

use of secular music in church, is the series of Catholic reforming councils that peaked, but certainly did not end, in the Council of Trent.[31] Craig Monson has emphasized the point that the Council of Trent's official pronouncements on music were limited both in subject matter and scope, in the interest – as was true also regarding other doctrinal issues – of avoiding extended discussion in the general congregation. The only dictum on music among the "abuses of the Mass" proscribed, following weeks of consultation and committee discussion, at the twenty-second session in September 1562 was as follows: "Let them keep away from the churches composition in which there is an intermingling of the lascivious or impure, whether by instrument or voice."[32]

This final pronouncement, however, was the distilled result of extended preliminary debate that resonates closely, as we shall see, with many earlier statements and proscriptions. Documentation surviving from that earlier discussion clarifies what was meant by "lascivious or impure." In the papers of the committee member Bartolomaeus a Martyribus, a list of recommended actions against perceived abuses includes one that reads: "Let not only profane songs be removed from the church or sanctuaries, but likewise singing that conceals the text, such as there is in polyphony."[33] Likewise the draft statement on a range of possible reforms of the Mass presented for the deliberation of the general congregation states: "In those Masses where measured music and organ are customary, nothing profane should be intermingled, but only hymns and divine praises."[34] The more detailed objections presented for consideration by the papal legates include a passage that points the finger more specifically, inveighing against the lascivious influences of singing in the Mass profanities "such as *della caccia* and *la battaglia*."[35] This dictum echoes, as Monson notes, Vicentino's disapproving remarks of only a few years earlier concerning those who would "compose a Mass upon a madrigal or upon a French chanson, or upon 'La Battaglia,'"[36] and also Bishop Bernardino Cirillo's famous letter of 1549, directed to the future chair of the committee on the abuses of the Mass, attacking the composition of Masses based on secular cantus firmi.[37] While these obvious references to the widely circulating chansons of Janequin may in some cases more specifically imply performance of Masses based on his *La guerre: escoutez tous gentilz*, no Mass survives on his similarly celebrated *La chasse: gentilz veneurs*, presumably the song referred to as *della caccia*. Moreover, the testimony of the great Spanish Dominican and scholar of the Salamanca school Navarrus (Martin de Azpilcueta, 1493–1586), as recorded in 1578, seems clearly to imply performance at Mass of Janequin's battle song, rather than a Mass setting constructed upon it. Navarrus bewails having heard, mixed in the spiritual dignity of the divine office a most profane and trifling song composed in France, now widely accepted in Spain, through which is represented, almost lifelike, the commotion of battle with the sound of drums and trumpets, and all the racket of war.

Not averse to such vivid musical depictions *per se*, Navarrus is nonetheless scandalized by the inappropriate air of profanity introduced by them when performed in the context of Mass:

Now although this representation may not in itself be shameful, and may be suitable to feasts and recreation, it is most inappropriate to the divine office.[38]

Here then are the first indications that the secular music targeted by the Council of Trent for removal from the divine office was far from limited just to secular cantus firmi, and indeed embraced some of the least ostensibly devotional songs in circulation. Even musical representations of the clamor of battle and the chase were, it would seem, fair game for use as adornments of the church's defining ritual.

The concern of many delegates to the council that its published reforms were too general to have any teeth seems borne out by the decrees of later church councils, in which the same issues as those debated in the Trent convocation surface again and again.[39] The continuing and repeated promulgation of the Council of Trend's strictures can only imply that the same abuses persisted long after the council had ended. This situation was surely encouraged by the reforms of the twenty-fourth session, which devolved responsibility for the specific expression of liturgical devotion, including music, to the provincial synods, and probably also by the realization of the difficulty of enforcing such strictures.[40] The dictum of the Synod of the Diocese of Trent in 1593 that "Musicians and organists should in church abstain from lascivious singing and profane songs suitable for dancing" gives some measure of how little the Council of Trent's position on secular music had apparently travelled by the end of the sixteenth century.[41] Still more striking is the persistence in the late 1560s of the performance, in the pope's own Cappella Giulia, of Masses based on secular songs, only two years after the commissioning from Animuccia, for the same chapel, of five Masses to be written "according to the requirements of the Council."[42] And Cappella Sistina MS 22, copied around 1565, combines within its covers two Masses on secular songs with none other than Palestrina's celebrated "reform" work the *Missa Papae Marcelli*.[43]

It would appear from general decrees repeated through the sixteenth century and beyond that organists were particularly impervious to the prohibition against secular elements.[44] Such strictures also provide substantial evidence that the presence of secular songs in the divine services was far from restricted to secular cantus firmi in polyphonic Mass settings. Navarrus specifically disapproves of "frivolous and sometimes wicked melodies; of this sort are those which they call *Baxae* and *Altae* and other ditties which the mob knows are base, obscene and passionate." Moreover, he notes, these are played "when the divine services are in progress."[45]

But without doubt the most pointed attacks against such abuses are found, both before and after the Council of Trent, in Reformist writings. Affirming the implicit presence, in the performance of melodies alone, of their originally attendant words, the Calvinist Martin Bucer, writing in 1553, allowed for the performance in church of sacred melodies on the organ and other instruments, since "the spirit, moved by such melody, can at least meditate privately by itself on the holy words." The reality, however, seems to have been far from this elevated ideal:

organists, instead of gravely playing holy things, mumble base and wanton songs on their organs: the which they play not only to give vain delectation to the ears of the hearers, but also for the pleasure of seducers and seductresses, whore-mongers and whores, and by which even the hearts of the most pure can be provoked to lewdness. Not only the ordinary people who profess themselves to be Christian, but also those who wish to be thought the highest governors of the church are not even slightly surprised to see and hear such things.[46]

By the same token that sacred melodies called to mind their similarly sacred texts, such melodies, at least in the absence of sacred contrafacta, could not have failed, as Harry Peter Clive notes, to conjure up their profane texts in the minds of their hearers.[47]

It is manifestly clear, though, that the performance of secular songs in church was far from limited to organ playing; neither, crucially, did it exclude the original, secular texts. Among those testifying to this is none other than Martin Luther. True to the commitment to deprive the devil of some good tunes, Luther expounds, in the preface to his *Begräbnis Lieder* of 1542, on the beauty of music and song to be heard in monasteries and churches, but deplores the "scurrilous and ungodly texts" with which they are adorned. He advocates the stripping of such texts and the reclothing of the melodies "with the living holy word of God," so that "such beautiful adornments of music may serve its dear creator and his flock, that he may be praised and honored, and that we, our hearts filled, through his holy word, with sweet song, will be improved and strengthened in faith."[48]

In this as in so many other respects advocating reforms far beyond those propounded by Luther, the early reformer Andreas Bodenstein von

Karlstadt, in his *De cantu Gregoriano Disputatio* of 1521–2, offers further specifics. Among the abuses listed in the 53 theses of the "Dispute," Karlstadt includes not only polyphony and the use of instruments in general, but also a particular secular piece that he claims to have heard performed at the moment of the elevation. The sacred climax of the Mass, he says, is made to coincide, in a sounding together "like the voices of sheep and wolves," with the "lustful song known as 'Wolauff gut gesell von hynnen'" played on the "cithara" (presumably the harp or another stringed instrument).[49] It is not of course possible to know which of the various versions of this song, which also embraced settings of the French text *Comment peut avoir joye*, Karlstadt had heard, nor, hence, what possible relevance, or lack thereof, may have been felt to attach to such a performance.[50] Certainly there is little about the German text, an evocation of the countryside in May, to suggest a meaning appropriate to the gravity of the moment of the elevation, with its message to earthly sinners of salvation via the risen Christ. The French text, a general lament at misfortune, presents a mood more ostensibly apt in its reflectiveness, but with nothing to suggest the penitence demanded by the focal point of the Mass.[51] Since versions of the song circulated, apparently as instrumental pieces, with only the German or French incipit, it is possible in any case that neither Karlstadt nor the performer he heard was familiar with anything beyond these first few words. Possibly germane to this issue may be the fact that, as Osthoff and Atlas have shown, Isaac's setting of *Comment peut avoir joye* and another setting of the German text are closely entwined musically with Isaac's two interrelated Masses on the same song.[52] Most relevant in the present connection is the appearance of Isaac's song in its entirety in the Credos of both Masses: in the six-voice Mass in a section that carries only the incipit "Et in spiritum," and in the four-voice Mass to the text of the "Et incarnatus est." With the obvious exception of the Benedictus, no part of the Mass carries a message more relevant to the act of transubstantiation than the "Et incarnatus." Thus it may be that this association had some role to play in the instance of elevation music lambasted by Karlstadt, or indeed that Isaac's "song" actually began life as a Mass section. But such speculation only serves to underscore the difficulties of unraveling the relationships and genealogy of this tangle of interlinked pieces.[53]

Far more pointed and scathing in its attack on musical abuses is *L'Histoire de la Mappe-Monde papistique*, a Calvinist satire published in Geneva in 1566 as the textual counterpart to an actual engraved "map."[54] Apparently emanating from the hand or at least the instigation of the expatriate Italian Jean-Baptiste Trento, the play reveals close acquaintance with the life and mores of his native region of the Veneto, including its musical life and repertory.[55] It takes as its conceit an imaginary world, each province of which is named after some abuse, from a Calvinist perspective, of Catholicism. The description of the musical carryings-on in the "province" of prayer comprises an attack as noteworthy for its specificity as for its biting sarcasm. After describing the action of "their comedies of Vespers," the author sets the scene for the greatest farce of all: that of Mass. Like Bucer, he speaks of "love songs, madrigals and sonnets" that are mumbled ("grignotés") on the organ, and, like Karlstadt, he points his finger at secular music accompanying the elevation; yet the gravity of Karlstadt's abuses pales beside that of those enjoyed in the "monde papistique":

and above all when they lift up high their God of dough, they play on their organs some love songs, such as some madrigals by Josquin, by Jaquet, by Verdelot, Arcadelt, Vincenzo Ruffo, Constanzo Festa, and principally those amorous things by Cypriano de Rore, such as those pretty madrigals which begin thus: "J'ay chanté tandis que j'ai bruslé"; and then "Tel se trouve devant vostre clarté, madame"; or then "L'oeil, la main, la bouche, le col, la poictrine"; or then "Amour, puisque tu me veux mettre en danger," and various others by this excellent musician. And when another act of the comedy is played, they take another break, and then these same personages present themselves performing other amorous madrigals of master Adrian Willaert, father of music, and above all a few little madrigals that certain lords, enamored with a Courtesan or public whore in Venice called "la Peccorina,"[56] had him compose, and which commence "D'elle vient l'amoureux pensement," and those fine madrigals "Amour, esprit, valeur, pitie & douleurs." They also play several dialogues by the same author, which they sing thus: "Pleurez yeux," etc.; which music completely hits the mark, and so amuses the people, that they don't miss a single note; and it all adds to give credit to the place, and water to the mill, as they say of it; and to entertain them and give them pleasure, ease and delight; and they are satisfied as by all the other pleasant comedies and farces that they can hear ordinarily; and they hang around with their mouths gaping, and turn their eyes in their heads like an aborting she-goat, so that it's a delight to see them.[57]

Even allowing for exaggeration, this damning evocation bears clear witness that secular music in the Mass was far from unknown. At least six of the seven named songs can be traced in the surviving repertory, and the fact that all were first published in collections by Scotto or Gardano in Venice in the 1540s and 1550s reveals that the author was familiar with a repertory that had a consistent circulation, a fact that may lend his statements a certain credence. Whether or not he had actually heard these specific pieces at Mass, a number lend themselves easily enough to Marian interpretation, a fact that may offer clues to their likely sacred use.[58] Festa's *Che si può più vedere Madonna*, presumably to be identified with *Tel se trouve devant vostre clarté, madame*, is a generic paean to a woman of otherworldly beauty whose rhetoric sits comfortably with that of fifteenth-century songs used as cantus firmi of Marian Masses. This perspective gains another dimension in the case of *Amor! senno! valor, pietate, e doglia*, the second part of Willaert's *I' vidi in terra angelici costumi* and presumably the madrigal referred to as *Amour, esprit, valeur, pitie & douleurs*. The piece sets number 156 of Petrarch's sonnets, a corpus mined repeatedly in the sixteenth century for Christian reinterpretation and adaptation.[59] The "heavenly beauty unmatched in this world" whose tears unite "love, wisdom, excellence, pity and grief" presents an image as potentially evocative of the grieving Virgin as that of *Comme femme desconfortée*.[60] Similarly the love and boldness engendered by seeing and hearing the loved one in Willaert's *Amor, da che tu vuoi pur ch'io m'arrischi* (presumably the satire's *Amour, puisque tu me veux mettre en danger*) lends itself easily to a Marian reading.

The fact that these pieces were apparently recognized by the author of the satire might well suggest that their textual associations were widely familiar, and may have had a direct role to play in their putative new context. On the other hand, since they were allegedly performed on the organ, further reasons for their possible use at Mass might be sought in their musical style. Here again *I' vidi in terra* offers perhaps the most fertile ground, presenting a picture of dignity, restraint and mournfulness entirely in keeping both with its text and with the mood of introspection and contrition appropriate for those gazing on their hoped-for redeemer. Likewise the simple declamation and repetitive imitative style of *Che si può più vedere Madonna*, a piece for three more or less equal voices, present a musical image of restraint appropriate to the most solemn moment of Mass, while its dirge-like rhythms and descending parallel passages would certainly fit it to a situation demanding feelings of repentance. Elsewhere, however, the message is decidedly mixed. It would be hard to imagine, for example, a more suitably dignified musical item than Willaert's *Occhi piangete*, presumably to be identified with *Pleurez yeux*, in which the funereal, homophonic opening sets a mood of deep lamentation. On the other hand the accusatory tone of the lover's lament to which it was set would seem to strike an oddly jarring note in the context of Mass. As in the cases already discussed, though, there is no way of knowing whether textual or musical aspects of this or any of the other named madrigals had any bearing on the performances putatively heard in the "province of prayer."

The particular value of such a polemic as the *Histoire de la Mappe-Monde papistique* lies in its remarkable level of detail: anti-Catholic diatribes are generally, for obvious reasons, far more likely to focus on such specifics than are the internal prohibitions of the Catholic church. Exceptions to this observation come in the form of censures by humanists which, while articulated, broadly speaking, from within the Catholic fold, are no less excoriating in their judgments. This is of course to be expected from a perspective by its nature deeply antipathetic to the kind of scholastic allegory whereby worldly melodies could be deemed meaningful in a sacred context. Thus it is unsurprising that humanist positions tend to focus strongly on the literal meanings of texts and their comprehensibility. Most prominent, and least unexpected, given the inspiration drawn from him by Luther and other reformers, are the typically extravagant attacks of Erasmus. The *Commentary on I Corinthians 14* inveighs against the introduction of:

a laborious and theatrical kind of music into our sacred edifices, a tumultuous bawl of diverse voices, such as I do not believe was ever heard in the theaters of the Greeks or the Romans. They crash everything out with trumpets, clarions, reeds, and sambukes, and human voices vie with these instruments. There are heard vile love ditties, to which harlots and mimes dance. People flock to the sacred edifice as to a theater to have their ears charmed. And for this purpose artisans of the organ are maintained at high salaries and troops of boys all of whose time is consumed in learning these things, and who study nothing good in the meanwhile.[61]

In the *Christiani matrimonii institutio* he holds forth against the tendency that "Nowadays the most frivolous tunes are given holy words, which is no better than if one put the jewelry of Thaïs on Cato. And given the whore-like shamelessness of the singers, the [secular] words are not even held back."[62] The wording here strongly suggests that he was responding to the use of secular cantus firmi in Mass settings; but at the very least it seems clear that he had heard secular songs performed in church complete with their original texts.

Agrippa von Nettesheim, in his *De incertitudine et vanitate scientiarum et artium* (1532), levels what seems to be a similar accusation:

Today there is such permissiveness in the music in our churches that certain obscene little polyphonic songs are sometimes placed on a par even with the canon of the Mass itself; and the divine rites themselves and prayers of holy supplication with wanton pieces of music paid for at great cost, not for the understanding of the hearers or for the elevation of the spirit, but to incite debauchery, not with human voices do they sing, but with the cries of beasts: boys neigh the discant, others bellow the tenor, others bark the counterpoint, others roar the altus, others gnash the bass; so that a certain multiplicity of sounds is heard, nothing is understood of the words and the prayer, but the authority of judgment is taken away from ears and mind alike.[63]

In a commentary extraordinary in its detail and specificity, Conrad von Zabern, as early as 1474, inveighs directly against the use of secular cantus

firmi in polyphonic Mass settings. In the fifth chapter of his treatise on singing, *De modo bene cantandi*, Conrad outlines the prerequisites necessary to
devotional singing, among them the following:

5. Item, singing devotionally is thus: that no melody that has come down to us not
from the devout holy fathers, but [rather has been] introduced by ministers of the
devil, as said below, shall ever be sung among divine songs of praise. Indeed impure
melodies of this kind are entirely to be rejected from the divine office. 6. And yet,
alas, in many churches [these] are almost daily in use. 7. I will speak by means of
example, that it will be understood: the leaders of some schools, wishing to satisfy
who knows whom, but in no doubt whatever that they serve the devil through this,
even if ignorant of certain worldly songs, took them up and adapted them, as far as
they were able, to those songs of divine praise that are among the most powerful,
that is, to the hymn of the angels Gloria in excelsis, and to the Symbolum Nicaenum
[Credo] and to the Sanctus and Agnus Dei, and, in singing these things to the same
worldly melodies, abandoning the devout melodies prescribed for us by the holy
fathers. 8. The which melodies of worldly songs, when they are sung in the office
of Mass, not only offend many of the faithful, as well I know, but also make the
common people, especially young and worldly men, ponder rather on the dance
hall than on the heavenly realm, no small impediment on their devotions, because,
evidently, they have often heard melodies of this kind, or similar ones, in the dance
hall. 9. Of this thing I have in truth heard the most striking complaints from not the
least of the laity, and, among the clergy, disorder and disgrace, such that by the good
action of the bishop and prelate, through the entire extent of his jurisdiction, melodies of this kind, which not without cause will be called diabolical, should be thoroughly prohibited, [and] which by this account I devoutly wish to have removed.[64]

Such detailed condemnation was clearly neither in the interests nor in the
nature of the reports of the church councils or other legislative documents of
the Catholic church. Yet such legislation bears repeated witness that, ecclesiastical proscriptions notwithstanding, abuses of this nature were of long and
persistent tradition. To whatever extent such objections arose in response to
reformational challenges – as was avowedly the case in some instances – or
to an internally perceived need for renewal, they provide ample evidence
that the diatribes of the reformers and humanists were far from groundless.

Among the clearest censures from the immediately pre-Trent period is
that found in the section on the abuses of singers in the 1543 *De praecipuis
quibusdam clericorum et laicorum abusibus pro ecclesia reformanda tollendis*
of the Bishop of Vienna Friedrich Nausea von Waischenfeld:

The final abuse of the singers is that sometimes in the singing and organ playing
they allow that which stirs up wantonness, and sometimes permit to be sung those
things which are not selected from the divine scriptures, but which are entirely

opposite from them or at least insufficiently spiritual, especially when they are in the habit of having them expounded not in the customary language, that is to say, in the vernacular, contrary to the mores and custom of the Catholic Church.[65]

The 1551 Council of Narbonne proscribes secular song in church in the context of an attack, found repeatedly beginning with the Council of Basel in the 1430s, against the Feast of Fools and other such spectacles – which were clearly almost impossible to stamp out, even on pain of excommunication:

By this edict it is decreed that in churches, when any feast days are cultivated, or spectacles in any other time (to wit, of Fools, of Innocents) are in the habit of being enjoyed, no stage tricks, secular songs, uproar, nor other things of this kind should take place; by means of which the populace is drawn away from religion and reduced to guffawing and immoderate laughter. And this edict of not performing spectacles in church will be precisely observed, lest the pain of excommunication which it elsewhere prescribes be imposed.[66]

Among the most detailed musical edicts of the earlier sixteenth-century church councils is that of the 1528 Council of Sens. The musical reforms of this council are of particular interest, moreover, in being motivated directly, as its records specifically state, "against Lutheran insurgencies and immoral customs" ("contra insurgentes Lutheranos & improbos mores"). The council affirms that "common wanton songs should not be heard in church under the pretext of musical chant" and, in common with a number of other councils, decrees that "no shameless or wanton music, but [rather] a sound altogether sweet, representing nothing except divine hymns and spiritual songs, should resound in church on the organs."[67] Perhaps partly in reference to secular cantus firmi, the 1492 Synod of Schwerin, listing the Gloria and Credo along with other parts of Mass that are to be "discanted," rules against "vulgar response or song in the place of those prescribed by organ or choir."[68]

The Chapter Acts of the cathedral of Breslau give a glimpse of how such edicts might have been enforced at the local level. At his reception, on December 16, 1502, by the chapter, the new organist Melchior Schondecher was told that he must be "diligent in his office and not play on the organ secular songs, which are more appropriate to dancing."[69] An anonymous late-fifteenth-century English manuscript treatise for the instruction of priests makes a detailed moral case against the vainglory that leads to the performance of secular music in the divine office:

Þere be iii maners of syngynges / oon is to preise god and his seyntes. / þe seconde for mannes honeste disporte and gladnesse of clene songes and honeste / and þe þridde is of flessheli loue. iolite. ribaudie or oþer folie suche as be towe or herdes [flax used for kindling] to lighte wiþ þe fire of lecherie in þe hertes of þe herers. /

to þise last syngers þe devel yeueþ [giveth] of his sugre roset [a concoction of rose petals and sugar used both in cooking and as a medicine] to swete [sweeten] wiþ þeire mouthes to make hem to synge in hault and as he wol be ela. [to make them sing high, up to E-la] / and aftre also / to þe syngers þat synge in chirch at divine service / he bloweþ a blast of vayne glorie / þat þei lose al þeire peyne and merite / for suche song pleseþ not oonli to god for þe noyse þat þe syngers make / but for þe hooli wordes in þe service / and þe deuocioun of þe people that here it / but in þise songes of loue and lecherie used at reuels and carolles is not oonli þe synnes of vaynglorie. but also þe service of chanons nonnes and monkes of þe devel / and þei þat use suche songes be professid to his rule and his service / which þei doo alle in gladnesse / and wiþ greet labour and cost.[70]

This quotation, and the general tone it takes, shows clearly that the danger of falling into ribaldry – and the wickedness attendant upon it – in music was perceived as ever present, and that the use of undignified music in a spirit of revelry, especially in church, was seen as an infringement of decorum and a revelation of lax morals.

Although (so far as it is possible to tell) becoming substantially less common as one proceeds ever further backwards into the fifteenth century, earlier musical proscriptions include, from the present perspective, some of the most striking. Two comments, both from outside the run of church councils and synods, offer particularly suggestive and tantalizing details.[71] In his *Summa theologica*, completed shortly before his death in 1459, St. Antoninus holds forth not only against polyphony in the divine office, but also against "the insertion of songs or balatas, and vain words, against which St. Jerome inveighs in *Distinction 92: Cantantes.*" Still more remarkable, however, and indeed among the most extraordinary of such proscriptions in its specificity, is a passage from Pierre Soybert's 1503 treatise *De cultu vinee domini liber inumere plenus com[m]oditatis*:

Item, the visiting bishop should reprove those who, with melodious and alluring voices, as may please the common people and the ladies, sing virolais or quick notes / notated music ["notulas"] at the elevation of the body of Christ or at least in the Mass, where the words are shameful or depraved, attractive to the vanities of women.

Here is direct confirmation, of a detailed and specific nature, of the existence of the practice addressed, laced with irony, in the *Histoire de la Mappe-Monde papistique*: namely the performance of secular songs not simply in the Mass, but at its focal and most sacred moment, and not just on the organ, as there, but – presumably with the attendant secular texts – with the full articulacy of voices.

I have found only two censures of this nature from the first half of the fifteenth century. The Synod of Breslau, foreshadowing the warning issued, some half a century later, to the new organist in the same city's cathedral, protests in 1446 against clerics of the diocese who,

little attending to sacred observance, dare to stir up playing on lutes, wind instruments and general clamor, [and] call forth the people gathered to hear the divine service, in Mass and votive rites, more through avarice and vainglory than for the praise and honor of God.[72]

Finally, in an edict that would be repeated and paraphrased in church councils and synods for more than a century, the great ecumenical Council of Basel in 1435 forbade "songs to be sung in the vernacular tongue, inserted during the solemn service of Mass."[73]

In the years before the Council of Basel, however, such proscriptions, at least in published records, are conspicuous by their absence. This might be taken to imply that in earlier years there had been nothing to object to: in other words that the introduction of secular song into the Mass was a new phenomenon in the 1430s. Or, alternatively, it may suggest quite the opposite: that earlier objections are absent because the practice was at that time considered unobjectionable, or at least tolerable. As it happens, tangible support for the latter hypothesis can be found in a quite different body of evidence. To consider this we must leave the realm of musical legislation and turn our attention instead to the library inventories of none other than the dukes of Burgundy.

Songs, motets and the rise of the cantus firmus Mass

The inventory drawn up, following the death of John the Fearless, in 1420, of the "books such as breviaries, missals, books of hours and other devotional books" of the ducal chapel includes, among the items listed under the heading "Missals and other books used for services of Mass," the following intriguing entries:

Item, a book covered in red, notated, in which there are polyphonic ANTIPHONS, VIRELAIS, and BALLADES.

Item, a large, flat book, notated, containing many MOTETS, VIRELAIS, and BALLADES, which begins *Colla jugo fidere*, and finishes *Bis dicitur*.

Item, another book of MOTETS, PATREMS, VIRELAIS, BALLADES, and other things, from which one sang in the chapel on the great feast days.[74]

Entries found in the inventory of chapel holdings of 1487, by then in the hands of Maximilian I and Philip the Fair in Brussels, add further detail in the form of the following descriptions, entered as consecutive items:

Item, another volume covered in greyish hide with two metal clasps, entitled "a book of song serving the chapel," beginning on the second leaf *Ma douleur ne cesse pas* and ending on the last *Le soleil luit la lune est rescousée*.[75]

Item, another covered with red leather with two metal clasps, entitled "a book of song serving the chapel," beginning on the second leaf "profondement" and ending on the last old [other?] contratenors.

Item, another, covered with parchment, entitled like the one above, beginning on the second leaf *Tabula baladarum, rondellorumque, vireleticorum*, and ending on the last leaf *Ma riche amour*.[76]

Item, another volume covered with white hide, with four large stitches [?] on each side and two latten clasps, entitled "serving the chapel for an entire year," beginning on the second folio *Alleluya ostende nobis*[77] and ending on the last, *contratenor*.

In other words the collection of chapel books included, besides a large body of liturgical manuscripts, a handful of polyphonic music books that embraced not only liturgical settings (including Credos, antiphons and an Alleluia), but also motets and, strikingly, secular songs. Most striking is the penultimate item, "entitled, like the one above" (i.e. "a book of song serving the chapel"), which is explicit in mentioning only ballades, rondeaux and virelais. It is highly unlikely that the scribes, whose entries are precise and detailed, simply misunderstood the purposes of the volumes they listed. This seems particularly so in the case of the 1420 inventory, for which one of the scribes was none other than Jacques de Templeuve, first chaplain of the Burgundian chapel under Philip the Bold, John the Fearless and Philip the Good, and immortalized in the text of Binchois's motet *Nove cantum melodie*.[78] But it seems similarly reasonable to take the later account, made by Martin Steenbergh and Charles Soillet, respectively Dean and school-master of St. Goedele in Brussels, at face value. The inventories, in other words, are documents drawn up by technically informed professionals, and they mean what they say.

The chapel inventory of 1404 adds further detail concerning the above entries: it would appear that the volumes it describes as "two books of MOTETS, one larger than the other" are to be identified with the second and third items given above from the inventory of 1420.[79] The second item is of particular interest since it has partially survived: this is the so-called Trémouïlle Manuscript, a source apparently copied in 1376, probably for a chapel of the French royal house, but bought in 1384 or later by Duke Philip the Bold.[80] While most of the musical contents of the manuscript have been lost, what has come down to us complete is its index. This is a document of great value, since the list of works, most of which have survived in other manuscripts, affords a rare glimpse into the repertory not only of the chapel for which it was compiled, but also of the ducal chapel under Philip the Bold and John the Fearless.[81] Further, given its position among the possessions of the chapel and its context in the above group of inventory entries, the conclusion seems inescapable that the contents of the Trémouïlle Manuscript were once used in Burgundian celebrations of Mass. Thus for the present investigation they become a focus of intense interest.

For our purposes here the primary point is the manuscript's spread of genres: seventy-one motets, five Mass movements and one hymn are joined by three chaces and no fewer than thirty-four songs.[82] In other words the great majority of the contents of this chapel manuscript – used, as the 1420 inventory quoted above clearly states, at Mass – were at least ostensibly secular (songs) or partly secular (most of the motets).

In turning to the songs, of which half have survived, it should be acknowledged at the outset that almost all were copied at the bottoms of openings, in spaces left beneath prior copies of motets. Were they, therefore, simply incidental "space-fillers," added perhaps as pastimes or learned amusements for chapel members? This seems unlikely for a number of reasons. First among these is the context offered by the third of the entries from the 1487 inventory cited above, which clearly describes a manuscript used in the chapel, yet which lists only songs. In simple practical terms, it should also be remembered that Trémouïlle, like its companion manuscripts, was kept in the chapel (wherever, on the Burgundian peregrinations, was assigned for that role) specifically for use there; further, in terms of the basic logistics of copying, it is easier to negotiate manuscript copying by first entering extended motets, leaving the remaining empty spaces for the much shorter songs. Briefly then, it seems likely that the songs in the Trémouïlle Manuscript constitute a corpus of secular works used, in accordance with the evidence presented above, at Mass. But what, if anything, in the texts of these pieces, ostensibly concerned with *amor courtois*, might have fitted them for use in the most sacred of contexts?

In at least two cases the answer seems obvious enough. There can be little doubt but that the text of the song *Quicumques vuet* which originally straddled folios 36v–7r (presumably the anonymous rondeau of that name that survives in a number of contemporary sources)[83] was conceived in direct reference to the so-called Athanasian Creed, generally known, from its opening words, as the "Quicumque vult," the great affirmation of faith in the Trinity.[84] Just as the Creed urges that "Whoever wishes to be saved must, above all, keep the Catholic faith," so the song affirms that "Whoever wishes to enjoy love must have faith and hope." Just as the Christian's faith in the Trinity keeps alive his hope for salvation, so faith "sustains the lover's desire" while hope "relieves his suffering." Like the love songs discussed in Chapter 3, with their potential, realized in Mass settings, to be directed to devotional purposes, *Quicumques vuet* could be read as an admonishment to earthly or spiritual love; yet in this case, that higher form of love is more directly invoked through its embrace of one of the central statements of faith.

The anonymous ballade *Comme le cerf* (ff. 44v–5r) draws still more directly on Psalm 42 (Vulgate Psalm 41), *Sicut cervus*. Here the lover's exclamation – "As the hart desires the spring, which the dogs have long pursued, my poor heart is drawn to the fountain of your grace, my Lady" – closely paraphrases the soul's longing in the psalm, "as the hart desires the spring," after God. In a parallel that, as will be seen, mirrors a key topos of courtly love lyrics, both lover and psalm narrator foresee only suffering or even death while the objects of their love remain obdurate. Comfort from the lady, on the one hand, or faith in God, on the other, offer the only hope of salvation. While the lamenting tone of the psalm complements its use as a canticle (in the form of a tract) for Holy Saturday (the Vigil of Easter), the day Christ lay dead in the tomb, its depiction of the stag/soul thirsting after water associates it with the new life awakened by baptism: indeed this is precisely its association on Holy Saturday, when it accompanies the procession of the celebrant and ministers to bless the font.[85] Like the stag who gains a new lease of life from drinking at the fountain, the faithful, just as Christ had done on the joyous day that succeeded Holy Saturday, gain the promise of new life through baptism. The same expectation of rebirth through faith surely also explains the use of Psalm 42 as the psalm for the third antiphon at Matins in the Office of the Dead, and, in some uses, for the tract of the Requiem Mass.[86] In his exposition on this psalm Augustine explains that:

> there is a certain Christian unity, whose voice thus speaks, "Like as the hart desireth the water-brooks, so longeth my soul after Thee, O God." And indeed it is not ill understood as the cry of those, who being as yet Catechumens, are hastening to the grace of the holy Font. On which account too this Psalm is ordinarily chanted on those occasions, that they may long for the Fountain of remission of sins, even "as the hart for the water-brooks."

Yet he is quick to observe that baptism is only the beginning, a setting out on a path that will be long and arduous, but glorious in its outcome:

> such "a longing" is not fully satisfied even in the faithful in Baptism: but … haply, if they know where they are sojourning, and whither they have to remove from hence, their "longing" is kindled in even greater intensity … "My soul is athirst for the living God" (verse 2). What I am saying, that "as the hart panteth after the water-brooks, so longs my soul after Thee, O God," means this, "My soul is athirst for the

living God." For what is it athirst? "When shall I come and appear before God?" This it is for which I am athirst, to "come and to appear before Him." I am athirst in my pilgrimage, in my running; I shall be filled on my arrival.[87]

In the first place a song of longing for the unattainable lady of *amor courtois*, then, the higher, sacred allusions of the song, with their salvific implications, would have been quickly perceived by the mind of any auditor familiar, as most surely were, with the psalms. Likewise, in its context in a manuscript of the Burgundian chapel, the song's deeper meaning would have been summoned up, or "activated," in any putative use, such as those documented above, at Mass.

But a much larger sacred context is provided by the principal group of works in the Trémouïlle manuscript, a repertory that by its very nature straddles, and negotiates, the conceptual distance between sacred and secular: its corpus of motets. The internal negotiation perceptible in at least some of these works between sacred tenors and secular upper voices provides, as we shall see, a key for further potential sacred meanings also in the songs.

In some motets the sacred function is unambiguous. Among the clearest instances, and surely the most obvious in its applicability to Mass, is *Post missarum solemnia / Post misse modulamina / Ite, missa est* (originally on ff. 11v–12r).[88] With its upper-voice texts exhorting the good effects – in actions and morals – to flow "after the sowing of the sweet *word*" of Mass, this piece is an elegant trope on the concluding valediction of Mass, *Ite, missa est*, heard in its tenor, whose function it must surely have been intended to assume in liturgical settings. In this it offers an interesting pendant to another piece in Trémouïlle, *Se grace / Cum venerint / Ite missa est* (originally on ff. 13v–14r), whose triplum text, in admonishing the wealthy to give alms to the poor, likewise focuses on the good works that should flow from the Mass. In the case of this piece, though, we can be more definite about contemporary functioning, since elsewhere it forms the closing number of the composite Mass of Tournai. Here its position in a Mass that was likely devised for the highest Marian devotions at the chapel to the Virgin in Tournai Cathedral offers a more specific context for its courtly French motetus text, whose Marian import, in its stock devotion to an intransigent lady, must in this context have been unambiguous.[89] Other motets in Trémouïlle, such as Machaut's motet 20, *Trop plus / Biauté paree / Je ne sui mie certains*, with its lyrics worshipping "the flower of ladies," were likewise easily applicable to Marian devotion.[90] In other cases potential sacred meanings are less immediately clear. Yet as recent scholarship has revealed, a key to such potential meanings can plausibly be found, as in the case of the *Ite missa est* settings, in the liturgical chant fragments that form their tenors.

Such work has focused particularly on the liturgical and biblical roots of the tenors of motets as a route to allegorical readings of their upper-voice texts, and thus as a means to negotiate the distance between sacred and secular spanned by their ostensibly contrasting textual registers.[91] Most relevant for present purposes, since it bears directly on a group of motets in Trémouïlle, is Anne Walters Robertson's study of the motets of Machaut. For Robertson the Latin tenors of Machaut's motets 1–17 provide a key to a reading of these motets – whose order is maintained almost consistently in the manuscripts of Machaut's works overseen by the composer himself – as a coherent allegory of the spiritual journey of the Christian in his quest for ultimate vision of Christ. She is encouraged in this interpretation by the many similar quests – with their analogous challenges, setbacks, and ultimate success – narrated in such works as Guillaume de Deguilleville's *Pelerinage de l'ame* and *Pelerinage de la vie humaine* and, particularly, the *Horologium sapientiae* of Machaut's contemporary Heinrich Suso.[92] The *Horologium* offers particularly attractive parallels in that, like Machaut's motets, it uses the language and conceits of *amor courtois*. Robertson notes that "the Lover's quest for a Lady is in many ways commensurate with the Christian's journey to be with Christ." She accounts for the obvious gender distinction by appeal to the personification, used by Suso and others, of Christ as Wisdom – the latter being characterized, following the female gender of the noun "sapientia" as a Lady.[93] Such an equation clears the way, she suggests, "for examining not just the tenors, but also the upper voices of Machaut's motets 1–17 from the dual perspective of courtly literature and medieval affective theology."[94]

Of the allegorical models she proposes for the motets, the largest group follows the typological method (that concerned with allegorical models for events in the life of Christ, most typically his Passion). Such allegory is typically addressed easily to the context of Mass, characterized – increasingly so, as we shall see in Chapter 8, in the later Middle Ages – as an allegory of the Passion. Most of the motets from nos. 1–17 found in the Trémouïlle Manuscript (nos. 8, 10, 14 and 15) fall into this category. Thus the obedience described in the tenor of motet 10, *Obediens usque ad mortem* ("obedient unto death") extracted from the Maundy Thursday liturgy, is set against the devotion, in the upper-voice texts, of the lover, burning with a love that threatens to consume him. Christ, as stated in the biblical source of the tenor, Paul's letter to the Philippians, was "obedient unto death, even the death of the cross," that we too may pass to eternal life, but only after a life of devotion of such intensity as that here depicted in the upper voices. Robertson notes how "the courtly and religious topoi complement one another and highlight the shared descriptive language of carnal and spiritual love."[95] Similarly in motet 8, the chant-derived tenor, *Et non est qui adjuvet* ("And there is no one to help"), its text drawn from Psalm 21: 12 and originally used in reference to the suffering of Christ in the responsory *Circumdederunt me* for Passion Sunday, is juxtaposed, in the upper voices, with the lover's complaints about his own suffering. An added layer of significance is supplied here by the fact that the *Circumdederunt* responsary was an important component of the Requiem Mass (as in the case of Richafort's *Requiem*, discussed above) and as a consequence was widely used in polyphonic *complaintes*. Here again, then – as noted in Chapter 4 in the specific context of the *Caput* Masses – a link is forged between the resurrection of Christ and its inherent promise of the resurrection of the body that is his Church. Yet in the synthesis formulated by motet 8, that combined message draws in also the ostensibly earthly desires of the courtly lover: both the quest of the soul as commended in the Requiem Mass and that of the suffering lover of the upper voices are set in the deeper, redemptive context of Christ's journey, articulated by the Passion Sunday liturgy, towards salvation.

The realization, surely unavoidable, that such motets as those in Trémouïlle must indeed have been sung at Mass opens up vision of an altogether new and more profound level of spiritual meaning for the courtly love texts which had already received a devotional *tinta* from their combination with sacred tenors. It also, intriguingly, prompts a reconsideration of two documents not referred to in the previous section, both of them much earlier than those already addressed and much better known. These are the famous decree *Docta sanctorum patrum* of Pope John XXII of 1324/5 and the *De musica* of Johannes de Grocheio of c.1300. Grocheio's oft-quoted definition of the motet, the focus already of controversy concerning the genre's intended audience,[96] holds that such pieces should be performed

coram litteratis et illis qui subtilitates artium sunt quaerentes. Et solet in eorum festis decantari ad eorum decorationem, quemadmodum cantilena quae dicitur rotundellus in festis vulgarium laicorum.

Christopher Page translates this as:

before the clergy [as he notes, the traditional sense of "litterati"] and those who look for the refinements of skills. It is the custom for the motet to be sung in their holiday festivities to adorn them, just as the *cantilena* which is called "rotundellus" [is customarily sung] in the festivities of the lay public.[97]

Yet there seems no reason in light of the evidence presented above to avoid the inference that the "festa" of the clergy carried here its most obvious meaning of ecclesiastical feasts. As Page has noted, the difference between liturgical feasts and public festivities was typically one of tone and register rather than of occasion, since they commonly marked the same days in the church calendar.[98] The social and cultural distinctions are real, but each arose in response to the same "festal moment." Moreover, as Page perceptively observes, the link is tightened by the musical comparison made by Grocheio between "high" and "low" repertories that share not only scale and subject matter but also source transmission and musical material. In the process Grocheio blends the two sides of the celebratory coin that were in any case both, as contemporary witnesses to caroling clerics testify, experienced and enjoyed by members of the clergy.[99] The opposition Grocheio draws between clerical and lay "feasts" surely makes best sense in this light. But it also makes sense of the attack, some quarter of a century later, of John XXII against the composers of the "new school" who

dismember melodies with hockets and sing lubricious discants, frequently inserting second and third voices in the vernacular …

We and our brethren long ago perceived that this is in need of correction, and we hasten to banish [these practices] more effectively: to throw them out completely, to do away with them from the Church of God. For this reason, we … specifically order that no one should presume to attempt these [practices] or ones like them in the aforementioned Offices, especially the Canonical Hours, or when Mass is celebrated.[100]

It seems unlikely that such "abuses" were new when Grocheio and John XXII were writing: Page draws attention to the warning of the early-thirteenth-century *Summa* of Robert of Courson, which, he argues, may well refer to the singing of motets:

In the same way we say that the services of masters of organum who set minstrelish and effeminate things before young and ignorant persons, in order to weaken their minds, are not licit; however, they can sell their services with respect to licit chants insofar as they are of use in churches. If, however, a wanton prelate gives benefices to such wanton singers in order that this kind of minstrelish and wanton music may be heard in his church, I believe that he becomes contaminated with the disease of simony. If, however, some sing any organa on a feast-day according to the liturgical customs of the region, they may be tolerated if they avoid minstrelish little notes.[101]

Neither, apparently, were such practices absent even from the most sacred parts of the rite. The Synod of Trier inveighed, in 1227, against traveling singers who would sing "verses" at Mass "super Sanctus and Agnus Dei":

Item precipimus ut omnes Sacerdotes non permittant trutannos, & alios vagos Scholares, aut goliardos cantare versus super *Sanctus, & Agnus Dei*, aut alias in missis vel in divinis officiis, quia ex hoc Sacerdos in Canone quamplurimum impeditur, & scandalizantur homines audientes.[102]

How broad, and how long-lasting, an effect the papal decree may have had cannot of course be gauged. As noted earlier, though, edicts against secular music in church seem to be otherwise absent before the Council of Basel, while the authority of *Docta sanctorum patrum* was still frequently being invoked in fifteenth-century proscriptions.

Such evidence of the potential role in Mass of motets lends weight to Frank Ll. Harrison's proposal, now more than half a century old, that it "seems most likely that the [English] motet of the thirteenth and fourteenth centuries was normally performed in the pulpitum [i.e. on the choir screen] after the Sanctus and Benedictus, during the Canon of the Mass."[103] But the same evidence adds the additional point that such motets need not have been fully sacred. Still more strikingly it also suggests further insights into the role of the songs with which, in the Trémouïlle Manuscript and elsewhere, such works rubbed shoulders, and which may likewise have been performed, where feasible, on the choir screen. Comparison between the two genres can allow us to see how the kinds of exegeses that can perceive Christological and ultimately salvific undercurrents in the macaronic motet repertory might, in appropriate circumstances, detect similar resonances in works that are ostensibly fully secular. Certainly there is little to separate the register of the upper-voice French texts of motets such as those of Machaut from that of such vernacular songs as those in the Trémouïlle Maniscript: both operate in the same theater of longing after the distant loved one, suffering of pains of rejection and, occasionally, ultimate vision of – though not of course consummation with – the beloved, peopled by a common cast of personified emotions derived from the *Roman de la rose* and its related lyric tradition. That beloved may be a source of hope and solace, as in Trémouïlle's *De fortune, Dame de qui* and Machaut's motet 6, or – more often – cruel and disdainful, as in *Phiton le merveilleux serpent* and motets 4, 5, and the whole series found in the Machaut manuscripts as nos. 10–15. The lovers of Machaut's *De toutes flours* and *De fortune*, as of his motets 3, 8 and 12, find themselves at the mercy of that age-old adversary of lovers, Fortune. Similarly Narcissus, condemned, as punishment for his coldness to Echo, to fall in love with his own reflection, becomes himself a painful reflection for the protagonists, belatedly struck down by remorse at their disdain of their would-be lovers, of both *De narcissus* and motet 7, *J'ai tant mon / Lasse! Je sui / Ego moriar pro te*. The singer of *Merci ou mort* (Trémouïlle ff. 28v-9r) desires mercy or death as the only available cures for his love-longing, while the voice of Machaut's motet 3, *Hé! Mors com tu / Fine Amour / Quare non sum mortuus?*, weighs the merits of death and mercy and opts for the former on the grounds that, in the absence of the loved one, life is bereft of joy. Love can be bitter and sweet in equal measure: thus the "sweetness bitter to my taste" ("Douceur fine a mon goust amere") of Machaut's *Biaute qui toutes autres pere* is echoed in the excessive love that, for the lover in motet 1, "makes a bitter thing of that which is most sweet to him" ("de son dous fac[e] on amer"). Standard metaphors can be co-opted for applications that are diametrically opposed: thus the "sweet prison" ("douce prison") of love so relished by the singer of Machaut's *Tant doucement* contrasts with the miserable bondage of the same composer's motets 1, 3 and 6.[104]

To add a sacred perspective to a similar parallel, one might propose, for example, that the mortal beloved whose "perfect form" ("parfaite figure") is held, by the female protagonist of *De Fortune*, to be "him on whom my desires are and will be always without end" ("celui, ou mi desire sont et seront a tous jours sans partir") could as easily be the redeemer whose grace is the final hope of all Christians. On the other hand the lady so venerated, as in Machaut's *Dame de qui*, by the more typically male voices of the songs could usually admit interpretation as either the Virgin, or, in accordance with the model proposed by Robertson, Wisdom/Christ. In at least one case, though, only one perspective seems viable: while either the Virgin or Wisdom can, in the words of Machaut's *En amer*, "satisfy everyone who begs her and prays her for her aid," only the latter can, as the song goes on, "without diminishing her treasure ... protect from death." In either case only faith and hope, as in the words of *Quicumques vuet*, can sustain the travail of the lover/Christian through the passage of pain and suffering characteristic of either songs or motets, a journey unavoidable for anyone who is to achieve eternal life.

One crucial difference separates the Latin/French motets from the songs, however: the latter lack the liturgical tenors from which the upper voices of the motets have been seen to derive their allegorical force. Yet precisely that force – absent, or at best latent, in the performance of songs in secular contexts – could, I am suggesting, become activated in the context of Mass. Here, and most particularly in cases – such as those documented above – of performance at the elevation, the sacred potential of songs would have been channeled through the same narrative conduit of redemption that has been seen to extend beneath the surfaces of motets. Songs used in this way would offer a close analogy to their thirteenth-century application, as discussed by Sylvia Huot, as lyric insertions in devotional texts,[105] commenting and casting new light on the sacred message being articulated, while at the same time uncovering sacred allegorical potential in the songs themselves and expounding, to return to the words of Aquinas quoted in Chapter 3, "spiritual truths ... by means of figures taken from corporeal things." Likewise, and more germanely for present purposes, they relate directly to the later use of secular songs as Mass cantus firmi. Context is key here, and in the later Middle Ages there was no more meaningful context than that of Mass. Such meaning, I propose, was nurtured in an environment characterized by consistency of – and fluidity between – the narrative frameworks that, according to context, could be made to bear allegorical weight. In some cases, indeed, it is clear that such context needed to comprise nothing more than a willingness, in Aquinas's words, to allow rather that "divine truths should be expounded under the figure of less noble than of nobler bodies." With such willingness, rhetorical consistency was clearly enough – with or without the context of Mass or even of a liturgical tenor – to sustain sacred allegorical import.[106]

But of course direct allegory is not the only strategy according to which the sacred and secular registers of medieval polyphony could be brought into dialogue: Kevin Brownlee's interpretation of Machaut's motet 15 (also in Trémouïlle) offers one of many potentially parodic readings of the interaction between the strata of the macaronic motet. Brownlee reads motet 15 as one of a number whose meanings turn on a deliberate opposition between an eternally truthful (Latin) tenor and profoundly contingent, and ultimately unreliable, (vernacular) upper voices. Indeed, as Huot notes, the multiplicity of textual interactions embraced by an individual polytextual motet can often admit both allegorical and parodic interpretations, a potential ambiguity that lies at the heart of the semantic play fundamental to the genre, and indeed of what we might call the late-medieval allegorizing "mental habit."

With parody we return full circle to the obscenely texted Mass cantus firmi discussed briefly at the beginning of Chapter 3: the musical analogue to the lewd carvings and marginal doodlings that Camille has so colorfully invoked as images "on the edge." Like Camille's doodlings, such cantus firmi are part of the cultural effusion of what he, like Huot and others following Bakhtin, have seen as reflections of the "carnivalesque": an element that, in apparently cocking a snook at established religion, at the same time paradoxically functions to reemphasize its unassailability.[107] It is in the nature of such ambiguity between potentially allegorical, parodic or downright obscene registers of meaning that there is unlikely in most cases to be any straightforward "solution" to a "higher" meaning of a given motet or song; indeed, as Huot demonstrates, different occasions for the performance of such pieces surely highlighted different and sometimes even opposing meanings. Yet such multivalency is of course precisely in the nature of the motet repertory's allusive richness, indeed its playfulness, an intellectual appeal in relation to which any putative blanket of unambiguous reference would be diminishing and stifling, as well as anachronous. What matters here is less whether this or that motet or song may be susceptible to a specific sacred reinterpretation than the recognition that sacred and secular forms of discourse were sufficiently intertwined that either may, in a given case or particular circumstance, be revealed as a potential reflection of the other. Such is surely the message of the many contemporary interactions – musical and otherwise – of the two registers discussed by Huot, and others, of Aquinas's appeal to the revelation of the spiritual by means of the earthly, and ultimately (to view the issue in terms of contemporary metaphor) of the indivisibility of the Church between Christ, its spiritual head, and its corporeal members here on earth.

Such fluidity between sacred and secular, motet and song, allegory and parody was mirrored in the late Middle Ages by a similar fluidity – by later fifteenth-century standards at least – of genre. The blend of motets and songs that comprised the majority of the Trémouïlle Manuscript also encompassed a handful of Mass movements, included in the manuscript's index in the list of "motets." This, as we saw in Chapter 2, is part of a larger pattern according to which a distinct genre of Mass music did not begin to be properly established until the mid fifteenth century; before that time, polyphonic settings of Mass texts were typically subsumed under the general rubric of "motet," a classification to which the index of the Trémouïlle Manuscript constitutes an early witness. Indeed it would be reasonable to propose that until the early fifteenth century – before the establishment of the cantus firmus Mass and before the advent of cycles of hymns and other minor liturgical items – "motet" was a term that could be applied to pretty much any polyphonic composition not based on a *forme fixe*.

In its absence of the kinds of clear genre distinctions familiar from later music, Trémouïlle is entirely typical of its time. This fact opens up the possibility that other sources, as for instance those – such as the Ivrea Codex, Cambrai 1328 and so on – with which it has close repertorial overlap, may also have found application within the context of Mass. The multiplicity of genre encompassed by these sources, and that multiplicity's reflection of the practices and habits of thought of the communities that produced and used them, was recognized long ago by Heinrich Besseler. Besseler distinguished such sources, in both size and function, from the "Folio Chorbücher" of the later fifteenth century, which latter stood as witnesses, as he put it, to "a division of musical spheres which announces itself strikingly already in the format of the manuscripts." With these he contrasted the picture of the "gemischte Quarthandschriften" ("quarto manuscripts of mixed repertory") predominant in the first third of the fifteenth century which, he noted,

makes manifest that a close interchange existed between the different realms. Not only were the forms of social music used for the church, but also the inner mindset of the music-making was similar. This led to the layout described, because people evidently did not feel the need to divide here that which was unified in life.[108]

That same distinction in the size of polyphonic music manuscripts may also, returning to Harrison's suggestion cited above, have had implications for the location of the singing: while performance from smaller quartos on the choir screen would clearly have presented no logistical problem, the natural home for the more unwieldy folio manuscripts was surely, as contemporary iconography attests, a lectern in the choir.

It was into this world, and as a reflection of its cultural, spiritual and musical mores, that the cantus firmus Mass was born. Its more clearly defined later ethos and social role have tended to obscure its origins in the much more fluid musical environment of the decades either side of 1400. Indeed the chanson-based Mass is in a number of fundamental ways the heir to the sacred/secular macaronic motet: both constituted an amalgam of Latin and – implicitly or explicitly – vernacular, with sacred and secular materials and ideas similarly drawn together in mutual commentary.

The crucial question that remains, though, is why did the cantus firmus Mass come into being at all? Why, if a contemporary urge for troping and allegory could be addressed by the performance of motets and even songs within the framework of Mass, was there a need for a new, more extended and technically involved type of linked compositions? Did this practice supersede the direct performance of secular songs in the Mass, and, if so, why? The answer to the latter question, at least to judge from the long history of continued proscriptions against precisely this practice, must surely be that it did not. But by the second third of the fifteenth century it would seem that the original considerations that had motivated the performance of secular pieces within the Mass had been joined by others. Most obviously, the 1435 edicts of the Council of Basel and their many echoes in the reports of later church councils would seem to reflect a mounting opposition, culminating but not ending with the Council of Trent, against the use of secular music in the Mass. Faced with such opposition but resistant to relinquishing the potential of this practice for particularization and personalization, composers and patrons may well have viewed the integration of songs, presumably for the most part without their words, within Mass settings as a more oblique route to similar ends. Such a solution may have appeared particularly attractive given that the subsuming of such items, typically in long notes and in a lower voice part, within a larger fabric meant that their melodic profiles were usually well concealed.

Yet this is only part of the story, some further threads of which will be gathered together in the next, final part of this book. First among these, taking us back to the opening of Chapter 3, is the enormous growth in the later fifteenth century, in both number and lavishness, of personal endowments of Mass. This development, revealed in countless wills, executors' accounts and other documents, provides ample evidence of a desire to personalize the rite, to stamp it with the individual "proxy" presence and personal plea for mercy of the endower who paid for it, and whose passage to paradise it was designed to expedite. Such desire could hardly have been more precisely addressed than by the cantus firmus Mass, whose very specific potential for particularization and emblematization clearly gave it great appeal as a vehicle for votive supplication.[109] The same desire may also, as we shall see, have been encouraged by a further consideration: the increasing contemporary tendency to view the entirety of Mass – not merely its canon – as an allegory of Christ's Passion, and hence as the representation of a single, overarching message of redemption. Such motivations would have acquired a grander and more politically assertive dimension in the case of a commission, as postulated in chapters 4 and 5, of a polyphonic Mass by a monarch or magnate of church or state, motivated by the desire to identify himself as a new "head" or "armed man" of the Christian church, or even as an anointed "christos." In this climate it seems reasonable to surmise that the endower of a polyphonic Mass would have felt driven to integrate his musical "proxy" into the tissue of the rite in as consistent and inextricable a manner as possible and hence to enfold his presence, as closely as could be imagined, into its redemptive essence.

In the end, therefore, any serious enquiry into the contemporary meaning of the polyphonic Mass must entail a more direct consideration of its operation *in situ*: how did polyphonic music function within the rite? How did it relate to other aspects of the Mass as celebrated in the time of its cultivation, and in particular to other modes of its ornamentation? More particularly, how did sounding adornments relate to, interact with, or reinforce visual ones, and what gave rise to the specific forms they took? How were the faithful expected to respond to them? And besides all these questions is one that precedes them all: what was it that gave rise to a perceived link between the five sections of the Mass Ordinary on which the polyphonic Mass is composed? When, how, and why did these textually and formally disparate items become conceived to be connected?

PART III

The cradle of the early polyphonic Mass

7 | The shape of the Mass

L'on peut en effet affirmer d'après toutes les données de l'histoire que le xiiie siècle fut un tournant dans les idées, les moeurs et la piété chrétiennes.[1]

If the flowering of the polyphonic Mass was an achievement of the fifteenth century, its seeds, as for so much else in late medieval spirituality, germinated in the fertile soil of the thirteenth.[2] This was the century that saw the crystalization of the doctrines of transubstantiation and purgatory, the dominant forces in devotional life, and arguably in life generally, during the later Middle Ages. The power of these notions over the public imagination was greatly enhanced by their mutual reinforcement: fear of purgatory sharpened focus on the redemptive power of Christ's presence in the consecrated elements of the Mass, while the grace that was believed to flow from that presence pushed into more urgent and dramatic relief the menace threatened by its absence.[3] Without the psychological and cultural conditions shaped by these twin beliefs the cyclic Mass, and the particular forms it took, would be barely imaginable.

If the cyclic polyphonic Mass created a space for compositional invention of remarkable range and fecundity, that range was nonetheless determined by the meaning and shape of the ritual it adorned. The substance of that meaning was the salvation promised by the resurrection of Christ, demonstrated through his bodily transubstantiation and manifested to the public in the elevation. Thus, as in the case of all other adornments of the Mass, the ultimate purpose of the cyclic Mass was to give prominence to, and in particular to harness, the power of the Real Presence of Christ, revealed at Mass as in no other event on earth until the Second Coming.[4] To the extent that the ritual had become, in the later Middle Ages, a means for the channeling of fear of purgatory (as well as a host of earthly calamities) and hope for redemption, the polyphonic Mass offered a means to express those sentiments with special intensity and precision. Thus it is not surprising that, as was observed in Chapter 3, its early history should mirror that of the endowed private Mass generally. Church and cathedral archives reveal a consistent pattern in the growth of such endowments: a relatively slow start, followed by increasingly rapid expansion in the fifteenth century. The evidence of private eucharistic prayers with personalized texts from the fourteenth century on suggests that the notion of individual redemption through the eucharist really began to take off at that time.[5] To these trends may be added the evidence of the similar history of other manifestations of personal piety, such as the growth in donations for the rebuilding, extension and elaboration of churches, and in the institution and cultivation of gilds, confraternities and chantries.[6] The growth of the polyphonic Mass was coincident with, and closely enmeshed with, these and related developments in the expression of personal piety.

For those with the means to afford them, Masses offered the most popular means of pleading for their souls, both through the ceremonies themselves and through the prayers of those attending them. To be present in a large church in the later fifteenth century must have been to be witness to an elaborate interchange of priests and attendant worshippers at devotions in chapels and at altars throughout the building. Never have ecclesiastical spaces been so fully and so variously used as at this time. Yet the scope for such development was not infinite. Typically paid for by rents from property, endowed Masses were meant to endure in perpetuity; thus at some point the growth in their numbers would inevitably become unsustainable. Signs that this point may have been approaching start to appear already in the later fifteenth century, with a growing number of "incorporations" in which earlier foundations are combined with new ones. While such conflation was often the result of insufficient funds to sustain expensive foundations indefinitely, it also seems clear that, as Barbara Haggh has noted, the system itself was beginning by the early sixteenth century to creak under its own weight.[7] Such perceived excess in the number and elaboration of observances for the welfare of souls surely added grist to the mill of reformers who, in the sixteenth century, inveighed against the general notion that earthly acts had the power to influence God's judgment. With the reforms of Luther and other protestants, and their counterparts in reforming tendencies within the Catholic Church culminating in the Council of Trent and its aftermath, "investments" in the welfare of posthumous souls through the invocations of private Masses, along with the polyphonic performances they sustained, seem increasingly to have fallen into obsolescence.[8]

Clearly the propagation of the polyphonic Mass, and the high expense and complex administrative mechanisms needed to sustain it, rested on a powerful belief system and a strong shared conviction in its efficacy. Yet if it was born of pressing eschatological concerns, both individual and collective, the forms it took and its wide circulation occurred in response to developments in the liturgy that framed and sustained it. Without the particular context and scaffolding of the larger ritual, the polyphonic Mass could never have taken the forms it did. Here again thirteenth-century developments were key. For the growth of the Mass these developments offered a mix of ostensibly opposing trends, balancing consolidation and renewal, conformity and diversity, which would prove remarkably propitious. Prominent among the former was a newly energized drive towards a streamlined, consistent and centralized liturgy. For historians of the polyphonic Mass, as we shall see, this had its most pregnant manifestation in the earliest widespread copying – long recognized as a harbinger of future groupings in polyphony – of Ordinary chants into fixed series, devised for days of particular liturgical rank.

In a number of ostensibly conflicting ways, the thirteenth-century codification of the liturgy provided the conditions necessary for the nature and forms taken by the polyphonic music fashioned to adorn it. It is important, therefore, however briefly, to explain the circumstances of that codification, and in particular the role within it of an institutional body whose work made it in many ways the defining movement of the thirteenth century: the Order of Friars Minor.

Liturgical change and the Franciscans

The rationalization of the liturgy conducted in the thirteenth century was not, of course, in itself anything new. In its goals of consistency and central control, and in its support by a larger political apparatus, it had much in common with the Carolingian reforms of some four centuries earlier. Yet the roots of the liturgical shifts that concern us here are to be found in the accelerated moves to centralized uniformity that, in the twelfth and thirteenth centuries, accompanied the codification of the practices of the new religious Orders. Here the desire for consistency was driven by the need for a common system of worship at general chapter meetings and during interaction between member houses. Such a requirement was pursued with unprecedented rigor by the Cistercians, whose directive for a common rite was affirmed by their Charter of Charity of 1119.[9] The Cistercian model set an important precedent not only in the degree of its strictness, however, but also in its emphasis on an exceptional brevity, enforced with the aim of returning the liturgy as closely as possible to the state of affairs stipulated by the Rule of St. Benedict.[10] Both these trends were to prove especially influential for later practice.[11]

Such uniformity was effected with particular thoroughness and durability by the Dominicans, where its exigency was accentuated by the extraordinarily rapid spread of the Order and by the regular and wide interaction of its members.[12] It seems clear that a uniform Dominican liturgy, whose chant shows strong Cistercian influence, had been arrived at by the early thirteenth century; but a particular circumstance appears, from the 1240s, to have stimulated the Dominicans into subjecting their liturgical observance to a hitherto unknown degree of consistency: this was the example set by, and competition inspired by, the liturgical reforms of the Franciscans.[13]

For the later development of the Mass, the key moment was surely the adoption by the Franciscans, through St. Francis's first rule of the Order of 1221, of the liturgy of the papal curia.[14] Though for different reasons, both the papal curia and the friars needed a liturgy that was concise and comparatively brief. For the curia, peripatetic and occupied primarily with administration, the complete *opus Dei*, with its evocation of the endless heavenly hymn of praise conducted with the aid of an array of liturgical books, was unfeasible;[15] for the friars, migrant and concerned first and foremost with proselytization through preaching, concision and – especially – portability were practical necessities. In its brisk delivery and drastic reduction in the length, complexity and – particularly regarding sequences, tropes, and other elements that were viewed as accretions to the basic pattern of worship – number of chants, this so-called *brevitas moderna* echoed in essence, if not necessarily in motivation, the work of other Orders, especially the Cistercians. Similarly the thirteenth-century trend towards the encompassing of the entire contents – texts, music, rubrics – necessary to the celebration of Mass, on the one hand, and Office, on the other, each within the covers of a single book is not without precedents.[16] But it is clear that this development became a significant and dynamic one through the work of the friars. Here the central figure, one through whose work the Order's stamp was set on the Western liturgy for centuries to come, was Haymo of Faversham, general of his adopted Order from 1240 until his death in 1244. The currency of Haymo's order of Mass *Indutus planeta* was maintained, via its subsequent habitual inclusion in Roman missals, in the Western church until well into the sixteenth century. Moreover, his revision, at the instigation of Innocent IV, of the Roman liturgy through his ordinals of the breviary and missal served to yoke together the Franciscan and papal liturgies from that time forth.[17]

Although, like the Cistercian reforms before them, these newly streamlined practices were not met with universal approval, they seem to have been viewed by many as a welcome corrective to ever-expanding – especially

votive – observance which, particularly in monastic houses, was leaving little time for other prescribed activities.[18] For the burgeoning desire of the
thirteenth-century papacy for consistency of liturgical observance through
propagation of the Roman curial rite, moreover,[19] the Order of Friars Minor
offered an opportunity that was to be impressively realized: through the
rapid expansion of the Order the papal liturgy was quickly propagated,
and its example taken up both by other Orders and by secular churches. In
turn, the further rationalizations of the friars were themselves subsequently
adopted by the papal curia, which enforced them on the churches of Rome.[20]
For its part, the incipient Order received, through its adoption of the curial
liturgy, the stamp of papal approval, and, more important, authority. For the
friars and for those with whom they brought it into contact, moreover, the
papal liturgy offered important practical advantages: it expressed the need,
as for the other Orders discussed above, for a common system of observance
according to which they could celebrate together, and on the basis of which
they could minister to the faithful on their peregrinations, spreading, as they
did, devotional orthodoxy and consistency far and wide.

But it would appear that the remarkable success of Haymo's codification
derived neither from a perceived authority of the curial liturgy nor from
that of Franciscan practice *per se*, but rather from the clarity of its presentation, and hence the easy comprehension it offered to celebrating clergy.[21]
Another reason for its quick uptake may have been its inherent flexibility,
and in particular the opportunities for individuation offered by its stipulations for private observances. Though clear and precise, Haymo's instructions for private Masses applied only to the liturgy of a church in its general,
public aspects, and to the basic ceremonial. Only these central, defining elements were fixed, while the other contents of the private Mass – foreshadowing the particularizing function of the cantus firmus in the polyphonic
Mass – could be selected freely from among the set formulas for the main
rite, without obligation to the cycle of the church year.[22] Thus while the
basic Mass ceremony as outlined in the ordinal was indeed to be observed
in votive and private Masses, the choice of their variable texts was left up to
their endowers.[23]

While Haymo's ordinal clearly explained the outline of the action of Mass,
Franciscan codification of its music had to wait until the publication of its
gradual in 1251. For the development and proliferation of the cyclic Mass the
promulgation of this book was of signal importance for two reasons. The first
of these was its adoption of the quintessentially thirteenth-century square
French-style chant notation which became increasingly standard from now
on, and obligatory in Franciscan, Dominican and Augustinian books.[24] The

same notation was in turn demanded as the norm in the late 1270s by the Franciscan pope Nicholas III, who ordered the destruction of older Roman chant books and their replacement by new books modeled on those of the Franciscans.[25] While the choice of the French-style notation was presumably due to its ease of legibility compared to earlier methods and hence its easier comprehensibility to the singing clergy,[26] it seems clear also that it was to prove a major stimulus to the performance – literally "on the book" – and composition of polyphony. Michel Huglo makes the important point that this was precisely the notation used for the first attempts at Parisian discant and organum. But he also notes the considerable increase in the physical dimensions of chant books in the thirteenth century, indicating, he suggests, a move away from singing exclusively from memory to (collective and solo) singing from a chant book placed on a lectern.[27] With this standardized notation and physical format and the coincident burgeoning of chant-based polyphony the conditions were in place for future, more elaborate polyphonic developments that relied for their existence on music as read.[28]

The second reason for the importance of the Franciscan gradual in the development of the polyphonic Mass concerns its kyriale. Besides its adherence to papal curial practice in expunging tropes almost entirely, the kyriale is of great historical significance for its layout: its chants are arranged in ten complete cycles comprising Kyrie, Gloria (except for those periods of the calendar during which this item was omitted), Sanctus, Agnus and "Ite missa est" or "Benedicamus domino," each pertaining to a different grade of liturgical observance from major double feast to ferial Mass and requiem, plus a separate cycle for Marian feasts and commemorations.[29] This was not the earliest kyriale to be organized in such a fashion: other surviving examples date back to the previous century, while the chants of at least one eleventh-century missal, albeit grouped into collections of Kyries, Glorias, etc., nonetheless appear to be arranged according to the sequence of the liturgical year.[30] But the Franciscan-Roman kyriale (since the two were effectively synonymous) was to have a decisive impact on future practice, setting the trend for such groupings up to and including the publication of the modern Roman gradual.[31] It also represents a key stage in the determination of the specific choice of chants for the various chant "cycles," a determination that, as attested by the enormously broad distribution of the Franciscan gradual from the mid-thirteenth to the fifteenth century, was widely adopted.[32]

As has been amply documented,[33] the sharing of musical material between sections was not a common feature of grouped monophonic Mass Ordinary chants. Yet such kyriale groupings set the scene for the growth of the polyphonic Mass in at least two significant ways: first, the very physical existence of the kyriale emphasized a view of music for the Ordinary as a separate, independently organized repertory. This was especially the case when, in the fifteenth century, it became common for it to be detached from its erstwhile parent missals and graduals to stand alone as a separate book of chants.[34] More particularly, though, the layout in chant "cycles" seems to have given rise, through its persistence and increasingly broad currency, to a habitual association between the various items of the Ordinary that in later, polyphonic groupings would receive directly musical expression.[35] Crucially also for polyphonic developments, such arrangements would appear to represent important signs of a shift in the role of the musical schola, in which earlier emphasis on soloistic chants of the Proper gives way to a new embrace of collective singing – largely unsynchronized with the ceremonial taking place at the altar – of the Ordinary.[36]

If the foundations of the cyclic Mass were laid by the paring down and rationalization of the standard components of the liturgy, however, its growth and development were enabled by concurrent shifts in spiritual emphasis that, as Pierre Salmon has noted, led elsewhere to considerable expansion. Salmon has drawn attention to the numerous additions in readings from scripture and in "pièces non organiques et sans structure liturgique": commemorations, suffrages, penitential psalms, litanies, the Athanasian Creed (*Quicumque vult*), and the offices of the Virgin and for the dead. His emphasis, then, is on "une évolution de la spiritualité, par le développement du culte de la Sainte Vierge et des saints, de la piété envers les morts, par la recherche de formules de prières plus vivantes ou plus dévotes, entretenant davantage la piété personnelle."[37] In other words reductions in the basic liturgy were counterbalanced by augmentations in those areas that were susceptible to particularization and personalization. The consequent and unprecedented proliferation and diversification in localized and personalized observance was a tendency to which the polyphonic Mass, with its broad potential for adaptability and particularization, was well placed to contribute. Most propitious for its development, and intimately intertwined, were piety towards the dead and piety towards the Virgin.

Devotions for the dead, a frequently recurring theme in this book, represent one of the oldest foci of votive observance in the Catholic ritual, and partial offices for the dead seem to have been fairly standard in monastic usage by the eleventh century.[38] Similarly the practice of reciting Saturday Masses and hours for the Virgin was already old by the time of the formation of the Franciscan liturgy, and complete *cursus* of votive offices for the Virgin are known from the same period.[39] Yet Marian devotion underwent

an altogether new level of expansion and codification in the thirteenth century, when it was cultivated with particular intensity by the religious Orders.
Here as elsewhere the Cistercians set trends that would subsequently be
taken up by others, instituting the communal Little Office at the general
chapter in 1185 and a daily *Missa de beata* (along with a daily Mass for
the dead) in 1194. Similar observances were instituted by the Franciscans,
Premonstratensians, and Dominicans, in all cases around the mid-thirteenth
century.[40] Sally Roper notes that the Saturday commemorative office of the
Virgin, though apparently not centrally stipulated, likewise became standard in Benedictine usage in the thirteenth century, while the same period
saw widespread adoption of communal celebration of the Little Office of
the Virgin. The elaboration of both offices via newly devised patterns of seasonal variation was a major concurrent trend, and Marian observance far
outweighed that devised for any other broadly "votive" purpose.[41]

The same strongly Marian emphasis is perhaps still more prominently
expressed in the emergence, around the same time, of observances centered on the performance of independent Marian antiphons. Here, as elsewhere, the initiative seems to have come from the religious Orders: the
Cistercians were seemingly the first, in 1218, to take up daily singing of
the *Salve regina* (although this did not apparently stabilize in communal
practice until 1251) while the Dominicans were responsible for the first
recorded performance, in 1221, of the singing of the *Salve* in what would
become its customary position after Compline. Here again the Franciscans
set an important benchmark by being the first, in 1249, formally to pre-
scribe the singing by seasonal alternation of what would become the four
standard post-Compline Marian antiphons (*Regina caeli*, *Alma redemptoris
mater*, *Ave regina caelorum* and *Salve regina*), a full century before similar
stipulation by the papacy for all churches following Roman Use.[42] Through
their contact with northern European observances, moreover, it seems that
the Franciscans were responsible also for introducing new enhancements
of Marian devotion within the Roman liturgy, though other thirteenth-century developments took place at the instigation of the papacy itself.[43]

There can be no question but that the enormous thirteenth-century
acceleration in Marian devotions is a reflection of the coincident growth
in awareness and fear of purgatory. The parallel emerges in particular relief
in the proliferation of votive rites, which would change the face of ritual
observance from this time forth. As the above details demonstrate, this
was true even in monastic settings, where the traditional ferial recitation
of the psalter yielded increasingly, as Roper has expressed it, to "devotional
observance not far removed from popular piety."[44] Such resemblance is to

be expected in rituals such as these, cultivated as they originally were in the context of private devotion and prayer; but their increasing visibility in communal worship is a measure of the degree to which concern for Marian intercession for the welfare of souls was overtaking the traditional round of temporal ritual even of religious houses whose original *raison d'être* had been precisely such observance.

The trend to votive expansion, once put into motion, only increased as ever more ardent and more personalized means were sought to appeal for saintly, and particularly Marian, intercession. That trend in due course proved a major force behind the cultivation of polyphonic Mass settings, a substantial proportion of them fashioned, through cantus firmus choice, for Marian worship. With the development of the cantus firmus, troping expunged by liturgical revision was effectively reintroduced – this time into the Ordinary items – in a fashion more directly responsive to changing trends in pious expression.[45] But the development of the polyphonic Mass received its most fundamental impetus from a particular circumstance, one for the most part unavailable to non-eucharistic observances. To appreciate this we must turn to the other principal theme announced at the beginning of this chapter: that of the transubstantiation of the host.

Like so many of the practices that have been discussed already, the doctrine of transubstantiation, at least in terms of its general acceptance, was a child of the thirteenth century. Its confirmation as church doctrine took place, at the hands of Innocent III, in 1215 at the Fourth Lateran Council, in many ways the defining church convocation of the later Middle Ages.[46] The instruction for the elevation of the consecrated host after the words "hoc est enim corpus meum" "so that all may see," which built on the slightly earlier statutes of the Synod of Paris presided over by Odo of Sully,[47] followed on in short order from the council.[48] With this new emphasis and the instruction of the people to adore the elevated host it quickly became, as we shall see in the final chapter, the prime focus of Mass, to which – as widely attested by contemporary evidence – access was sought by a public eager for the palliative effect of gazing on its maker. It also, not surprisingly, became the single most potent focus for personalized observance, as individuals and corporations sought ways to bring their plea, usually via saintly (most commonly Marian) intercession, into direct contact with their redeemer, present before them on the altar.

Such personalization was subject, of course, to certain strictures: the ritual of Mass, especially in its strictly codified Franciscan-Roman organization, was fixed and consistent in its basic components. Yet the fixing of the essentials of the liturgy, restrictive on one level, was liberating on another: strict codification of its words and their succession (the "ordo missae") served to focus efforts at the particularization of Mass on its elaboration, both visible and sonic. At the same time the fixed pattern of the liturgical year at public Masses proved a powerful stimulus for private Masses, where no such restrictions applied, and for the tremendous growth of gilds and confraternities founded primarily to celebrate Masses for departed brethren (a subject of Chapter 4).

These circumstances – along with the enhanced focus on the veneration of saints, and particularly the Virgin, in the context of a new and universally shared emphasis on personal piety and piety towards the dead – created conditions fundamental to the development and proliferation of the polyphonic Mass. And behind all this was the central, fundamental emphasis on the Real Presence and its manifestation in the elevated host: it was that Presence that gave the various pleas framed through particularizations of the Mass their special efficacy.

8 | Counterpoint of images, counterpoint of sounds

The entire edifice of the late-medieval Mass turned on a single event: the transubstantiation whereby the communion wafer was believed to be transformed into the living body of Christ. Sights and sounds – along with attendant allegory and imagery – lent increasing point and emphasis to this transformation and its visible manifestation, the elevation by the officiating priest of the consecrated host.[1]

For late medieval worshippers the host was more than just a symbol: the presence before them of the risen Christ was believed to bestow all manner of benefits in their daily lives, from forgiveness of sins and protection from sudden death on the day of seeing the host to the safe delivery of children and good digestion.[2] Most crucial, though, was the hope it offered of deliverance from purgatory, that fearful place of retribution that, after death, awaited all but the most saintly. Thus it was for the vouchsafing of the soul in the afterlife that its vision was most eagerly sought. It is unsurprising, then, that the commemoration of the dead was placed, in the celebration of Mass, shortly after the consecration, when the presence of Christ on the altar promised it maximum potency.[3] And the association, for the worshipping faithful, of seeing the host with the final communion, the *viaticum* through which the dying person's soul would be commended to its maker, was rehearsed again and again in Latin and vernacular prayers composed to be uttered at the time of the elevation.[4]

This, then, is the nature of the characteristic late-medieval emphasis – addressed in John Bossy's classic "The Mass as a Social Institution" – on the "sacrificial" aspect of Mass: the atoning, through reenactment of Christ's Passion in the consecration, for the sins of humanity.[5] The climactic role of the elevation was dramatically heightened by the fact that, for most, the actual taking of communion – the "sacramental" act whereby the Christian participated in symbolic union with Christ and his church – occurred only annually (at Easter) and directly preceding death.[6] Thus vision of the host was as close as one would normally get to it, a fact that contributed greatly to its mystery and prestige.[7] At the same time it was a vivid reminder of the moment when – so one hoped – one would cast eyes on it for the last time. Yet such *Augenkommunion*, a shared wonderment on the part of believers at vision of their maker, was not the only aspect in which the socially unifying, "sacramental," aspect of the rite joined the sacrificial in the late medieval experience of Mass: Bossy emphasized the counterweight – coinciding, at the end of the ritual, with the priest's actual consumption of the consecrated elements – of the pax, the celebration, by ritual kissing, of a community cleansed and reaffirmed by the preceding sacrifice. One of the key elements, as he notes, in the expression of this "ritual of social peace," to whose significance in this regard we will return, was the Agnus Dei.[8]

Conviction in the transformative power of the host led to ever greater proliferation not only of celebrations of Mass, but also of its adornments, both concrete and sounding, paid for frequently by individuals seeking spiritual succor for themselves and their own. Focus on the host had implications beyond the moment itself, its deep meaning "spilling" into and embracing the larger ritual, including the polyphonic Mass. As might be expected, though, these adornments were concentrated with particular intensity on the moment of the elevation. Thus an understanding of the function of the polyphonic Mass entails an understanding also of its relation to other kinds of accoutrement devised to elaborate the Mass – and particularly this, its focal point – and of the narratives and allegories that gave it its social and psychological meaning. The most fundamental of these, and the "seed" for all the others, was the gesture of the elevation itself.

The act of elevation

The practice of physically elevating the host grew from modest roots: the ancient procedure whereby the priest, taking the bread into his hands as Christ himself had done, raised it slightly above the altar table. How and why this developed, apparently around the end of the twelfth century, into a more dramatic, publicly visible lifting is the subject of debate.[9] But there can be little doubt that it derives ultimately from the shift in emphasis, dating back to Carolingian times, from communal, "sacramental" experience to a sacrificial action conducted alone, on the people's behalf, by the priest.[10] This change, with its concomitant development towards a more hierarchized articulation of church space, created a distance between sacrifice and faithful whose bridging – via sights, sounds and personal endowments – became ever more urgently sought as the notion of transubstantiation and its perceived benefits took hold.[11] For the church as an institution the host thus became a source of great power, its sacramental nature being subject to a centralizing control unavailable from the veneration of saints and pilgrimages, with their contexts of local affiliations and devotions.[12] Only a priest could effect the transformation of bread into the body of Christ, his hands literally framing it in the moment of exhibition; thus only the agency of the church permitted access to its sacramental power. This transformative function emphasized also the role of the priest as vicar of Christ, divinely empowered as his representative in the performance of the sacraments and particularly of the reenactment of the Last Supper which was the essential substance of Mass. And that focus, as we saw in Chapter 5, gave rise in turn to richly allusive networks of Christological allegory surrounding his person, actions and vestments.[13] More prosaically, but offering an undoubted premium for the exercise of ecclesiastical power, the host also had the advantage of being easily and cheaply available.

With the growing desire of the people – attested in countless documents from the later fourteenth and fifteenth centuries – for vision of their maker, that power only increased. Spiritual gain perceived to flow from the elevated host took more quantifiable form in the practice of granting indulgences for its veneration;[14] and desire to gaze upon it, if possible on a daily or even more frequent basis, was a vital force behind the late medieval proliferation of Masses, and the reason for the unseemly scramble for a view of it so critically remarked upon by Cranmer and others.[15]

As the host overtook the relics of saints as the most powerful sacred object at the church's disposal, pressure increased to extend its visibility. Ever longer expositions following the consecration were joined by further showings elsewhere in the Mass and outside it, especially in connection with the Feast of Corpus Christi. In processions, blessings, exorcisms, invocations against poor weather and for the protection of crops, and in all manner of healings and enchantments, exposure of the host spread yet further during the course of the fourteenth and fifteenth centuries as its hold on the public imagination continued to increase.[16]

Along the way it became the focal point of an increasingly elaborate network of prayer, contemplation, ceremony, physical gesture, paraphernalia, music and iconography deriving partly from institutional, and, more particularly, from corporate and personal devotions. It was also the focal point of a wide range of narratives and images fashioned to invoke, via associated indulgence prayers, the power of the Real Presence so as to reduce the time of the soul in purgatory and hasten its progress to heaven.[17]

Reverencing the host: the visual frame

The focus of a rich array of devotions and symbolism, the consecrated host also stood at the pinnacle of a hierarchy of proximity and distance shaped by the desire to frame it with maximum reverence and mystery. This was the source of what Joseph Jungmann referred to as "the centrifugal tendency of the Gothic period," a tendency towards diversification and splitting off of functions for which he saw evidence, for example, in the diverging roles of priest and singing schola in the thirteenth century.[18] This tendency acquired a particular momentum in the later Middle Ages, emanating from the priest and radiating out through the officiating clergy and singing choir to the worshipping laity. For its participants and observers, the functions of the late-medieval Mass were founded upon, as Eamon Duffy has expressed it, "a complex and dynamic understanding of the role of both distance and proximity, concealment and exposure."[19] Of course this was particularly true for Mass at the high altar: Masses in princely and other private chapels, and at side chapels in larger churches afforded – as contemporary iconography repeatedly attests – much closer access, a fact that, I will argue, gave them special appeal in this time of ever greater eschatological concern. Yet the fundamental model remained one of distance and separation. What one saw, where one saw it, and what one was able to perceive of the speech and music that carried its message depended on one's situation: as lay worshipper, singer in the schola, assisting cleric or server, or as the celebrant himself. All these perceptions, and their intended interpretations, were calibrated with respect to these different positions, the roles of the various participants in the sacred drama and their proximity – conceptual as well as spatial – to the God who was to appear, in person, on the altar.[20] Most of the action, the business of the celebrant and assisting clergy, occurred – beyond the choir – around the altar, while at the climactic moment the celebrant faced the altar alone, supported by the deacon and subdeacon, to encounter, as his earthly mediator, Christ himself.

For the enactment of High Mass in the later Middle Ages a key role in this social and spatial hierarchy was played by a screen that separated the realm of the laity from that of the clergy and the sacred ritual they were to perform.[21] Thus a fundamental tenet of such Masses was that their action was conducted not just apart from the people, but in a different realm, in the sanctuary from which they were physically separated and by a priest who, for the most part, was facing away from them in the direction of the altar.[22] The degree to which screens articulated that separation varied: while some, as for example earlier German examples from the thirteenth century, might be solid across their width,[23] others, especially those from the later phase of screen development in the fifteenth and sixteenth centuries, could be light and porous.[24] In the majority of cases a central doorway admitted a sight line to the high altar, permitting vision of the action of Mass and, crucially, the elevation.[25]

Presence of a screen did not preclude its transgression: documentation and iconographical evidence from across western Europe attests to the presence of laity in the choir,[26] including at Mass, albeit in the latter case frequently in the form of censures against it.[27] Duffy notes how parishioners of Eye in the fifteenth century carried torches up to the high altar on All Saints' Day and knelt there at the elevation, a practice probably duplicated elsewhere.[28] A similar procedure was surely more common at private Masses in side chapels, as for instance those mounted by gilds and confraternities. And the approach of the laity to the altar seems to have been a widespread custom at the offertory when, in acknowledgment of their position in the community of Mass, they processed to the altar with gifts of candles, bread and alms for the poor.[29] At least notionally though, as well as generally in practice, the division drawn by the screen seems to have been closely observed, a situation that was also articulated administratively and financially: while the clergy maintained the chancel and its accoutrements, responsibility for the upkeep of the nave typically rested with the laity.[30] In a state of affairs whose implications for the development of polyphonic Mass music were – as we shall see – surely considerable, that division was increasingly underscored, especially in the fifteenth century, by the presence of numerous nave altars, many of them maintained, or at least supported, by private citizens. Most prominent of these was the main "public" altar, commonly dedicated to the Holy Cross or – in fifteenth-century England – the Holy Name of Jesus, against the west face of the screen.[31]

To the faithful at worship, then, the experience of Mass at the high altar, visible, if at all, through apertures in the screen and far beyond their reach, was of an order entirely distinct from that of the participants in its ritual action.[32] Yet from their perspective the screen (and the distance it articulated) appears to have been more than simply a barrier: it could also function as a frame for the action of Mass, and particularly for its central mystery. That mystery, moreover, was frequently glossed and enhanced by a sculptural program whose redemptive message became activated and vivified by the ritual that took place beyond it in the sanctuary.[33] And crowning it all was the great crucifix, its message of redemption articulating the symbolic border, drawn by the screen, between this world and the next, and drawing the eyes forward to the enactment of the means of that redemption at the high altar. This, as Jacqueline Jung has expressed it, was the screen's central function: to dramatize this sense of dynamism, of transition to a better world, beckoning the hearts and minds of the faithful to the moment when, at the elevation, crucifix and embodied Christ would be linked in a vertical axis. There can be no clearer expression of that dynamism than her quotation from the fourteenth-century Carthusian Ludolf of Saxony. Explaining the statement of Acts, 14: 21 – "through many tribulations we must enter into the kingdom of God" – Ludolf notes that:

This statement is well illustrated by the fact that a cross is placed between the choir and the outer limits of a church [that is, the nave], so that whoever wants to go into the choir must pass beneath the cross; for no one can enter from the Church militant into the Church triumphant except by means of the cross.[34]

Besides the obvious distance it articulated, this combined function of the screen as frame and place of transition does much to explain the heavy emphasis on the gestures of the priest, and especially his signs of the cross, in late medieval Mass commentaries: these visible gestures were intended to form the principal markers in the progress of the liturgy for attentive observers, for whose salvation it was being enacted. Most obvious was the parallel between the raising of the priest's arms at the elevation with the raising up of Christ onto the cross, a link frequently articulated in contemporary images. The most famous example is surely the central panel – with its diagonal interaction of elevation and crucifixion scene – of the Antwerp *Seven Sacraments* altarpiece by van der Weyden (Plate 4).[35] But the parallel is still more immediately illustrated (in this case – unusually – involving the elevated chalice) in the panel, by the Master of St. Ulrich, of the *Mass of St. Ulrich* in the Catholic parish church of Sts. Ulrich and Afra, Augsburg. Here the elevated cup is linked, in a vertical axis, with crucifixes both on the celebrant's chasuble and on the altar, the latter appearing, from the direct rear perspective, as if actually lifted by the priest from within the chalice (Plate 5).[36] This same parallel finds widespread expression in illuminated missals, with the initial "T" of the opening of the Canon ("Te igitur") appearing, in an image of the crucifixion, as the cross, or, still more commonly, in the juxtaposition, opposite the opening of the Canon, of a full-page illuminated image of the crucifixion. The carefully calibrated progress of the late medieval Mass towards its inward, privately enacted climax was to be observed – and absorbed – by the laity, and marked by shifts in their observed devotions, contemplation and physical posture.[37] Members of the schola, on the other hand, were drawn more closely to the act of transformation not only by their closer proximity to it but – as we shall see – by the special function, in its articulation, of singing. As metaphors for mystery and venerability, then, concealment and distance defined the rhythm of Mass, from outward to inward, a rhythm that was geared towards highlighting, in the elevation, a brief moment of accessibility to which all observers' eyes were to be drawn.

Plate 4 *Altarpiece of the Seven Sacraments*, Rogier van der Weyden, 1453–5, central panel, detail

Reverencing the host: enhancing the visible

The centrality of the elevation and – especially in Masses at the high altar – its distance from the laity explains the various efforts, traceable in contemporary documents, to maximize its visibility. An obvious example can be seen in the practice documented in English, French and Spanish churches,

Plate 5 *Mass of St. Ulrich*, Master of the Legend of St. Ulrich, central panel

especially from the fifteenth century onwards, of drawing a dark cloth over
the reredos at this point in order that the white wafer could stand out as
starkly as possible.[38] In bearing, as they sometimes did, an image of the crucified Christ, these cloths might themselves have been imbued with something of the visual hierarchy of Mass: though scarcely visible to the distant
congregation, such an image could focus the attention of the celebrant on
the crucifixion at the very moment when, in lifting the consecrated wafer,
he invoked the hoisting up of Christ onto the cross.[39] The same desire for

visibility prompted the stipulation of some religious Orders that the door in the screen should be opened at the moment of the elevation (see note 25), and led to warnings to the thurifer to beware of obscuring the host with clouds of incense.[40] A more extravagant gesture towards the same end is attested by the endowment in 1502, by an alderman of Hull, of money to pay for a machine via which angels would descend to the altar at the elevation, and be raised back into the roof after the Pater noster.[41]

But vision of the host could most obviously be enhanced by good lighting. Provision of light came to offer one of the commonest (and cheapest) means of lay access to the altar at the moment of transubstantiation. If personal access was largely proscribed, vicarious association through donations was not. Thus individuals or gilds frequently provided torches to burn from the elevation to the Agnus Dei. Endowments such as these could be brought into direct association with the plea for mercy after death when, as frequently happened, individuals specified in their wills that torches used at their funerals be donated afterwards to the church to burn around the altar at the time of the consecration.[42] Such a donation was conceived, as Duffy has termed it, as a "proxy" for the endower, the next best thing to standing before the consecrated host oneself. A similar conviction lay behind the frequent donation of personal items of linen for altar cloths and corporals, and, for those with more money at their disposal, vestments, vessels, liturgical books and so on.[43] Association with the parish Mass was particularly desirable, linking as it did the "private" desire of the endower to harness the prayers of the community for the salvation of his or her soul with the "public" urge for association with a community-wide plea for salvation. Similarly, these endowments, like others, some of which I will address below, combined the plea for salvation with the provision to the community of an actual service, concerns which from a later medieval perspective were intimately related.

The sonic frame

For the late medieval experience of High Mass the screen was the clearest sign of the visual counterpoint of Mass. But the nature of the screen also affords access to an understanding of the roles in the rite of its various kinds of sound. If the screen, and the distance it articulated, functioned as a filter for the visible – alternately a frame for and a barrier to what could be seen or not seen – this role was still more strongly defined in the case of what could be heard. Duffy notes that, at least in larger churches, "parishioners would have been well out of earshot of anything said, as opposed to sung, at the altar."[44] In other words their aural experience of High Mass and particularly, as we shall see, its central mystery, seems likely in many cases to have been chiefly a musical one.[45] That point literally gains an extra dimension from evidence of the widespread construction, under late medieval choir stalls, of resonating chambers designed to augment the sound of the singing above. Although there is no evidence that this phenomenon arose explicitly to enhance audibility beyond the screen, this, along with an enhanced sense for the schola of the power of its contribution and of its audibility to the heavenly court, would clearly have been one of its effects.[46] The limited space and inconducive nature of choir stalls for the propping up of folio-size choirbooks suggest that the presence of resonance chambers beneath the choir stalls would more typically have affected chant than polyphony: though specific inferences are seldom possible, contemporary iconography would seem to imply characteristic performance of polyphony from a free-standing lectern, in *medio chori*. Yet the depiction of adult singers tightly clustered around lecterns,[47] and in particular (as in Plate 6, from the early-sixteenth-century Prayerbook of Joanna of Ghistelles) the presence of lecterns clamped, in choir stalls, to the carpentry below, reveals at least the possibility in such a setting of performance from a choirbook.[48]

Better known, and of more general relevance to the augmentation of sound in the choir, is the presence throughout Europe of acoustic jars, modeled after Vitruvian principles, that were sometimes a feature of such resonating chambers, but were more commonly embedded in various locations in the walls of choirs.[49] The widely quoted 1432 *Chronicle of the Celestins of Metz* clarifies their intended purpose: "Ode le Roy, priour de seans ... fit et ordonnoit de mettre les pots au cuer de l'église ... et pensant qu'il y fesoit milleur chanter et que il ly resonneroit plus fort." The author's own codicil reveals his own skepticism, however: "je ne seay si on chante miez que on ne fasoit."[50] Clearly this acoustical function was still known in the seventeenth century: a satire by Claude Pithoys, published in 1662 at St. Léger, Luxembourg, notes, in berating clerical negligence, that "Of fifty singing men that the public maintain in such a house, there are sometimes not more than six present at the service; the choirs are fitted with jars in the vaults and in the walls that six voices there make as much noise as forty elsewhere."[51]

While, as we know from eyewitness accounts, attention to the progress of Mass could be variable, contemporary guides, particularly those in the vernacular, leave no doubt that the sights and sounds of Mass were geared to express its hierarchies with maximum precision. This is revealed also in the degree of audibility of what the priest said: thus it was natural, within

Plate 6 Chanting the Office of the Dead, Simon Bening and Workshop, Prayerbook of Joanna of Ghistelles, South Netherlands (Ghent) c.1516 (before 1529)

the scheme of things, that the words of the Canon, embracing the central mystery, should be uttered by the priest under his breath, inaudible even to the assisting clergy; natural also that, on returning from his sacred and solitary duty in the Canon, he should recite the Pater noster aloud.[52] But while the experience of Mass differed in accordance with one's position in the hierarchy, it was also natural that the key moment, its supporting words guarded and protected such that access to them beyond the altar was strictly circumscribed,[53] should be the one point at which the complex of images and sounds would coincide. To ensure that they did, the practice was adopted of signaling the elevation by the sounding of a bell. In this combined gesture aural and visual were united in a single climactic moment.

This use of the bell offers a means of access to an understanding of the function of sound, and particularly music, in the Mass as a whole: if sound, in its various gradations, was a conduit through which the various stages of ritual could be signaled to attentive observers, an outward, public commentary on inward, priestly action, it was also, at least in design, a means of drawing them in, directing their thoughts and prayers to the key moments of the Mass that, verbally, were beyond their reach. This much is clear from contemporary guides, and especially the widely circulating vernacular treatises aimed at the laity. Thus the late-fourteenth-century *Lay Folks Mass Book*, revealingly subtitled *Manner of Hearing Mass*, instructs the reader:

> How Þou shulde Þi messe here.
> when Þo preste saies he, or if he singe,
> to him Þou gyue gode herknynge;
> when Þo preste praies in priuete,
> tyme of prayere is Þen to Þe. [54]

Sound – whether spoken, sung, or resounding from an inanimate object – was a vital force in activating the mystery of Mass, and in articulating the import and depth of its concrete fixtures, including (at High Mass) the screen and its sculptural program, and the altar itself. That fifteenth-century sensibilities – at least of the liturgically aware – were indeed attuned to such functioning is demonstrated visually by the setting, in devotional panel paintings of the period such as that by van der Weyden cited above, of sacred imagery within the space of a church, and by the role within that space of the screen.

For music, that functioning receives unusually eloquent expression in the Berlin *Madonna in a Church* by Jan van Eyck (see Plate 7). Here, from a central Virgin and child, two pools of light direct the eyes through a doorway in the screen to the high altar, where two angels clad in bright liturgical vestments stand singing from an open book. As Jacqueline Jung has elaborated it, this image expresses in particularly concise and potent form the link between sacred image and its ecclesiastical symbols.[55] She emphasizes the visual dynamism whereby the Virgin – both *porta caeli* via which

Plate 7 *Madonna in a Church*, Jan van Eyck, 1437–8

the redeemed will enter heaven and *porta mundi* through whom Christ descended to earth – and Christ – the door to salvation according to John 10: 9 – are linked to the physical door, behind them, into the sanctuary, which thus symbolizes the transition, via salvation, to the world to come. Here, as she notes, Christ's unnaturally tiny dimensions that directly – on the panel – accord with the size of the aperture itself underscore that relationship with unusual literalism.

Yet the dynamism of this image is given a further charge by an aspect of its symbolism that seems not to have received attention: the presence of the singing angels around the altar is a clear reference to their role at the moment of transubstantiation, when, in the words of Gregory the Great, "at the words of the Priest, the heavens be opened, and the quires of Angels are present in that mystery of Jesus Christ."[56] That the angels stand alone is another clue to the functioning, within the image, of the Christ child, his gaze aimed directly into the door that he so perfectly fits: it is his arrival, in flesh, that their singing heralds, an arrival facilitated by the celebrating priest who, as we saw in Chapter 4, was himself, according to late medieval understanding, a type of Christ. Thus the power of the image lies in a suggestiveness that, typically for late medieval imagery, relies for its effect on the cultural knowledge of its viewer. Host and celebrant are absent from the sanctuary because both are implicitly present already in the foreground, in the Virgin's arms, in the form of a figure whose gaze and physical proportions draw him forward to the altar where, alone on earth until his Second Coming, he can be made flesh. This is the source both of the dynamism of the image and of its fundamental message. In its depiction of the yearning of the Christ child for access to the altar it articulates more than just the mystical status of the realm beyond the screen: it adumbrates the transcendence through which, by his sacrifice, memorialized at Mass, Christ will open the gate of heaven for all believers. Distance and attraction, presence and beyondness are collapsed, on a single flat surface, into an allegory of the promise of the life to come. In its exemplification, then, of music's heavenly role in drawing attentive listeners from the earthly realm – symbolized by the nave – to the salvation embodied within the sacred space beyond, the panel expresses the role of music in the Mass with an eloquence that words alone could scarcely achieve.

The function of the singing schola – those angels' earthly counterpart – as intended mediator between people and clergy, earthly and heavenly, is clear from the key moments of Mass that Duffy, following the sixteenth-century *Instructions for Parish Priests* of Richard Mirk, enumerates as follows: "intense prayer at the elevation, preceded and followed by private prayers keyed to a few significant moments in the ceremony – the confession of sins, the Gloria and the Sanctus, the offertory, the commemorations of the living and of the dead before and after the sacring, the receiving of the pax."[57] Music played a crucial role in most of these moments: indicating, accentuating, accompanying, framing; but nowhere was its role more integral than in the Canon, with its central consecration or "sacring," which had become, as we shall see, the location of the musical Sanctus.

The increasing emphasis on the sacring was accompanied by a corresponding drive to frame it with an appropriate level of elaboration and solemnity. For those worshipping, that drive, as contemporary witnesses repeatedly attest, was charged by the distance and mystery of the host and the consequent urge – surely felt ever more insistently as fear of purgatory increased its grip on the popular imagination – to breach that distance. Yet elaborations at this point had to be accommodated to the fact that the Canon, the part of the Mass with which the desire for association was most powerfully felt, was also its most inviolable: fixed in most of its particulars by the seventh century,[58] its words were (with the obvious exception of the commemorations of the living and the dead) largely immune to alteration. While the text itself remained sacrosanct, though, it was increasingly surrounded by layers of elaboration – visual, textual and musical – all motivated by the desire to highlight the moment of the elevation.

If scope for visible elaboration of the Canon – beyond the prescribed moves and gestures of the celebrating clergy – was necessarily limited, that for audible embellishment was almost limitless. Here again personal endowment found an avenue for expression. When Baugois le Beghin, a canon of the great collegiate church of St. Omer in Saint-Omer, northern France, died in 1475, he endowed a bell "called Julienne" to be rung, among other specified times,[59] at High Mass every day at the precise moment of the elevation, "as is customary in notable churches of this kingdom." Records beginning in the late thirteenth century detail the use of a large church bell, of which this was one, to signal the impending elevation in addition to, or in place of, the smaller bell that had been part of the history of the elevation since its inception.[60] From a late medieval perspective, Baugois's bequest was a masterstroke: by imprinting his sounding proxy upon the key moment of the principal devotion of his own church he was able to harness the prayers not only of all those present in the building, who would have turned to face the anticipated elevation, but also of anyone within earshot in the surrounding city and beyond. Moreover, the sound of his memorial was set to outlast by far that of those instituted by his contemporaries: his bell continues to hang – and sound – in the tower to this day.[61] One function of such bells was to forewarn those in the environs of the church, who could then rush into the building in time to view their maker, and to instruct those working roundabout to pause, face the church and worship the risen Christ being made present within its walls.[62]

The sound of the Sanctus

A more extended embellishment – and one much more conducive to particularization – could be had from the endowment of music. The most obvious locus for this was the oldest component of the Mass Ordinary: the Sanctus.[63] Recalling the singing of the multitudes of the seraphim as related in the vision of Isaiah,[64] the words of the first part of the Sanctus (as far as "gloria tua") served in the Mass to signify the joining of the earthly church with the heavenly hosts in the song of praise. This emphasis is enhanced by the form of the text used in the liturgy: the untranslated "sabaoth" embraces not only the armies of angels but the whole assembly of God's creation, while "heaven and earth," rather than just the "whole earth," are filled with his glory.[65] With this hymn of praise the church militant here on earth could cast itself as participating already in the endless song of the heaven to which it sought ultimate admission. But this binding of earthly with heavenly forces was considerably tightened when – as first codified by the Western Church in the eighth century[66] – the words from Isaiah were joined in the Mass by a paraphrase of the acclamation – of Benedictus with two surrounding Osannas – with which the crowd greeted Christ at his entry into Jerusalem on Palm Sunday.[67] With this embrace of God's corporeality, brought by Christ's earthly presence, as sealed by him in the New Covenant and ritualized in the Mass, the Sanctus evolved into an appropriately universal paean with which to celebrate the impending arrival of Christ on the altar.[68]

It is not surprising, then, that from an early stage the Sanctus functioned as a collective hymn sung by all those present, clergy and congregation alike.[69] Its traditionally joyful nature was underscored by its incorporation in the later Middle Ages, according to some witnesses, of the organ: indeed this is the only place in the great *Rationale divinorum officiorum* of Durandus, the most voluminous and influential compendium of liturgical practice from the late thirteenth to the early sixteenth century, in which the organ is mentioned at all.[70] The so-called Sanctus, or sacring, bell, rung originally to signal the beginning of the Sanctus but whose use seems, from the thirteenth century, to have been confused or conflated with the bell to signal the consecration, was apparently introduced as an expression of the same general mood.[71]

Subject, however, like so much else in the Mass, to Jungmann's "centrifugal tendency," the singing of the Sanctus was in the course of the Middle Ages cleaved increasingly away from both officiating clergy and laity, becoming instead the province of a separate group of singing clerics.[72] Congregational singing seems clearly precluded by the development, from the ninth century on, of more elaborate, frequently troped, settings. With the performance of such compositions the singing group became representatives of a now tacit laity, offering up the hymn of praise on their behalf. "Vicars" of the people in joining with the angelic choirs, this earthly choir functioned here, as elsewhere in the Mass, as a conduit between priestly action and lay reception: the commencement of singing signaled that a particular point in the sacred rite had been reached; at the same time, like the elevation bell, it was placed to draw the attention of the laity inward to the impending elevation, and to the prayers and meditations that increasingly, in books of hours and private primers, came to be prescribed for this moment.

Yet these functions of the Sanctus to communicate and display were combined, paradoxically, with a contrary function: to mask. The supreme sanctity of the moment of transubstantiation engendered various strategies designed to surround it with an appropriately heightened degree of mystery. Part of this aim could be achieved, as for most of the Mass, through distance and/or (in Masses at the high altar) the physical interposition between laity and clergy of the screen. But the heightened focus on the Real Presence in the later Middle Ages encouraged further layers of concealment. Most obviously, this could take the form of direct physical obstruction. In the Use of Sarum a veil suspended in the sanctuary, evoking the veil of the temple, gave point to the devotional rhythm of Lent and Passiontide, articulating the various degrees of solemnity of different days. On ferial days the entire Canon – including the elevation – was conducted behind it, depriving all but the officiating and assisting clergy, in a manner fitting to this time of deprivation, of sight of the host; on higher days, by contrast, the veil shrouded the entire ritual action of Mass with the exception of the Canon, for which it would be raised. Thus was formed a pattern of revelation and concealment that gave particular impetus towards the impending salvation of Easter.[73] Similar Lenten veils, often decorated with scenes from the Passion or other biblical themes, are documented across Europe.[74] Still greater degrees of concealment were effected when, as in Plate 8, a scene from a Flemish church interior in the later fifteenth century, substantial further covering was added. Here the entire rood screen, the altar on its west face and the surmounting figures of the crucifix with the Virgin and St. John are draped with white hangings, concealing from the people the familiar symbols of their redemption. Similar "Lenten arrays," frequently adorned with images befitting the season, were widespread in England.[75]

Of longer standing and much wider application than such physical veils, however, was a veil of words and music. This followed a long earlier history, beginning perhaps in the eighth century, during which the recitation by the priest of the Canon proper (beginning at "Te igitur") was customarily surrounded by reverent stillness, the words themselves conducted quietly or indeed in silence.[76] Yet at some point it seems to have become clear that words and music presented a dual advantage: first, of concealing the priest's words – so sacrosanct that they were to be audible only to himself and to God – behind a wall of sound; and, second, of avoiding the disruption in the visual rhythm of Mass that would result from the physical obstruction of its telos in the elevation. In the eleventh and twelfth centuries this sounding wall could take the form of the loud chanting of psalms and other prayers by a gathering of clerics around the altar.[77] With the increasing division of the roles of those present at Mass and the greater emphasis on the singing choir, however, the same role came instead to be filled by the Sanctus.

The performance of the Sanctus by the singing group alone, once established, was traditionally attended by the officiating clergy, who recited the same words privately, in bowed silence, after which the celebrant faced the altar to recite the Canon. In a shift of great importance to later polyphonic developments, however, the increasing elaboration of its melodies seems to have led this originally separate musical item to overlap with the words of the Canon, its musical veil concealing what had earlier been cloaked in silence.[78] At the same time the presence already of the unadorned words of the Sanctus in the recitation of the officiating clergy opened up the possibility, beginning in the ninth century but cultivated particularly from the eleventh to the thirteenth, for the verbal and musical adornment of its sung performance in the form of tropes. While these were often addressed to the Passion, they also – in a further harbinger of later polyphonic developments – opened up opportunities to associate the Canon, and its central consecration, with other venerations. Trinitarian texts, in accordance with traditional interpretations of the threefold Sanctus, are common, but tropes venerating Christ and the Virgin attest to widespread votive adaptations.

Historical ambiguities remain concerning the temporal organization of this central part of the Mass. Yet it is clear that the net effect of such additions to the Sanctus was to push performance of the Benedictus far beyond the beginning

Plate 8 The Lenten array, Book of Hours, South Netherlands, c.1492

of the Canon. More specifically, elaboration and extension of the Sanctus led to – or arose in tandem with – a development that was to prove of considerable importance also for polyphony: the coordination of the Benedictus with the elevation.[79] This link between action and text, for him "who comes in the name of the Lord," was not formalized until the *Ceremoniale episcoporum* of 1600, but it was clearly of long tradition by then, and could scarcely have been more fitting.[80] Plate 9, a Bolognese Mass scene by the Master of the Brussels Initials, from a Missal prepared for Cosimo de' Migliorati, bishop of Bologna before his elevation to the papacy as Innocent VII, is a particularly clear late-fourteenth-century witness to the practice: here the illumination combines the moment of the elevation with the depiction of a group of clerics singing the Sanctus, while the rest of the page carries the text of the Canon.[81] The point of desired coordination was often further articulated by the pattern of added text in troped settings, their concentration in the first Osanna being situated precisely so as to set the scene for the following Benedictus.[82]

The polyphonic Sanctus

This development underwent a still more heightened degree of articulation with the introduction of polyphony. The use of polyphony during the Canon brought with it some distinct advantages: in the first place it added another layer of elaboration to this climactic point in the liturgy; it also gave a richer dimension to the "greater music" in which men and angels joined forces, in the Sanctus, in a hymn of praise. But perhaps still more advantageously, the polyphonic Sanctus was infinitely malleable: it could be extended and shaped so that the musical "veil" could be made to fit any given situation or level of solemnity. It seems possible that, particularly during earlier periods when polyphony was uncommon, priestly action and vocal performance were not perfectly coordinated at this point. Haberl noted that, in what may have been a remnant of a much earlier practice, in the papal liturgy even in the seventeenth century the polyphony of the Sanctus, along with that of the Kyrie and Agnus Dei, could be slowed down, speeded up or even broken off by the magister at whatever point the action of Mass dictated.[83] Similar considerations, albeit in a much earlier setting, may explain the common practice in the early to mid fifteenth century, particularly in English settings, of dividing the long duos of the Sanctus and Agnus into short passages separated by simultaneous rests or fermatas, a feature that would have enabled the music to be curtailed quickly and efficiently as need arose. Direct practical evidence on this point is limited before 1600; but it seems probable that, over time, polyphony came to be shaped to give ever finer point to the expression of the mystery it was shaped to adorn, and to the social considerations that gave that expression its particular profile.

For our purposes, though, the central point comes with the consecration itself: a break in the singing may well have been allowed here to permit the desired coordination between Benedictus and elevation. Such a gap would also have been an appropriate remnant of the silence that long tradition had

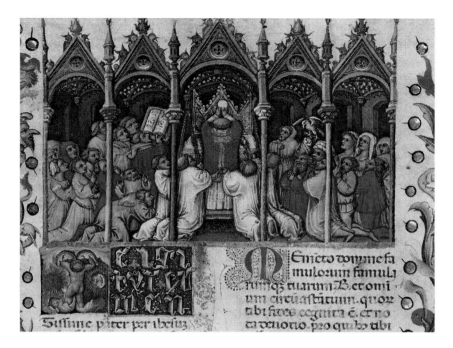

Plate 9 A Mass scene with chanting clerics, Master of the Brussels Initials, Italian, Bologna, 1389–1404

earlier decreed should surround the action of the Canon as a whole. It may even be the case that the bipartite division – customary for us – of Sanctus and Benedictus each with a concluding Osanna was itself motivated by this desire for coordination between the Benedictus and the elevation.[84] Certainly this runs counter to the original division of the Sanctus – in accordance with the distinct scriptural origins of its component parts – before Osanna I. In fact this latter division persisted in some quarters well into the age of polyphony, as revealed in the late-fifteenth-century *Canonis Misse Expositio* of Gabriel Biel: focusing on the liturgical origins of the two constituent texts of the Sanctus, Biel draws a distinction between the first part, up to "gloria tua," which is "of the angels" and the second part, beginning at Osanna I, "of men."[85] This same division – as Michael Long notes and as I will elaborate below – reveals itself also in some polyphonic settings which presuppose a coordination of the elevation not with the Benedictus, but with Osanna I.[86] In either case the joyful "clamor" of the repeated Osanna formed a frame for what had come to be characterized as the more inward expression of the Benedictus; the difference was simply that in cases where the biblical division was observed, the frame and what it surrounded assumed the status of a single, uninterrupted statement. At any rate, polyphonic practice at least from the fourteenth century provides widespread evidence of a strong point of division before the Benedictus,[87] a procedure formalized in numerous settings of the early fifteenth century by the presence of separate chant intonations on the words "Sanctus" and "Benedictus."[88]

Gilding the lily? The elevation motet

In the context of late medieval practice the link between elevation and Benedictus is sometimes revealed, paradoxically, by the interpolation of something else altogether. This happens when, particularly from the early sixteenth century on, elevation prayers, traditionally assigned by primers and commentators on the Mass to be uttered by worshippers at the elevation, are introduced into the ceremonial itself in sung settings. As for the Sanctus before them, then, the history of such items traced a path that led beyond their original functions as general expressions of devotion by members of the laity to the assumption of a new, more elaborate musical role in the choir.[89] In the same manner that the celebrant, as sole communicant in most late medieval celebrations of Mass, had assumed the role of the people as the church's "body," so the choir had increasingly become its "voice."

Surely the most widely discussed case in point is that described in a decree issued by Louis XII of France in 1512. This concerns the first verse of *O salutaris hostia*, an elevation prayer of wide circulation from the fifteenth century onwards.[90] The decree stipulates that this is henceforth to be sung ("decantetur") at daily Mass in Notre Dame of Paris and in its subject churches precisely "in elevationem Corporis Christi … inter pleni sunt caeli et benedictus qui venit."[91] This clearly testifies to an existing custom of placing the Benedictus after the elevation. But it also bears witness to a particular musical attempt to harness for earthly benefit the grace that was perceived to emanate from the consecrated host: part of the *O salutaris hostia* text was to be replaced by new words beseeching God to protect and preserve France and its monarch.[92]

Endowment records reveal evidence of similar procedures elsewhere. The 1450 will of a Strasburg canon includes payment for the singing of the antiphon *O sacrum convivium* "at the elevation directly after the Benedictus."[93] Singing of the *O salutaris hostia* at daily Mass was instituted in 1503 by a bourgeois of Langres and his wife, while a 1507 endowment at Ste.-Éminie in the diocese of Mende stipulated the performance at the elevation of *Gaudete flores*.[94] When Nicolas Rembert, dean of the collegiate church of St. Omer and former *contratenorista* of St. Peter's, Rome, died in 1504 he endowed funds for the choir to perform – almost certainly in polyphony – "before the high altar each day at High Mass in the presence of God their *O salutaris hostia* or *O sacrum convivium*, which may be performed before or as soon as possible after the Pater noster, and before the Agnus Dei if my lords do not wish to permit it here."[95] The timing of Rembert's antiphon was surely dictated by the expectation that the elevation itself would be marked by the singing of the Benedictus, which – given the date of his endowment and the fact that it was for High Mass – would likely on at least some occasions have been in polyphony.[96] Certainly there would be no reason, other than the priority of an existing custom, to perform motets on such texts anywhere other than at the elevation itself: Rembert, anxious to gain maximum possible benefit for his soul, clearly wished to place his motet as near to the moment of grace as circumstances allowed.[97]

Such documents record instances from a long history of the use of elevation chants or motets in place of, before, or after the Benedictus.[98] Like Sanctus tropes, these items must have functioned dramatically to set the scene, or to provide an extended gloss on the Benedictus and the associated moment of transubstantiation. Similar motivation can be inferred from the frequent interpolation into the Sanctus from the fourteenth century on, typically as a continuation of the text of the first Osanna, of the thirteenth-century sacramental prayer *Ave verum corpus*.[99] Surviving examples of this are not confined to chant. Du Fay's Sanctus "Papale," probably composed in the 1430s, combines the standard text with *Ave verum corpus*, but in a novel and apparently unique way: the three "Sanctus" invocations alternate with phrases from the prayer to the holy sacrament, which is then completed after "gloria tua," leaving the text from Osanna I to the end free of interpolated material. This textual layout might seem at first blush to imply that Du Fay was following the ancient division of the Sanctus before Osanna I. However, a chant intonation for "Benedictus" makes a clear break at that point, suggesting that, as in the examples already cited, the interpolated text functioned as a scene-setter, preparing the ground for the Benedictus, which then assumed what was surely by this time its customary climactic position at the elevation.

Locating the elevation: substitute motets and the *motetti missales*

As already mentioned, though, remnants do survive of a tradition of coincidence between the elevation and Osanna I. A particularly clear example is the *Missa de Venerabili Sacramento* by Hottinet Barra, as copied in the large opening section of music for the Holy Sacrament in the Occo Codex.

Here three of the five voices in the Osanna carry eucharistic texts from the Corpus Christi liturgy as tropes: two voices sing lines from the sequence *Lauda Sion* (whose melody is also paraphrased in the tenor) while another sings *O salutaris hostia*. The texting in the rest of the Sanctus, with the sole exception of the tenor of its first section, which also carries a verse from *Lauda Sion*, is standard.[100] The same phenomenon has left its trace, as Michael Long has noted, in the *Missa de Sancta Anna* by Pierre de la Rue, where Osanna I has been replaced by a setting of *O salutaris hostia*.[101] Similarly the quotation in the Osanna I of Obrecht's *Missa Graecorum* of the Easter sequence *Victimae paschali laudes* seems clearly to indicate the intended coincidence of that moment with the manifestation in the elevation of the paschal victim himself, perhaps, given the choice of quotation, specifically in an Easter Mass.[102]

A broader *ersatz* view of an association between Osanna I and elevation is offered by a group of "Masses" that for the most part eschew the standard liturgical texts: the Milanese *motetti missales* that, instead of the standard Ordinary settings, comprise series of motets.[103] Two of these groupings signal the position of the elevation explicitly,[104] while another, the series of Christmas *motetti missales* by Compère copied on folios 170v–9r of Milan 2269, preserves a "Sanctus" outline in which the elevation clearly falls at the position normally occupied by Osanna I. The succession of motets that comprises this latter grouping is interrupted at the Sanctus by regular Mass text. Yet this movement sets the standard liturgical text only as far as "gloria tua"; after this, following a double bar, the music proceeds not, as usual, to the Osanna, but to a Christmas responsory text concerning the incarnation whose relevance to the miracle of transubstantiation could scarcely be more direct: "Verbum caro factum est et habitavit in nobis, et vidimus gloriam eius." The liturgical point, as in the *Adoramus te Christe* "ad elevationem" of the Mass *sostituita da 8 mottetti* a few folios earlier, is underscored by the musical setting: like so many motets and other musical passages destined for the elevation, the section embraces a succession of block chords marked with fermatas.[105] In contrast to these three cycles, however, a similar substitution occurs in Josquin's *Missa D'ung aultre amer* at the point of the Benedictus, which in various copies is replaced by parts of the same composer's elevation motet *Tu solus, qui facis mirabilia*.[106]

Some details of the patterns of temporal coincidence between the Sanctus and the elevation are likely to remain obscure. But one thing is clear: this musical item came to express the meeting of earth and heaven not only in the song of their respective choirs, but in the descent of the King of Heaven himself.

The question that remains, though, is what does any of this have to do with the cyclic polyphonic Mass? If attention was so heavily focused on the transubstantiation why was there any need for multipartite compositions extending across the rite that enclosed it? Why not focus instead simply on settings of the Sanctus and elevation prayers? But the musical Sanctus functioned in the Mass as more than a celebration and elaboration of its crowning moment: its role within the ritual as a whole, I will argue, provides a key to an explanation of the cyclic Mass as a general phenomenon. To understand this we need to grasp the significance not only of the climactic moment of the consecration itself, but also of its symbolic extent, as conceived in the later Middle Ages, across the rite that frames it.

The embrace of the Passion

From its origins in the ninth century, allegorical exegesis had interpreted the Mass primarily as a representation of events in the life of Christ, and principally of his Passion. Hence it had focused above all on the actions of the Canon and its central sacrament.[107] For ordinary worshippers, the incomprehensibility of Latin already threw exegetical weight strongly onto the visible, and the cues thereby offered for a proper understanding of the various stages of this defining phase of the Mass liturgy. And yet, notwithstanding their frequent access to private primers or books of hours, this was almost equally true of their more educated brethren.[108] The words of the Canon and indeed – as we have seen – most of the spoken words of the public Mass at the high altar would have been inaudible to the assembled laity. The aura of heightened value conferred by concealment was clearly an essential factor in the lay experience of Mass; yet that principle reached its apex in the Canon, the mystery of mysteries through which the miracle of transubstantiation was effected, and whose words were, in the later Middle Ages, to be hidden from everyone except the celebrant himself, uttering them, *sotto voce*, at the altar. This circumstance surely does much to explain the heavy emphasis in Mass commentary from the eleventh century onwards on the signs of the cross made by the priest in the Canon, and on his actions, clothing and person more generally.

In fact this emphasis was not merely a concomitant of the inaudibility of the Canon: it was a stated requirement. Strict proscription of lay access to its words and the more intimate details of its enactment was complemented by the recommendation, in commentaries on the Mass, to focus its exegesis on the visible details of the celebrant's vestments and actions, including, as we have seen, his numerous prescribed signs of the cross.[109] From the thirteenth century onwards, though, as we saw in Chapter 5, interpretation of the vestments came to signify the actual garments worn at the various stages of Christ's suffering. With this shift came a more direct identification of the priest with Christ himself, and, in turn, the spread of Passion imagery beyond the boundaries of the Canon: clothed in the Passion garments, items of the "arma Christi" so venerated particularly in the fifteenth century, the priest could be seen to represent not simply Christ, but the suffering Christ of the Passion, throughout the course of the rite.

Such a development grew out of the conception of the church fathers – whose methods of biblical exegesis provided a model for later commentators' expositions of the liturgy – of the Mass as a representation of the sacrifice of Christ. From the twelfth century on, though, and particularly following the codification of the doctrine of transubstantiation at the Fourth Lateran Council in 1215, allegory fashioned to explicate and magnify that central point gathered powerful momentum: every gesture in the Canon was imbued with symbolic significance as a recollection – indeed a reenactment – of a moment in the suffering and death of Christ. The most widespread summary of this model, one whose influence was to become ubiquitous and would reach its peak in the later fifteenth century, was, as we have seen, the compendious late thirteenth-century *Rationale divinorum officiorum* of Guillelmus Durandus.[110] The following two centuries saw an increasing accumulation of guides – ranging from detailed scholarly considerations to smaller handbooks designed to prepare priests for their pastoral duties – all propagating and expanding on this same fundamental view of the Mass as an embodiment and reenactment of the process of the Passion. From these sources of priestly teaching the broader outlines of that message were conveyed, through sermons and prayers, to the worshipping laity. It is surely unsurprising that some of the most simplistically and pervasively Passion-oriented manuals, geared as they are to the less scholarly end of the priesthood, are in the vernacular. Striking in this regard is a mid-fifteenth-century Stuttgart Mass commentary discussed at length by Franz, in which, as he notes, "jeder Akt in der Messe repräsentiert einen Vorgang in der Leidenszeit." Likewise, for "Langforde's Meditations in the Time of the Mass," associated with the late medieval English Brigittine house of Syon, "the processe of masse representyd the verey processe of the Passyon of Cryst."[111]

The expansion of Passion allegory into the Mass as a whole followed easily from the overwhelming emphasis on the consecration – ritually conceived (as eloquently explained by Bossy) as sacrifice – as the prime locus of its meaning.[112] This central transforming moment thus became the focal point for the theological underpinning of the Mass as a whole, and the guiding principle behind its elaboration. Stated at its most extreme, as in the early-fourteenth-century *Pastorale novellum* of the Beromünster choirmaster and later Dean of Constance Rudolf von Liebenegg, such a view held that "the whole liturgy was properly only a decorative frame-work for the accomplishment of the Sacrament."[113] The overflowing of Passion imagery into the rest of the Mass was clearly encouraged also by popular desire, already discussed, for more extended vision of the host. In Jungmann's words, "There was … a desire that this moment and the cor-responding elevation of the Host might be stretched out through the whole Mass."[114]

It is not hard to see how the spread of imagery – and on occasions such as Corpus Christi the embodiment – of the redeemer throughout the Mass could have encouraged a similar consistency in physical phenomena devised to enhance and adorn its message, including its music. This, I propose, is the ultimate force behind the creation of the cyclic cantus firmus Mass and its celebrated musical unity. A sung polyphonic Ordinary setting embodied a series of advantages, integrated with great elegance. First and foremost, it could be linked to a specific occasion, and here we return to a theme of the previous chapter: following the streamlining of the liturgy and decline of troping, the cantus firmus offered new, and newly specific, possibilities for particularization; second, the specific message embodied in the cycle as a whole could be brought into contact, in the Sanctus, with the moment of grace, and hence its plea made, symbolically, directly to the redeemer; and third, like the ostension of the host in the Feast of Corpus Christi and like the consistent message of the exegeses just discussed, it was extended across the rite, bringing the entire ceremony under the aegis of an all-en-compassing plea. In addition to these more general characteristics it also, in its embrace of both Sanctus and Agnus Dei, had the advantage of tightening the link between private and public, sacrifice and sacrament: Bossy makes the important observation that the Agnus Dei provided the musical adorn-ment – as well as the textual illustration – of the moment when, concur-rently with the priest's communication on their behalf, the public affirmed, in the ritual kissing of the *pax* board, the peace and renewal of commu-nity achieved by the preceding sacrifice. As he further notes, moreover, "its 'dona nobis pacem' provided an appropriate conclusion for the Mass as a musical genre."[115]

Through the agency of the cyclic Mass, the unity that was felt to envelop the ritual as a whole in a consistent message received the enhancement of a sonic marker that bound together its various parts: it seems clear enough even from the encouragement of close hearing (noted above) found in such basic texts as *The Lay Folks Mass Book* that there was no need for musical literacy to perceive the distinction between the sound of polyphony and what that polyphony surrounded; indeed the prominence of polyphony was surely enhanced by the fact that, for most hearers, it was probably a comparatively rare experience. And the more specific message articulated by choice of model and particularity of construction was known, at the very least, to those who paid for it and to God.

Yet questions remain: why, if the Sanctus and, to some extent, the Agnus Dei represented the climactic phases of the cyclic Mass in terms of their relation to the surrounding rite, was it not customary to make them similarly climactic musically? There are clear cases, as we saw in Chapter 3, in which the point of the elevation in the Sanctus does indeed receive musical delineation; and some form of musical climax in the Agnus Dei, especially in the third invocation with its imploration for peace, is memorably articulated in a number of Masses, including some particularly striking examples by Josquin. Given the above considerations, though, it seems unsurprising that the overriding concern in most Mass settings, as in the message of the ritual they were composed to adorn, seems to have been with a consistency and unity of utterance across the five component movements.

More ostensibly paradoxical is the fact that the Benedictus, coinciding as it commonly did with the elevation, was one of the few sections of the cantus firmus Mass that was typically free of borrowed material. Surely, it might be objected, this is the one place where the presence of an endower's proxy, in the form of a specially chosen theme, would have been especially desirable. It may well be that the removal of outside music from this most sacred moment was a reflection of the increasing objections (discussed in Chapter 6) to just such a practice. That situation may itself have encouraged the growth of the cantus firmus Mass, its individual identity within a broader unity perhaps in turn making such direct engagement with the moment of the elevation seem less urgent than hitherto. From a practical viewpoint, on the other hand, the usual setting of this section as a duo with frequent cadential articulation may reflect, as discussed earlier, a need for flexibility of timing at this most critical moment, allowing for the possibility of coherent yet quick curtailment of the music at short notice.

It seems clear from church accounts that many personal endowments involved extemporized polyphony; yet it is also beyond reasonable doubt

Plate 10 *Portrait of a Young Man*, Master of the View of St. Gudule, detail

that – notwithstanding the limited quantity of direct evidence linking specific endowments with specific pieces – desire for personalization was a major force in the growth of composed polyphony. One need think only of Du Fay's Mass for St. Anthony of Padua (discussed in Chapter 3) or of the carefully tailored composition, by Obrecht, of his Mass of St. Donatian for the endowment for the Bruges furrier Donaes de Moor to be aware of the remarkably efficacious link that existed in such cases between needs and available means.[116] By aural analogy with the tangible objects – torches, personal linen for making corporals, vestments, books, etc. – already discussed, endowed music could bring the donor, via personal proxy, into the presence of the host. Such personalization, for which polyphony on the book was inherently unsuited, was manifestly available to tailor-made compositions, most obviously when particularized by the use of specifically chosen cantus firmi.

As already noted, there was clearly a particular value attached to association with the public High Mass, where endowed music could serve to associate its donor with the prayers of the entire community. That cachet was obviously sufficient to inspire donations, such as that of Rembert discussed above, involving huge expense. But such endowments had other disadvantages besides cost: they were restricted – as, presumably, in the case of Rembert's endowment – by prevailing customs concerning services at the high altar, and, most important, they were bound by the annual liturgical cycle of the church year. It is this situation that best explains the growth, which acquired particular momentum in the fifteenth century, of private Masses, where no such restriction applied, and where votive devotions to favored saints, especially the Virgin, could proceed unimpeded by the church calendar.[117] Also, while the model of spatial relation between priestly enactment and lay observation remained one of distance, or at least separation, Masses at subsidiary or private altars offered the considerable advantage of much closer access to the liturgical action and, crucially, the transubstantiated host. That observation is widely corroborated by contemporary visual representations of private Masses depicting celebrant and observer(s) in close physical proximity: Plates 4 (on page 183) and 10 show this juxtaposition in details from the *Altarpiece of the Seven Sacraments* by van der Weyden and the Metropolitan Museum, New York's *Portrait of a Young Man* by the Master of the View of St. Gudule. In both these cases the single lay observer assumes the clerical role normally assigned to an acolyte, carrying a torch with one hand while, with the other, supporting the hem of the celebrant's chasuble to avoid having its weight impede his lifting of the host.[118] The appeal of such Masses to those who paid for them was surely matched by their attractiveness to a broader public: desire to gaze on the host, and to do so with a minimum of interposed distance, fed the availability of worshippers (as in the late fifteenth-century Mass celebration, apparently at an altar on the west face of a choir screen, depicted on the cover of this book) whose prayers, reciprocally, benefited the souls of the endowers.

These same forces were likewise instrumental in the intensive contemporary growth of the privately endowed and supported altars at which such devotions were conducted, and in the development of their various adornments, including – as in cases such as those of Du Fay and Donaes de Moor – polyphony. In this climate of particularized and personalized devotion it is easy to comprehend how the cantus firmus Mass, whose scope and adaptability allowed it to be fitted to individual devotional needs with special precision, would have found a particular purchase. Given such circumstances, it seems likely that music at privately funded Masses, paid for by wealthy clerics and citizens for performance in side chapels and chantries, must commonly have outshone even that at the public High Mass, where *ex tempore* performance of polyphony on the book was probably commonplace, particularly in churches of more limited means. Thus a work such as Obrecht's Mass for Donaes – likely performed in front of the surviving triptych depicting him and his wife being presented by their patron saints to the Virgin and Child – might be said to have constituted the audible counterpart to personalized altarpieces of which van Eyck's *Mystic Lamb*, painted for the Ghent side chapel of Joos Vijd and Elizabeth Borluut, is the most celebrated example.[119]

Last things

A common thread runs through the separate sections of this book: this concerns not the internal structures of the cyclic Mass, but rather the perspectives of its users. As with any cultural artifact, different users – from different times, different social backgrounds, and acting with different priorities – have inevitably approached the same settings of the polyphonic Mass with different eyes and ears. To enquire after these various priorities affords insights not only into the societies in which those users moved, but also into the compositions themselves, and the very different responses and evaluative models they can sustain. It is thus to attempt, culturally speaking, a truly deep appreciation of their significance. But to step back from the interpretation of observable structures is also to open up the field of vision to new, and substantial, interpretative questions. Most particularly, what common ground might there be between these ways of seeing and evaluating the early polyphonic Mass? Can the diverse uses to which it has been put in the past suggest new, and newly relevant, ways of appreciating it today? Two general topics suggest themselves: first, the notion of unity, and second, that of pathos, and particularly the pathos associated with death.

The topic of unity is the more familiar one to students of the forms and structures of the cyclic Mass, given classic expression in the quotation from Bukofzer cited at the beginning of this book. I have traced the route whereby this particular model of internal, structural unity, rooted in the Enlightenment instantiation of the work of art and refined subsequently by Hegelian dialectics, grew out of intellectual priorities of the times in which it was coined. Yet there can be no doubt that the unity embodied in the form of the cyclic Mass was of great concern also to its original users; indeed one might claim that it was of much more urgent importance, more profoundly rooted in their societal needs and aspirations. Unity, as I sought to demonstrate in the final chapter, is indeed the very lifeblood of the cyclic Mass in its expression of the eschatological needs of those who paid for its production and enactment in sound. In spanning the ritual of Mass, the repeated statement of a cantus firmus offered a means both of embracing its sacramental message as a unified celebration and reenactment of Christ's Passion, and of particularizing its plea to the Redeemer, made flesh, at the point of climax, on the altar. The unity it imposed served, then, a more than merely aesthetic purpose, however lofty: it offered the prospect of a quicker release, after death, from purgatory, and consequently a quicker passage to paradise.

But the sacramental import of performances, *in situ*, of cyclic Masses extended beyond the province of those individuals or institutions that paid and provided for them. It embraced the corporate body of all those present, reminding us (to revisit a phrase used earlier in this book) that there was no such thing, in the later Middle Ages, as a truly private Mass. All who were present at a particular Mass shared in the attendant nourishment of the Real Presence, and all, conversely, bestowed benefit, by their prayers, on those who had ordered and paid for it. Such unity of purpose is nowhere more obviously expressed than in the organized rituals of confraternities, their primary *raison d'être* being specifically to offer prayers for the souls of their departed brethren. This priority is clearly embodied in the opening sermon, quoted in Chapter 4, of the register of the York gild of Corpus Christi: "as Christ unites the members to the Head by means of his precious Passion, so we shall be united in faith, hope and charity by the daily celebration of this sacrament of remembrance."

In this sense, then, the central concern of the Mass was always with unity, a unity that received just one of its expressions, albeit an especially eloquent one, in the cyclic polyphonic Mass. As Eamon Duffy has written, "the Eucharist could only be used to endorse existing community power structures because the language of Eucharistic belief and devotion was saturated with communitarian and corporate imagery."[1] To be present at Mass was, at least notionally, to be part of a social nexus unified in adoration of the risen Christ and to experience the unity of being bound to him, as a member of the church, in one body. As the defining expression of the Christian message of redemption, then, the Mass was the universal, and ultimately unifying, act of the church militant here on earth.

The topic of pathos associated with death is revealed in particular relief, to return to a theme from Chapter 3, in the Masses of Du Fay. There can be no more vivid or familiar meeting place between modern preoccupations with affective musical pathos and the medieval concern with death than the Agnus Dei II of Du Fay's late masterpiece, the *Missa Ave regina caelorum*. And this is a significance which gains added depth from fore-echoes including those in the Mass for St. Anthony of Padua and *Missa La belle se siet*. The musical gesture that links these works must have carried an intensely personal meaning: one personal enough, indeed, to straddle Du Fay's entire Mass-writing career from youthful essay through early maturity to late stylistic summation. Moreover, in the Mass for St. Anthony of Padua, it found its place in a work specified for annual performance for the benefit of his soul, both during his earthly life and, in perpetuity, after it had ended.

This deeply personal musical gesture (at least in the form in which it occurs in the two musically linked works on *Ave regina caelorum*) is so well known, and so seemingly natural from a modern aesthetic stance, that it is easy to miss what must surely have been its revolutionary quality when considered against its contemporary reportorial backdrop. Such overtly personal musical utterances have been associated more often with Josquin, widely acknowledged as a composer given to individualized expressive responses to his texts; in fact a similar motivation, as I argued in Chapter 3, may perhaps have lain behind a series of related musical gestures in Masses that likewise seem to span that composer's career. Indeed, the very familiarity of affective strategies in music by Josquin and his successors may perhaps have obscured their truly radical status in the work of a composer born some half a century earlier. Yet the presence of such procedures in later repertory offers the possibility of deeper insight into their use by Du Fay and, consequently, into their contemporary meanings in the context of the early polyphonic Mass.

Some pertinent insights are expressed in Bernhard Meier's work on modal theory and practice, and it is worth invoking them briefly here. Meier cites a series of cases, beginning with examples drawn from works by Josquin, to demonstrate an incipient affective use, in sixteenth-century music, of the contrast between "major" and "minor" to heighten text expression.[2] The affective power of such contrast derives, he emphasizes, not from the intrinsic nature of the intervals concerned, but from the act of sudden change.[3] He further notes that these exceptional uses of major and minor are thrown into particular relief in the context of their time by the prevailing normativity of the modal system. In other words to be "attuned" to the exceptionality, or even aware of its presence, means being attuned first to the nature of pervading normality.[4]

Timothy McKinney has made the latter point with particular clarity in his study of Glarean's response to Josquin's *Planxit autem David*.[5] He notes that a present-day listener to this work, famously praised by Glarean for its depiction of lamentation, would likely miss its affective import because of its predominantly "major" sound. Yet for Glarean – as for others at least as far back as Johannes Afflighemensis around 1100 – rooted in the classically derived notion of modal ethos, the dolefulness traditionally associated with the Hypolydian mode makes it the ideal choice for this motet. Similarly the import of the use at key points in the motet of the psalm tone (also Hypolydian) deriving from the recitation of the Lamentations of Jeremiah during Holy Week, surely striking to contemporary hearers, would generally be lost on modern ones. Various other features, their affective properties observable from a contemporary viewpoint but not from a modern one, emphasize the point.[6]

Such observations underscore the need for constant vigilance against confusing culturally instilled associations of musical sounds with their "natural" properties.[7] But they also give some sense of the likely effect, at least on learned ears, of the sudden, and clearly affective, interjection in Du Fay's Masses of such a radical intervallic shift. Arresting to today's ears, these moments must have been truly shocking in their own time, and that shock, in its textual contexts, would surely have left no doubt concerning the depth of the composer's fear for the welfare of his soul.

Of course affective responses to texts could be articulated and underscored by other tactics, many of them familiar to modern scholarship.[8] A battery of signifiers of lamentation, traceable through the history of laments at least as far back as Andrieu's *Armes, amours* on the death of Machaut and embracing settings of the Requiem, the many songs on "regretz" themes, and so on, are drawn on frequently and with clear affective intent, particularly from the later years of the fifteenth century onwards.[9] Clearly Du Fay's case is exceptional to the extent that his motet and Masses, backed up by his own words and concerns as voiced in his surviving will and executors' account, make up a unique aggregate of information. Yet the use by Du Fay of such unambiguous musical tactics to emphasize moments of intensely personal concern in the texts of the Mass ordinary seems to lack direct parallels in other Mass settings.

Where to from here?

What does this mean for the relation between donors and the Masses fashioned for the welfare of their souls? Have the concerns that led to such endowments left material traces in other Mass settings, and how might such traces be recognized? Clearly Du Fay was not alone in his fears for his posthumous fate: such concerns, to judge from contemporary wills and executors' accounts, and from the sheer scale of material and monetary investment in preparation for the afterlife generally, seem to have been more or less universal. And that universality is surely what led to the dissemination of cantus firmus Mass cycles far beyond their places of origin: a Marian Mass, say, composed for a particular endowment could as easily be appropriated for another. Perhaps that very universality discouraged, in the case of the Mass Ordinary, the kinds of responses that, in laments and in requiems, were occasioned – actually or presumably – by specific individual deaths. Further instances will probably emerge, as in the example discussed by McKinney, from an increasingly enhanced "feel" for such signifiers deriving from an improved awareness of contemporary perceptions of musical style.[10]

Yet it seems likely that new insights into the contemporary meaning of polyphonic Mass settings will, as in the past, continue to emerge most fruitfully when situated in a broader cultural and contextual perspective. Larger constructional elements seem likely to yield further clues concerning contemporary meanings. For example, such clues may well emerge from further instances, such as those discussed in Chapter 3, of sudden shifts in the treatment of borrowed material, shifts presumably effected to reflect and enhance the unfolding of the message articulated by the rite in which they are embedded. Gestures of this nature beg questions concerning the ways in which such melodies were intended to be, or actually were, perceived: was such change meant to be heard by those present, or was its message considered more subliminal – directed, via Christ and/or some favored saint, to God? Seeds for discussion are clearly to be found in the ways in which the melody is highlighted – or not – by the surrounding texture, a question recently revisited by Bonnie J. Blackburn.[11] What reasons lay behind the choice of aurally perceptible quotation, on the one hand, or of texturally embedded cantus firmus usage on the other? For whose "ears," besides those of the divine company, were the latter intended? We may hope that new insights into this question will emerge as we refine our awareness of the cultural functioning of polyphonic Masses and the ways they were tailored to address it.

That such melodies were indeed, at least some of the time, intended to be heard seems clear enough from the many and varied censures against their use discussed in Chapter 6. And at least one sixteenth-century witness attests to the role of such recognition in enhancing the aural impact of the polyphonic settings in which they are clothed. Writing in 1577, Francisco Salinas made the following observations concerning the familiarity of borrowed material:

And Aristotle in his *Problems* [Bk. XIX, sec. 5], inquiring why we tend to listen with greater pleasure to a song that we already know than to one that is unknown to us, among other reasons, gives these: that when we know what is sung, it is more obvious that the singer is performing what the composer intended; just as the familiar attracts the eye with more pleasure, so also the familiar is sweeter to the ear

than the unfamiliar. Furthermore, when a familiar song is heard, we more pleas-
urably perceive in its sounds the various modes which the good writer of music
uses. Wherefore, those highly celebrated motets of Josquin des Prez, "Inviolata,"
"Benedicta es caelorum regina," and "Praeter rerum seriem," are held in greater
esteem than those of which he himself was entirely the composer, since to the songs
that have been used for centuries in the church and are familiar to all, the intertwining of many parts was added.[12]

Salinas's comments direct us back to the discussion of Chapter 3, and to a
possible route towards the understanding of musical quotations of a range
extending far beyond the sacred melodies encased in Josquin's chant-based
motets. They invite us to see, in Aquinas's advocacy of the value of metaphor in scripture, a rationale for the use in Mass settings not only of secular
pieces *per se*, but of popular and even bawdy songs, one that goes further
and deeper than that of incidental decoration or *Randerscheinungen*. Such
songs, to paraphrase Aquinas, might be viewed in this context as examples
of the "less noble bodies" that invite the contemplation of "those who could
think of nothing nobler than bodies," "similitudes drawn from things farthest away from God" possessing the power to awaken in the listener "a
truer estimate that God is above whatsoever we may say or think of him."[13]
From this perspective the functioning of such borrowings could operate by
stealth, drawing the listener in, through a combination of their familiarity
and their distance from God, to an awareness that God is present in all
things, and perhaps even a realization, along the way, of the adroitness of
the composer in exemplifying that presence. Could it be that the very familiarity and ostensible unsuitability of such tunes may have constituted their
most potent weapon in drawing the listener into an enhanced love of God?

It seems at any rate that future insights into musical borrowing will continue to derive most abundantly from speculation, as in chapters 4 and 5,
concerning the choice of melodies used. Such speculation seems unlikely
in most cases to yield definitive results: the "smoking gun" of documentary confirmation (as in the case of the valedictory statements of Du Fay)
is seldom the stuff of cultural history. What it can and will do, however, is
to suggest circumstances in which the polyphonic Mass may plausibly have
been meaningful to its users, if only to some of them some of the time. It
can thus add to the rich tissue of cultural awareness against which the polyphonic Mass may stand out more vividly and meaningfully, offering us new
ways, via enhanced sensitivity to the world that created it, of enjoying and
appreciating it.

Some things will, and must, of course remain closed to us. Every Mass
setting had its own rationale, both for coming into being and for surviving

beyond its first performance: it was written for a particular place, occasion, individual or purpose, and further, changing, purposes sustained its subsequent passage. Even if those specifics could be recovered, the broader social circumstances that gave them their meaning in given times and places would still be at least partially irretrievable, prisoners of societies long since past.[14] This is at the same time the limitation and the challenge of a study such as this one: if the goal is ultimately unreachable, its pursuit still offers the thrill of an enhanced sense of contact with those who created the objects we admire; and the thrill of that dialog can grow and change with each generation, at least so long as our interest in the music persists. A human desire for contact with the past has been fundamental to our appreciation of the early polyphonic Mass since its reemergence in the late eighteenth century; it seems set to continue as we strive to comprehend the world for which the music was fashioned, and, at the same time, to have that comprehension enrich our own.

Appendix 1: Texts relating to *L'homme armé*

1 Guillelmus Durandus

Guillelmi Duranti Rationale divinorum officiorum, ed. A. Davril and T. M. Thibodeau, Corpus Christianorum, continuatio mediaevalis CXL, CXL A, CXL B, 3 vols. (Turnhout: Brepols, 1995, 1998, 2000), Book III, 1

[3.] Rursus pontifex, uersus aquilonem respiciens, quamuis uersus orientem, seu uersus altare, si sit magis accomodum respicere possit, tanquam aduocatus et pugil cum hoste pugnaturus antiquo uestibus sacris, quasi armis induitur, iuxta Apostolum, ut iam dicetur.

4. Primo, sandalia pro ocreis habet ne quid macule uel pulueris affectionum inhereat. Secundo, amictus pro galea caput contegit. Tertio, alba pro lorica totum corpus cooperit. Quarto, cingulum pro arcu, subcingulum pro pharetra assumit, et est subcingulum illud quod dependet a cingulo, quo stola pontificis cum ipso cingulo colligatur. Quinto, stola collum circumdat, quasi hastam contra hostem uibrans. Sexto, manipulo pro claua utitur. Septimo, casula quasi clypeo tegitur; manus libro pro gladio armatur. De singulis etiam aliter infra dicetur. Hec itaque sunt arma quibus pontifex seu sacerdos armari debet, contra spirituales nequitias pugnaturus; nam, ut inquit Apostolus: *Arma militie nostre non sunt carnalia, sed ad destructionem muniminum potentia.* Et in alia epistola, ad Eph. VI *c.: Induite,* inquit, *uos armatura Dei, ut possitis stare aduersus insidias dyaboli. State ergo succincti lumbos uestros in ueritate, et induti loricam iustitie, et calciati pedes in preparatione euangelii pacis: in omnibus sumentes scutum fidei, in quo possitis omnia tela nequissimi ignea extinguere: et galeam salutis assumite: et gladium spiritus quod est uerbum Dei.* Hec quidem armatura est premissa, septiplex uestis sacerdotalis; significatiua septemplicis uirtutis sacerdotis, et representatiua uestium Christi, quibus indutus fuit tempore passionis, prout infra dicetur. ...

6. Sic itaque, munitus ad certamen contra spiritualia nequitie in celestibus, et pro sedanda in subditos iudicis ira, ad altare procedit; et per confessionem dyaboli renuntiat dominio, et seipsum accusat. Populus uero quasi pro suo pugile oraturus, in profestis diebus terre prosternitur; dum autem ille orationes et alia recitat, quasi totis uiribus contra dyabolum pugnat. Dum dyaconus in ieiuniis ante euangelium casulam super humerum replicat, quasi gladium contra hostem uibrat. Dum epistola legitur uoce preconis, imperatoris edicta dantur. Cantus sunt tubicine, precentores chorum regentes sunt duces exercitum ad pugnam instruentes, quibus lassescentibus alii subueniunt. Cantus autem sequentie est plausus, seu laus

215

uictorie. Dum euangelium legitur, hostis quasi gladio uulneratur; aut exercitus post uictoriam dispersus adunatur. Episcopus predicans est imperator uictores laudans. Oblationes sunt spolia que uictoribus diuiduntur. Cantus offertorii est triumphus qui debetur imperatori. Pax autem in fine datur, ut populi quies, hoste prostrato, insinuetur. Et deinde populus, data licenti[a] per "Ite missa est," cum gaudio, de uictoria et pace obtenta, ad propria redit.

2 Innocent III, from *De sacro altaris mysterio libri sex*

Opera Omnia Innocentii III *(Patrologia Latina, vol. 217)*. Innocentii III Romani Pontificis Operum Pars Altera: Sermones, Opuscula. II. Opuscula: Innocentius III Romani Pontificis Mysteriorum Evangelicae Legis et Sacramenti Eucharistiae Libri Sex *(Edit. Opp. Innocentii III, Colon., 1575, in-folio.)*

[Book I: Chapter LXIV] De armatura virtutum

Ista sunt arma quae pontifex debet induere, contra spirituales nequitias pugnaturus. Nam, ut inquit Apostolus: *Arma militiae nostrae non sunt carnalia, sed ad destructionem munitionum potentia Deo* (2 Corinthians 10) De quibus idem Apostolus in alia dicit Epistola: *Induite vos armaturam Dei, ut possitis stare adversus insidias diaboli. State ergo succincti lumbos vestros in veritate, et induti loricam justitiae, et calceati pedes in praeparationem Evangelii pacis, in omnibus sumentes scutum fidei, quo possitis omnia tela nequissimi ignea exstinguere, et galeam salutis assumite, et gladium spiritus, quod est verbum Dei* (Ephesians 6).

[Book II: Chapter XXVIII] De extensione manuum sacerdotis in missa

Nam et Christus cum expandisset manus in cruce, pro persecutoribus oravit, et dixit: *Pater, dimitte illis, quia nesciunt quid faciunt* (Luke 23), moraliter instruens, quia Christus semper paratus est recipere poenitentes, juxta quod ipse promisit: *Omnis qui venit ad me, non ejiciam foras* (John 6). Cum autem verus Moyses, id est Christus elevat manus, id est impendit auxilium et solatium, vincit Israel, id est Ecclesia. Nam *si Deus pro nobis, quis contra nos?* (Romans 8). Sin autem paululum manus remittit, id est si, peccatis exigentibus, subtrahit auxilium et solatium, superat Amalech, id est diabolus. Quia *non est volentis, neque currentis, sed Dei miserentis* (Romans 9). Quia vero Christus promisit Ecclesiae: *Ecce ego vobiscum sum omnibus diebus usque ad consummationem saeculi* (Matthew 28), ob hoc Aaron, id est mons fortitudinis, et Hur, id est ignis charitatis, sustentant manus ipsius, ut in fortitudine ferat auxilium, et ex charitate solatium, ne manus ejus lassentur usque ad solis occasum, id est usque ad finem mundi. Sicque Josue duce, id est Christo ductore Israel fugat Amalech et populum ejus, id est Ecclesia superat diabolum et exercitum daemonum in ore gladii, id est per virtutem orationis.

Gladius enim est verbum Dei (Ephesians 6). Si quis ergo vult orationis virtute superare diabolum, debet elevare manus, id est actus ad Deum, ut ejus conversatio sit in coelis (Philippians 3).

3 Johannes Beleth

Johannis Beleth, Summa de ecclesiasticis officiis, *ed. Herbert Douteil, 2 vols., Corpus Christianorum, continuatio mediaevalis 41–41A (Turnhout: Brepols, 1976)*

32 De officiis altaris

Sacerdos ergo tamquam advocatus et pugil cum hoste antiquo pugnaturus uestibus sacris quasi armis induitur, sandalia pro ocreis assumens, ne quid macule vel pulveris affectioni etiam inhereat. Amictu caput pro galea contegit. Totum corpus alba pro lorica cooperit. Cingulum pro arcu, subcingulum pro pharetra assumit. Et est subcingulum quiddam in stola, quo ligatur cum cingulo. Cum stola collum circumdat, quasi hastam contra resistentem uibrat. Mappula sine manipulo pro claua utitur. Casula quasi clipeo protegitur. Manus libro pro gladio armatur.

33 De confessione sacerdotis ante missam

Sic itaque ad certamen munitus contra spiritualia nequitie in celestibus et pro sedanda iudicis ira in subditos ad altare procedit, et populus quasi pro suo pugile oraturus in profestis diebus terre prosternitur. Cum cantat orationes et reliqua recitat, quasi totis viribus contra dyabolum pugnat. Dum in euangelio casulam super humerum replicat, quasi gladium contra hostem preparat. Dum euangelium legitur, tanquam gladio percutitur diabolus. Pax in fine datur, ut populi quies hoste prostrato insinuetur. Inde data licentia reuertendi gratias Deo referens populus cum gaudio remeat ad propria.

4 Honorius Augustodunensis

Honorii Augustodunensis Operum Pars Tertia Liturgica *(Patrologia Latina, vol. 172)*. Honorius Augustodunensis: Gemma animae sive De divinis officiis et antiquo ritu missarum, deque horis canonicis et totius annis solemnitatibus *(Bibl. Patr. XX, p. 1046, ex edit. Melchioris Lotteri, Lipsiensis urbis typographi, anno 1514 data)*

69 Significatio processionum

Populus a Pharaone per Moysen ereptus, est Christianus populus a diabolo per Christum redemptus. Tabulae Testamenti a monte accipiuntur, et libri Evangelii ab altari ad portandum sumuntur; populus ibat armatus, et populus Christianus vadit fide et baptismate signatus. Prae turmis illorum signa ferebantur; et ante nos cruces et vexilla portantur. Eos columna ignis praecessit, et nos candelae lumen praecedit. Ille populus sanguine aspergebatur, iste aqua benedicta aspergitur; levitae tabernaculum foederis portaverunt, et hic diaconi et subdiaconi plenaria et capsas gerunt. Arca testamenti a sacerdotibus portabatur; et scrinium vel feretrum cum reliquiis a patribus portatur. Aaron summus sacerdos sequitur ornatus, et apud nos episcopus, summus scilicet sacerdos, sequitur infulatus. Rex si adest cum sceptro rector populi, significat Moysen cum virga ductorem populi. Si rex non aderit, tunc pontifex utrumque exprimit, Moysen, baculum portando; Aaron, mitra caput velando. Clangor tubarum exprimitur per sonum campanarum.

72 De pugna Christianorum spirituali

Missa quoque imitatur cujusdam pugnae conflictum, et victoriae triumphum, qua hostis noster Amalech prosternitur, et via nobis ad patriam per Jesum panditur. Jesus quippe imperator noster cum diabolo pugnavit, et coelestem rempublicam ab hostibus destructam hominibus reparavit: cui cum posset producere duodecim legiones angelorum (Matthew 26), vel septuaginta duo millia militum, instruxit tantum agmen duodecim apostolorum, et expugnavit septuaginta duo genera linguarum. Pontificis namque et cleri, populique processio, est quasi imperatoris, et cujusdam exercitus ad bellum progressio. Hi cum subtus albis et desuper cappis, vel aliis solemnibus vestibus induuntur, quasi milites pugnaturi subtus loricis, desuper clypeis muniuntur. Cum de choro exeunt, quasi de regia curia procedunt. Quasi imperiale signum et vexilla a signiferis anteferuntur, cum ante nos crux et vexilla geruntur. Quasi duo exercitus sequuntur, dum hinc inde ordinatim cantantes gradiuntur. Inter quos vadunt magistri et praecentores quasi cohortium ductores ac belli incitatores. Sequuntur priores, quasi exercitus duces atque agminum ordinatores.

73 Quod episcopus spiritualiter agat vicem imperatoris

Procedit pontifex cum baculo, quasi imperator cum sceptro. Ante pontificem portantur sancta, sicut ante regem imperialia. Ante archiepiscopum crux portatur, sicut ante imperatorem gestatur; qui pallio decoratur, sicut rex corona perornatur. Comitatur turba plebis, quasi exercitus pedestris. Cum de basilica procedunt quasi de regia urbe turmae proruunt. Cum ad aliam ecclesiam procedimus, quasi ad castellum expugnandum pergimus: quod cum cantu intrabimus, quasi in dedicationem accipimus et inde auxiliarios nobis accimus; cum vero ad monasterium redimus, quasi ad locum certaminis tendimus. Scrinium cum reliquiis portamus contra daemones, sicut filii Israel portaverunt arcam Dei contra Philistiim hostes. Cum ecclesiam intramus, quasi ad stationem pervenimus. Cum campanae sonantur quasi per classica milites ad praelium incitantur. Quasi vero acies ad pugnam

ordinantur, dum utrimque in choro locatur. Qui crucem cum vexillo coram archi-
episcopo tenet, est signifer, qui vexillum coram imperatore in pugna fert.

74 Quod cantor sit signifer et tubicina

Cantor qui cantum inchoat, est tubicen qui signum ad pugnam dat. Praecentores
qui chorum utrinque regunt, sunt duces qui agmina ad pugnam instruunt. Cantores
capita piliolis tegunt, baculos vel tabulas manibus gerunt; quia praeliantes caput
galeis tegunt, armis bellicis se protegunt.

75 De bello spirituali

Bellum cum tubarum clangore et turbarum clamore committitur; et nostrum spir-
ituale bellum cum campanarum compulsatione, et cleri cantatione incipitur. Geritur
namque bellum non contra *carnem, et sanguinem; sed adversus principes, et potestates, adversus rectores tenebrarum harum, contra spiritualia nequitiae in coelestibus*
(Ephesians 6). Quasi ergo strenui milites pugnant, dum totis viribus utrinque cantant.
Ignea tela concupiscentiae nequissimi hostes immittunt, quae fortes viri fortiter scuto
fidei repellunt, hostes vitiorum acriter insistentes gladio verbi Dei prosternunt.

76 Quod cantores vicem ducem agant

Cantores manu et voce alios ad harmoniam incitant, quia et ducere alios manibus
pugnando, et voce hortando ad certamen instigant. Interim stat pontifex ad altare,
et pro laborantibus orationem recitat, sicut et Moyses in monte pro pugnantibus
orabat (Exodus 17).

77 De cantore, quod vicem praeconis agat

Lector qui Epistolam recitat, est praeco qui edicta imperatoris per castra praedicat.
Meliores voces ad *Graduale* vel *Alleluia* cantandum eliguntur, et fortiores manu
ad duellum producuntur. Jam deficientibus in cantu, alii succurrunt; ita multum
laborantibus in praelio, alii constantes corde subveniunt. Deinde sequentiam cum
voce et organis jubilant; quia victoriam cum plausu et cantu celebrant. Diaconus
qui Evangelium in alto recitat, est praeco qui peracto bello agmina dispersa cum
tuba convocat. Quod episcopus populum exhortando alloquitur, significat quod
imperator victores laudando affatur. Quod tunc oblationes offeruntur, significat
quod spolia victoribus coram imperatore dividuntur. Cantus offertorii, est laus
quam offerunt imperatori.

78 De David cum Christo et Goliath cum diabolo comparatis

Multiplici itaque hoste, ab Jesu, qui et Josue, superato, et victori populo ob pacis
abundantiam negligentia resoluto, rursus Philistaei adversus Israel conveniunt,

crudele bellum indicitur. Ex quibus Goliath procedit, duellum petit. Cui David
cum pastorali pera occurrit funda, et lapide cum dejecit, proprio mucrone perfo-
dit. Populus autem liberatus, pro victoria Deo immmolat victimam, pro gratiarum
actione laudes jubilat. David Hierusalem venienti turba populorum obviam ruit,
salvatorem populi hymnis excepit. Sic quoque vitiis a Christiano populo superatis,
denuo consurgit, negligenti animae acrius bellum infertur. Ex quibus gigas Goliath,
scilicet diabolus, procedit, duellum petit, dum quemlibet Christianum ad singularia
vitia allicit. Cui fortis animus cum sacra Scriptura, ut David, cum mulc[t]ro lactis
[note: Id est, cum ephi polenta et panibus decem (1 Kings 17: 17)] occurrit funda,
et lapide, dejecit: dum per humanitatem Christi quae sitienti populo erat petra, et
credentibus populis lapis angularis eum devincit, proprio ense prostratum jugulat,
dum hostem malignum fragili carne superat.

79 Mysterium

Cum ergo a subdiacono, et aliis sacrificium instituitur quasi David a Saul et populo armis induitur (1 Kings 17). Cum oblationes super altare ponuntur, quasi
arma David deponuntur. Porro cum pontifex ad altare venit, quasi David adversus Philistaeum procedit. Per calicem mulctrale accipitur, per corporale funda, per
oblatam petra intelligitur. Praefatio quae cantatur, fuit clamor quo pugil gigas ad
duellum provocabatur, per Canonis deprecationem, intelligimus populi orationem.
Sacerdotis inclinatio, est fundae lapide imposito rotatio. Panis elevatio est lapidis jac-
tatio. Ubi denuo inclinatur, significat quod hostis prosternitur. Ubi autem diaconus
ad sacerdotem venit, et calicem cum eo elevans deponit, designat quod David ad
prostratum cucurrit, extracto gladio caput abstulit. Deinde data pace populus com-
municat quia accepta per David pace populus Deo sacrificans participat. Cantus in
communione, est laus populi pro victoriae exsultatione. Oratio et benedictio quae
sequitur, est trophaeum quo David a populo Jerusalem veniens excipiebatur. His
peractis, populus ad propria remeat, quia populus tunc post victoriam cum gaudio
ad propria repedabat.

(80 Item de missa et de judicio)

81 De pugna Philistaei

Hoc ut dictum est in figura praecesserat, quando David cum Goliath congressus
populum a tyrannide ejus eruerat (1 Kings 17), quia et Christus cum diabolo duellum subierat et populum oppressum ab eo eripiebat. Philisthim namque Israel
impugnabat, et daemonum caterva humanus genus vexabat; hostes contra populum
Dei aciem direxerant, et daemones contra justos tyrannos incitaverant; hostes se
vallo munierant, et daemones per philosophos errores firmaverant. Goliath agmini-
bus Dei exprobrabat, et diabolus cultoribus Dei per idolatriam insultabat. David a
patre suo ad pugnam mittitur, et Christus a Patre in mundum ad certamen dirigitur.
David oves pavit, et Christus innocens ad pascua vitae congregavit. David ursum

vel leonem superavit, et Christus diabolum se tentantem superavit. David ovibus derelictis ad locum certaminis tendit, et Christus a discipulis derelictus ad conciliabula hostium venit. Veniente David clamor in castris oritur, et Christo inter Judaeos veniente clamor *reus est mortis* exoritur. David a militibus armis Saul induitur, moxque eisdem exuitur (1 Kings 17), et Christus a militibus vestibus Pilati, scilicet purpura et Chlamide coccinea induitur, moxque eisdem exuitur. David contra Philistaeum baculum portavit, et Christus crucem contra diabolum bajulavit. David mulctrum et Christus accepit vas aceto plenum. Hostis funda et lapide prosternitur, et diabolus Christi carne vincitur. Per fundam quippe, Christi caro; per lapidem, ejus anima, per David, deitas intelligitur. Petra itaque de funda excussa frontem superbi penetrat, quia anima Christi, de carne tormentis excussa, regnum tyranni penetrans infernum spoliat. Proprio ense victum jugulat, quia per mortem auctorem mortis vicit. Reverso David populus laetatur, et Christo ab inferis regresso populus fidelium congratulatur. David Jerusalem veniens a turbis cum cantu excipitur, et Christus ab Jerusalem coelos ascensurus ab angelis hymnologis laudibus suscipitur.

82 De armis sacerdotis

Sacerdos itaque pugil noster cum hoste populi congressurus, armis munitur spiritualibus, quia pugnaturus est contra spiritualia nequitiae in coelestibus (Ephesians 6: 12). Denique sandaliis se pro ocreis induit, caput humerali pro galea tegit, totum corpus alba pro lorica vestit. Cum stolam collo circumdat, quasi hastam ad resistendum vibrat. Cingulo pro arcu se cingit, sub cingulum pro pharetra sibi appendit. Casula pro clypeo protegitur, manipulo pro pugili clavo utitur. Porro libro, in quo est verbum Dei pro gladio armatur, per confessionem diaboli Domino renuntiatur, sicque hostis ad singulare certamen provocatur, quasi enim totis viribus pugnat, dum cantum et orationes et reliqua contra diabolum recitat. Dum ad Evangelium super humerum projicit, quasi gladium arripit. Dum legitur Evangelium quasi ense petit diabolum.

5 Sicard of Cremona

Opera Omnia Sicardi *(Patrologia Latina, vol. 213) Sicardus Cremonensis,* Sicardi Cremonensis Episcopi Mitrale seu de Officiis Ecclesiasticis Summa

Book III: De Officiis Ministrorum Ecclesiae, Chapter IX: Brevis Recapitulatio Missae

Judicasti, Domine, causam meam (Lamentations 3). Nulli dubium quod missa pugnae sit repraesentativa, repraesentans cujusdam pugnae conflictum et victoriae triumphum. Et quod repraesentat nobis triplicem pugnam: unam figurantem, duplicem figuratam; unam in capite, aliam in membris. Figurans fuit cum Moyses Amalec prostravit (Exodus 17), Josue septem populos expugnavit (Joshua 6 et infra). David Goliam, Saulem et Philisthaeos superavit. Figurata in capite est, quia

Christus cum diabolo pugnans, ipsum superavit et infernum exspoliavit; figurata in membris est, quia impugnamur, non solum a mundo, sed a carne et a diabolo; non est enim nobis colluctatio adversus carnem et sanguinem, sed adversus principes et potestates (Ephesians 6). Sacerdos itaque celebrans missam ex his quae facit, et quae circa eum fiunt, breviter et velociter habeat in mente, figurantia quae praecessere, figurata quae sunt in capite completa, et quae sunt a nobis moribus adimplenda. Cum processionem facimus cum vexillis, reliquiis, libris, cereis et thuribulis, recolamus Moysen, qui signis et prodigiis de Aegypto populum per desertum ad terram promissionis perduxit (Exodus 7 et infra.). Ibi populus armatus, hic clerus sacris vestibus. Ibi arca, hic scrinium reliquiarum. Ibi tabulae Testamenti de monte Sinai, hic liber Evangelii de altari. Ibi columna ignis, hic cereus igneus. Ibi virga, hic sceptrum regis vel baculus pontificis. Ibi Moyses et Aaron, hic rex et episcopus, vel episcopus repraesentans utrumque; in baculo regem, in mitra pontificem. Recolamus et Josue qui Jericho circuivit (Joshua 6), quae corruit, et populus regnum obtinuit. Ibi clangor tubarum, hic strepitus campanarum. Recolamus David (2 Kings 6) et Salomonem (3 Kings 8), qui arcam Dei hymnis et canticis reduxerunt, et in templo locaverunt. Simus memores Jesu Christi, qui de sinu Patris venit in mundum (John 8; I Timothy 1); de praesepi ad templum (Luke 2); de Bethania in Hierusalem (John 12); de Hierusalem in montem (Matthew 27; John 19): optantes ut de mundo revertamur ad patriam, quasi de una Ecclesia ad aliam; de militanti ad triumphantem: sequentes crucem, id est vestigia Crucifixi, et nos vitiis et concupiscentiis crucifigentes (Galatians 5). Sequentes vestigia sanctorum, praecepta Evangeliorum; induti loricam justitiae, cingulum continentiae, scutum fidei, galeam salutis aeternae (Ephesians 6). Unde sacerdos pugnaturus contra spiritualia nequitiae in coelestibus, sacris vestibus quasi induitur armis, sumens sandalia pro ocreis, ne quid pulveris inhaereat pedibus, amictum pro galea, albam pro lorica, cingulum pro arcu, subcingulum pro pharetra, stolam pro hasta, mapulam vel manipulam pro clava, casulam pro clypeo, librum pro gladio. Sic armatus pro omnibus ad altare procedit, et per confessionem diabolo renuntiat, et se accusat; quia sapiens in principio sermonis accusator est sui (Proverbs 18). Per orationes et cantus diabolum incitat, dum casulam super humerum complicat, gladium contra hostem parat. Dum legitur epistola voce praeconis, imperatoris dantur edicta. Cantor est tubicen, praecentores, qui chorum regunt, duces qui exercitum ad pugnam instruunt: quibus lassescentibus alii subveniunt. Cantus sequentiae, plausus est victoriae. Dum evangelium legitur, adversarius vulneratur, aut exercitus dispersus post victoriam adunatur; quem dum praedicat episcopus, imperator laudans victores affatur; oblationes sunt spolia, quae victoribus dividuntur. Cantus offertorii, triumphus qui exhibetur imperatori. Sed rursus populo negligentia resoluto, Philisthaeus consurgit adversus Israel. Unde inter Goliam et David duellum indicitur (Kings 17): haec est torpens anima, vel genus humanum, cui diabolus bellum indicit, sed a Christo, qui pro nobis pugnat, vincitur; hic est enim verus David, *manu fortis et visu desiderabilis,* qui a Patre ad pugnam mittitur; qui oves pavit, qui ursum et leonem superavit (Kings 17); qui baculum contra Philisthaeum portavit, dum crucem contra diabolum bajulavit.

6 Nikolaus Stör (?)

6 Nikolaus Stör (?), Officij misse sacrique canonis expositio
(Strasbourg: Henricus Arimensis, c.1476), Book I, Tract 5, Chapter 1

Allegorice autem vestes sacerdotales generaliter loquendo significant virtutes quibus sacerdotes armari debent contra spirituales nequicias pugnaturi. De quibus
armaturis dicit apostolicus ad ephe. ult. *Induite vos armatura dei … et gladium spiritus quod est verbum dei.*

7 John Lydgate, *Vertue of the Masse*

John Lydgate, Vertue of the Masse, *from Thomas F. Simmons (ed.),*
The Lay Folks Mass Book, or The Manner of Hearing Mass, *Early
English Text Society, Original Series 71 (London: Trübner, 1879;
reprint London, New York, Toronto: Oxford University Press, 1968),
pp. 167–8.*

The morallisacioun of þe prist whan he gothe to masse

Vpon his hede, an Amyte, the prist hathe,
Whiche is a signe. tokene of figure,
Outwarde a shewyng. grounded on the faithe.
The large Awbe …[etc.]
A prist made stronge. withe this armure
A fore the Awtier. as cristis champioun
Shal stonde vpright. make no discomfiture,
owre thre enemyes. venquysshe and bere downe
The flesshe the world. Sathan the felle dragoun.
First to begynne. or he further passe
Withe contrite. and lowe confessioun,
And so procede. devoutly to the masse.

8 Thirteenth-century Pontifical of the Roman Court

Michel Andrieu (ed.), Le Pontifical Romain au moyen-âge, *vol. 2:*
Le Pontifical de la curie Romaine au XIIIe siècle *(Vatican City:
Biblioteca Apostolica Vaticana, 1940), pp. 385–403. The text below
follows one of the variant readings given in the edition.*

Ordo ad benedicendum seu coronandum imperatorem.

1. Cum rex in imperatorem electus pervenerit ad portam Collinam, que est iuxta
castellum Crescentii, recipiatur honorifice a clero urbis cum crucibus et turibu-
lis et processionaliter deducatur usque ad gradus basilice sancti Petri, cantantibus

universis Resp. *Ecce mitto angelum meum*, camerariis eius missilia spargentibus ante ipsum et prefecto urbis gladium preferente.

…

5. Quo demum surgente, rex ipse a parte dextera et prior diaconorum (cardinalium) a parte sinistra deducant eum usque ad ecclesiam sancte Marie in Turribus, ubi ante altare, subdiacono evangelii tenente, rex super eum corporaliter prestet huiusmodi iuramentum:

6. *Ego enim N[omen], rex romanorum, annuente domino futurus imperator, promitto, spondeo et polliceor (atque iuro) coram Deo et beato Petro me de cetero protectorem ac defensorem fore summi pontificis et sancte romane ecclesie in omnibus necessitatibus et utilitatibus suis, custodiendo et conservando possessiones, honores et iura eius, quantum divino fultus adiutorio fuero, secundum scire et posse meum, recta et pura fide. Sic me Deus adiuvet et hec sancta Dei evangelia.*

…

15. Post hec procedant ad altare sancti Mauritii, ubi Hostiensis episcopus ungat ei de oleo exorcizato brachium dextrum et inter scapulas et hanc orationem dicendo …

…

23. Cumque lecta fuerit epistola et graduale et *Alleluia* cantatum, interpolata cantilena, imperator procedat processionaliter ad altare et ibi summus pontifex gladium evaginatum de altari sumit eique tradit, curam intelligens imperii totius in gladio sic dicendo:

24. *Accipe gladium de super beati Petri corpore sumptum, per nostras manus licet indignas, vice tamen et auctoritate sanctorum apostolorum consecratas, imperialiter tibi concessum nostreque benedictionis officio in defensionem sancte Dei ecclesie divinitus ordinatum, ad vindictam malefactorum, laudem vero bonorum. Et memento de quo psalmista prophetavit dicens: "Accingere gladio tuo circa femur tuum potentissime," ut in hoc per eundem vim equitatis exerceas, molem iniquitatis potenter destruas et sanctam Dei ecclesiam eiusque fideles propugnes ac protegas, nec minus sub fide falsos quam christiani nominis hostes execres ac dispergas, viduas ac pupillos clementer adiuves ac defendas, desolata restaures, restaurata conserves, ulciscaris iniusta, confirmes bene disposita, quatenus hec agendo, virtutum triumpho gloriosus iustitieque cultor egregius cum mundi salvatore, cuius tipum geris in nomine, sine fine regnare merearis. Qui cum …*

25. His verbis expletis, accingit illi ensem in vagina repositum, ita dicens:

Accingere gladio tuo super femur tuum, potentissime, et attende quia sancti non in gladio, sed per fidem vicerunt regna.

26. Mox autem accinctus eximit gladium de vagina viriliterque ter illum vibrat et vagine continuo recommendat.

27. Eo igitur sic accincto et beati Petri milite mirabiliter facto, subsequenter apostolicus imponit ei mitram clericalem in capite, ac super mitram imperatorium diadema de altari sumptum, dicens:

28. *Accipe signum glorie, diadema regni, coronam imperii, in nomine patris et filii et spiritus sancti, ut spreto antiquo hoste spretisque contagiis vitiorum omnium, sic*

iustitiam, misericordiam et iudicium diligas, et ita iuste et misericorditer et pie vivas, ut ab ipso domino nostro Iesu Christo in consortio sanctorum eterni regni coronam percipias. Qui cum ...

...

41. Post hec, evangelio decantato, imperator, corona et manto depositis, accedat ad summum pontificem et offerat ad pedes eius aurum quantum sibi placuerit.

42. Ipsoque pontifice descendente pro perficiendis missarum misteriis ad altare, imperator more subdiaconi offerat [ei] calicem et ampullam et stet ibi donec pontifex ad sedem reversus communicet, sacramque communionem de manu eius suscipiat cum osculo pacis et sic ad thalamum rediens in ambonem resumat mantum pariter et coronam.

9 Tenth-century Romano-German pontifical

Cyrille Vogel and Reinhard Elze (eds.), Le Pontifical Romano-Germanique du dixième siècle, *2 vols. (Vatican City: Biblioteca Apostolica Vaticana, 1963), vol. I, pp. 379–80.*

Benedictio ensis noviter succincti

1. *Exaudi, quesumus, domine, preces nostras, et hunc ensem, quo hic famulus tuus N[omen] se circumcingi desiderat, maiestatis tue dextera benedicere dignare, quatinus defensio atque protectio possit esse aecclesiarum, viduarum, orphanorum omniumque Deo servientium contra sevitiam paganorum, aliisque insidiantibus sit pavor, terror et formido. Per [Jesum Christum dominum nostrum.]*

2. Alia. *Famulum tuum N[omen], quaesumus, domine, piaetatis tuae custodia muniat, ut hunc ensem, quem te inspirante desiderat suscipere, te adiuvante illesum custodiat. Per [Jesum Christum dominum nostrum.]*

3. Alia. *Benedic, domine, sancte pater omnipotens, per invocationem sancti nominis tui, et per adventum filii tui, dom. n. Iesu Christi, atque per donum spiritus paracliti, hunc ensem, ut is, qui hodierna die tua pietate eo precingitur, visibiles inimicos sub pedibus conculcet victoriaque per omnia potitus semper maneat illesus. Per [Jesum Christum dominum nostrum.]*

4. (Tunc cantetur antiphona ista): *Speciosus forma pre filiis hominum. Diffusa est gratia in labiis tuis. Accingere gladio tuo super femur tuum, potentissime.*

5. Oratio unde supra. *Omnipotens sempiterne Deus, qui famulum tuum N[omen] eminenti mucrone circumcingi iussisti, fac illum contra cuncta adversantia ita caelestibus armari praesidiis, quo nullis hic et in evum tempestatibus bellorum turbetur. Per [Jesum Christum dominum nostrum.]*

Oratio pro exercitu

Praebe, domine, misericoridiae tuae opem exercitui nostro, et sub aeris claritate presta eis optatum proficiscendi auxilium, et, sicut Israeheli properanti ex Egypto securitatis prebuisti munimen, ita populo tuo in prelium pergenti lucis auctorem dirige angelum, qui eos die noctuque ab omni adversitate defendat. Sit eis itinerandi sine labore profectus, ubique providus eventus, meatus sine formidine, conversatio sine fastidio, moderata fragilitas sine metu, fortitudo sine terrore, copia rerum et proeliandi recta voluntas, et, cum, tuo angelo duce, victor extiterit, non suis tribuat viribus, sed ipsi victori Christo filio tuo gratias referat de triumpho, qui humilitate suae passionis de morte mortisque principe in cruce triumphavit. Qui tecum vivit ...

10 Pontifical of Durandus

Michel Andrieu (ed.), Le pontifical Romain au moyen-âge, *vol. 3:* Le Pontifical de Guillaume Durand *(Vatican City: Biblioteca Apostolica Vaticana, 1940), pp. 447–50; 549–50*

XXVIII. De benedictione novi militis

1. In benedictione novi militis hoc modo proceditur. Pontifex enim priusquam dicatur evangelium benedicit ensem eius, dicens:

2. Benedictio ensis. *Exaudi, quesumus, domine, preces nostras, et hunc ensem, quo hic famulus tuus circumcingi desiderat, maiestatis tue dextera dignare benedicere, quatenus esse possit defensio ecclesiarum, viduarum, orphanorum, omniumque Deo servientium contra sevitiam paganorum, aliisque sibi insidiantibus sit terror et formido, prestans ei eque persecutionis et iuste defensionis effectum. Per Christum ...* Resp.: *Amen.*

3. Alia benedictio. *Benedic, domine sancte, pater omnipotens, eterne Deus, per invocationem sancti tui nominis et per adventum Christi filii tui domini nostri et per donum spiritus sancti paracliti hunc ensem, ut is, famulus tuus, qui hodierna die hoc, tua concedente pietate, precingitur, invisibiles inimicos sub pedibus conculcet victoriaque per omnia potitus semper maneat illesus. Per [Jesum Christum dominum nostrum.]* Resp.: *Amen.*

4. Possent etiam hic dici alie benedictiones armorum quas require infra, sub benedictione armorum. Armis itaque benedictis, priusquam cingat illi ensem, premittit:

5. *Benedictus dominus Deus meus, qui docet manus meas ad prelium.* Et dictis primis tribus versibus, cum *Gloria patri,* dicit:

V[ersus] *Salvum fac servum tuum. Esto ei, domine, turris. Domine exaudi. Dominus vobiscum. Oremus.*

6. Oratio. *Domine sancte, pater omnipotens, eterne Deus, qui cuncta solus ordinas et recte disponis, qui, ad cohercendum malitiam reproborum et tuendum iustitiam, usum gladii in terris hominibus tua salubri dispositione permisisti et militarem ordinem ad populi protectionem institui voluisti, quique per beatum Ioannem militibus ad se in deserto venientibus, ut neminem concuterent sed propriis contenti essent stipendiis, dici fecisti, clementiam tuam, domine, suppliciter exoramus, ut, sicut David puero tuo Goliam superandi largitus es facultatem et Iudam Machabeum de feritate gentium nomen tuum non invocantium triumphere fecisti, ita et huic famulo*

tuo, qui noviter iugo militiae colla supponit, pietate celesti vires et audaciam ad fidei et iustitie defensionem tribuas, et prestes fidei, spei et caritatis augmentum et Dei timorem pariter et amorem, humilitatem, perseverantiam, obedientiam et patientiam bonam et cuncta in eo recte disponas, ut neminem cum gladio isto vel alio iniuste ledat, et omnia cum eo iusta et recta defendat, et, sicut ipse de minori statu ad novum militie provehitur honorem, ita, veterem hominem deponens cum actibus suis, novum induat hominem, ut te timeat et recte colat, perfidorum consortia vitet et suam in proximum caritatem extendat, proposito suo in omnibus recte obediat et suum in cunctis iuste officium exequatur. Per [Jesum Christum dominum nostrum.] Resp.: *Amen.*

7. Post hec pontifex ensem nudum sumit de altari et ponit illum in dextera manu illius, dicens: *Accipe gladium istum, in nomine patris et filii et spiritus sancti, et utaris eo ad defensionem tuam et sancte Dei ecclesie et ad confusionem inimicorum crucis Christi et fidei christiane et corone regni Francie, vel talis, et, quantum humana fragilitas tibi permiserit, cum eo neminem iniuste ledas. Quod ipse prestare dignetur, qui cum patre et spiritu sancto vivit et regnat per omnia secula seculorum.* Resp.: *Amen.*

8. Deinde, ense in vagina reposito, cingit illi ensem cum vagina et cingendo dicit: *Accingere gladio tuo super femur tuum, potentissime, in nomine domini nostri Iesu Christi, et attende quod sancti non in gladio sed per fidem vicerunt regna.*

9. Ense igitur accincto, miles novus illum de vagina educit et evaginatum ter in manu viriliter vibrat et, eo super brachium terso, mox in vaginam reponit.

10. Quo facto, insigniens illum caractere militari, dat sibi osculum pacis, dicens: *Esto miles pacificus, strenuus, fidelis et Deo devotus.*

11. Et mox dat sibi alapam leviter, dicens: *Exercitus a sompno malitie et vigila in fide Christi et fama laudabili.* Amen.

12. Tunc nobiles astantes imponunt sibi calcaria, ubi hoc fieri mos est, et cantatur antiphona: *Speciosus forma pre filiis hominum, accingere gladio tuo super femur tuum potentissime.*

13. Oratio. *Omnipotens sempiterne Deus, super hunc famulum tuum N[omen], qui eminente mucrone circumcingi desiderat, gratiam tue benedictionis infunde et eum dextere tue virtute fretum fac contra cuncta adversantia celestibus armari presidiis, quo nullis in hoc seculo tempestatibus bellorum turbetur. Per [Jesum Christum dominum nostrum.]*

14. Ultimo dat illi vexillum, ubi hoc fieri mos est. Cuius vexilli benedictionem require infra, sub benedictione armorum.

XXXVIII. De benedictione armorum

1. Armorum et vexilli bellici benedictio fit hoc modo: *Adiutorium nostrum in nomine domini. Dominus vobiscum. Oremus.*

Oratio. *Signaculum et benedictio Dei omnipotentis, patris et filii et spiritus sancti sit super hec arma et super induentem ea, quibus ad tuendam iustitiam induatur, rogantes te, domine Deus, ut illum protegas et defendas. Qui vivis.* Resp.: *Amen.*

2. Oratio. *Deus omnipotens, in cuius manu victoria plena consistit, quique etiam David ad expugnandum rebellem Goliam vires mirabiles tribuisti, clementiam tuam humili prece deposcimus, ut hec arma almifica pietate benedicere dignare et concede famulo tuo N[omen] eadem gestare cupienti, ut ad munimen ac defensionem sancte matris ecclesie, pupillorum et viduarum, contra visibilium et invisibilium hostium impugnantionem, ipsis libere et victoriose utatur. Per Christum [dominum nostrum].* Resp.: *Amen.*

3. Benedictio gladii. *Benedicere digneris, quesumus, domine, enses istos et hos famulos tuos, qui eos te inspirante suscipere desiderant, pietatis tue custodia muniat et illesos custodiat. Per [Jesum Christum dominum nostrum.]* Resp.: *Amen.*

4. Benedictio vexilli bellici. Oratio. *Omnipotens sempiterne Deus, qui es cunctorum benedictio et triumphantium fortitudo, respice propitius ad preces humilitatis nostre et hoc vexillum, quod bellico usui preparatum est, celesti benedictione sanctifica et contra adversarias et rebelles nationes sit validum tuoque munimine circumseptum; sitque inimicis christiani populi terribile atque in te credentibus solidamentum et victorie certa fiducia. Tu es, Deus, qui conteris bella et celestis presidii sperantibus in te prestas auxilium. Per [Jesum Christum dominum nostrum.]* Resp.: *Amen.*

5. Ultimo aspergat eum cum aqua benedicta.

6. In traditione vero vexilli ita dicitur: *Accipe vexillum celesti benedictione sanctificatum, sitque inimicis populi christiani terribile. Det tibi dominus gratiam, ut ad ipsius nomen et honorem cum illo hostium cuneos potenter penetres incolumis et securus.* Resp.: *Amen.*

7. Tradendo autem illud vexillifero det ei osculum pacis.

11 Naples, Biblioteca Nazionale, MS VI. E. 40 *L'homme armé* Masses 2–6: canons and Kyrie tropes

Mass 2: cantus firmus text: *L'homme armé, L'homme armé, L'homme armé*

Canon

Ambulat hic armatus homo, verso quoque vultu arma rapit; dexteram sequitur, sic ut vice versa ad levam scandat. Vultus sumendo priores ipse retrograditur; respondent ultima primis.

Here the armed man walks, and with his face turned too. He seizes arms, and pursues a rightward course in such a way that when the times are changed he may climb to the left. Assuming his prior countenance he retreats: the end corresponds to the beginning.

Kyrie

Kyrie virtutis auctor, virique creator, celi terre ponthique sator, eleyson.

Kyrie fidei miro, arma donans viro, quis cum hoste dimicet diro, eleyson.

Kyrie cuius virtute, vir armatus tute, hostem vincit gaudet salute, eleyson.

Christe salvator, viri potens armator, armorum dator, quibus hostis fit vir trium-phator, effugatus abit temptator, eleyson.

Kyrie spiritus alme, viro donans arma palme, dono septemplice, patris nati nexus unice, eleyson.

Lord, author of virtue and creator of man, maker of heaven, earth and sea, have mercy upon us.

Lord, by the miracle of faith giving arms to man with which he might fight with the obstinate enemy, have mercy upon us.

Lord by whose virtue the armed man conquers the enemy in safety and rejoices in salvation, have mercy upon us.

Christ, Savior, powerful armer of man, giver of arms by which man is made trium-phant over the enemy, and the tempter retires, chased away, have mercy upon us.

Lord, nourishing Spirit, giving man arms of the palm by a sevenfold gift, single bond of the Father and Son, have mercy upon us.

Mass 3: cantus firmus text: *doibt on doubter, doibt on doubter*

Canon

Sic metuendus eat gressum rependendo ne pausat. Demum scandendo per dyates-saron it. Ast ubi concendit vice mox versa remeabit. Descensus finem per diapen-tem facit.

Thus let the one to be feared proceed, retracing his step. He pauses. Then, ascend-ing, he passes through a fourth. But where he has climbed up, he will remain in reverse. He makes his final descent by a fifth.

Kyrie

Kyrie summe Pater timuit te spiritus ater, Israel in pelago salvato pertimuit te pharao, gente mala timida salvato fideles eleyson.

Christe timende Deus sola moriturus iniquos voce subegisti presenti parce cat-erne eleyson.

Kyrie vivificum da sacri pneuma timoris quem dudum sanctis electis sponte dedisti eleyson.

Lord, Father most high, the dark spirit feared you; when Israel was saved in the sea, Pharaoh feared you greatly, who saved the fearful faithful from a cowardly evil race; have mercy upon us.

Christ, God who art to be feared, with your voice alone thou has subjugated the iniquitous at the hour of death. Spare your ready army, have mercy upon us.

Lord, give the quickening spirit of a holy fear, which you once gavest freely to your holy elect, have mercy upon us.

Mass 4: cantus firmus text: *On a fait partout crier*

Canon

Buccina clangorem voces vertendo reflectit, subque gradu reboat iterum clamando quaterno.

The trumpet reflects the sound, turning the pitches around; it echoes, calling out again at the fourth degree below.

Kyrie

Kyrie altitonans genitor Deus orbis conditor alme eleyson.
Qui Moysem revocare tuba populum voluisti, eleyson.
Te tuba cuncta canat nostra quoque suscipe vota, eleyson.
Christe, Deus homoque judex ultor vitiorum eleyson.
Cuius judicium tuba precinet alta futurum eleyson.
Voce tube populis indulge vivificandis eleyson.
Qui sonitu magno veniens tua dona dedisti eleyson.
Spiritus immense Patri natoque coeve eleyson.
Ultima soleris nos cum tuba fine sonabit eleyson.

Lord, God thundering from on high; nourishing creator of the world, have mercy upon us.
Who wished Moses to revive his people with the trumpet, have mercy upon us.
May every trumpet sing to you, and also receive our prayers, have mercy upon us.
Christ, God and man, judge and punisher of sins, have mercy upon us.
Whose coming judgment the trumpet shall sing from on high, have mercy upon us.
At the sound of the trumpet be merciful to your awakening people, have mercy upon us.
Who, coming with a great noise, gave your gifts, have mercy upon us.
Boundless Spirit with Father and Son coeval, have mercy upon us.
May you comfort us at the end when the final trumpet shall sound, have mercy upon us.

Mass 5: cantus firmus text: *d'un haubregon de fer*

Canon

Per dyapente sonat subter remeando lorica. Post ubi finierit gressum renovando resumit. Tuque gradu sursum cantando revertere quinto. Principio finem da qui modularis eundem.

The breastplate sounds, returning a fifth below; then, where it has stopped, it resumes its step once again. And do you, in singing, return in the fifth degree above; You who make music, give an end that is the same as the beginning.

Kyrie

[Kyrie] O Deus excelse lorica casside tali protege Christicolas famulosque tuos velud olim David Goliam vicit et Israel hostem eleyson.

   Christe spei galea scuto fideique salutis contritis tenebris nos indue lucis et armis eleyson.

   [Kyrie] Spiritus optime da loricam dulcis amoris obstantem jaculis nos quis ferit immundus hostis, eleyson.

Lord, O exalted God, with such a breastplate and helmet protect Christians and your servants, just as once David vanquished Goliath and Israel her enemy, have mercy upon us.

   Christ, clothe us with the helmet of hope, with the shield of faith in salvation from the penitent shadows, and with the armor of light, have mercy upon us.

   Lord, perfect spirit, give the breastplate of sweet love that resists the javelins with which the foul enemy strikes us, have mercy upon us.

Mass 6: cantus firmus text: *entire song*

Arma virumque cano vincorque per arma virumque
Alterni gradimur hic ubi signo tacet.
Sub lychanos hypaton oritur sic undique pergit
Visceribus propriis conditur ille meis.

I sing of arms and a man, and am conquered by arms and a man. We step in alternation; here where I sign [at the *signum congruentiae*], he is silent. He rises up beneath the *lichanos hypaton* and thus proceeds everywhere. He himself is formed from my own inmost being.

Kyrie

[Kyrie] alme Pater summeque Deus celi quoque rector, eleyson.
Principium finis immensi conditor orbis, eleyson.
Ne pereat da plasma tuum sed pace fruatur, eleyson.
Christe coeterne splendor sapientia virtus eleyson.
Lumen imago Patris lux verbum nate redemptor, eleyson.
Sanguine perfuso proprio tu parce redemptis, eleyson.
[Kyrie] spiritus une Dei nexus spiramen amorque, eleyson.
Igne sono linguis qui missus dona dedisti, eleyson.
Munere tu nostra septemplice complue corda, eleyson.

Lord, nourishing father and God most high, also ruler of heaven, have mercy upon us.
Beginning, end, creator of the boundless world, have mercy upon us.
Grant that your created one may not perish, but delight in peace, have mercy upon us.

Christ, coeternal splendor, wisdom and virtue, have mercy upon us.

Ornament, image of the father, light, word incarnate, redeemer, have mercy upon us.

Through the shedding of your own blood, you spare the redeemed, have mercy upon us.

[Lord] one spirit, bond, breath and love, have mercy upon us.

Through fire, sound and tongues, you who were sent gave gifts, have mercy upon us.

Shower upon our hearts with your sevenfold gift, have mercy upon us.

Appendix 2: Texts concerning secular music in church

For sources of the texts cited, see p. 246

Navarrus on secular music in church

Martin de Azpilcueta (Navarrus) (1493–1586), testimony recorded by
Cardinal Caietanus, De horis canonicis *(1578), XVI, n. 43 (quoted in*
Gerbert, p. 226)[1]

… spirituali gravitati divini officii profanam quandam & levem in *Galliis* inventam
cantilenam, iam nimis in *Hispaniis* receptam, qua fere ad vivum repraesentantur
tumultus praelii cum sonitu tympanorum, & tubarum, & toto strepitu bellico. Nam
licet haec repraesentatio de se non sit inhonesta, & conviviis recreationique seculari
sit apta; inepta tamen valde est officiis divinis, quiete dicendis, & eorum fini, qui
est, erigere animas & spiritus ad meditandum divina, & ad Deum super omnia dili-
gibilia diligendum, & peccatum mortiferum, quod nos ab eo separat, super omnia
odibilia odio habendum: ad quae parum promovet strepitus ille bellicus, magis
ferociens, quam leniens animos.

Organs/instruments in church

Chapter acts of the Cathedral of Breslau, 1502 (Alfred Sabisch [ed.], Acta
Capituli Wratislaviensis 1500–1562: Die Sitzungsprotokolle des Breslauer
Domkapitels in der ersten Hälfte des 16. Jahrhunderts, Erster Band,
1500–1516, *Erster Halbband, 1500–1513 [Cologne and Vienna: Böhlau,*
1972], p. 128, statute 186, 1502. [dec. 16. fer. VI])

(2) Eodem die Melchior Schondecher [note: Organist der Domkirche] organista
novus capitulariter susceptus est et dictum est sibi, quod sit diligens in officio suo et
cantilenas saeculares non cantet in organis, quae magis pertinent ad choreas.

Council of Sens, 1528 (Mansi XXXII, p. 1190; also quoted in Gerbert,
p. 195 and Clive, III, 99; partial translation in Fellerer, 578)

Organorum usum ecclesia a patribus ad cultum servitiumque divinum recepit.
Nolumus itaque quod organicis instrumentis resonet in ecclesia impudica aut lasciva melodia, sed sonus omnino dulcis, qui nihil praeter hymnos divinos & cantica
spiritualia repraesentet.

Synod of Cologne, 1536 (Schannat VI, p. 255; see also Mansi XXXII, p. 1227; translation in Fellerer, 578)

Organorum melodia quemadmodum temperanda. Cap. XV.
Organorum melodia in templis sic adhibebitur, ne lasciviam magis, quam devotionem excitet; neve praeter Hymnos Divinos ac cantica spiritualia quicquam resonet, ac repraesentet.

The music of organs should be used in churches in such a manner that it should not arouse more titillation than devotion; nor should it produce any sound or representation other than divine hymns or spiritual chants.

Synod of Augsburg, 1548 (Mansi XXXII, p. 1309)

Organa ad populi aures nullum alium sonitum, aut numerum deferant, quam qui religiosus ac pius ab omnibus habeatur. Melodiae lascivae aut alio pertinentes, procul absint: profani etiam rhythmi ecclesiasticis sonis, aut verba sentientiaeve ecclesiasticae profanis numeris aut rebus ludibrii causa non accommodentur. Nam cum aut melodiae aut orationes sententiaeve sacrae in profanam consuetudinen [*sic*] abeunt, fieri non potest, quin ad suum usum in ecclesiis depromptae animis audientium memoria illius ludibrii aut scommatis pungant, atque avocent a devotione.

Synod of Cologne, 1550 (Schnannat VI, p. 632; also quoted in Gerbert, pp. 195–6; translation in Fellerer, 578)

Num organa quid saeculare resonent, seu aliud, quam cantum Ecclesiasticum: Et, sileantne ab elevatione Eucharistiae, usque ad Agnus Dei: quo interea ab omnibus, sub alto silentio, devota Dominicae Passionis & Redemptionis nostrae memoria recolatur?

Should organs produce any secular sound? Should they produce any other than ecclesiastical? Should they not remain silent from the elevation of the host to the Agnus Dei, during which interval the thoughts of all should contemplate in deep silence the passion of our Lord and our redemption?

Synod of Cologne, 1550; Synod of Haarlem, 1564 (Schannat VI, p. 756; Schannat VII, p. 8; translation in Fellerer, 591)

Organa nihil lascivum sonent, aut saeculare, sed quod ipsa etiam plebs intelligat religiosum ac pium esse. Et praestiterit, Symbolum totum cani similiter Praefationem, & Orationem Dominicam, quam partem reliqui organis, sicut magno abusu alicubi consuetum est fieri.

Organs should produce no lascivious or secular sound but what the common people themselves know to be religious and pious, and it is better for the whole symbol

[Credo] to be sung like the Praefatio and the Lord's Prayer than for part of it to be left to the organs, as is customarily done in some places with great abuse.

Council of Arras, 1570 (Schannat VIII, p. 255)

Ubi organa sunt, efficiatur, ut nihil seculare sonent, seu aliud, quam Cantum Ecclesiasticum: omnino autem non pulsentur ab elevatione Eucharistiae usque ad Agnus Dei: quo interea ab omnibus, sub alto silentio, religiosa ac devota Dominicae Passionis, & nostrae Redemptionis memoria recolatur.

Synod of Tournai, 1600 (Schannat VIII, p. 479)

In solemni Missae Sacrificio praefatio, Dominicaque Oratio a Celebrante, Gloria in excelsis, & Symbolum Apostolorum a Clero integre decantentur, nec organis suprimantur, nec aliis caeremoniis, quam in Missali Romano praescriptis, utantur.

Synod of Augsburg, 1567 (Schannat VII, p. 164)

Organorum usus multis in locis est immodicus, atque corrigendus, ne sacras preces, & audientium pietatem impediat lasciva modulatio, neve musica intempestiva, quae neque simplex, neque gravis videatur, turpes vel profanas cantiones referens, effaeminatos potius demulceat, quam pios animos pascat. Nec decet sacros Hymnos, ut sunt: *Gloria in excelsis, Praefatio, Sanctus, Agnus,* abrumpi, vel aliis canticis aut modulationibus impediri, quo minus integre exaudiantur.

A nostris Ecclesiis arceri volumus, nullumque illic locum habere cantiones haereticorum, quantalibet modulationis & pietatis specie vulgo blandiantur. Antiquas vero & Catholicas cantilenas, praesertim, quas pii majores nostri Germani majoribus Ecclesiae festis adhibuerunt, vulgo permittimus, & in Ecclesiis, vel etiam Processionibus retineri probamus.

Council of Poissy, 1561 (refers back to the Council of Basel) (Monson, 30)

Laudes itaque divinae non festinanter, sed tractim servatis intervallis, dierum tamen festorum a profestis distinguendorum habita ratione, nec in altum sublata voce decantentur, quin etiam molles omnes fractique cantus, quos discantus vocant, quorum tumultus et strepitus potius auditur quam pronunciatio, tollantur vel emendentur aut in melius reformentur … Porro autem clerici et sacerdotes cantum suum ita instituant, ut ad pietatem et ad Deum populi animum excitent, et organa quidem, quorum usus est in templis, nihil praeter hymnos divinos et spiritualia cantica repraestentent, impudicas autem cantilenas et christianis auribus indignas modulando non referant. Dum autem et symbolum, quod est ab omnibus audiendum, recitatur, conticescant, neque evangelii et verborum propheticorum aut apostolicorum, quam vocamus epistolam, et praefationem, quae gratiarum actio dicitur, et precationem dominicam, quominus a populo audiantur, impediant, ut episcopus cum consilio seniorum capituli poterit decernere.

Synod of Constance, 1567; Provincial Council of Cambrai, 1565 (Schannat VII, pp. 488, 103–4; see also Gerbert, p. 186)

Organorum usum in Missis sic servari statuimus, uti Concilio Tridentino mandatum est: id est, ne modulatione lascivas cantationes imitentur. Caeterum, quae in Choro cani debent ad instructionem, ea canantur voce, ut intelligantur mente, non autem organis, quae aeque aedificare nequeunt, ut viva vox, piae mentis interpres, & nuncia. Licet tamen ad ornatum cultus Divini his modulis organicis uti in Kyrie eleyson, Gloria in excelsis, in Prosis, Offertorio, Sanctus, & Agnus Dei.

Synod of the Diocese of Augsburg, 1567 (Schannat VII, p. 164; see also Gerbert, pp. 186–7)

Organorum usus multis in locis est immodicus, atque corrigendus, ne sacras preces, & audientium pietatem impediat lasciva modulatio, neve musica intempestiva, quae neque simplex, neque gravis videatur, turpes vel profanas cantiones referens, effeminatos potius demulceat, quam pios animos pascat. Nec decet sacros hymnos, uti sunt: *Gloria in excelsis, Praefatio, Sanctus, Agnus*, abrumpi, vel aliis canticis aut modulationibus impediri, quo minus integre exaudiantur.

Navarrus (Martin de Azpilcueta [Navarrus], 1493–1586) (testimony recorded by Cardinal Caietanus, De horis canonicis *(1578), c. XVI, n. 53, etc.; translation in Fellerer, 579; original in Gerbert, p. 194)*

Multi organistae faciunt sonare saepius organo cantiones profanas in ecclesiis, imo & vanas, & quandoque malas; cuiusmodi sunt, quas vocant baxas, & Altas, & alias cantilenas, quas vulgus novit esse turpes, obscoenas, & petulantes: quod palam est peccatum, praesertim cum id faciunt, quando officia divina fiunt, tam ob irrev[er]entiam, quae loco sacro fit, quam propter occasionem, quae praebetur avertendi mentes ab attentione rerum divinarum & spiritualium, & ad intendendum easdem temporalibus, vanis, & malis. Tum quia est causa, quod multis in locis non canuntur, nec audiuntur *Credo*, & *Gloria* a populo in festis, quibus non iubetur cani, ut pro his audiantur fistulae, & harmoniae; sed ut animo & ore confiteamur sanctam fidem catholicam, & ut gratias Domino ob suum adventum agamus. Tum quia multi organistae, quo suam artem ostentent, & plene audiantur, tamdiu pulsant (cum tamen ille pulsus non sit aliud, quam, ut ille ait, sine mente sonus) ut nonnunquam Missa una hora diutius aequo protrahant …

Many organists too frequently cause profane organ melodies to resound in the churches, nay, even frivolous and sometimes wicked melodies; of this sort are those which they call Baxae and Altae and other ditties which the mob knows are base, obscene, and passionate. This is manifestly sinful, especially when they do this thing when the divine offices are in progress, both on account of the irreverence which thus occurs in a sacred place and because of the occasion that is given for turning minds away from attention to divine and spiritual matters and directing them to frivolous and wicked temporal matters. Moreover it is the reason why, in many places, the Credo and Gloria are neither sung nor heard by the people on festal days, on which they are ordered not to be sung so that reeds and harmonies may be heard instead…Moreover many organists, in order to make a display of their skill and be heard at greater length, pound away so long (though that pounding, as the distinguished man said, is nothing more than sound without sense) that sometimes they draw the Mass out a whole hour longer than is proper.

Sacra Congregatione del Consilio, deliberations of 1564–1626 ("Very short communications to the Most Holy Supreme Pontiff and our Lord, Sixtus V [1587–88]," with the note, "To Cardinal Carafa, that he may consider everything well and then report to our Lord." Archivio Segreto Vaticano, Sacra Congregazione del Concilio, posiz. 5 [1587–8], f. 178r–181v, from the bishop of Barcelona, who offers eighteen points concerning good Christian life in his diocese; translation in Monson, 33)

15. De sonis et organis, alijsq[ue] musicis inst[rument]is

Rationi quidem, et rei de qua tunc agitur et tempori videtur consentaneum: ut in hebdomada sancta nullum audiretur in templis in officioru[m] celebratione aut alias, musicum instrume[n]tum; sed sola vox non rispons, non afferata [efferata?], sed pia humilis, lachrimosa atq[ue] utinam organicus omnis tunc cessaret cantus. Deinde non videtur decens: ut in templo, maximè dum aguntur divina officia, vel organo, vel alio instrumento sonet quid prophanum neque deberent sonare tibicines in ecclesijs, in locis sanis et pijs, vel ante templorum aedes.

15. Concerning sounds and organs, and other musical instruments

It seems agreeable to reason and to the matter then in hand and the time: that in Holy Week no musical instrument should be heard during the celebration of the services in churches, or on another occasion; but a single voice, not responding, not uncontrolled, but devout, modest, tearful; and would that organ music then might cease. Then it does not seem proper that anything profane be played on either the organ or another instrument in church, especially while divine services are performed; and wind players should not play in churches, in chaste and devout places, or in front of the buildings of the churches.

Council of Bordeaux, 1583 (Gerbert, pp. 229–30; from Conc. ed. Labb. T. XV. p. 775)

Ab organis & omni ecclesiastico cantu quaevis musica, lascivum quidpiam & vulgares cantilenas, aut levitatem similesque ineptias referens, omnino arceatur; sit gravis ubique, sit & divinis laudibus accommodata, ut ea circumstantium fidelium animi ad maiorem pietatem, devotionem, ac religionem ardescant. In Symbolo & passione Domini nulla penitus adhibeantur organa, neque etiam musica, nisi admodum simplex, & fusa, quaeque talis sit, ut singula verba intelligantur.

Musicians to abstain from secular music in church

Council of Sens, 1528, (Mansi XXXII, p. 1190; also quoted in Clive, III, 99; partial translation in Fellerer, 578):

Propterea praecipimus, ut in ecclesiis sint musici cantus distincti ac discreti, moventes cor ad devotionem compunctionemque. Porro in ecclesiis praetextu musici cantus non sunt audiendae publicae cantilenae & lascivae. Neque enim, inquit Hieronymus, in tragoediarum modum guttur & fauces medicamine sunt leniendae, ne, dum blanda vox quaeritur, congrua vita negligatur. Nam ut cantor minister Deum moribus stimulat, cum populum vocibus delectat, ita lascivus animus dum lascivioribus delectatur modis, eos saepe audiens emollitur & frangitur. Curent ergo sacerdotes & clerici sic suos cantus instituere, ut modesta honestaque psallendi gravitate, placidaque & grata modulatione, sic audientium aures deliniant, ut provocent excitentque ad devotionem compunctionemque; non ad lasciviam, cordisve aut animi titillationem.

Council of Reims, 1564 (Mansi XXXIII, p. 1316; also quoted in Clive, III, 101)

Se quidem esse in hac sententia ut existimet esse providendum ne sit in ecclesia lasciva, mollis, fracta et enervata musica: & ne in canendo symbolo apostolorum & in canticis angelorum nempe Gloria in excelsis, & Sanctus, ullus sit usus organorum; in aliquibus aliis, ut in prosis, poste eis dati locum.

Constitutiones almae domus for the Holy House of Loreto, promulgated by Cardinal Giulio della Rovere, 1576; stipulations for maestro di cappella (Monson 25–6, quoting Floriano Grimaldi, La Cappella Musicale di Loreto nel Cinquecento *[Loreto: Ente Rassegne Musicali, 1981], p. 106)*

Sia nominato inoltre un maestro di cappella il quale non solo ottomperi alle leggi prescritte dal concilio tridentino a i musici di chiesa, cioè di non mischiare alcunché di lascivo o d'impuro nei loro canti, ma pensi di trovarsi nella chiesa dove le angeliche armonie risuonarono delle lodi di Cristo Signore, e della sua Vergine Madre.

A chapel master should be appointed, moreover, who would obey the laws laid down by the Council of Trent for church musicians, namely, not to mix in anything indecent or impure in their songs; but let him remember his presence in the church, where angelic harmonies echo the praises of Christ the Lord and of his Virgin Mother.

Bucer on secular music on organ and other instruments, 1553

Martin Bucer, Familiere Declaration du livre des Pseaumes
(Geneva, 1553), p. 472 (quoted in Clive, III, 94)

Mais voicy une chose horrible à dire: que cecy est receu par tout, que les organistes en lieu de chanter choses sainctes gravement, ils gringotent en leurs orgues des chansons villeines & impudiques: lesquelles non seulement ils iouent pour donner une delectation vaine aux oreilles des auditeurs, mais aussi pour le plaisir des maquereaux & maquerelles, des putiers & putains, desquelles aussi les coeurs de ceux qui sont les plus purs peuvent estre provoquez à impudicité. Voila un merveilleux abbrutissement, de dire que non seulement le populaire qui s'appelle Chrestien, mais aussi ceux qui veulent estre reputez les principaux gouverneurs de l'Eglise, ne sont point tant peu soit estonnez de voir & ouyr telles choses …

Luther on secular song in church

Martin Luther (1483–1546); Luthers Werke: Schriften, 35. Band, Lieder, Haupttext: [Die Lieder Luthers] IV. Certe. 2. Die Gesangbuchvorreden. 4. *Die Vorrede zu der Sammlung der Begräbnis Lieder (1542) (from http:// luther.chadwyck.com/english/frames/werke/fulltext), p. 480, lines 1–9:*

Also haben sie auch warlich viel treffliche schoene Musica oder Gesang, sonderlich in den Stifften und Pfarrhen, Aber viel unfletiger abgoettischer Text da mit geziert. Darumb wir solche abgoettische todte und tolle Text entkleidet, und jnen die schoene Musica abgestreifft, und dem lebendigen heiligen Gottes wort angezogen, dasselb damit zu singen, zu loben und zu ehren. Das also solcher schoener schmuck der Musica in rechtem Brauch jrem lieben Schepffer und seinen Christen diene, Das er gelobt und geehret, wir aber durch sein heiliges wort, mit suessem Gesang jns Hertz getrieben, gebessert und gesterckt werden im glauben. Das helffe uns Gott der Vater mit Son und heiliger Geist, Amen.

Bodenstein von Karlstadt on polyphony in church

Andreas Bodenstein von Karlstadt (1486–1541); 53 Thesen "De Cantu Gregoriano Disputatio" (1521–2) (Neubrandenburg: Anthonius and Walther Brenner, 1556); see Hermann Barge, Andreas Bodenstein von Karlstadt *vol. I,* Karlstadt und die Anfänge der Reformation *(2nd edn. Nieuwkoop: B. De Graaf, 1968), p. 492*

Thesis 18: Sic cum illo et organa, tubas et tibias in theatra chorearum et ad principum aulas relegamus.

Thesis 19: Nam elevatio panis coelestis et cantus organi lasciuus, vulgo, "Wolauff gut gesell von hynnen," ut ovinae chordae et lupinae, concordant in cithara.

Histoire de la Mappe-Monde papistique

Jean-Baptiste Trento (?), Histoire de la Mappe-Monde papistique,
en laquelle est declairé tout ce qui est contenu & pourtraict en la grande
Table, ou Carte de la Mappe-Monde: Composée par M. Frangidelphe
Escorche-Messes *(Luce Nouvelle: Brifaud Chasse-diables, 1567)*
(quoted in Clive, III, 96)

Chapter on prayer, "Province IX"

En leurs comedies de Vespres, & en leurs Scenes tant bien entretaillees & ornees,
qui'ils appellent Coeurs ou grandes chappelles, ils y ont mis plusieurs chantres &
ioueurs de farces qui vont & viennent desguisez & vestus de velours … & puis,
enrichis, de badinages en la fin, après qu'ils ont ioué le premier acte de la farce de
leurs Vespres, ils font une pause, & puis sortent d'autres personnages, qui iouent
des chansons amoureuses, de madrigals, & sonnets qu'ils font gringuenoter sur les
orgues par quelque excellent ioueur: & ainsi en font-ils en leurs autres comedies de
la Messe: & sur tout quand ils levent en haut leur dieu de paste, ils iouent sur leurs
orgues quelques chansons d'amours, comme des madrigales de Iosquin, de Iaquet,
de Verdelot, Arcadelt, Vincent Rouf, Constant Feste, & principalement des choses
amoureuses de Cyprian Rore, comme ces beaux Madrigales, qui commencent ainsi,
I'ay chanté tandis que i'ay bruslé: & puis, Tel se trouve devant vostre clarté, madame, ou bien l'oeil, la main, la bouche, le col, la poictrine: ou bien, Amour, puis
que tu me veux mettre en danger, & plusieurs autres de cest excellent musicien.
Et quand un autre acte de la comedie est ioué, ils font une autre pause, & puis ces
mesmes personnages se presentent sonnant d'autres madrigales amoureux de mais-
tre Adrian Villaert, pere de la musique, & sur tout quelques petits Madrigalins que
luy firent faire aucuns Seigneurs amoureux d'une Courtisane ou putain publique, à
Venise, qui s'appeloit la Peccorina, qui commencent, D'elle vient l'amoureux pensement, & ces beaux Madrigales, Amour, esprit, valeur, pitie & douleurs. Ils iouent
aussi quelques Dialogues du mesme autheur, qu'ils chantent ainsi, Pleurez yeux, &c.
laquelle musique vient fort à propos, & amuse tellement les gens, qu'ils n'en perdent
point une note: & le tout se fait pour donner credit au lieu, & amener l'eau au mou-
lin, comme dont dit: & pour les entretenir & leur donner plaisir, soulas, & contente-
ment: & en sont repeus comme de toutes les autres comedies & farces plaisantes,
qu'ils pourroyent ouir ordinairement: & demeurent la gueule bée, & tournent les
yeux en la teste comme une chievre qui avorte, tellement que c'est un plaisir de les
voir.

Erasmus

Commentary on 1 Corinthians 14 *(from Gerbert, p. 222)*

Non his contenti operosam quandam & theatricam musicam in sacras aedes
induximus, tumultuosum diversarum vocum garritum, qualem, non opinor, in

Graecorum aut *Romanorum* theatris unquam auditum fuisse. Omnia tubis lituis, fistulis ac sambucis perstrepunt: cumque his certant hominum voces. Audiuntur amatoriae foedaeque cantilenae, ad quas scorta mimique saltitant. In sacram aedem velut in theatrum concurritur ad deliniendas aures. Et in hunc usum aluntur magnis salariis organorum opifices, puerorum greges, quorum omnis aetas in perdiscendis his consumitur, nihil interim bonae rei discentium.

Christiani Matrimonii Institutio, *Opera (ed. Lugd. Bat.), V, col. 718c
(quoted in Johan Huizinga* The Autumn of the Middle Ages, *trans.
Rodney J. Payton and Ulrich Mammitzsch [University of Chicago Press,
1996], pp. 417–18)*

Nunc sonis nequissimis aptantur verba sacra, nihilo magis decore, quam si thaidis ornatum addas Catoni. Interdum nec verba silentur impudica cantorum licentia.

Agrippa von Nettesheim

Agrippa von Nettesheim, De incertitudine et vanitate scientiarum et artium
*(Cologne: [printer unknown], 1532), Chapter 17. In Karl Gustav Fellerer,
"Agrippa von Nettesheim und die Musik,"* Archiv für Musikwissenschaft
16 (1959), 81

Hodie vero tanta in ecclesiis musicae licentia est, ut etiam una cum missae ipsius canone obscoene quaeque cantiunculae interim in organis pares vices habeant ipsaque divina officia et sacrae orationum preces conductis magno aero lascivis musicis non ad audientium intelligentiam, non ad spiritus elevationem, sed ad fornicatriam pruriginem non humanis vocibus, sed belvinis strepitibus cantillant, dum hinniunt discantum pueri, mugiunt alii tenorem, alii latrant contrapunctum, alii boant altum, alii frendent bassum faciuntque, ut sonorum plurimum quidem audiatur, verborum et orationis intelligatur nihil, sed auribus pariter et animo iudicii subtrahitur autoritas.

Conrad von Zabern (Mainz: Peter Schöffer, 1474)

Karl-Werner Gümpel, Die Musiktraktate Conrads von Zabern, *Akademie
der Wissenschaften und der Literatur: Abhandlungen der geistes- und
sozialwissenschaftlichen Klasse Jahrgang 1956, No. 4 (Wiesbaden: Franz
Steiner, 1956), p. 271 (127)*

(5) Item etiam sic est cantandum devotionaliter, ut nulla melodia, quae a devotis sanctis patribus nobis non est tradita, sed a diaboli ministris introducta, ut infra dicetur, inter divinae laudis carmina umquam cantetur; huiusmodi enim melodiae adulterinae penitus sunt reiciendae a divino officio. (6) Et tamen heu

in plerisque ecclesiis quasi cotidie sunt in usu. (7) Exemplariter loquar, ut intelligar: Nonnulli scolarium rectores placere nescio cui cupientes, sed haud dubium diabolo per hoc servientes, etiamsi nescii, quorundam mundialium carminum melodias sumpserunt et illas super his, quae de potioribus sunt inter divinae laudis carmina, hoc est super hymnum angelicum *Gloria in excelsis* et super Symbolum Nicaenum ac super *Sanctus* et *Agnus Dei*, ut poterant, aptarunt haec sub eisdem mundialibus melodiis cantando dimissis devotis sanctorum patrum melodiis nobis praescriptis. (8) Quae mundialium carminum melodiae dum cantantur in officio missae, non solum plurimos christifideles, ut sciens scio, scandalisant, sed etiam multos praesertim iuvenes vel carnales homines plus de domo choreae quam de regno caelorum cogitare faciunt in devotionis impedimentum non modicum, nimirum quia huiusmodi melodias vel eis similes in domo choreae saepe audierunt. (9) De re hac in veritate notabilem audivi laicorum non minimorum querelam in cleri confusionem et notam, ut merito episcopi et praelati per totum suae iurisdictionis ambitum huiusmodi melodias non immerito diabolicas nominandas penitus prohibere deberent, quas per litteram devotionaliter hic volo exclusisse etc.

Friedrich Nausea von Waischenfeld, Bishop of Vienna

Friedrich Nausea von Waischenfeld, Episcopus Viennensis, De praecipuis quibusdam clericorum et laicorum abusibus pro ecclesia reformanda tollendis, *Book V (June 1543) (quoted in Monson, 29)*

De cantorum abusibus

Denique cantorum abusus est, quod aliquoties in cantibus et organis in templo permittunt, que magis lasciviam quam devotionem excitant, sinantque aliquando cani, que non modo non ex divinis sunt desumpta scripturis, sed que sunt ab eis omnino diversa vel certe minus spiritualia, maxime cum in lingua non consueta, utpote vernacula, legi soleant contra catholice ecclesie morem et consuetudinem.

Council of Narbonne, 1551

Mansi XXXIII, p. 1270 (quoted in Clive, III, 99–100)

Hoc edicto praescribitur, ne in templis, cum aliqui dies festi coluntur, vel alio tempore spectacula (quibus stultorum, puerorumque animi solent delectari, artes ludicrae, cantilenae saeculares, strepitus, a clericis vel laicis, neque alia hujusmodi fiant: quibus a religione populus revocatur: & in cachinnationes immodicosque risus solvitur. Itaque edictum de spectaculis in ecclesia non faciendis exacte observatur: ne poena excommunicationis quas que alias praescribit infligantur.

Synod of Schwerin, 1492

Schannat V, p. 655; translation in Fellerer, 578

XLVII. Que cantica in Missa integre cantari debent, statutum

Item statuimus, & mandamus, ut quilibet Sacerdos nostre Diocesis, cum gratia Dei dispositus, Missarum solemnia decantaverit, Gloria in excelsis, Credo, Offertorium, Prefationem cum Pater noster, juxta Sacrorum Canonum sanxiones a principio usque ad finem decantet, nullo abstracto, diminuto, vel refecto: aut aliud responsorium, vel carmen vulgare loco premissorum in organis, aut choro, qui presentes fuerint Clerici resonent. Et in Credo tractatim cantetur: Ex Maria Virgine, & Homo factus est, genibus flexis.

We likewise decide and order that whatever priest of our diocese, appointed by the grace of God, shall descant the solemnity of the Mass, should chant the Gloria in excelsis, Credo, Offertorium, Praefatio, along with the Pater Noster, in accordance with the sanctions of the sacred canons from the beginning to the end, with nothing subtracted, diminished, or revised; nor shall there be any vulgar response or song in the place of those prescribed, by organ or choir; the clerics who may be present shall intone it.

St. Antoninus (1389–1459)

St. Antoninus, Summa theologica, *4 vols. (completed a few years before his death) (Graz: Akademische Druck- und Verlagsanstalt, 1959), 3: cols. 321–2 (pt. 3, tit. 8, cap. 4, par. 12); translation by Rob C. Wegman*

De ministerio musicorum in cantando & pulsando

Et cantus quidem firmus in divinis officiis a sanctis doctoribus institutus est, ut Gregorio Magno, & Ambrosio, & aliis. Biscantus autem in officiis ecclesiasticis quis adinvenerit, ignoro: pruritui aurium videtur magis deservire quam devotioni, quamvis pia mens etiam in his fructum referat audiendo. Qui tamen huic operi insistunt, videant *ne dum blanda vox quaeritur, congrua vita quaeri negligatur, & Deum moribus irritet, dum populum vocibus delectat,* ut ait Gregorius Dist. 92. *In sancta.* Communiter tamen tales solent esse leves & dissoluti. Praecipue autem redarguendam est in officiis divinis, ibi misceri cantiones seu balatas & verba vana, contra quod etiam Hieronymus invehit, Dist. 92. *Cantantes.*

Of the ministry of music in singing and playing

Cantus firmus has been instituted in the divine offices by the Holy Doctors [of the Church], by Gregory the Great, and St. Ambrose, and others. I do not know who was the first to introduce biscantus in the ecclesiastical offices: it seems to be dedicated to the titillation of the ears rather than [the engendering of] devotion, although a pious mind may reap profit even from hearing those [songs]. However, they who persist in such practices should see to it that "the right life not be neglected while the alluring voice is sought after, and that what delights the people in vocal sounds should not anger God in moral conduct," as St. Gregory says in Distinctio 92: *In sancta.* Generally, however, such people tend to be frivolous and dissolute. What must be particularly condemned in the divine offices, moreover, is the insertion of songs or balatas, and vain words, which St. Jerome also inveighs against in Distinction 92: *Cantantes.*

Later in the same passage Antoninus writes about the organ in church:

Pulsare … in organis vel aliis ad Dei laudem non est prohibitum, & juste recipiunt salarium pulsantes; tamen pulsare balatas, ut frequenter fit, valde detestabile est.

Pierre Soybert (d. 1454)

Pierre Soybert, De cultu vinee domini liber inumere plenus com[m]oditatis *(Paris, 1503), f. 23v, quoted in Vital Chomel, "Droit de patronage et pratique religieuse dans l'archevêché de Narbonne au début du XVe siècle,"* Bibliothèque de l'école des chartes, *115 (1957), 58–137, at 105, n. 3*

Item reprehendere debet episcopus visitans eos qui cum modulatis et blandis voci-bus ut placeant laicis vel mulieribus cantant virolays seu notulas circa elevationem Corporis christi vel in missa, ubi sunt verba turpia seu corrupta, attractiva ad vani-tates mulierum …

Synod of Breslau, 1446

Schannat V, pp. 289, 300

Item, ut ad aleas, & ad taxillos non ludant, nec hujusmodi ludis intersint, etiam ut plausus manuum more gentili, vel cantilenas seculares cantare non presumant: quia in uno ore laudes Chisti, una cum laudibus Jovis non concordant.

Item didicimus: quod quidam Ecclesiarum Rectores, ac Monasteriorum nos-tre Diocesis tam seculares, quam Religiosi, honestati Clericali, ac cultui Divino minime intendentes, ludos in lutinis, tubis & clamoribus excitare presumunt, pop-ulum, plus propter lucrum & vanam gloriam audiendum Divina congregatum, in Missis solennibus, aut votivis provocant, quam ad laudem & honorem Dei. Cum vero in Ecclesia non alia, nisi que honestatem & devotionem introducere videantur, exerceri debent; Quare statuimus & ordinamus, quod nullus Ecclesiarum tam secu-laris, quam religiosus Rector, sive Plebanus, & presertim Monasteriorum & nostre Diocesis inantea quovis modo de talibus Missis votivis, aut solennibus nuncupatis, indiscretis, ac honestati Clericali contrariis, & derogantibus attentare presumat sub pena excommunicationis, & decem florenorum, Fisco Camere nostre irremissi-biliter applicandorum.

Council of Basel, June 9, 1435

Gerbert, Liber IV, Caput I, p. 176 (according to testimony of Augustinus Patricius [see Conc. Ed. Labb. p. 1532])

Illarum ecclesiarum abusum, in quibus in sacrificio solemnis Missae symbolum fidei, praefatio, sive oratio dominica [Lord's prayer] inchoata cantilena non perficiuntur, aut omnino sine cantu dicuntur, damnavit, atque abolevit; vetuitque, inter Missarum solemnia cantilenas vulgari sermone conditas cantari, & in privatis Missis iussit omnia pronuntiari alta & intelligibili voce, praeter ea, quae Secreta nuncupatur.

Entries in the inventories of the Burgundian ducal library

Inventory of 1420

See Georges Doutrepont, *Inventaire de la "librairie" de Philippe le Bon (1420)* (Brussels: Commission royale d'histoire, 1906), pp. 27–8

Item, un livre couvert de rouge, noté, où il y a Anthenes Deschanteés, Virelaiz et Balades. [The inventory of 1477 describes the same volume as "Ung liure en parchemin ouquel sont plusieurs Motez à deschant pour dire en vne chapelle' (see Doutrepont, p. 27)]

Item, ung grant livre plat, noté, de plusieurs Motez, Virelaiz et Balades, qui se commence *Colla jugo fidere*, et se fenit *Bis dicitur.*

Item, ung autre livre de Motez, Patrens, Virelaiz, Balades et autres choses, où l'en chantoit aux grans festes en la chapelle.

Inventory of 1487

Jean Baptiste Joseph Barrois, Bibliothèque protypographique, ou Librairies des fils du roi Jean Charles V, Jean de Berri, Philippe de Bourgogne et les siens (Paris, Strasbourg, London: Treutel et Würtz, 1830), pp. 287–8, plus personal copy of original source (Lille, Archives départementales du nord, B 3501, no. 123.744, ff. 31r–81v) provided by David Fiala

Item ung autre volume couvert de cuir grisatre a deux cloans de leton intitulé ung livre de chant servant a la chapelle commencant au second feuillet Ma douleur ne cesse pas et finissant ou derrenier Le soleil luit la lune est rescousee.

Item ung autre couvert de cuir rouge a deux cloans de leton intitulé ung livre de chant servant a la chapelle commencant ou second feuillet profondement et finissant ou derrenier ancien [autres?] contratenores.

Item ung autre couvert d'ung parchemin intitulé comme le dessus commencant ou second feuillet Tabula baladarum rondellorumque vireleticorum et finissant ou derrenier feuillet Ma riche amour.

Item ung autre couvert de cuir blanc a quatre gros bouts sur chascun costé et deux cloans de leton intitulé ung an tout entier servant a la chapelle commencant ou second feuillet Alleluya ostende nobis et finissant ou derrenier contratenor.

Sources cited above

Clive, Harry Peter "The Calvinist Attitude to Music, and Its Literary Aspects and Sources," *Bibiothèque d'Humanisme et Renaissance* 19 (1957), 80–102, 295–319; 20 (1958), 79–107 (Clive).

Fellerer, Karl Gustav, "Church Music and the Council of Trent," *Musical Quarterly* 39 (1953), 576–94 (Fellerer).

Gerbert, Martin, *De cantu et musica sacra a prima ecclesiae aetate usque ad praesens tempus* (San Blasien: Typis San-Blasiensis, 1774; repr., 2 vols., ed. Othmar Wessely: Graz: Akademische Druck- und Verlagsanstalt, 1968).

Mansi, Giovan Domenico, *Sacrorum conciliorum nova et amplissima collectio, cujus Joannes Dominicus Mansi et post ipsius mortem Florentinus et Venetianus editores ab anno 1758 ad annum 1798 priores triginta unum tomos ediderunt, nunc autem continuata et absoluta*, 53 vols. (Florence, 1759–98; repr. Paris: H. Welter, 1901–1927).

Monson, Craig, "The Council of Trent Revisited," *Journal of the American Musicological Society* 55 (2002), 1–38.

Schannat, Johann Friedrich, *Concilia Germaniae*, 11 vols. (Cologne: Simon, 1759–90; repr. Aalen: Scientia, 1970–96).

Appendix 3: Madrigals listed in *L'Histoire de la Mappe-Monde papistique*

"des choses amoureuses de Cyprian Rore"

I'ay chanté tandis que j'ai brulé

Cantai, mentre ch'i arsi, del mio foco, in Cipriano Rore *I madrigali a cinque voci nuovamente posti in luce* (Venice: Scotto, 1542). Edition in Cipriano de Rore, *Cipriani Rore Opera Omnia*, II: *Madrigalia 5 vocum*, ed. Bernhard Meier, Corpus Mensurabilis Musicae 14 (n.p.: American Institute of Musicology, 1963), pp. 1–4 (Giovanni Brevio, *Rime e prose volgari* [Rome: Blado, 1545])

Cantai, mentre ch'i arsi, del mio foco
La viva fiamma ov'io morendo vissi,
Ben che quant'io cantai e quant'io scrissi
Di madonna e d'amor fu nulla o poco.
Ma se i begli occhi ond'il mio cor s'accese
Del lor chiaro divin almo splendore
Non m'havessero a torto fatto indegno,
Col canto havrei l'interno e grave ardore
Agl'orecchi di tal fatto palese,
Che pietà fora ov'alberga ira e sdegno.
A gl'amorosi strali fermo segno sarei,
pieno di dolce aspro martiro
Ov'hora in libertà piango e sospiro:
Ahi, pace in cor d'amanti non ha loco.

While I burned, I sang
the living flame of the fire in which I lived dying,
even though what I sang and wrote
about my lady and love was little or nothing.
But if the fair eyes which lit my heart
with their bright, divine, and dear splendor
had not wrongfully made me unworthy,
by my song I would have revealed
my inner grievous ardor to someone's ears,
so that there would be mercy where now dwell anger and disdain.
I would be a fixed target for the arrows of love,
filled with sweet and bitter torment,

247

where now I weep and sigh in liberty.
Alas, there is no place in lovers' hearts for peace.

Tel se trouve devant vostre clarté, madame

Che si può più vedere, Madonna, in *Di Constantio Festa il primo libro di madrigali a tre voci novamente da Antonio Gardano ristampati & corretti* (Venice: Gardano, 1556 [RISM 1556²⁶]). Contents of this print are the same as those of RISM 1551¹⁴ (Venice: Scotto: only tenor part book surviving), plus subsequent reprints, 1559²², 1564¹⁷; same piece is anonymous in 1537⁷ (also Scotto: only bass part book surviving) and [c.1537]⁸ (place and date of publication unknown): only cantus and tenor part books surviving). Edition in Costanzo Festa, *Costanzo Festa Opera Omnia*, vol. VII: *Madrigali,* ed. Albert Seay, Corpus Mensurabilis Musicae 25 (Neuhausen-Stuttgart: American Institute of Musicology, 1977), pp. 19–21.

Che si può più vedere, Madonna,
che vostr'occh' e'l chiaro viso.
Che mostrate fra noi è'l paradiso,
Et cert' al mio parere,
Dirò che Giov' assai più belle cose,
Habbia di voi più belle et gloriose,
Ma non dirò che più ne regni suoi,
Sia'l paradiso perchè qui fra noi,
Hor dica pur chi vuol quel che gli piace,
Che'l ciel e'l paradiso, i Dei, le stelle,
Son vostri lumi e'l viso et le mammelle.

What can be better seen, my lady,
than your eyes and your fair face?
For you show that paradise is among us,
And surely, in my opinion,
I will say that Jove may have much more beautiful things
than you, more beautiful and glorious,
but I will not say that paradise is more in his realms,
because it is here among us.
Now let anyone say what he pleases,
for heaven, paradise, the gods, the stars,
are your eyes and your face and your breasts.

L'oeil, la main, la bouche, le col, la poictrine

L'occhio, la man [anon.] in *Cipriano il secondo libro de madregali a cinque voci insieme alcuni di M. Adriano et altri autori a misura comune*

novamente posti in luce a cinque voci (Venice: Gardano, 1544
[RISM 1544[17]]. Reprints: 1551[15], 1552[24], 1563[14]]). No modern edition.

L'occhio la man la bocca il coll'il petto
e cio che vegg'in voi d'invidia pieno
che non verrebbe a vostri assalti meno?
L'occhio si queto 'sconde che m'invola,
La man invoglia e la bocca m'uccide.
Si dolce sona e dolce canta e ride
L'aura soave e poichè dalla gola spira
Mi porta in loco dolc'e ameno
fra due bei colli ond'io vi moro in seno.

Your eye, hand, mouth, neck, and breast
and that which I see filled with envy in you,
What would not succumb under your attacks?
Your eye hides so quietly that it robs me.
Your hand allures me, and your mouth kills me.
So sweetly sounds and sweetly sings and laughs
The sweet breeze, and after it breathes from your throat
It bears me to a sweet and pleasant place
Between two hills where I die on your breast.

Amour, puis que tu me veux mettre en danger

Amor, da che tu vuoi pur ch'io m'arrischi (actually by Willaert, not
Rore as stated in *L'Histoire de la Mappe-Monde papistique*), in *Di
Cipriano Rore et di altri eccellentissimi musici il terzo libro di madrigali
a cinque voce novamente da lui composti et non più messi in luce.
Con diligentia stampati. Musica nova & rara come a quelli che la
canteranno & udiranno sara palese* (Venice: Scotto, 1548 [RISM
1548[9]]). Edition in Adrian Willaert, *Adriani Willaert: Opera Omnia*,
vol. XIV: *Madrigali e Canzoni Villanesche*, ed. Helga Meier, Corpus
Mensurabilis Musicae 3 (Neuhausen-Stuttgart: American Institute of
Musicology, 1977), pp. 92–6.

Amor, da che tu vuoi pur ch'io m'arrischi
In udir e vedere Sirene e Basilischi?
Fammi gratia, signore,
S'egli avvien che mi strugga lo splendore
Di due occhi sereni,
e ch'io sia preda
D'un ragionar accorto,
Che chi n'ha colpa creda

Che per udir e per veder sia morto.

Seconda parte:
Gentil coppia eccellente,
Chi vi mira et ascolta
Solamente una volta,
E non mor di piacere,
Può gir arditamente
Ad udir e vedere
Le Sirene d'amor e i Basilischi.

Love, since you want me at risk
hearing and seeing sirens and basilisks,
Grant me this favor, O Lord:
if it happens that the splendor
of two serene eyes consumes me
and I fall prey
to clever speech,
let the guilty person believe
that I am dead through hearing and through seeing.

Second part:
Noble, excellent couple,
whoever sees and hears you
only once,
and does not die of pleasure,
may boldly go
to hear and see
the sirens of love and the basilisks.

"de maistre Adrian Villaert"

D'elle vient l'amoureux pensement Unknown.

Amour, esprit, valeur, pitie & douleurs

Secunda pars (*Amor! Senno!*), of *I' vidi in terra angelici costumi*, in *Musica Nova* (Venice: Gardano, 1559 [RISM 1559[b]]). Edition in Adrian Willaert, *Adriani Willaert: Opera Omnia* vol. XIII: *Musica Nova, 1559: Madrigalia*, ed. Hermann Zenck and Walter Gerstenberg, Corpus Mensurabilis Musicae 3 (n.p.: American Institute of Musicology, 1966), pp. 85–90. (Francesco Petrarcha, Sonnet no. 156)

I' vidi in terra angelici costumi,
E celesti bellezze al mondo sole;
Tal che di rimembrar mi giova, e dole:

Che quant'io miro, par sogni, ombre, e fumi.

E vidi lagrimar que' duo bei lumi,
Ch'han fatto mille volte invidia al sole;
Ed udì' sospirando dir parole
Che farian gir i monti, e stare i fiumi.

Amor! senno! valor! pietate! e doglia!
Facean piangendo un più dolce concento
D'ogni altro, che nel mondo udir si soglia.

Ed era 'l cielo all'armonia s'intento
Che non se vedea in ramo mover foglia.
Tanta dolcezza avea pien l'aer e 'l vento.

I beheld on earth angelic grace,
and celestial beauty on terrestrial soil,
such that remembering it thrills me and saddens me
so much that I see it through dreams, shadows, mists.

And I beheld tears spring from those two lovely eyes,
which a thousand times have made the sun jealous,
and heard spoken sighing words,
that stirred the mountains and stayed the rivers.

Love, wisdom, worth, pity and grief
made in weeping a sweeter chorus
than any other to be heard on earth.

And heaven on that harmony was so intent
that not a leaf upon a branch was seen to stir,
so filled with sweetness were the air and wind.

Pleurez yeux

Occhi piangete, in *Musica Nova* (Venice: Gardano, 1559 [RISM 1559[b]]).
Edition in Adrian Willaert, *Adriani Willaert: Opera Omnia* XIII: *Musica
Nova, 1559: Madrigalia*, ed. Hermann Zenck and Walter Gerstenberg,
(Corpus Mensurabilis Musicae 3) (n.p.: American Institute of Musicology,
1966), pp. 119–24. (Francesco Petrarcha, Sonnet no. 84)

Occhi piangete: accompagnate il core
Che di vostro fallir morte sostene.
"Così sempre facciamo; e ne conviene
Lamentar più l'altrui, che'l nostro errore."

"Già prima hebbe per voi l'entrat'Amore,
Là ond'anchor come in suo albergo vene."
"Noi gli aprimmo la via per quella spene

Che mosse dentro da colui che more."

"Non son, com'a voi par, le ragion pari:
Ché pur voi foste nella prima vista
Del vostro e del suo mal cotanto avari."

"Hor questo è quel che più ch'altro n'attrista,
Ch'i perfetti giudicii son sì rari,
E d'altrui colpa altrui biasmo s'acquista."

Weep, eyes: accompany the heart
that is about to die for your failings.
"So do we always: we must
mourn more for another's fault than our own."

"Yet it was through you that Love first entered,
where he still lives as if it were his home."
"We opened the way because of that hope
that came from within that one that is to die."

"These reasonings are not, as they may seem, equal:
for it was you, so eager at first sight,
who did harm to yourself, and to that one."

"Now that is what saddens us more than anything,
that perfect judgment is so rare,
and we are blamed for another's fault."

Notes

Preface

1 "Die musikalische Form der Messe ist die edelste Frucht des segensreichen Bundes, der Liturgie und Kunst seit nunmehr fast zweitausend Jahren aneinander schließt. Musikalische Interessen und Bestrebungen allein hätten sie niemals zustande gebracht; außerhalb des Rahmens der Liturgie wäre kein Künstler darauf verfallen, Texte aneinander zu reihen, wie diejenigen der Messe. Die Liturgie hat diese geschaffen, die Künstler aber bauten aus den lose nebeneinander stehenden Stücken eine innerlich zusammenhängende, zyklische Form, das Gefäß für ihre genialsten Inspirationen" (Peter Wagner, *Geschichte der Messe: I Teil: Bis 1600* [Leipzig: Breitkopf und Härtel, 1913], p. v).

2 For the latter, see for example Jennifer Bloxam's essays "In Praise of Spurious Saints: The *Missae Floruit Egregiis* by Pipelare and La Rue," *Journal of the American Musicological Society* 44 (1991), 163–220, and "Sacred Polyphony and Local Traditions of Liturgy and Plainsong: Reflections on Music by Jacob Obrecht," in Thomas Forrest Kelly (ed.), *Plainsong in the Age of Polyphony* (Cambridge and New York: Cambridge University Press, 1992), pp. 140–77.

3 For hidden programs see for example Michael P. Long, "Symbol and Ritual in Josquin's *Missa di Dadi*," *Journal of the American Musicological Society* 42 (1989), 1–22. For direct comparison with another aspect of contemporary culture, see for instance Bloxam's highly persuasive analogy between Obrecht's motet *Factor Orbis* and contemporary guides to sermon writing developed in "Obrecht as Exegete: Reading *Factor Orbis* as a Christmas Sermon," in Dolores Pesce (ed.), *Hearing the Motet: Essays on the Motet of the Middle Ages and Renaissance* (New York: Oxford University Press, 1997), pp. 169–92. A view of musical output as an expression of a particular composer's career forms the backbone of Rob C. Wegman, *Born for the Muses: The Life and Masses of Jacob Obrecht* (Oxford University Press, 1994).

4 Hence James Haar's comment that "as historians concerned not only with cultural artifacts but also with the intellectual and artistic outlook of the past we want to know not just how music was made but why it took the shapes it did, and especially how it was heard and criticized by those who first performed and listened to it" ("A Sixteenth-Century Attempt at Music Criticism," *Journal of the American Musicological Society* 36 [1983], 191).

5 As Anmon Linder has vividly expressed it, the intelligibility of that rite "depends on both cognition and sensation: … on seeing the unfolding ritual

act in forms, movement, colours, and light, on hearing the tolling bells, the spoken word, and the sung melody, on sensing the environing space and the closeness of fellow-worshippers in prostration, genuflection, kiss of peace, and other physical actions, on smelling incense and smoking candles, on tasting the Eucharist" (*Raising Arms: Liturgy in the Struggle to Liberate Jerusalem in the Late Middle Ages* [Turnhout: Brepols, 2003], p. 365).

6 Miri Rubin has observed that "Because we never encounter an utterance in isolation, be it picture, ritual, or word, the range of uses is inscribed before the use actually takes place. It is therefore necessary in critical practice to capture and differentiate the meanings of uses within the range of possibilities, to make sense of action within the sphere of possibilities, rather than to ascribe preordained meanings to them" (*Corpus Christi: The Eucharist in Late Medieval Culture* [Cambridge University Press, 1991], p. 3).

Chapter 1 Enlightenment and beyond

1 Manfred Bukofzer, *Studies in Medieval and Renaissance Music* (New York: Norton, 1950), pp. 218–19. See also pp. 225–6: "The Renaissance musicians recognized the cyclic Mass as the most dignified form of composition and thus *indirectly* [my italics] also recognized its liturgical dignity, but in their essentially artistic approach to the problem, which put musical unity above all, they were no longer guided by the strictly liturgical attitude of medieval musicians. It may seem paradoxical that the Mass cycle, the most extended composition before the advent of the opera and the symphony, and regarded today as liturgical music *par excellence*, was actually the result of the weakening of liturgical ties at the oncoming of the Renaissance."

2 See Leo Schrade's essays "The Mass of Toulouse," *Revue Belge de Musicologie* 8 (1954), 84–96; "The Cycle of the Ordinarium Missae," in H. Anglès *et al.* (eds.), *In Memoriam Jacques Handschin* (Strasburg: P. H. Heitz, 1962), pp. 87–96; "News on the Chant Cycle of the *Ordinarium Missae*," *Journal of the American Musicological Society* 8 (1955), 66–9; and Kurt von Fischer, "Neue Quellen zum Einstimmigen Ordinariumszyklus des 14. und 15. Jahrhunderts aus Italien," in Albert Linden (ed.), *Liber Amicorum Charles van den Borren* (Antwerp: Lloyd Anversois, 1964), pp. 60–8.

3 Geoffrey Chew, "The Early Cyclic Mass as an Expression of Royal and Papal Supremacy," *Music and Letters* 53 (1972), 254. For more on this see Chapter 7.

4 For some cases in point see the Preface to this book.

5 For the general development of the history of early music before Ambros, traced through the achievements of Burney, Forkel, Baini, Kiesewetter and Brendel, see my "'Under Such Heavy Chains': The Discovery and Evaluation of Late Medieval Music before Ambros," *Nineteenth Century Music* 24 (2000), 89–112.

6 Peter Wagner, *Geschichte der Messe* (Leipzig: Breitkopf und Härtel, 1913).

7 Charles Burney, *A General History of Music, From the Earliest Ages to the Present Period* (London: Printed for the Author, 2nd edn., 1789; repr. London: G. T. Foulis, 1935); and Johann Nicolaus Forkel, *Allgemeine Geschichte der Musik*, vol. II (Leipzig: Schwickertschen, 1801; repr. Graz: Akademische Druck- und Verlagsanstalt, 1967).

8 For a summary of the philosophical and ideological background to the earliest music histories, see Elisabeth Hegar, *Die Anfänge der neueren Musikgeschichtsschreibung um 1770 bei Gerbert, Burney und Hawkins* (Strasbourg: Heitz, 1933; repr. Baden-Baden: Valentin Koerner, 1974). See also my "'Under Such Heavy Chains.'"

9 For more on this see Jessie Ann Owens, "Music Historiography and the Definition of 'Renaissance,'" *Notes* 47 (1990), 305–30.

10 For more on this and other details sketched in this section, see my "'Under Such Heavy Chains.'"

11 For Ambros's view see his *Geschichte der Musik*, vol. III (Leipzig: Leuckart, 1868; 3rd. edn., revised by Otto Kade, 1893), p. 23.

12 "The brief musical examples provided up to now – with which authors wished to illustrate their rules of counterpoint – can already give a sense of the level of purity which they were able to apply to the combination of individual chords; but of the construction of complete phrases and the forms of complete pieces they still teach us nothing" (Forkel, *Allgemeine Geschichte*, vol. II, p. 515). For more on this see my "'Under Such Heavy Chains.'"

13 Giuseppe Baini, *Memorie storico-critiche della vita e delle opere di Giovanni Pierluigi da Palestrina*, 2 vols. (Rome: Società Tipografica, 1828; repr. Hildesheim: Georg Olms, 1966).

14 Baini's privileged access, as administrator of the college of papal singers, to papal records led him to the conclusion that Du Fay's period of service in the papal choir ended in 1432. While this was not dramatically wide of the mark (he actually left the choir for the last time in 1437: see for example David Fallows, *Dufay* [2nd rev. edn., London: Dent, 1987], pp. 48, 219), Baini's interpretation was significantly inaccurate in concluding that the composer began his service in 1380 (see Baini, *Palestrina*, vol. I, pp. 399–400). A consequence of this was that 1432 came to be presumed to be the date of Du Fay's death, while it was inferred that he must have been born about 1350. This misapprehension, almost universally accepted by his successors, was not definitively refuted until Haberl published the first results of his research in the papal archives in 1885 (see Franz X. Haberl, "Wilhelm du Fay. Monographische Studie über dessen Leben und Werke," *Vierteljahrschrift der Musikwissenschaft* I [1885], 397–530).

15 Raphael Georg Kiesewetter, *Geschichte der europäisch-abendländischen oder unserer heutigen Musik* (Leipzig: Breitkopf und Härtel, 1834); trans. Robert Müller, as *History of the Modern Music of Western Europe, from the First Century of the Christian Era to the Present Day* (London: T. C. Tenby, 1848), p. 120.

16 *Ibid.*, p. 120.

17 *Ibid.*, p. 131.

18 Franz Brendel, *Geschichte der Musik* (Leipzig: Heinrich Matthes [F. C. Schilde], 1851). Brendel's history ran to nine editions, frequently (though not in the sections under consideration here) revised, between 1851 and 1906. I have used the fifth edition, of 1875.

19 G. W. F. Hegel, *Vorlesungen über die Philosophie der Geschichte,* in *Sämtliche Werke* vol. XI ed. H. Glockner (Stuttgart: F. Frommann, 1928), p. 518. See Ernst Gombrich, "In Search of Cultural History," in his *Ideals and Idols: Essays on Values in History and in Art* (London: Phaidon, 1979; originally published 1969), p. 33.

20 See Brendel, *Geschichte*, p. 115. Similarly Hegel describes a process whereby Christian art, through its accruing of the "sensual" and "spiritual," came to detach itself from the church which had nurtured it (see *Vorlesungen über die Philosophie der Geschichte*, p. 516; quoted in Gombrich, "In Search of Cultural History," p. 33).

21 "Denn kaum gereift, kaum zu höherem, selbstständigem Dasein entfaltet, verlässt sie [die Kunst] die Hallen des Tempels und eilt hinaus in die Welt" (Brendel, *Geschichte*, p. 114).

22 This view of music only truly finding its feet through breaking away from the church has a history extending back at least to Burney. For Burney, however, reflecting the high status he accords opera, the "long infancy and childhood" bounded by music's reliance on chant was only ended once it "broke loose from the trammels of the church, and mounted the stage as a secular amusement" (Burney, *A General History*, vol. I, p. 425; see also Hegar, *Die Anfänge*, p. 42).

23 August Wilhelm Ambros, *Geschichte der Musik*, vol. II (Leipzig: Leuckart, 1864; 3rd edn., revised by Heinrich Reimann, 1891), and vol. III. Citations from the *Geschichte* will be given in translation with insertion of original text where there is potential for ambiguity. References, given in the main text, will be to volume number and page.

24 See for example Julian Schmidt, *Geschichte der deutschen Nationalliteratur* (1853, p. 341) as translated and quoted in the following passage by Philipp Naegele: "More or less the entire generation which today claims a literary education has to some extent gone through the philosophical school [of Hegel and his followers]. One is tempted to say that its influence lies in the air and that those who concern themselves the least with it also remain the least immune to it, for the influence of a power which one does not comprehend is the hardest to ward off" (Philipp Otto Naegele, "August Wilhelm Ambros: his Historical and Critical Thought," unpublished PhD dissertation, Princeton University, 1954, Chapter 2, p. 38).

25 Ernst Gombrich, "In Search of Cultural History," pp. 34–42.

26 For Hegel the unifying operation is itself yet another instance in which the general "resolves" or "synthesizes" what is essential in the particular; the means

is inherent in the end. This is a characteristic which, as he makes clear, is (or should be) a fundamental property of the work of art: "Where the particular appears only as a means to a specific end, it neither has nor should have any validity and life of its own, but on the contrary is to manifest in its entire existence that it is there only for the sake of something else, i.e. the specific end. The category of means and end makes obvious its dominion over the objective world in which the end is realized. But the work of art differentiates the fundamental topic that has been selected as its center by developing its particular features, and to these it imparts the appearance of independent freedom; and this it must do because these particulars are nothing but that topic itself in the form of its actually corresponding realization" (G. W. F. Hegel, *Aesthetics: Lectures on Fine Art*, 2 vols., trans. and ed. T. M. Knox (Oxford University Press, 1975), vol. II, p. 984).

Observing the linkage between *particular* artwork and *general* universal system, Robert Wicks notes that "The principle of organic unity ... clearly exemplifies how a beautiful artwork renders perceivable Hegel's metaphysical vision of the total systematicity of the universe: the organic unity of the artwork visually represents the metaphysical interconnectedness of all things, perceptual and non-perceptual. The beautiful artwork is a microcosm and perceptually reveals one aspect of 'the divine' through its perceivable exemplification of organic structure. The most-beautiful artworks offer us a vision of what is perfect, what is 'divine,' by means of their perfected, idealized, systematically unified appearance" (Robert Wicks, "Hegel's Aesthetics: An Overview," in Frederick C. Beiser [ed.], *The Cambridge Companion to Hegel* [Cambridge University Press, 1993], p. 368).

27 To quote Wicks again: "The principle of *organic unity* ... determines beauty as a mode of perfection. According to this well-known principle, the beauty of an artwork or natural object corresponds to its degree of organization or integration. In the ideal case, no elements of an artwork or natural object appear arbitrary, unplanned, accidental, or irrational. The best artworks have no 'dead spots.' Beauty thus becomes identified with systematicity, or an intense 'unity in diversity' in the field of appearance" (*ibid.*, pp. 367–8).

28 The coincidence that led to the location of the musical Renaissance in the early fifteenth century is elucidated in Owens, "Music Historiography."

29 Ambros himself was clearly well aware of this process. Quoting Burney via Kiesewetter, he offers a clear instance of its operation during the eighty or so years leading up to his own *Geschichte*. For Burney, Palestrina's music reveals everywhere "the fire of genius ... in spite of the cramping limitations of cantus firmus, of canon, of fugue, of inversions which would be enough to freeze others or turn them to stone" (vol. III, pp. 207–8). For Ambros, on the other hand, writing in a time by which the prevailing idioms of Palestrina's time had become much more familiar, "this remark would apply incomparably better to Josquin. With him – far more strongly than with Palestrina – one perceives

beneath the limiting constraints of the contrapuntal style the powerfully driving fire of genius" (vol. III, p. 208).

30 For a detailed consideration of the eighteenth- and nineteenth-century rediscovery of Josquin and its relation to his sixteenth-century reputation, see my "From Humanism to Enlightenment: Reinventing Josquin," *Journal of Musicology* 17 (1999), 441–58.

31 A particularly colorful view of this by Gustav Schilling casts Josquin himself in this role, operating as a kind of composing Pied Piper. Josquin's "folk-like" melodies made even his church music "an object for the entertainment of merry companies, who sang his Masses and danced to his melodies ..." He is thus endowed with the responsibility for leading music out of the church and into the realm of the people: "Josquin, through his Masses, became a folk composer in the true sense of the word, and thus the first who led harmonic music, and new music generally, out of the Church and into the circles of the people ..." (*Geschichte der heutigen oder modernen Musik. In ihrem Zusammenhang mit der allgemeinen Welt- und Völkergeschichte* [Karlsruhe: Christian Theodor Groos, 1841], p. 165. Quoted in Jürg Stenzl, "'In das Reich der schönen Kunst ganz einzutreten, war ihm nicht beschieden': zur Josquin-Reception im 19. Jahrhundert," in Heinz-Klaus Metzger and Rainer Riehn [eds.], *Musik Konzepte* 26/27: *Josquin des Prés* [Munich: Johannesdruck Hans Pribil, 1982], p. 94).

32 For Burckhardt's view see Gombrich, "In Search of Cultural History," p. 37: "These demands [of the church] ... are [for Burckhardt] largely negative. The spirit of worship must not be deflected and diverted by anything that reminded the beholder of the realities of secular life. Wherever these are deliberately brought into art the picture will no longer look devout." See also the quotations at the opening of this chapter for Bukofzer's view of the relation between the "Renaissance" composer and the church.

33 Commenting, in one of his typical analogies to the visual arts, on Ockeghem's earlier status as the "forefather" (*Stammvater*) of music, Ambros observes how research has now opened up the music of earlier generations: "It became customary to view him as the patriarch – even the forefather – of music, roughly as Cimabue had for a long time been seen as the forefather of Christian painting, until deeper research also established a significant artistic practice before his time" (*Geschichte*, vol. III, pp. 173–4).

34 For Ambros's role in the promulgation of the notion of the "Netherlandish" schools, following Kiesewetter, and in face of the fact that many of the composers under discussion received their training elsewhere, see Paula Higgins, "Antoine Busnois and Musical Culture in Late Fifteenth Century France and Burgundy," unpublished PhD dissertation, Princeton University, 1987, pp. 222–5.

35 "In the works of this school a fully developed art finally steps forth. It is no contradiction if in its details elementary and undeveloped [elements] can

frequently be shown, and if this art described as completely developed appears only as the beginning of an almost two hundred year long development. It is completely developed in the sense that its composers are no longer seeking – testing and experimenting – the rules of art, but, in fully conscious possession of the rules of art, are capable of creating the artwork corresponding to them. Here for the first time step forward musicians who are not scholastics, not acousticians, not mathematicians, not archaeologists, but true artists" (Ambros, *Geschichte*, vol. II, p. 453).

36 Ambros's rhetoric is closely aligned to that of such Romantic authors as Jean Paul and E. T. A. Hoffmann (see for example Stenzl, " 'In das Reich,' " 97–8). He directly invokes Jean Paul, for example, in his praise of Josquin's *Missa La sol fa re mi*, a work displaying "that deep, almost passionate longing that, according to the opinion of many enthusiastic friends of music (as for example Jean Paul), constitutes the profoundest nature of all music and permits it to become understood as an art of higher longing [*als eine Art höheren Heimwehes verstanden worden ist*]" (vol. III, p. 213; see Stenzl, " 'In das Reich,' " 100). For a strong advocacy of this aspect of Ambros's history and its value in opening up modern access to music of the period, see Friedhelm Krummacher, "Wissenschaftsgeschichte und Werkrezeption: Die 'alten Niederländer' im 19. Jahrhundert," in Hermann Danuser and Friedhelm Krummacher (eds.), *Rezeptionsästhetik und Rezeptionsgeschichte in der Musikwissenschaft* (Laaber: Laaber Verlag, c.1991), pp. 205–22. See for example p. 215, where Ambros and Spitta are yoked together in this common aim: "What united the two authors, however, was the urgent attempt to open up the music of the past by means of the aesthetic categories of their current music. And behind this stood the intention to make old music accessible not only as a historical object, but as an effective art for the present. While Ambros may from time to time have proceeded incautiously in the transfer of aesthetic categories, it is clear that access to Renaissance music was possible only under this condition."

37 Thus "Even meager two-part counterpoint acquires warmth, color and life in the hands of Du Fay (Benedictus of the Mass *Ecce ancilla*)" (Ambros, *Geschichte*, vol. II, p. 498).

38 "Du Fay was the first whose works show true style, and who gave to musical works that form, that organic construction, which, centuries later (albeit expanded and modified in various ways) remain both rule and law" (*ibid.*, p. 496). In this context it is worth pointing out that for Kiesewetter, writing thirty years earlier, "manifest design" was only observable in compositions as far back as Ockeghem. Before that composers contented themselves with "mere premeditated submissions to the contrapunctic operation" (Kiesewetter, *Geschichte*, p. 128; for more on this see my " 'Under Such Heavy Chains' ").

39 See Naegele, "Ambros," Chapter 2, p. 81; Chapter 3, pp. 70, 75–6.

40 This "way back" of course already embodies the notion of some sort of Renaissance through its implicit assumption of a concept of musical "art"

during antiquity, to which the music of the pre–Du Fay era was forging a return. Ambros's view reveals its lineage from such anticipations of the notion of a Renaissance as that of Hegel, for whom the "revival of learning" of the study of antiquity was an essential factor in the ending of the Middle Ages (see Gombrich, "In Search of Cultural History," p. 33).

41 For more on this process see Jessie Ann Owens, "Music Historiography," 328.

42 In the words of Forkel, "All things have a small beginning, and grow upwards only gradually to that goal which, in accordance with their original nature, they are capable of attaining" (Forkel, *Allgemeine Geschichte*, vol. II, p. 486).

43 Thus just as the transformations of ecclesiastical doctrine (*Kirchenlehre*) into other areas of thought "are no mere exegeses of that which had been handed down" ("keine blosse Exegese des Gegebenen"), so "in a closely analogous way the Netherlands composers built on Gregorian chant as a Holy [tradition], and from its elements [built] a rich musical world. The church modes, in their original state scarcely more than formulas for singing within single species of fifth and fourth, developed only in the multi-voiced, artful tonal fabrics of the masters the full extent of their hidden potential for cultivation and their profound meaning; Gregorian melody, already in its naked state like a pure, original folk melody, imbued with a peculiar elemental power [gleich jeder urwüchsig-echten Volksweise voll eigenthümlicher Urkraft], allowed only here the recognition of the full extent of its higher musical meaning" (Ambros, *Geschichte*, vol. III, p. 14).

44 See the discussion above. As in so many areas, Ambros is not entirely consistent in his application of the idea of "organicism." His direct, and acknowledged, source for his notion of an "organic" style in music was Burckhardt's revision and expansion of Kugler's *Geschichte der Baukunst*, where the *organischer Stil* of northern "Gothic" architecture (a style allegedly consisting of the working out of small details) is contraposed against the *Raumstyl* (a style evincing a new concern with large-scale architectonic proportions) of Italian Renaissance buildings. In Ambros's analogue, the music of the Netherlanders pertains to the former while the latter finds its musical counterpart in Italian music's "emancipation" from its Netherlandish models. Significantly, he sees the most extreme development of this "organicism" in the construction of an entire Mass deriving from a brief succession of notes: he gives the example of Josquin's *Missa Faisant regretz* (see Ambros, *Geschichte*, vol. III, p. 503; quoted and discussed in Naegele, "Ambros," Chapter 2, p. 71 and Chapter 3, pp. 119–21).

45 Ambros goes on to sharpen his view of this dialectical process via reference to imitation, the stylistic aspect of music beginning in the late fifteenth century that is probably most susceptible to a dialectical interpretation: "Imitation builds the innermost core of polyphony. It emphasizes with clarity the inner cohesion of the tonal fabric; the voices, while answering one another, proceed under each other in direct interchange; at length the melody performs the

dialectical process on itself and within itself, as its own elements become subject and counter-subject; what is otherwise temporally divided in it is allowed to sound together simultaneously, and brings to consciousness the multi-faceted connections of its individual elements in a new, higher meaning" ("endlich vollzieht die Melodie den dialektischen Prozess an sich und in sich selbst, indem sie ihre eigenen Glieder zu Satz und Gegensatz werden, das sonst in ihr zeitlich Getrennte gleichzeitig zusammenklingen lässt und die wechselseitige Beziehung ihrer einzelnen Glieder in einer neuen, höheren Bedeutung zum Bewusstsein bringt") (Ambros, *Geschichte*, vol. III, pp. 9–10).

Thus dialectic is used to describe imitation's characteristic of bringing together the different parts of a melody temporally, in order to make processes in time appear simultaneous or even static. In this way Ambros sharpens the atemporalizing focus which, through such notions as "unity" and "cyclicity," helped to draw pieces of music towards the material condition of the other fine arts and thereby to hypostatize them as musical "works."

46 For a discussion and critique of Ambros's relation to Burckhardt, see Naegele, "Ambros," Chapter 2, pp. 71–9 and *passim*.

47 Thus for Hegel, as for Burckhardt and Ambros, the "new spirit" was characterized by a new sense of sensuality, beauty and individualism: "These three facts, the so-called revival of learning, the efflorescence of the fine arts, and the discovery of America ... may be compared to the dawn, the harbinger of a new fine day after the long, fateful and terrible night of the Middle Ages ..." (Gombrich, "In Search of Cultural History," p. 33).

48 For more on the Hegelian frame of Brendel's history and its likely influence, see my " 'Under Such Heavy Chains.' "

49 Such had not always been the case in his writings: Naegele ("Ambros," Chapter 2, p. 12) observes the clear and acknowledged Hegelian framework of a number of Ambros's earlier tracts. Notwithstanding Hegel's sometimes more shadowy presence in the *Geschichte* and his frequent infiltration via younger Hegelians (including A. B. Marx), it is never in doubt that (as Naegele puts it) "both his own statements and his frequent unacknowledged quotations and paraphrases of Hegelian sentences point to the Hegelian philosophy as the most important single source of Ambros' philosophical orientation" (*ibid.*, Chapter 2, p. 15).

50 This stance is the entirely logical outcome of two basic considerations that Ambros, as he himself observes, took over from Burckhardt (for a discussion of this see *ibid.*, Chapter 3, pp. 104, 119). First, like other manifestations of the Renaissance, monody originated in Italy. Second, monody is characterized by subjectiveness and individualism, in contrast to the more collective ethos Ambros sees behind "Netherlandish" polyphony. Only by the time, at the end of the sixteenth century, that the natural course of northern polyphony had been run and Italy was ready and waiting in the wings was monody able truly to assert itself as the "delayed birth of the 'new age,' the age of the Renaissance, in its most particular sense, which freed man from those medieval associations

and emancipated him as an individual" (Ambros, *Geschichte*, vol. III, p. 11). Further support for this later "Renaissance" is supplied in the preface to volume II, where Ambros adds that monody constituted a Renaissance "insofar that, in contrast to music arising out of Gregorian chant, it emerged through a systematic restoration of ancient music" (vol. II, p. XXII).

51 This discrepancy may in any case have caused Ambros less anxiety than might be imagined: it is of a piece with his general notion of a "time-lag" in the development of music vis-à-vis the other arts. This is a putative phenomenon which, in his earlier *Die Gränzen der Musik und Poesie* (1856), he had rationalized – under the influence of Hegel and A. B. Marx – as a reflection of music's dual status as both the most vivid expression of "the spirit" and an "architectural" art with all the "purely constructive" demands that this entails (see Naegele, "Ambros," Chapter 3, pp. 59–60). These views of music lagging behind the other arts and being weakened by its communion with them were not unique to Ambros: Burney had similarly seen music as a slow developer, a factor which already in ancient Greece was accountable to its dependence on another art form, in this case poetry.

52 See Owens, "Music Historiography," 328.

53 See above. In drawing a chronological distinction between the beginning of the "Neuzeit" and the "Renaissance," Ambros may have taken his cue from Burckhardt's apparent division between a "new spirit" and a "Renaissance" expression of that spirit. See for example the latter's remark that "it was the Italian of the Renaissance ... who had to withstand the first tremendous surge of the new age" (see Gombrich, "In Search of Cultural History," p. 40).

54 See Ambros, *Geschichte*, vol. III, pp. 8–9.

55 *Ibid.*, p. 9. See for example Ambros's judgments on the repertory of the Squarcialupi Codex (*Geschichte*, vol. II, pp. 534–7).

56 In the realm of the Hegelian absolute spirit, as Naegele eloquently puts it, "the subject – the individual – recognizes the identity of his will and of objective necessity as the measure of his freedom and of his self-consciousness ... Freedom and necessity become identical inasmuch as the highest form of freedom consists in the conscious recognition of necessity" (Naegele, "Ambros," Chapter 2, p. 16).

57 Friedrich Blume, *Renaissance and Baroque Music: A Comprehensive Survey*, trans. and ed. M. D. Herter Norton (London: Faber and Faber, 1969), p. 30 (translations of articles originally published in *Die Musik in Geschichte und Gegenwart*).

58 Franz X. Haberl, "Wilhelm du Fay," 397–530. Baini's dating of Du Fay's career was, however, strongly opposed in 1867 by F. W. Arnold. See his "Das Lochemer Liederbuch nebst der Ars Organisandi von Conrad Paumann," in Friedrich Chrysander (ed.), *Jahrbuch für musikalische Wissenschaft*, vol. II (Leipzig: Breitkopf und Härtel, 1867), pp. 47–58. Basing his conclusions on Tinctoris, Martin le Franc, Adam von Fulda and later theorists, along with a

careful consideration of more circumstantial evidence, Arnold dates Du Fay's life with remarkable accuracy. He proposes a birth date between 1400 and 1405 and even – on the basis of Tinctoris's remark in 1476 that Du Fay, along with Dunstaple and Binchois, was "novissimus temporibus vita functos" – correctly guesses the year of his death. He thus concludes that Baini's singer and the composer must have been two different people. His views were also adopted by Arrey von Dommer (*Handbuch der Musik-Geschichte*, [Leipzig: Grunow, 1868], pp. 75–6), who briefly, and accurately, adumbrated some of the revisions this would imply for the history of polyphony.

59 For discussion of this priority as articulated by Burney, Forkel, Baini, Kiesewetter and Brendel see my "'Under Such Heavy Chains.'"

60 See pages 17–20, and Owens, "Music Historiography," which addresses in depth the historical coincidence that led to the location of the musical "Renaissance" in the early fifteenth century.

61 Indeed, the "unity" and "coherence" perceived in the Mass were of a much more obvious or surface nature than the underlying unity traditionally imputed to the eighteenth- and nineteenth-century symphonies and sonatas in the context of which such principles had been first applied. In the words of Richard Cohn and Douglas Dempster, the "principal and most persistent canon governing our Western aesthetic is that successful works of art, including the 'masterpieces' of Western art music, exhibit unity, coherence, or 'organic' integrity. Music theory upholds this canon in its seminal commitment to the presupposition that musical unity is to be found not 'exposed on' the complex, sometimes bewildering phenomenal 'surface' of a composition, but rather 'hidden in' some 'underlying' structural simplicity" ("Hierarchical Unity, Plural Unities: Toward a Reconciliation," in Katherine Bergeron and Philip V. Bohlman (eds.), *Disciplining Music: Musicology and Its Canons* (Chicago and London: Chicago University Press, 1992), p. 156). One might have expected the distinction between the "underlying" unity claimed for common-practice works and the very different "unity" perceived in fifteenth- and sixteenth-century polyphony to have brought the application of the notion of "organic unity" to early repertories into question; yet any such concern was easily overridden by the inextricable linkage traditionally assumed to exist between the notion of unity and that of artistic value, and the desire to associate earlier repertories with both.

62 The application of the notion of "cyclicity" to Western music in general, and the Mass in particular, is too large and ramified a topic to be addressed here. As noted above, the application to musically linked settings of the five movements of the Mass Ordinary of the word "cycle" or "Zyklus" seems to have occurred for the first time in 1913, in the *Geschichte der Messe* of Peter Wagner.

63 For discussion of some implications of these issues in the context of a range of Masses in these categories see my essays "Innovation, Stylistic Patterns and the Writing of History: The Case of Bedyngham's Mass *Deuil angouisseux*,"

in Peter Wright and Marco Gozzi (eds.), *I Codici Musicali Trentini: Nuove scoperte e nuovi orientamenti della ricerca* (Trento: Provincia autonoma di Trento, 1996), pp. 149–76 and "Quinti toni in Context: Currents in Three-voice Mass Writing in the Later Fifteenth Century," in Philippe Vendrix (ed.), *Johannes Ockeghem: Actes du XIe Colloque international d'études humanistes* (Paris: Klincksieck, 1999), pp. 481–98.

64 See most obviously Edgar H. Sparks, *Cantus Firmus in Mass and Motet* (Berkeley: University of California Press, 1963), pp. 119–90, 239–41, where the cantus firmus and other procedures of some composers, such as Ockeghem, are dubbed predominantly "irrational," as opposed to the "rational" practices favored by Busnoys and others.

65 Here again, as in such notions as that of a musical "Renaissance" beginning in the early fifteenth century, we see the tenacity with which such notions, once rooted, can persist.

66 Thomas Brothers has suggested that the *Missa Alma redemptoris mater* is not "truly analogous to isorhythmic practice" because it "lacks a repetition of pitches within each movement." Yet some single "isorhythmic" Mass movements by the same composer in the Old Hall manuscript similarly lack such repetitions. (See Thomas Brothers, "Vestiges of the Isorhythmic Tradition in Mass and Motet, ca. 1450–1475," *Journal of the American Musicological Society* 44 [1991], 3. See also the editions of and commentary on Credos nos. 84 and 85 in Andrew Hughes and Margaret Bent, *The Old Hall Manuscript*, Corpus Mensurabilis Musicae 46, 3 vols. [(Rome): American Institute of Musicology, 1969–73].) Conversely, the movements of many early "cantus firmus" Masses, Du Fay's *Se la face ay pale*, for example, do involve repeats of the cantus firmus. All this goes to show is that, as Margaret Bent has demonstrated, "isorhythm," a term devised by Friedrich Ludwig in the early years of the twentieth century, has been too narrowly conceived to respond to the scope of rhythmic and melodic manipulation perceptible in motet (in which one might reasonably include Mass-movement) writing of the fourteenth and early fifteenth centuries. (see Margaret Bent, "The Late-medieval Motet," in Tess Knighton and David Fallows [eds.], *A Companion to Medieval and Renaissance Music* [London: Dent, 1992], pp. 114–19).

67 Support for this conclusion may be seen in the source tradition of many early Masses, such as the *Missa Rex seculorum* variously ascribed to Dunstaple and Power, whose movements are scattered across manuscripts and indeed between sources.

68 Interestingly, Bukofzer's insistence that the "cyclic tenor Mass is the most influential achievement of the English school of Renaissance music" did not prevent him from emphasizing the continuity between the "isorhythmic" Mass movements of Old Hall and early Mass movements, pairs and the *Missa Alma redemptoris mater*: "The idea of writing a Mass setting on a tenor not borrowed from plainsongs of the Ordinary was prompted by a medieval

form, the isorhythmic motet. The fountainhead of the development is the transfer of the isorhythmic technique to the Mass, to which many single isorhythmic Mass sections in OH and LoF [the Fountains Fragments] attest" ("*Caput*: A Liturgico-Musical Study," pp. 221 and 223). See also Bukofzer's contribution, "English Church Music of the Fifteenth Century," to Anselm Hughes and Gerald Abraham (eds.), *The New Oxford History of Music*, vol. III (London: Oxford University Press, 1960): "This significant innovation [the cyclic tenor Mass] was obviously prompted by isorhythmic methods of composition; it is no accident that we find so many isorhythmic Masses [*sic*] in the Old Hall manuscript" (pp. 203–4).

69 Terry Eagleton, *The Ideology of the Aesthetic* (Oxford: Blackwell, 1990), p. 8.

70 Gombrich, "In Search of Cultural History," pp. 41–2.

Chapter 2 Contemporary witnesses

1 The complete definition reads "Missa est cantus magnus cui verba Kyrie, et In terra, Patrem, Sanctus et Agnus, et interdum caeterae partes a pluribus canendae supponuntur, quae ab aliis officium dicitur." See Johannes Tinctoris, *Tinctoris: Dictionary of Musical Terms*, trans. and ed. Carl Parrish (New York: Free Press of Glencoe, 1963), p. 41.

2 Manuel Erviti, "The Motet as an Expression of Sociocultural Value circa 1500," unpublished PhD dissertation, University of Illinois at Champaign-Urbana, 1997, pp. 33, 38–9. For an excellent overview and bibliography of the enormous importance of Cicero in the late medieval academy and of Tinctoris's wide and deep familiarity with his treatises, see *ibid.*, pp. 26–9. See also Sean Gallagher, "Models of Varietas: Studies in Style and Attribution in the Motets of Johannes Regis and His Contemporaries," unpublished PhD dissertation, Harvard University, 1998, pp. 49–71. For the sociocultural significance of Tinctoris's definitions see Erviti, "The Motet," *passim*, but particularly pp. 46–90. On Tinctoris's Ciceronianism specifically, see Ronald Woodley, "Johannes Tinctoris: A Review of the Documentary Evidence," *Journal of the American Musicological Society* 34 (1981), 217–48. The same preeminence of music for the Mass over that for motets and (in this case improvised) songs in Paolo Cortese's similarly Ciceronian *De cardinalatu libri tres* (see p. 29) seems, as for Tinctoris, to be a reflection of its superior social status at the focal point of medieval ritual, and indeed of life generally. See Nino Pirrotta, "Music and Cultural Tendencies in 15th-century Italy," *Journal of the American Musicological Society* 19 (1966), 142–3. Pirrotta further proposes, however, that "The songs accompanying the sacrifice of the Mass ... are highest in his esteem because of the humanist's prejudice that the importance of the text essentially determines the esthetic value of its music."

3 "Hanc autem diversitatem optimi quisque ingenii compositor aut concentor efficiet, si nunc per unam quantitatem, nunc per aliam, nunc per unam perfectionem, nunc per unam proportionem, nunc per aliam, nunc per unam coniunctionem,

nunc per aliam, nunc cum syncopis, nunc sine syncopis, nunc cum fugis, nunc sine fugis, nunc cum pausis, nunc sine pausis, nunc diminutive, nunc plane, aut componat aut concinnat. Verumtamen in his omnibus summa est adhibenda ratio, quippe ut de concentu super librum taceam qui pro voluntate concinentium diversificari potest, nec tot nec tales varietates uni cantilenae congruunt quot et quales uni moteti, nec tot et tales uni moteti quot et quales uni missae.

Omnis itaque res facta pro qualitate et quantitate eius diversificanda est prout infinita docent opera ..." (*Liber de arte contrapuncti* [1477], III. p. viii. See Johannes Tinctoris, *Johannis Tinctoris opera theoretica*, ed. Albert Seay, Corpus scriptorum de musica, no. 22/2 [Rome: American Institute of Musicology, 1975], p. 155).

4 "Quemadmodum enim in arte dicendi varietas, secundum Tullii sententiam, auditorem maxime delectat, ita et in musica concentuum diversitas animos auditorum vehementer in oblectamentum provocat ..." (*ibid.*).

5 See Horst Weber, "Varietas, variatio / Variation, Variante," in Hans Heinrich Eggebrecht (ed.), *Handwörterbuch der musikalischen Terminologie*, 14. Auslieferung (Stuttgart: Franz Steiner, Winter 1986–7), p. 17.

6 For a facsimile, translation and commentary on the relevant parts of the treatise see Pirrotta, "Music and Cultural Tendencies," 142–4 and 146–61.

7 The translation combines aspects of that by Pirrotta (*ibid.*, 154) with a detailed translation kindly supplied by Leofranc Holford-Strevens. The original, from Pirrotta (*ibid.*, 150) is as follows: "litatoria enim sunt ea / in quibus omnia pthongorum / prosodiarum analogicarumque mensionum genera versantur / & in quibus musicorum generi laus cantus praeclare struendi datur: ex quo non sine causa Io. Medices senator homo in musicis litterata pervestigatione prudens / neminem in praestantium musicorum numerorum referendum esse censet / qui minus gnarus litatorii modi faciendi sit. Itaque ob id unum inter multos Iuschinum Gallum praestitisse ferunt / propterea quod ad litatoria cantus genera plus doctrinae sit ab eo adiectum / quam addi a / recentium musicorum ieiuna sedulitate soleat."

8 See Rolf Dammann, "Geschichte der Begriffsbestimmung Motette," *Archiv für Musikwissenschaft* 16/4 (1959), 337–77, *passim*. See for example 347, from the anonymous *Discantus positio vulgaris*: "Mothetus vero est super determinatas notas firmi cantus mensuratas, sive ultra mensuram diversus in notis, diversus in prosis multiplex consonans cantus."

9 As Margaret Bent has observed, the French predilection for motet construction based on a *cantus prius factus* in the tenor was not shared by Italian or English composers. See her "The Late-medieval Motet," in Tess Knighton and David Fallows (eds.), *Companion to Medieval and Renaissance Music* (Oxford and New York: Oxford University Press, 1992), p. 117.

10 Hence Grocheio's distinction between "laying out" (*ordinare*) the tenors of motets and organum and "composing" (*componere*) the tenors of conductus. See Christopher Page, "Johannes de Grocheio on Secular Music," *Plainsong and Medieval Music* 2 (1993), 17–41, at 39, and Dammann, "Motette," 351.

11 For stipulations of this nature from Grocheio, Jacques de Liège and the Quatuor principalia, see Dammann, "Motette," 353.

12 See Martin Staehelin, "Beschreibungen und Beispiele musikalischer Formen in einem unbeachteten Traktat des frühen 15. Jahrhunderts," *Archiv für Musikwissenschaft* 31 (1974), 238 and 242; see also Erviti, "The Motet," p. 17, who points out that sets of instructions as to how to compose motets disappear from music theory until the end of the sixteenth century, when they resurface in the treatises of such theorists as Pontio, Cerone and Morley.

13 Erviti, "The Motet," pp. 44.

14 See Margaret Bent, "A Note on the Dating of the Trémouïlle Manuscript," in Bryan Gillingham and Paul Merkley (eds.), *Beyond the Moon: Festschrift Luther Dittmer* (Ottawa: Institute of Medieval Music, 1990), pp. 217–42. Further songs are listed in the contents of Part 2 of the source, something which did not deter the scribe of the note indicating its ownership from using the umbrella term "motet" to cover the collection as a whole: "*Iste liber motetorum pertinet capelle illustrissimi principis Philippi ducis Burgondie et comitis Flandrie*" (see Bent, "A Note," pp. 217, 218).

15 See Maria del Carmen Gómez Muntané, *La Música en la casa real Catalano-Aragonesa durante los años 1336–1432*, 2 vols. (Barcelona: Antoni Bosch, 1977), vol. I, pp. 207–8. I wish to thank Rob Wegman for this and a number of the other references of this nature presented here.

16 Enrico Peverada, *Vita musicale nella chiesa Ferrarese del quattrocento* (Ferrara: Capitolo Cattedrale, 1991), p. 135. The comma added in Peverada's transcription of this document after "Mutetis" is editorial.

17 Alfons Dewitte, "Boek- en bibliotheekwesen in de Brugse Sint-Donaaskerk XIIIe–XVe eeuw," in *Sint-Donaas en de voormalige Brugse Katedraal* (Bruges: Jong Kristen Onthaal voor Toerisme, 1978), p. 85. Reinhard Strohm makes the same point concerning terminology in connection with this record. For more on the record and on Couterman, who was also a composer, see Strohm, *Music in Late Medieval Bruges* (Oxford University Press, 2nd rev. edn., 1990), p. 21.

18 See Craig Wright, "Dufay at Cambrai: Discoveries and Revisions," *Journal of the American Musicological Society* 28 (1975), 226.

19 Transcribed in *ibid.*, 228.

20 See Fiona Kisby, "Music and Musicians of Early Tudor Westminster," *Early Music* 23 (1995), 226. The sum paid for the copying, 16*d*, was the same as that paid two years previously for the "prykyng of a masse in the prykedsong boke" (both records are transcribed in *ibid.*, 237).

21 See Jules Houdoy, *Histoire Artistique de la Cathédrale de Cambrai*, Mémoire de la Société des Sciences de l'Agriculture et des Arts de Lille 4th series, vol. VII (Lille: L. Danel, 1880), pp. 188–93.

22 Strohm, *Bruges*, p. 23. For the copying records of St. Donatian see Dewitte, "Boek- en bibliotheekwesen," pp. 83–95.

23 This record is quoted and briefly discussed in my articles "La musique à la collégiale à la fin du moyen âge," in Nicolette Delanne-Logié and Yves-Marie

Hilaire (eds.), *La cathédrale de Saint-Omer: 800 ans de mémoire vive* (Paris: Centre Nationale de la Recherche Scientifique, 2000), pp. 135–6; and "Musical Life at the Collegiate Church of Saint-Omer, Northern France, in the Fifteenth Century," *Humanas* (*Revista do Instituto de Filosofia e Ciências Humanas da Universidade do Rio Grande do Sul*), 21/1, pt. 2 (1998), 324.

24 The Mass is found on folios CClxxxiijv–CCxcvjr. For a brief discussion see Daniel Leech-Wilkinson, *Machaut's Mass: An Introduction* (Oxford University Press, 1990), p. 9; Leech-Wilkinson notes that, perhaps significantly, this manuscript is the most accurate source for the Mass.

25 "... domino Johani Filiberti cantori cappellano domini florenos duos auri donandos duobus francigenis qui dederunt prefato domino nostro librum unum cantus sex missarum novarum ..." See Lewis Lockwood, *Music in Renaissance Ferrara* (Oxford University Press, 1984), p. 52.

26 Suparmi Saunders, "The Dating of the Trent Codices from Their Watermarks, with a Study of the Local Liturgy of Trent in the Fifteenth Century" (New York and London: Garland, 1989), pp. 91, 197–8; Saunders's evidence is refined in Peter Wright's essays "Johannes Wiser's Paper and the Copying of His Manuscripts," in Peter Wright (ed.), *I Codici Musicali Trentini: Nuove scoperte e nuovi orientamenti della ricerca* (Trento: Provincia autonoma di Trento, 1996), pp. 31–53, and "Watermarks and Musicology: The Genesis of Johannes Wiser's Collection," *Early Music History* 22 (2003), 247–332.

27 See Margaret Bent, "A Contemporary Perception of Early Fifteenth-Century Style: Bologna Q15 as a Document of Scribal Editorial Initiative," *Musica Disciplina* 12 (1987), 186, 191–3.

28 Such separation can take a systematic form, as in the case of the six cycles whose individual movements head the sections of Glorias, Credos and so on in Trent 93 and Trent 90, or an apparently haphazard one, as in the case of the *Missa Rex seculorum* variously ascribed to Dunstaple and Power. The movements of the latter are scattered in various copies between six manuscripts, the only movements appearing anywhere contiguously being the Credo and Sanctus on folios 46v–9r of Trent 92. For the later end of this trend see for example the various movements detached from cycles and transmitted in Trent 89 (copied c.1460–8: see Peter Wright, "Johannes Wiser's Paper," specific watermark datings on pp. 36–7) and the Strahov Manuscript (Prague, Museum of Czech Literature, Strahov Library D.G. IV. 47, compiled between c.1460 and c.1480: see Charles Hamm and Herbert Kellman [eds.], *Census Catalog of Manuscript Sources of Polyphonic Music 1400–1550*, vol. III [(n.p.): Hänssler, American Institute of Musicology, 1984], p. 61).

29 Strohm suggests that the treatise was "written well before 1482" (*Bruges*, p. 123).

30 For the passage in Gaffurius see *Practica musice Franchini Gafori Laudensis* (Milan: Ioannes Petrus de Lomatio, 1496; repr. New York: Broude Brothers, 1979), *De Genere Superparticulari & eius speciebus. Caput Quintum: De Proportione sesqualtera.* For Tinctoris's usage see for example his definition in

the *Diffinitorium*: "Cantilena est cantus parvus: cui verba cuiuslibet materiae sed frequentius amatoriae supponuntur" (*Dictionary*, p. 13).

31 For the specifics of Ott's debt to Bembo, see Weber, "Varietas," p. 17.

32 "Primum enim ingentem copiam requirit ratio carminis, cujus forma per omnes partes, quas sane multas habet, debet esse sui similis. Alicubi quatuor temporibus absolvitur melodia totius Missae, alicubi paucioribus. Quis autem non videt, quam magna, & ea tamen accurata ac diligenti copia opus sit, ut eadem clausula per totam cantionem, non solum sine molestia, sed etiam cum suavitate et laude ingenii repetatur? Atque haec quoque caussa [*sic*] est, cur plurimum artis in Missis artifices ostenderint. Artis enim hoc proprium est opus, condire illam copiam, ne pariat fastidium, & nimia esse videatur. Hinc, quod in aliis cantionibus rarissimum est, tanta signorum varietas, tam mirabilis numerorum quasi distributio in Missis cernitur. Longe autem errant, si qui haec ostentandi gratia ab otiosis ingeniis adinventa putant. Necessitas fuit, quae coegit artifices ad has quasi praestigias querendas, quibus similitudinem melodiae occultarent, et eosdem sonos, subinde alia atque alia forma, sicut in scena histriones mutato cultu ostenderent" (*Missae tredecim quatuor vocibus* [Nuremberg: Hieronymus Graphaeus, 1539], preface by Johannes Ott, quoted from Ambros, *Geschichte der Musik*, vol. III [Leipzig: Leuckart, 1868; 3rd edn., rev. Otto Kade, 1893], p. 40, with minor corrections from the facsimile of the preface, provided, together with the author's own translation, in Royston Gustavson, "Hans Ott, Hieronymus Formschneider, and the *Novum et insigne opus musicum* [Nuremberg, 1537–1538]," unpublished PhD dissertation, 2 vols., University of Melbourne, 1999, vol. II, pp. 562–5).

33 In this Josquin was closely aligned with such contemporary German theorists as Glarean and Sebald Heyden. See for example Patrick Macey, "Josquin as Classic: *Qui habitat, Memor esto*, and Two Imitations Unmasked," *Journal of the Royal Musical Association* 118 (1993), 6–8.

34 It is possible, as Pirrotta observes, that Cortese's "modes of one kind (*uniusmodi modi*), on which the propitiatory songs [Masses] unremittingly insist ..." ("uniusmodi servarentur in canendo modi / quibus litatoria continuata cadunt ...") is also a reference to the repeated cantus firmi of Mass settings. In Pirrotta's view, the humanist context of Cortese's description suggests approval of the resulting uniformity and moderation ("Music and Cultural Tendencies," 160; original text 151).

Chapter 3 "Faisant regretz pour ma dolente vie": piety, polyphony and musical borrowing

1 Take heed, O man of worldly mien,
  Replete with pride and vanity,
  Leave off from your high-handed will
  And your desire to act in sin

You'll die: mark well what is certain,
And have remorse within your heart:
Make sure you know the sober truth:
That there's nothing more sure than death.

Jean Molinet, *Dictier pour penser a la mort*, in Jean Molinet, *Les faictz et dictz de Jean Molinet*, ed. Noël Dupire, vol. II (Paris: Société des anciens textes Français, 1937), p. 428. Translation by Philip Weller.

2 The standard literature on purgatory is too well known and too extensive to rehearse in detail here. The touchstone study remains Jacques Le Goff, *The Birth of Purgatory* (English edn., translated by Arthur Goldhammer, University of Chicago Press, 1981); on the link between purgatory and the penitential focus of Mass, see especially pp. 213–20, 289–98. The first fully to recognize the role in the fifteenth century of foundations with polyphony in the attempt to access the power of the Real Presence in seeking deliverance from purgatory was Barbara Haggh. See her pioneering PhD dissertation "Music, Liturgy and Ceremony in Brussels, 1350–1500," 2 vols., University of Illinois at Urbana-Champaign, 1988, particularly the Conclusion, pp. 503–26.

3 Jacques Chiffoleau makes the important point that the period from the mid fourteenth century on saw a greatly increased emphasis on a high density of Masses immediately following death, as opposed to devotions set to recur periodically in perpetuity. He sees this as a result of a greater emphasis by endowers on the quickest possible curtailment of their own personal expiation of sins in purgatory, as opposed to the collective desire – expressed by recurring devotions – to hasten the moment of grace ushered in by the Last Judgment (see his *La comptabilité de l'au-delà: les hommes, la mort et la religion dans la région d'Avignon à la fin du Moyen Âge [vers 1320–vers 1480]* [Rome: École française de Rome, 1980], pp. 339–56).

4 This point is emphatically underscored by Joel Rosenthal: "It is essential that we do not attempt to make any distinction between money and bequests given to the church for what we would today call spiritual purposes, for example the purchase of prayer services, and what we would see as secular charity, for example alms to the poor or to prisoners." See his *The Purchase of Paradise: Gift Giving and the Aristocracy, 1307–1485* (London: Routledge and Kegan Paul/ Toronto: University of Toronto Press, 1972), p. 9.

5 To quote Rosenthal again, "Almost all forms of medieval philanthropy had the purchase of prayers as their ultimate goal" (*ibid.*, p. 10).

6 For more on this issue see my essay "Personal Endowment: The Economic Engine of the 'Cyclic' Mass?" in Bruno Bouckaert (ed.), *Yearbook of the Alamire Foundation* 7 (2008), 71–81.

7 Reinhard Strohm, *Music in Late Medieval Bruges* (Oxford University Press, 2nd, rev. edn., 1990), pp. 40–1, 146–7.

8 Du Fay's will has been well known to musicology since its publication in transcription by Jules Houdoy in 1880 (*Histoire artistique de la cathédrale de*

Cambrai, ancienne église métropolitaine Notre-Dame: Comptes, inventaires et documents inédits [Mémoires de la Société des sciences, de l'agriculture, et des arts de Lille, 4th series, VII], pp. 409–14. The executors' account (Lille, Archives départementales du Nord 4 G 1313) has been widely discussed, primarily by Craig Wright and David Fallows (Craig Wright, "Dufay at Cambrai: Discoveries and Revisions," *Journal of the American Musicological Society* 28 [1975], 175–229; David Fallows, *Dufay* (London: Dent, 2nd, rev. edn., 1987), especially pp. 79–85).

9 A similar interaction likely involved Obrecht's Mass for St. Donatian, commissioned, as Strohm has shown (see above, note 7), for the benefit of the soul of the Bruges furrier Donaes de Moor. The purpose of the Mass was annual performance in the private chapel of Donaes and his wife in the Bruges church of St. James, probably before the (surviving) triptych, by the Master of the St. Lucy Legend, which depicts the couple being presented by their patron saints to a central depiction of the Lamentation (see Colin T. Eisler, *Early Netherlandish Painting: The Thyssen-Bornemisza Collection* [London: P. Wilson for Sotheby's Publications, 1989], pp. 116–23, 273; see also M. Jennifer Bloxam, website on the St. Donatian Mass [http://obrechtmass.com/home.php]). Pierre Henry's monthly *Ave Maria gratia dei plena per secula*, endowed at Notre Dame of Paris in 1486, and surely, as Craig Wright infers, implying performance (at least by 1501) of Brumel's surviving motet set to the same otherwise unknown text, represents a rare further link between a specific foundation and a known polyphonic piece (see Craig Wright, *Music and Ceremonial at Notre Dame of Paris 500–1550* [Cambridge University Press, 1989], pp. 185–6, 349). A further, and particularly vivid, example can be seen in the setting, in its unusually rich private chantry, of the tomb of Richard Beauchamp, Earl of Warwick in St. Mary's Church, Warwick. Beauchamp's tomb is surmounted by his life-size effigy in gilded latten (an alloy similar to bronze) surrounded by a cage-like hearse which would originally have been draped with a fabric cover, to be removed only during Masses celebrated for his soul. This practice reveals the reason behind the most unusual feature of the effigy: in contrast to the customary pressing together of the hands in prayer, the hands on Beauchamp's figure are held apart, focusing his gaze directly onto a ceiling boss depicting Mary as Queen of Heaven, an image nonetheless "visible" to the figure only during the progress of such Masses. The praying figure of Edward Despenser (the so-called "kneeling knight") in Tewkesbury Abbey, perpetually facing the high altar and hence also the regular transubstantiation, at Mass, of his maker, offers a similarly striking example of the same phenomenon.

10 Kirkman, "Personal Endowment," 79.

11 The same can be said of the anonymously surviving Mass for St. Anthony Abbot, which must almost certainly be Du Fay's documented Mass for that saint. See the liner notes, by Philip Weller, to the recording of that Mass by the Binchois Consort, conducted by Andrew Kirkman (Hyperion CDA 67474).

12 On Huizinga's views see M. Jennifer Bloxam, "A Cultural Context for the Chanson Mass," in Honey Meconi (ed.), *Early Musical Borrowing* (New York: Routledge, 2003) p. 19. I am grateful to Professor Bloxam for sending me a copy of her essay in advance of its publication.

13 Text and music found in a Gloria (paired with a closely related Credo) in Bologna Q15, ff. 35v–7r. The reading given by Besseler – "Tu m'as monté su[s] la pance et riens n'a[s] fait" (see Guillaume Du Fay, *Guilielmi Dufay: Opera Omnia* IV: *Fragmenta missarum*, ed. Heinrich Besseler, Corpus Mensurabilis Musicae 1 [Rome: American Institute of Musicology, 1962], p. 24.) – is present only in the contratenor; the superius has "asoté" in place of "monté." The meaning, though not entirely clear, must be something along the lines of "You have seduced me on the paunch / jumped on my paunch and done nothing."

14 See Bloxam, "A Cultural Context."

15 For another, more spiritually rooted, possible explanation, see "Last Things" (pp. 212–13).

16 See Michael Camille, *Image on the Edge: The Margins of Medieval Art* (Cambridge, MA: Harvard University Press, 1992). Bloxam describes such uses as "in-jokes," in which the ribald songs function as irreverent parodies of the loftier material more typically drawn into Marian devotion, and as invitations to contemplate the shift in register undergone by the songs in their new contexts (Bloxam, "A Cultural Context," pp. 26–7).

17 Michael Long, "Symbol and Ritual in Josquin's *Missa Di dadi*," *Journal of the American Musicological Society* 42 (1989), 3.

18 Anomalies of style and transmission have led a number of scholars to doubt the attribution of the *Missa Di dadi* to Josquin (see M. Jennifer Bloxam, "Masses on Polyphonic Songs," in Richard Sherr [ed.], *The Josquin Companion* [Oxford University Press, 2000], pp. 158–9). The authorship of the Mass has limited bearing on the present argument, however.

19 For a detailed consideration of the ritual interaction of the elevation with polyphony, see Chapter 8.

20 Long sees this process as a more dynamic one: "the symbolic process in late medieval devotional art did not involve merely the replacement of a sacred concept, person, or object by a secular stand-in. For the symbolic entity itself was simultaneously transformed into something more than it once was, and that metamorphosis justified its presence in a new, non-secular context" ("Symbol and Ritual," 2). Awareness of the same allegorical interaction of sacred and secular underpins, *inter alia*, Sylvia Huot's exegesis of the thirteenth-century motet and Anne Walters Robertson's of Machaut's motets. See respectively Huot, *Allegorical Play in the Old French Motet: The Sacred and the Profane in Thirteenth-century Polyphony* (Stanford University Press, 1997), especially the Introduction (pp. 1–18) and Conclusion (pp. 189–95), and Robertson, *Guillaume de Machaut and Reims: Context and Meaning in his Musical Works* (Cambridge University Press, 2002), especially chapters 3–6 (pp. 79–186). We will return to

issues raised by these studies in Chapter 6. For a more "inherent" perspective see also David Rothenberg, "Marian Feasts, Seasons, and Songs in Medieval Polyphony: Studies in Musical Symbolism," unpublished PhD dissertation, Yale University, 2004, p. 72, which draws in this connection on Rachel Fulton, "'Quae est ista quae ascendit sicut aurora consurgens?' The Song of Songs as the *Historia* for the Office of the Assumption," *Mediaeval Studies* 60 (1998), 76.

21 Thus it is no surprise that this same passage from Aquinas has been invoked in at least two other musical contexts: the juxtaposition of liturgical chant with the Fauvel story in the *Roman de Fauvel*, and the use of lyrics from *amor courtois* in the motets of Machaut (see, respectively, Susan Rankin, "The Divine Truth of Scripture: Chant in the *Roman de Fauvel*," *Journal of the American Musicological Society* 47 [1994], 242, and, in reference to Rankin, Robertson, *Guillaume de Machaut*, p. 181).

22 See the (slightly different) translation in *Pseudo-Dionysius: The Complete Works*, ed. Colm Luibheid and Paul Rorem (Mahwah, NJ: Paulist Press, 1987), p. 146: "However, the divine ray can enlighten us only by being upliftingly concealed in a variety of sacred veils which the Providence of the Father adapts to our nature as human beings." The same chapter offers further elucidation: "For it is quite impossible that we humans should, in any immaterial way, rise up to imitate and to contemplate the heavenly hierarchies without the aid of those material means capable of guiding us ... as our nature requires. Hence, any thinking person realizes that the appearances of beauty are signs of an invisible loveliness." On the interpretation of these passages see Paul Rorem, *Pseudo-Dionysius: A Commentary on the Texts and an Introduction to Their Influence* (New York and Oxford: Oxford University Press, 1993), p. 53. As Rorem notes, "The veils, or 'material means capable of guiding us' are immediately identified as, among other things, the beautiful sights, odors, lights, examples, and Communion itself in the Eucharist." On the influence of *The Celestial Hierarchy* on the medieval interpretation of symbols see *ibid.*, pp. 77–90. Here as in the other works ascribed to him, Pseudo-Dionysius is, Rorem states, "consistent and emphatic on this point: the material world is anagogically (or upliftingly) symbolic of the immaterial world, not just concerning the angels but also and especially concerning God" (*ibid.*, p. 78).

23 www.newadvent.org/summa "... conveniens est sacrae Scripturae divina et spiritualia sub similitudine corporalium tradere. Deus enim omnibus providet secundum quod competit eorum naturae. Est autem naturale homini ut per sensibilia ad intelligibilia veniat, quia omnis nostra cognitio a sensu initium habet. Unde convenienter in sacra Scriptura traduntur nobis spiritualia sub metaphoris corporalium. Et hoc est quod dicit Dionysius, I cap. caelestis hierarchiae, *impossibile est nobis aliter lucere divinum radium, nisi varietate sacrorum velaminum circumvelatum.* Convenit etiam sacrae Scripturae, quae communiter omnibus proponitur (secundum illud ad Rom. I, *sapientibus et insapientibus debitor sum*), ut spiritualia sub similitudinibus corporalium

proponantur; ut saltem vel sic rudes eam capiant, qui ad intelligibilia secundum se capienda non sunt idonei" (www.ccel.org/ccel/aquinas/summa.FP.html). The ultimate source of Aquinas's position, like his embedded quotation, is St. Paul's Epistle to the Romans: "For the invisible things of him from the creation of the world are clearly seen, being understood by the things that are made" (Romans 1: 20). See also Augustine, *De doctrina christiana*, I, 4: "if we wish to return to our Father's home, this world must be used, not enjoyed, that so the invisible things of God may be clearly seen, being understood by the things that are made – that is, that by means of what is material and temporary we may lay hold upon that which is spiritual and eternal" (www.ccel.org/ccel/augustine/doctrine.toc.html).

24 As Rorem notes, "*The Celestial Hierarchy* [regards] the anagogical interpretation of all symbols, whether beautiful or not, as part of the overall Dionysian method of ascending to union with God ... When Dionysius mentions beauty ... it is in the larger context of understanding all perceptible symbols, most of which are artistically neutral." As for many other aspects of Dionysian reception, the influence of this notion on late medieval thought was effected particularly through the agency of the ninth-century John Scotus Eriugena, for whom "'every visible and invisible creature can be called a theophany, that is, a divine apparition' or 'a self-manifestation of God.' This means that the world as a whole is a metaphor for God, and must be interpreted anagogically as an uplifting to God. 'For everything that is understood and sensed is nothing else but the apparition of what is not apparent, the manifestation of the hidden, the affirmation of the negated, the comprehension of the incomprehensible'"(Rorem, *Pseudo-Dionysius: A Commentary*, pp. 78–83; quotation at p. 79).

25 www.newadvent.org/summa. Objection 3: "quanto aliquae creaturae sunt sublimiores, tanto magis ad divinam similitudinem accedunt. Si igitur aliquae ex creaturis transumerentur ad Deum, tunc oporteret talem transumptionem maxime fieri ex sublimioribus creaturis, et non ex infimis. Quod tamen in Scripturis frequenter invenitur." Answer: "sicut docet Dionysius, cap. II Cael. Hier., magis est conveniens quod divina in Scripturis tradantur sub figuris vilium corporum, quam corporum nobilium. Et hoc propter tria. Primo, quia per hoc magis liberatur humanus animus ab errore. Manifestum enim apparet quod haec secundum proprietatem non dicuntur de divinis, quod posset esse dubium, si sub figuris nobilium corporum describerentur divina; maxime apud illos qui nihil aliud a corporibus nobilius excogitare noverunt. Secundo, quia hic modus convenientior est cognitioni quam de Deo habemus in hac vita. Magis enim manifestatur nobis de ipso quid non est, quam quid est, et ideo similitudines illarum rerum quae magis elongantur a Deo, veriorem nobis faciunt aestimationem quod sit supra illud quod de Deo dicimus vel cogitamus. Tertio, quia per huiusmodi, divina magis occultantur indignis" (www.ccel.org/ccel/aquinas/summa.FP.html).

26 Jacqueline E. Jung, "Beyond the Barrier: The Unifying Role of the Choir Screen in Gothic Churches," *Art Bulletin* 82/4 (December, 2000), 646.

27 *Ibid.*, 647. Original on 656, quoting Jean-Thiébaut Welter, *L'Exemplum dans la littérature religieuse et didactique du moyen âge* (Paris and Toulouse: Occitania, 1927; repr. Geneva: Slatkine, 1973), p. 68: "Ad edificationem rudium et agrestium erudicionem, quibus quasi corporalia et palpabilia et talia que per experienciam norunt frequencius sunt proponenda, magis enim moventur exterioribus exemplis quam auctoritatibus vel profundis sentenciis." Similarly, "for lay people it is more fitting to show everything clearly, as it were directly before their eyes and perceptible with their senses, so that the preacher's words might be as completely open and lucid as that precious stone, the carbuncle" (Jung, "Beyond the Barrier," p. 646). Original in Welter, *L'Exemplum*, p. 120: "Laici autem oportet quasi ad oculum et sensibiliter omnia demonstrare ut sit verbum predicatoris apertum et lucidum velut gemmula carbunculi."

28 Robertson, *Guillaume de Machaut*, p. 186, quoting Heinrich Suso, *Wisdom's Watch upon the Hours* [*Horologium Sapientiae*], trans. Edmund Colledge, The Fathers of the Church, Medieval Continuation 4 (Washington DC: Catholic University of America Press, 1994), pp. 119–20.

29 Widening the lens, Reynolds notes that "The rhetorical impulse to discuss divine matters in the popular language led painters to portray biblical stories with modern images ...; and it caused composers to base their Masses on chansons" (Christopher Reynolds, "The Counterpoint of Allusion in Fifteenth-century Masses," *Journal of the American Musicological Society* 45 [1992], 249–50).

30 *Ibid.*, pp. 234–48.

31 Bloxam sees a direct parallel in the Mass based on a song-derived cantus firmus, "the sonorous conjuring of the secular song within the Mass effecting a similar meshing of expressive elements usually confined to separate spheres. In the chanson Mass as in Gerson's theology, a codified poetical/musical language of secular love suggests to the reader/listener the paradigmatic relationship of his or her personal experience of corporeal love to the mystical experience of divine love" ("A Cultural Context," p. 24).

32 James H. Stubblebine, *Assisi and the Rise of Vernacular Art* (New York: Harper and Row, 1985). Quotations at pp. 113 and 88.

33 Wolfgang Kemp, *The Narratives of Gothic Stained Glass*, trans. Caroline Dobson Salzwedel (Cambridge University Press, 1997), first published in German, as *Sermo Corporeus: Die Erzählung der mittelalterlichen Glasfenster* (Munich: Schirmer/Mosel, 1987).

34 Jung, "Beyond the Barrier," 634–50; quotation at 647.

35 *Ibid.*, 628–9, 648–9.

36 See Bloxam, "A Cultural Context," *passim*, and Howard Mayer Brown, "Music and Ritual at Charles the Bold's Court: The Function of Liturgical Music by Busnoys and His Contemporaries," in Paula Higgins (ed.), *Antoine Busnoys: Method, Meaning, and Context in Late Medieval Music* (Oxford University Press, 1999), pp. 53–70. Most recently, see Rothenberg's discussion

of a series of applications of secular music in Marian polyphonic settings in "Marian Feasts."

37 For this aspect of the thirteenth-century motet see particularly Sylvia Huot, *Allegorical Play in the Old French Motet: The Sacred and the Profane in Thirteenth-century Polyphony* (Stanford University Press, 1997). Maria Rika Maniates outlined the same parallel in the context of a group of late-fifteenth- and early-sixteenth-century motets that draw on preexistent courtly songs (see her "Combinative Techniques in Franco-Flemish Polyphony: A Study of Mannerism in Music from 1450–1530," unpublished PhD dissertation, Columbia University, 1965, pp. 188–93). See also Bloxam, "A Cultural Context," pp. 13–15. Rothenberg ("Marian Feasts") analyzes the nature and foci of Marian symbolism in the late Middle Ages and addresses them in a series of case studies from the thirteenth to the sixteenth century.

38 See Bloxam, "A Cultural Context," pp. 24–7 and the earlier literature cited by her.

39 *Ibid.*, pp. 26–7.

40 See the list of works based on this song in Honey Meconi, "Art-Song Reworkings: An Overview," *Journal of the Royal Musical Association* 119 (1994), 27–8.

41 See most recently the detailed discussion in Rothenberg, "Marian Feasts," Chapter 9.

42 For a series of examples see, for instance, my essay "Personal Endowment."

43 For recastings following this disposition see the *Salve Regina* settings by Divitis (using Josquin's *Adieu mes amours*), de la Rue (Du Fay's *Par le regard* and Binchois's or Du Fay's *Je ne vis onques*), Ghiselin (*Je ne vis onques*), Bauldewyn (Ockeghem's *Je n'ay dueil*), Vinders (Ghiselin's *Ghy syt die wertste bovenal*), anon. (de la Rue's *Myn hert altyt heeft verlanghen*) and, also anon., (the Dutch song *O werde mont*) (all in Munich, Bayerische Staatsbibliothek MS 34), and "Ar. Fer" (a series of French and German songs, in Munich, Bayerische Staatsbibliothek MS 3154). My thanks for information on these settings to Jacobijn Kiel, who kindly supplied me with information and transcriptions from her forthcoming doctoral dissertation, to my student Christine Petsu, who produced a master's project at Rutgers University on *Salve Regina* settings involving song quotation, and to Herbert Kellman, for the kind loan of his microfilm of Munich 34. See the listings of motets based on songs in Meconi, "Art-Song Reworkings," and under the individual song listings in David Fallows, *A Catalogue of Polyphonic Songs, 1415–1480* (Oxford University Press, 1999).

44 "D'ung aultre amer mon cueur s'abesseroit. Il ne fault pas penser que je l'estrange, Ne que pour rien de ce propos me change, Car mon honneur en appetisseroit. Je l'aime tant que jamais ne seroit Possible a moi consentir l'eschange. D'ung aultre amer ... l'estrange. La mort par dieu avant me defferoit Qu'en mon vivant j'acointasse ung estrange. Ne cuide nul qu'a cela je

me range. Ma leaulte trop fort je mefferoit. D'ung aultre amer ... appetisseroit" ("To love another my heart would demean itself. It should not be thought that I estrange myself from him/her, nor that I would change myself in this regard for anything, for my honour would thereby be diminished. I love him/her so much that it would never be possible for me to agree to exchange him/her. To love another ... Would that I would die before, by God, betraying myself, by, alive, becoming familiar with another. Let none think that I would yield to this; my loyalty is too strong for me to so offend. To love another ..." On this group of works see Rothenberg, "Marian Feasts," pp. 240–4.

45 Josquin des Prez, *The Collected Works of Josquin des Prez*, ed. Thomas Noblitt, vol. VII: *Masses Based on Secular Polyphonic Songs* (Utrecht: Koninklijke Vereniging voor Nederlandse Muziekgeschiedenis, 1997), p. xii.

46 "The devotional reference to the Virgin Mary, 'De tous biens plaine est ma maistresse,' and the implication of pious, rather than worldly love, 'D'ung aultre amer mon coeur s'abesseroit,' are subtly revealed through the union of these two melodies with a liturgical chant concerning the Paschal Lamb" (Maniates, "Combinative Techniques," p. 188).

47 Rothenberg, "Marian Feasts," pp. 244–50. Rothenberg makes the important point that while the Mary referred to in the biblical source of this passage is Mary Magdalene, in this context – as in various similar equations admitted by the common name "Mary" – she is reinterpreted in the new, liturgical, context as the Virgin Mary. This is underscored by Josquin's quotation in his motet of a song (and one commonly harnessed for Marian devotion) about a woman "full of all goodness" (*ibid.*, pp. 179–87, 249–50). Rothenberg also notes the possibility, admitted by the exact quotation of the songs, that the superius may have admitted underlay of the secular texts. That option is actually adopted, in tandem with the motet text, in Ross Duffin's edition of the piece (see Josquin des Prez, *A Josquin Anthology: 12 Motets*, ed. Ross Duffin, [Oxford University Press, 1999], pp. 119–23). Duffin also notes that the song texts comment on their corresponding parts of the motet text (*ibid.*, p. ix). The text of the motet reads as follows: [Part 1] "Victimae paschali laudes immolent christiani. Agnus redimit oves; Christus innocens patri reconciliavit peccatores. Mors et vita duello conflixere mirando, dux vitae mortuus regnat vivus. [Part 2] Dic nobis Maria, quid vidisti in via? Sepulcrum Christi viventis et gloriam vidi resurgentis. Angelicos testes, sudarium et vestes. Surrexit Christus spes mea; praecedet suos in Galilaeam. Credendum est magis soli Mariae veraci quam Judaeorum turbae fallaci. Scimus Christum surrexisse ex mortuis vere; tu nobis Christe rex, Miserere. Alleluia." [Part 1] "Let Christians sacrifice praises to the paschal victim. The lamb has redeemed the sheep; innocent Christ has reconciled sinners to the father. Death and life have clashed in a miraculous duel, the slain leader of life reigns living. [Part 2] Tell us, Mary, what did you see on the road? I saw the tomb of the living Christ and the glory of the risen one, the angelic witnesses, the shroud and clothing. Christ my hope is risen;

he goes before his own in Galilee. Truthful Mary alone is more to be believed than the lying crowds of Jews. We know Christ truly to have risen from the dead. Christ, our king, have mercy on us. Alleluia.")

48 Josquin des Prez, *Josquin des Prez*, ed. Noblitt, vol. 7, p. xiii.

49 Noblitt proposes that the motet originated as a bipartite piece, in tandem with the Mass, only later becoming detached and acquiring the third part, its use of the same song providing an emblematic link to the parent Mass (*New Josquin Edition* vol. VII: *Masses Based on Polyphonic Songs* I: Critical Commentary [Utrecht: Koninklijke Vereniging voor Nederlandse Muziekgeschiedenis, 1997], p. 29).

50 [Part 1] "Tu solus qui facis mirabilia. Tu solus creator qui creasti nos. Tu solus redemptor qui redemisti nos Sanguine tuo preciosissimo." ("Thou alone art the One who performs wondrous deeds. Thou alone art the One who created us. Thou alone art the One who redeemed us with thy most precious blood.") [Part 2] "Ad te solum confugimus. In te solum confidimus, Nec alium adoramus, Iesu Christe. Ad te preces effundimus. Exaudi quod supplicamus, Et concede quod petimus, Rex benigne." ("In Thee alone we seek refuge. In Thee alone we fully trust, And adore no other, Jesus Christ. To Thee we pour forth our requests. Harken to what we humbly pray, And grant what we desire, Benevolent King.") (translation from Noblitt, *ibid.*, p. 38).

51 Rothenberg, "Marian Feasts," p. 244.

52 Edition in Josquin des Prez, *Werken van Josquin des Près*, ed. Albert Smijers, Motetten i: 7, no. 24 (Amsterdam and Leipzig: Vereniging voor Nederlandse Muziekgeschiedenis, 1924), pp. 130–1. The song quotation was first noted in Richard Taruskin (ed.), *J'ay pris amours: Twenty-eight Settings in Two, Three, and Four Parts* (Miami: Ogni Sorte, 1982), p. 5.

53 Aspects of the style, layout and source tradition of *Vultum tuum* have led Jeremy Noble and Richard Taruskin to propose that it belongs with the repertory of *motetti missales* cycles (see Noble, "The Function of Josquin's Motets," *Tijdschrift van de vereniging voor nederlandse muziekgeschiedenis* 35 [1985], 16–17, and Taruskin, liner notes to recording of "Josquin des Prez, Motets for the Blessed Virgin," Musical Heritage Society 4647L [Tinton Falls, New Jersey, 1982]). Patrick Macey has suggested that the shorter of the two *Ave Maria* settings by Josquin and the elevation motet *Tu lumen, tu splendor Patris* were also originally members of the cycle that subsequently became detached. Restoring them – the former in "loco Offertorii" and the latter as an appendage, "ad elevationem," to *O Maria, nullam* (the proposed motet "loco Sanctus") – as he proposes results in a grouping with all eight components of a complete *motetti missales* cycle. Macey also advocates some reordering of the individual items, including, following Taruskin, the placement of *Christe, fili Dei* in the position of the Agnus Dei. This location for the motet is supported not only by its division into three sections, two of them concluding "miserere nobis," but also by the coincidence that it would provide between

the Mass's direct plea for mercy and the plea for the intercession of the Virgin, invoked not only through her prayers but also through her presence in the proxy song (Patrick Macey, "Josquin's 'Little' *Ave Maria*: A Misplaced Motet from the *Vultum tuum* Cycle?" *Tijdschrift van de Vereniging voor Nederlandse Muziekgeschiedenis* 29 [1989], 38–53).

54 Taruskin suggested that the song, in this context, "seems to be intended ... as a secret love letter to the Virgin Mary" (*J'ay pris amours*, p. 5).

55 This is in stark contrast to the freer borrowing procedures found in some motets that, as Rothenberg has demonstrated, afford opportunities for dialogue – semantic and symbolic – between the borrowed material and its new setting (see his "Marian Feasts," *passim*).

56 See Rob C. Wegman, *Born for the Muses: The Life and Masses of Jacob Obrecht* (Oxford University Press, 1994), pp. 204–7. My thanks to Philip Weller for reminding me of this.

57 For an edition see *Guglielmi Dufay: Opera Omnia II: Missarum Pars Prior*, ed. Heinrich Besseler, Corpus Mensurabilis Musicae 1 (Rome: American Institute of Musicology, 1960), pp. 105–23. On the borrowing pattern see Murray Steib, Introduction to Johannes Martini, *Johannes Martini: Masses: Part 1: Masses without Known Polyphonic Models*, ed. Murray Steib and Elaine Moohan (Madison A-R Editions, 1999), p. xv.

58 John 1: 14. On the word and its particular meaning in the Johannine books of the Bible, see for example "Logos," in F. L. Cross and E. A. Livingstone (eds.), *The Oxford Dictionary of the Christian Church* (Oxford University Press, 1997), pp. 992–3 and William A. Beardsley, "Logos," in Bruce M. Metzger and Michael D. Coogan (eds.), *The Oxford Companion to the Bible* (Oxford and New York: Oxford University Press, 1993), pp. 463–4. Anonymous Masses on *Le serviteur* are found in Trent 88, ff. 267r–75v and Trent 89, ff. 153v–60r, a Mass in Trent 88 (ff. 411v–422v) is ascribed to Ockeghem, but usually given, on Tinctoris's evidence, to Faugues, and a Mass by Agricola is found in Jena, Universitäts- und Landesbibliothek, Chorbuch 22, ff. 128v–141r. A Credo *Le serviteur* by De Orto also survives in Vienna, Österreichische Nationalbibliothek, MS 1783, ff. 197v–201r.

59 "Le serviteur hault guerdonné, Assouvy et bien fortuné, L'éslite des heureux de France Me treuve par la pourvoiance D'ung tout seul mot bien ordonné. Il me semble a prime estre né, Car après deul desordonné Suys fait par nouvelle alliance. Le serviteur ... Je estoie un homme habandonné Et le dolent infortuné Lors quant vostre humble bienveullance Voult confermer mon esperance, Quant ce beau mot me fut donné. Le serviteur ..."

60 See my discussion of this work in "Innovation, Stylistic Patterns and the Writing of History: The Case of Bedyngham's Mass *Deuil angouisseux*," in Peter Wright and Marco Gozzi (eds.), *I Codici Musicali Trentini: Nuove scoperte e nuovi orientamenti della ricerca* (Trento: Provincia Autonoma di Trento, 1996), pp. 149–75.

61 Ff. 273v–281r. The Mass is edited in Louis Gottlieb, "The Cyclic Masses of Trent 89," 2 vols., unpublished PhD dissertation, University of California at Berkeley, 1958, vol. II, pp. 500–17.

62 Robert J. Mitchell, "The Paleography and Repertory of Trent Codices 89 and 91, together with Analyses and Editions of Six Mass Cycles by Franco-Flemish Composers from Trent Codex 89," unpublished PhD dissertation, University of Exeter, 1989, p. 89.

63 Kirkman "Innovation," p. 163, with examples on p. 175.

64 "Adieu m'amour, adieu ma joye, Adieu le solas que j'avoye, Adieu ma leale maistresse! Le dire adieu tant fort me blesse Qu'il me semble que morir doye.

De desplaisir forment lermoye. Il n'est reconfort que je voye, Quant vous esloigne, ma princesse. Adieu m'amour, Adieu ma joye …

Je prie a dieu qu'il me convoye, Et doint que briefment vous revoye, Mon bien, m'amour et ma deesse! Car adquis m'est, de ce que laisse, Qu'apres ma payne joye aroye.

Adieu m'amour … morir doye."

65 Christopher Reynolds, "The Counterpoint," 228–60, and his *Papal Patronage and the Music of St. Peter's, 1380–1513* (Berkeley, Los Angeles and London: University of California Press, 1995).

66 See the argument and musical examples in Reynolds's *Papal Patronage*, pp. 258–9; for his case for the authorship of Faugues see *ibid.*, pp. 172–81. See also his "The Counterpoint," 233.

67 The text, which survives only in Seville, Biblioteca Capitular y Colombina, MS 5-1-43, ff. 86v–7r, is provided in Howard Mayer Brown (ed.), *A Florentine Chansonnier from the Time of Lorenzo the Magnificent: Florence, Biblioteca Nazionale Centrale MS Banco Rari 229*, Monuments of Renaissance Music vii, 2 vols. (Chicago University Press, 1983), vol. I, p. 250. Brown declines to translate the text, on grounds of its likely corruption.

68 François Cornilliat has suggested to me that this may well be a corruption, the more likely original verb here being "convient il."

69 Possible text source cited in Fallows, *A Catalogue*, p. 319. The song text itself is found in Eugénie Droz and Arthur Piaget (eds.), *Le Jardin de plaisance et fleur de rethorique*, 2 vols., Société des Anciens Textes Français, 59 (Paris: Firmin-Didot, 1910 [facsimile] and 1925 [commentary]), f. 78v (song no. 183): "Pour lamour dune qui est cy / Chanson nouvelle chanteray / Pour envieux ie ne serray / Ne pour son amoureux aussi. Loyal vueil estre par tel si / Que iamais autre ne seray / Pour lamour &c. Et si seray hors de soussy / Dont mesdisans creuer feray / Et oultre plus quant ie pourray / Venir les feray a mercy / Pour lamour &c." "For the love of one who is here present / I shall sing a new song. For envious I shall not be, / Nor even of her love. Loyal I wish to be, in such fashion / That never shall I be other. For the love … And I shall be free of care, From which [state] I shall deflate the evil-sayers./ And even more, if I am able, I shall make them come to forgiveness. For the love …"

70 Reynolds, *Papal Patronage*, p. 260 and "The Counterpoint," 236–7, with musical quotations on 233.

71 Reynolds, "The Counterpoint," 233–4, 237.

72 *Ibid.*, 240.

73 Reynolds, *Papal Patronage*, pp. 266–75.

74 I have elsewhere argued that the attribution of this – for Ockeghem – stylistically anomalous work, which occurs only in Verona, Biblioteca Capitolare, MS 759, a source compiled far from Ockeghem's sphere of activity and long after the work's composition, is erroneous. In that study I compared the Mass with contemporary cycles, finding stylistic similarities with the three-voice Masses of Johannes Touront (see my *The Three-voice Mass in the Later Fifteenth and Early Sixteenth Centuries* [London and New York: Garland, 1995], pp. 249–60). Taking his cue from this argument, Jaap van Benthem has more recently argued that the composer of the cycle was in fact Touront, suggesting that the attribution to Ockeghem, a composer working in Tours, may have been an error based on a mistaken toponymic (i.e., putatively, something like "Johannes, Master of Tours"). See the commentary to his edition: Johannes Ockeghem, *Johannes Ockeghem: Masses and Mass Sections III: Masses Based on Secular Settings, Fascicle 1: Missa Primi toni Presumably by Johannes Touront, Missa Quinti Toni*, ed. Jaap van Benthem (Utrecht: Koninklijke Vereniging voor Nederlandse Muziekgeschiedenis, 2004), pp. vii–xvi.

75 Reynolds, "The Counterpoint," 245, and Howard Mayer Brown, *A Florentine Chansonnier*, vol. I, p. 281.

76 Reynolds, "The Counterpoint," 234–5, 247.

77 *Ibid.*, 241.

78 Reynolds, *Papal Patronage*, p. 258.

79 Bloxam, "Masses on Polyphonic Songs," p. 174.

80 See for example Alejandro Enrique Planchart, "Masses on Plainsong Cantus Firmi," in Richard Sherr (ed.), *The Josquin Companion*, pp. 130–2.

81 See Patrick Macey, "An Expressive Detail in Josquin's *Nimphes, nappés*," *Early Music* 31 (2003), 401.

82 John Milsom, "Sense and Sound in Richafort's Requiem," *Early Music* 30 (2002), 449–53.

83 For more on *Nimphes, nappé* and the relevant bibliography, see Chapter 6.

84 The same impression is reinforced by the occurrence of several statements of the same figure in Josquin's lament for Ockeghem *Nimphes des bois*, as well as its occasional appearance in others of his lamenting chansons such as *Cueur langoreulx* and *Parfons regretz*.

85 The fact that the Mass was recorded as having been copied for Cambrai Cathedral in the year 1473/4 suggests that it may have been composed within a year or two of its composer's death. For a discussion of this record and speculation concerning the possible date of composition see Fallows, *Dufay*, pp. 79 and 289.

86 As I first noted in the sleeve notes to my recording of this work with the Binchois Consort (*Dufay: Music for St. Anthony of Padua*, on Hyperion CDA66854).

87 My thanks to my student Yifat Shohat for pointing this out to me. The Mass was formerly known as the *Missa Sine nomine*, but was christened *La belle se siet* by Fallows on account of its quotations of Du Fay's song on that text (see Fallows, *Dufay*, pp. 165–8). The accidentals are notated in the copies in Bologna Q15, Aosta, and Venice, Biblioteca Marciana, Cod. it. IX, 145. They are absent only in the later Trent 93 and Trent 90 (see the *Apparatus criticus* of Du Fay, ed. Besseler, *Guglielmi Dufay: Opera Omnia,* vol. II, p. xviii). While this passage is isolated in its direct context, F♯ and B♭ occur closely together at a number of other points in the cycle, most obviously towards the end of the same movement, where, at bars 98–9, the diminished fourth is again outlined directly in the superius. The notes occur in close vertical proximity in the "Jesu Christe" of the Gloria, another point of intensified supplication, where their effect is underscored by fermata chords.

88 Bologna Q 15 ff. 133v–4r and Trent 92, ff. 219v–20r. Edition in Du Fay, ed. Besseler, *Dufay: Opera Omnia*, vol. IV, p. 43.

89 Anmon Linder, *Raising Arms: Liturgy in the Struggle to Liberate Jerusalem in the Late Middle Ages* (Turnhout, Belgium: Brepols, 2003), pp. 292, 123.

90 *Ibid.*, p. 292.

Chapter 4 "Head of the church that is his body": Christological imagery and the *Caput* Masses

1 See for instance Rob C. Wegman, "Petrus de Domarto's *Missa Spiritus almus* and the Early History of the Four-voice Mass in the Fifteenth Century," *Early Music History* 10 (1991), 295–7.

2 Manfred Bukofzer, *Studies in Medieval and Renaissance Music* (New York: Norton, 1950), pp. 309–10; see also Wegman, "*Missa Spiritus almus*," 241.

3 This began with Thomas Walker, "A Severed Head: Notes on a Lost English *Caput* Mass," paper read at the Thirty-fifth Annual Meeting of the American Musicological Society, St. Louis, MO, December 27–29, 1969. It proceeded with Margaret Bent and Ian Bent, "Dufay, Dunstable, Plummer: A New Source," *Journal of the American Musicological Society* 22 (1969), 394–434, and Alejandro Enrique Planchart, "Guillaume Dufay's Masses: Notes and Revisions," *Musical Quarterly* 58 (1972), 1–23.

4 "(1) Ante diem autem festum paschae sciens Iesus quia venit eius hora ut transeat ex hoc mundo ad Patrem cum dilexisset suos qui erant in mundo in finem dilexit eos (2) et cena facta cum diabolus iam misisset in corde ut traderet eum Iudas Simonis Scariotis (3) sciens quia omnia dedit ei Pater in manus et quia a Deo exivit et ad Deum vadit (4) surgit a cena et ponit vestimenta sua

et cum accepisset linteum praecinxit se (5) deinde mittit aquam in pelvem et coepit lavare pedes discipulorum et extergere linteo quo erat praecinctus (6) venit ergo ad Simonem Petrum et dicit ei Petrus Domine tu mihi lavas pedes (7) respondit Iesus et dicit ei quod ego facio tu nescis modo scies autem postea (8) dicit ei Petrus non lavabis mihi pedes in aeternum respondit Iesus ei si non lavero te non habes partem mecum (9) dicit ei Simon Petrus Domine non tantum pedes meos sed et manus et caput."

5 Bukofzer, *Studies*, p. 238.

6 *Ibid.*, p. 242; Reinhard Strohm, *The Rise of European Music* (Cambridge and New York: Cambridge University Press, 1993), p. 236.

7 Geoffrey Chew, "The Early Cyclic Mass as an Expression of Royal and Papal Supremacy," *Music and Letters* 53 (1972), 256–7.

8 *Ibid.*, 260.

9 Anne Walters Robertson, "The Savior, the Woman, and the Head of the Dragon in the *Caput* Masses and Motet," *Journal of the American Musicological Society* 59 (2006), 537–630. Robertson's case is built on these two unquestioned facts, both of which have nevertheless been interpreted differently – and arguably more persuasively – by others. Reinhard Strohm has suggested that the heading in the Lucca Codex reveals a misapprehension by a scribe who, upon seeing the word "caput" beneath the cantus firmus in the tenor, erroneously assumed that it referred to the fifth antiphon, "Caput drachonis," at Lauds on Sunday in the octave of the Epiphany (*Music in Late Medieval Bruges* [Oxford University Press, 2nd, rev. edn., 1990], p. 124). Support for this view is found in Planchart's observation that the Northern European chant from which the "Caput" melisma was drawn was most likely unknown to the Italian scribe of Lucca, who therefore (and understandably) assumed that the word "caput" was the incipit of the well-known Epiphany antiphon (see Alejandro Enrique Planchart, "Guillaume Dufay's Masses: Notes and Revisions," *Musical Quarterly* 58/1 [1972], 13). The same verbal association between "Caput" and the antiphon "Caput drachonis" could also be adduced as an explanation for the presence of the dragon-slaying scene in the Chigi Codex, though it could equally refer, as Herbert Kellman noted, to the dragon-slaying name saint –St. Philip – of the nobleman Philippe Bouton, for whom the manuscript was prepared (*Vatican City, Biblioteca Apostolica Vaticana, MS Chigi VIII.234* [New York and London: Garland, 1987], vi–viii). This would certainly explain the sundry dragons depicted elsewhere in the source, just as the same patron's rebus of the rosebud ("bouton") is liberally scattered through its pages.

But perhaps the main question concerns the choice of cantus firmus itself: if the composers had indeed wanted to refer to the "caput drachonis," why did they not set their Masses to the antiphon of that name? Robertson (568) suggests that composers chose the *Caput* melisma over the antiphon because they sought a link with the Easter season that follows Maundy

Thursday. Yet cantus firmi were frequently used in the fifteenth century in contexts different from those of their original functions, a point she makes herself in support of her own interpretation (544–6). Further questions arise from the layout of the Ockeghem and Obrecht cycles. The presence of the cantus firmus in the bass in the former is viewed by Robertson as evidence of the composer forcing down the devil into the lowest register, while the shifting cantus firmus of the latter is seen to depict the swirling shape of the dragon's tail. No explanation is offered, though, for the position, in its standard tenor location, of the chant in the anonymous progenitor of the series. Moreover, the suggestion that Ockeghem set a B-natural-heavy chant in the bass in order to let the devil sound out in his interval (the tritone) begs the question as to why so often an F above a bass B is actually notated as F♯ in the earliest source of the Mass (on this point see Jaap van Benthem, Communication, *Journal of the American Musicological Society* 61 [2008], 238–41). A simpler explanation might be that this is one of many cases of the phenomenon, widely acknowledged for this period, of compositional "one-upmanship," with Ockeghem's display in placing a heavily "B-centered" chant in the bass being answered in Obrecht's Mass by setting the tune in all four textural registers. For further objections see Reinhard Strohm, *Mass Settings from the Lucca Choirbook*, Early English Church Music 49 (London: Stainer and Bell, 2007), p. 34, and "John Hothby, the Lucca Codex – and Further Dragons' Heads?" *Acta Musicologica* 80 (2008), 64–5.

10   Bukofzer, *Studies*, p. 242.

11   On this point see Alejandro Enrique Planchart, "Parts with Words and Parts Without Words: The Evidence for Multiple Texts in Fifteenth-century Masses," in Stanley Boorman (ed.), *Studies in the Performance of Late Medieval Music* (Cambridge University Press, 1983), pp. 242–3.

12   David Rothenberg, "Marian Feasts, Seasons, and Songs in Medieval Polyphony: Studies in Musical Symbolism," unpublished PhD dissertation, Yale University, 2004, p. 91; see also pp. 75 and 89, where he illustrates the point with regard to the *Ecce ancilla domini* Masses of Du Fay, Ockeghem and Regis.

13   *Ibid.*, p. 91: "Primo accipe tenorem alicuius antiphone vel responsorii vel alterius cantus de antiphonario et debent verba concordare cum materia de qua vis facere motetum." On the treatise *De modo componendi tenores motetorum*, see Daniel Leech-Wilkinson, *Compositional Techniques in the Four-part Isorhythmic Motets of Philippe de Vitry and His Contemporaries*, 2 vols. (New York and London: Garland, 1989), vol. I, p. 21. Also discussed in Alice V. Clark, "*Concordare cum Materia*: The Tenor in the Fourteenth-century Motet," unpublished PhD dissertation, Princeton University, 1996, pp. 3–6, and Anne Walters Robertson, *Guillaume de Machaut and Reims: Context and Meaning in His Musical Works* (Cambridge University Press, 2002), p. 146. For some late-fifteenth-century English examples of similarly motivated cantus firmus choice, see for example Magnus Williamson, "Royal Image-making

and Textual Interplay in Gilbert Banaster's *O Maria et Elizabeth*," *Early Music History* 19 (2000), 237–78, at 237 and *passim*.

14 The classic case of this is the series of Masses on *L'homme armé*, the topic of Chapter 5.

15 Ephesians 1: "(20) [Deus] operatus est in Christo suscitans illum a mortuis et constituens ad dexteram suam in caelestibus (21) supra omnem principatum et potestatem et virtutem et dominationem et omne nomen quod nominatur non solum in hoc saeculo sed et in futuro (22) et omnia subiecit sub pedibus eius et ipsum dedit caput supra omnia ecclesiae (23) quae est corpus ipsius plenitudo eius qui omnia in omnibus adimpletur."

16 Ephesians 4: "(15) veritatem autem facientes in caritate crescamus in illo per omnia qui est caput Christus (16) ex quo totum corpus conpactum et conexum per omnem iuncturam subministrationis secundum operationem in mensuram uniuscuiusque membri augmentum corporis facit in aedificationem sui in caritate."

17 Colossians 2: "(17) … corpus autem Christi (18) nemo vos seducat volens in humilitate et religione angelorum quae non vidit ambulans frustra inflatus sensu carnis suae (19) et non tenens caput ex quo totum corpus per nexus et coniunctiones subministratum et constructum crescit in augmentum Dei."

Other references are as follows:

Colossians 1: (18) He [Christ] is the head of the body, the church; he is the beginning, the firstborn from the dead, so that he might come to have first place in everything. (et ipse est caput corporis ecclesiae qui est principium primogenitus ex mortuis ut sit in omnibus ipse primatum tenens.)

Colossians 2: (9) For in him [Christ] the whole fullness of deity dwells bodily, (10) and you have come to fullness in him, who is the head of every ruler and authority. ([9] quia in ipso inhabitat omnis plenitudo divinitatis corporaliter [10] et estis in illo repleti qui est caput omnis principatus et potestatis.)

Ephesians 5: (22) Wives, be subject to husbands as you are to the Lord. (23) For the husband is the head of the wife just as Christ is the head of the church, the body of which he is the Savior. ([22] mulieres viris suis subditae sint sicut Domino [23] quoniam vir caput est mulieris sicut Christus caput est ecclesiae ipse salvator corporis.)

1 Corinthians 11: (3) But I want you to understand that Christ is the head of every man, and the husband is the head of his wife, and God is the head of Christ. (volo autem vos scire quod omnis viri caput Christus est caput autem mulieris vir caput vero Christi Deus.)

18 *Expositions on the Book of Psalms. By Saint Augustine, Bishop of Hippo*, translated, edited, with brief annotations, and condensed from the six volumes of the Oxford translation, by A. Cleveland Cox, from Philip Schaff (ed.), *A Select Library of the Nicene and Post-Nicene Fathers of the Christian Church* (8 vols., New York: Christian Literature Publishing Co., 1886), Psalm 66, 1. In *Early Church Fathers: Nicene and Post-Nicene Fathers Series I*, vol. 8 (www.ccel.

org/ccel/schaff/npnf108.html). "Resurrectionem enim Christiani novimus in Capite nostro jam factam et in membris futuram. Caput Ecclesiae Christus est, membra Christi Ecclesia. Quod praecessit in Capite sequetur in corpore. Haec est spes nostra" (*Sancti Aurelii Augustini Hipponensis Episcopi Enarrationes in Psalmos*, Patrologia Latina 36, Col. 0786).

19 *Dogmatic Treatises, Ethical Works, and Sermons: Exposition of the Christian Faith*, Book V, Ch. 14: 180; English translation from *Ambrose: Selected Works and Letters. Early Church Fathers: Nicene and Post-Nicene Fathers Series II*, vol. 10 (www.ccel.org/ccel/schaff/npnf210.toc.html). "Scriptum est, inquies, quia *cum mortui essemus peccatis, convivificavit nos in Christo, cujus gratia estis salvi facti; et simul suscitavit, simulque fecit sedere in coelestibus, in Christo Jesu* (Ephesians 2: 5–6). Agnosco scriptum: sed non ut homines sedere ad dexteram sibi patiatur Deus, sed ut in Christo sedere; quia ipse est omnium fundamentum, et ipse est caput Ecclesiae (Ephesians 5: 23), in quo communis secundum carnem natura praerogativam sedis coelestis emeruit: in Christo enim Deo caro, in carne autem humani natura generis omnium hominum particeps honoratur" (*Sancti Ambrosii Mediolanensis De Fide Ad Gratianum Augusti Libri Quinque*, 181, Patrologia Latina 16, Col. 0685A).

20 *Dogmatic Treatises, Ethical Works, and Sermons: Two Books Concerning Repentence*, Book I, Ch. 6: 28; English translation from *Ambrose: Selected Works and Letters. Early Church Fathers: Nicene and Post-Nicene Fathers Series II*, vol. 10 (www.ccel.org/ccel/schaff/npnf210.toc.html). "Vos autem dicitis: *Noli me tangere*. Vos dicitis volentes justificare vos ipsos: Non est proximus noster, superbiores quam legisperitus ille qui Christum tentare cupiebat; ille enim dixit: *Quis est meus proximus* (Luke 10: 29)? Ille interrogat, vos negatis; sicut sacerdos ille descendentes, et sicut levita praeterientes, quem curandum suscipere debuistis, nec recipientes hospitio, pro quo Christus duo numeravit aera, cujus te proximum fieri Christus jubet, ut facias in eum misericordiam. Ipse enim est proximus, quem non solum conformis natura conjunxerit, sed etiam misericordia copulaverit. Ab eo te alienum superbia facis, extollens te frustra inflatus mente carnis tuae, et non tenens caput. Si enim caput teneres, adverteres non tibi eum deserendum, pro quo Christus mortuus est. Si caput teneres, adverteres corpus omne compaginando potius quam solvendo, in incrementum Dei per copulam charitatis, et redemptionem crescere peccatoris" (*Sancti Ambrosii Mediolanensis De Poenitentia Libri Duo* [Patrologia Latina 16, Col. 0475A-B]).

21 For more on Mass commentaries as interpretative sources for the fifteenth-century Mass, see Chapter 5.

22 "Potest et aliter hoc mysterium explanari. Est enim corpus Christi universalis Ecclesia, scilicet caput cum membris, juxta quod dicit Apostolus: Unus panis et unum corpus multi sumus (1 Corinthians 10). Et inveniuntur in isto corpore quasi tres partes, ex quibus totum corpus consistit. Una pars est ipsum caput videlicet Christus, qui et caput est et pars corporis. Altera pars sunt illi quorum

corpora requiescunt in tumulis, et animae regnant cum Christo" (Innocent III, *De sacro altaris mysterio libri sex*, Liber VI, Caput III: Quid significant partes illae quae fiunt de sacrificio. Patrologia Latina 217, Col. 907C).

23 "[Pugna] Figurata in capite est, quia Christus cum diabolo pugnans, ipsum superavit et infernum exspoliavit; figurata in membris est, quia impugnamur, non solum a mundo, sed a carne et a diabolo" (*Sicardi Cremonensis Episcopi Mitrale seu de officiis ecclesiasticis summa*, Liber Tertius. De officiis ministrorum ecclesiae. Caput IX: Brevis recapitulatio missae. Patrologia Latina 213, Col. 144D).

24 "'...nemo ascendit in coelum, nisi Filius hominis' (John 3) cui quasi capiti membra corporis adnectuntur omnes qui in fide hujus sacramenti efficiuntur filii Dei, et sic corpus unum, caput cum membris, ascendit in coelum" (*ibid.*, Caput VI: De quinta parte missae. Patrologia Latina 213, Cols. 130C).

25 "Sacerdos itaque celebrans missam ex his quae facit, et qua circa eum fiunt, breviter et velociter habeat in mente, figurantia quae praecessere, figurata quae sunt in capite completa, et quae sunt a nobis moribus adimplenda" (*ibid.*, Caput IX: Brevis recapitulatio missae. Patrologia Latina 213, Col. 144D-145A).

26 See for example the liturgy of the Chair of Peter, whose *Oratio* (collect) states: "Deus, qui hodiernâ die beatum Petrum post te dedisti caput ecclesiæ, cum te ille vere confessus sit" ("O God, who didst this day give us as head of the Church, after Thyself, the Blessed Peter, etc.") (*Catholic Encyclopedia* [www.newadvent.org/cathen/], "Chair of Peter").

27 "Petrus enim secutus est Christum, non solum genere martyrii, sed et in ordine magisterii. Quod Christus ostendit, cum ait: Tu vocaberis Cephas (John 1). Licet enim Cephas secundum unam linguam interpretetur Petrus, secundum alteram tamen exponitur caput. Nam sicut caput habet plenitudinem sensuum, caetera vero membra partem recipiunt plenitudinis; ita caeteri sacerdotes vocati sunt in partem sollicitudinis, sed summus pontifex assumptus est in plenitudinem potestatis" (Innocent III, *De sacro altaris mysterio libri sex*, Liber I, Caput VIII: De primatu Romani pontificis. Patrologia Latina 217 Col. 0778D-0779A). For a further example regarding this inherited status of the pope, see the proceedings of the Second Council of Nicaea (the Seventh Ecumenical Council, held in 787) where Adrian I is referred to as "most holy head" (www.newadvent.org/fathers/3819.htm; Zabbe and Cossart, Concilia, Tom. VII., col. 32). On the Holy See, see for example the *Liber Pontificalis* (ed. Duchesne, II, Paris, 1892, p. 7), issued under the pontificate of Leo III (795–816): "Nos sedem apostolicam, quae est caput omnium Dei ecclesiarum, judicare non audemus" ("We dare not judge the Apostolic See, which is the head of all the Churches of God") (see *The Catholic Encyclopedia*, "Holy See"). This characterization of the Holy See as head of the universal church was no doubt bolstered by the papal assumption of the mint of the Senate of Rome, its coins traditionally, as late as the twelfth century, emblazoned with the rebus "Roma caput mundi" (see *The Catholic Encyclopedia*, "Papal Mint").

28 Charles Caspers, "The Western Church during the Late Middle Ages: *Augenkommunion* or Popular Mysticism?" in Charles Caspers, Gerard Lukken and Gerard Rouwhorst (eds.), *Bread of Heaven: Customs and Practices Surrounding Holy Communion* (Kampen: Kok Pharos, 1995), pp. 83–97, at 89.

29 "in Ecclesia militante summus pontifex, sicut Christi uicarius et caput omnium prelatorum, perfectius Christum representat …" "quia non ita proprie Christum caput Ecclesie representant." See Guillelmus Durandus, *Guillelmi Duranti Rationale divinorum officiorum*, ed. A. Davril and T. M. Thibodeau, Corpus Christianorum, continuatio mediaevalis CXL, CXL A, CXL B, 3 vols. (Turnhout: Brepols, 1995, 1998, 2000), CXL (I–IV), p. 549.

30 "Papa elegitu in caput totius Ecclesiae … Capitis autem est influere viam omnibus membris" (*De Potestate Ecclesiastica* I, qu. v, art. 1). Augustinus Triumphus as quoted in Ralph E. Giesey, "The French Estates and the Corpus Mysticum Regni," in *Album Helen Maud Cam* (Louvain and Paris: University of Louvain/Éditions Béatrice-Nauwelaerts, 1960), p. 166.

31 www.newadvent.org/summa. "… Christus est caput omnium eorum qui ad Ecclesiam pertinent secundum omnem locum et tempus et statum, alii autem homines dicuntur capita secundum quaedam specialia loca, sicut episcopi suarum Ecclesiarum; vel etiam secundum determinatum tempus, sicut Papa est caput totius Ecclesiae, scilicet tempore sui pontificatus; et secundum determinatum statum, prout scilicet sunt in statu viatoris." (Aquinas, *Summa theologiae*, III, Q.8, article 6 [www.ccel.org/ccel/aquinas/summa.FP.html].)

32 "… vergißt … fast bei keinem Gegenstand, gleich seinem Vorgänger Innocenz III, Beziehungen zu suchen auf Christum, das Haupt der Kirche. Da dieses geistige Reich materiell verkörpert am Gotteshaus uns entgegentritt, wird sich noch Gelegenheit bieten, zu sehen, welch reiche und lebensvolle Entfaltung und welch großartige Auffassung dieser mittelalterlichen Anschauung von der Kirche gegeben wird. Ficker hat als Zentralgedanken der Sicardschen Symbolik Christus und die Kirche bezeichnet. Wir glauben indes für Sicard wie für Durandus diese Bestimmung noch präciser fassen zu können, wenn wir die Vorstellung von der Kirche als Leib Christi als den tiefsten Gedanken mittelalterlicher Symbolik wie überhaupt der ganzen damaligen Weltanschauung hinstellen. Christus erscheint diesen Menschen nur in seiner Verbindung mit und in seinem Fortleben und Wirken in der Kirche" (Joseph Sauer, *Symbolik des Kirchengebäudes und seiner Ausstattung in der Auffassung des Mittelalters, mit Berücksichtigung von Honorius Augustodunensis, Sicardus und Durandus* [Freiburg im Breisgau: Herder, 1924; repr. Münster: Mehren u. Hobbeling, 1964], p. 36). The work referred to in the above quotation is Gerhard Paul Ficker, *Der Mitralis des Sicardus. Nach seiner Bedeutung für die Ikonographie des Mittelalters*, Beiträge zur Kunstgeschichte, Neue Folge IX (Leipzig: Ramm, 1889).

33 My thanks to John Caldwell for this information.

34 My thanks to John Caldwell and Magnus Williamson for these details, and for pointing out relevant references. On the growth of devotions, including

Masses, to the Holy Name in England see particularly Richard Pfaff, *New Liturgical Feasts in Later Medieval England* (Oxford University Press, 1970), pp. 62–83; on the elevation of the Mass of the Holy Name to canonical status see *ibid.*, pp. 73–4. On musical responses see David Mateer and Elizabeth New, "'In Nomine Jesu': Robert Fayrfax and the Guild of the Holy Name in St. Paul's Cathedral," *Music and Letters* 81 (2000), 507–19, and particularly 508–9. See also the general discussion in Eamon Duffy, *The Stripping of the Altars* (New Haven and London: Yale University Press, 1992), p. 113.

35 On the great wealth of the more prominent Corpus Christi gilds see for instance Miri Rubin, *Corpus Christi: The Eucharist in Late Medieval Culture* (Cambridge University Press, 1991), pp. 239–40. Rubin notes that "The creative possibilities inherent in this occasion were many – and were realised and expressed for as long as Corpus Christi was celebrated." On the patterns of founding of Corpus Christi gilds in fourteenth-century England, see *ibid.*, pp. 233–4. On the huge number of gilds of one kind or another in fifteenth-century England alone, see Gervase Rosser, "Going to the Fraternity Feast: Commensality and Social Relations in Late Medieval England," *Journal of British Studies* 33 (1994), 430–1, where the number is estimated to have been as high as 30,000.

36 "Sicut enim in uno corpore multa membra habemus, omnia autem membra non eundem actum habent: ita multi unum corpus sumus in Christo, singuli autem alter alterius membra" (Romans 12: 4–5). My thanks to John Harper for drawing my attention to this passage.

37 Paula Ložar (trans.), "The Prologue to the Ordinances of the York Corpus Christi Guild," *Allegorica* 1 (1976), 104–9, which also gives the original text as follows: "vt quemadmodum Christus vniret membra cum capite sua passione preciosa. sic nos erimus vniti fide spe et caritate huius sacramenti recordacione diei uersaria" (*ibid.*, 104). "… hac vnitate insuper fraternali omnes confratres erunt membra Christi … Vnde sicut membrorum naturalium hominis ad caput est naturalis compassio. sic omnium confratrum ad Christum erit reciproca amatio" (*ibid.*, 106, 108).

38 Duffy, *The Stripping of the Altars*, p. 92.

39 Mervyn James, "Ritual, Drama and Social Body in the Late Medieval English Town," *Past and Present* 98 (1983), 4. See also *ibid.*, 6–10, where James offers a more general and speculative assessment of the "corporal" aspect of the Feast. For critiques of this emphasis on the notion of the body linking host and society, see Charles Zika, "Hosts, Processions and Pilgrimages in Fifteenth-century Germany," *Past and Present* 118 (1988), 43–5 and Rubin, *Corpus Christi*, pp. 269–71.

40 See Zika, "Hosts, Processions and Pilgrimages," 38.

41 See *ibid.*, 40. Rubin notes that the Corpus Christi procession in Mainz had children representing angels singing responses *en route* (*Corpus Christi*, p. 251). Similar practices were surely widespread. Kenneth Kreitner has chronicled

the same feature in Barcelona from the fifteenth century on. However, the fact that, as he notes, the cathedral there had a monopoly until the late sixteenth century on polyphony would seem to preclude, at least in this case, any kind of direct musical connections between the music of Mass and procession ("Music in the Corpus Christi Procession of Barcelona," *Early Music History* 14 [1995], 153–204, at 159–61, with commentary on 172–83).

42 James, "Ritual, Drama and Social Body," 11. For more on civic and ecclesiastical hierarchies as mirrored in Corpus Christi processions see Zika, "Hosts, Processions and Pilgrimages," 41–2, Rubin, *Corpus Christi*, pp. 247–71, and Duffy, *The Stripping of the Altars*, pp. 92–3.

43 For Coventry, York and Lérida see Rubin, *Corpus Christi*, p. 267. For Barcelona see Kreitner, "Music in the Corpus Christi Procession," 164, 169, 194. Kreitner notes that, from the mid fifteenth century, such entries could even incorporate parts of the dramatic actions and accoutrements of the Corpus Christi procession and that, by the 1460s, the procession itself could even be postponed to coincide with royal visits.

44 This parallel was directly drawn in London, where every royal entry from the coronation entry of Richard II in 1377 to that of Edward VI in 1547 was marked by at least one pageant representing the New Jerusalem (see Gordon Kipling, "'He That Saw It Would Not Believe It': Anne Boleyn's Royal Entry into London," in Alexandra F. Johnson and Wim Hüsken [eds.], *Civic Ritual and Drama* [Amsterdam and Atlanta, GA: Rodopi, 1997], p. 52).

45 See Gordon Kipling, *Enter the King: Theatre, Liturgy, and Ritual in the Medieval Civic Triumph* (Oxford University Press, 1998). In other instances, the entry route underscored juridical legitimacy by following town boundaries (see Rubin, *Corpus Christi*, p. 247); in still others, as in Würzburg, it took in parish and collegiate churches and outlying boroughs, symbolically affirming their links – and subordination – to church and civic authorities in the cathedral and town square (see Zika, "Hosts, Processions and Pilgrimages," 38–9).

46 Coventry, City Archives MS BA/E/F37/1. On the wealth and extravagance of the Coventry Corpus Christi gild see Rosser, "Going to the Fraternity Feast," 439–40. The discovery of the *Caput* fragment was announced in Manfred F. Bukofzer, "*Caput Redivivum*: A New Source for Dufay's *Missa Caput*," *Journal of the American Musicological Society* 4/2 (1951), 97–110.

47 On this point see Duffy, *The Stripping of the Altars*, p. 92: "it is important to grasp that the Eucharist could only be used to endorse existing community power structures because the language of Eucharistic belief and devotion was saturated with communitarian and corporate imagery." Likewise James, "Ritual, Drama and Social Body," 9: "the archetypal symbol was the mass, which both affirmed and created the symbol of social body, which was the body of Christ. The Corpus Christi procession involved the application of this theme to a specific community and place, presenting in visual form the structure of social differentiation taken up into the social wholeness which was the town itself."

48 Quoted in James, "Ritual, Drama and Social Body," 9. In the same vein, James goes on to quote another lesson, also read at Matins during Corpus Christi: "Let him come near, let him enter that Body, that he may be quickened. Let him not sever himself from the fit joining together of all the members ... let him be goodly, and useful, and healthy."

49 In discussing the church's offering Jungmann quotes Augustine's *De civitate Dei*: "ipse offerens, ipse et oblatio. Cuius rei sacramentum quotidianum esse voluit Ecclesiae sacrificium, quae cum ipsius capitis corpus sit, se ipsam per ipsum discit offerre" (Joseph Jungmann, *The Mass of the Roman Rite: Its Origins and Development* [translation, by Francis A. Brunner, of *Missarum Solemnia*], 2 vols. [Westminster, MD: Christian Classics, 1986], vol. I, p. 190). See also, more generally, Jungmann's discussion of the "Meaning of Mass" (*ibid.*, vol. I, pp. 175–95).

50 Translation from Duffy, *The Stripping of the Altars*, p. 93. For the original see C. Wordsworth (ed.), *Horae Eboracenses: The Prymer or Hours of the Blessed Virgin Mary, According to the Use of the Illustrious Church of York*, Surtees Society 132 (Durham and London: Quaritch, 1919), p. 73.

51 Innocent III, *De sacro altaris mysterio libri sex*, Liber I, Caput XXXIV. De pontificalibus indumentis, secundum quod Christo convenient: "Pontifex ergo in altaris officio capitis sui Christi, cujus membrum est, repraesentans personam ..." (Patrologia Latina 217 Col. 0787A).

52 For more on this see Chapter 5.

53 Ernst H. Kantorowicz, *Laudes Regiae: A Study in Liturgical Acclamations and Mediaeval Ruler Worship* (Berkeley and Los Angeles: University of California Press, 1946), p. 143.

54 "In capite uero pontificis sacramentalis est delibutio obseruata quia personam capitis, scilicet Christi qui est caput Ecclesie, in pontificali officio representat" (*Rationale*, Liber I, Caput VIII). See Durandus, *Guillelmi Duranti* CXL, I–IV (1995), p. 106.

55 Kantorowicz, *Laudes Regiae*, pp. 143, 141.

56 See Ernst H. Kantorowicz, *The King's Two Bodies: A Study in Mediaeval Political Theology* (Princeton University Press, 1957), pp. 202–3. For Kantorowicz, a key text in this regard is Pope Boniface VIII's 1302 bull *Unam sanctam*: "Urged by faith we are bound to believe in one holy Church, Catholic and also Apostolic ..., without which there is neither salvation nor remission of sins ..., which represents one mystical body, the head of which is Christ, and the head of Christ is God." As Kantorowicz has interpreted this: "Pope Boniface was bent upon putting political entities in what he considered their proper place, and therefore stressed, and overstressed, the hierarchical view that the political bodies had a purely functional character *within* the world community of the *corpus mysticum Christi*, which was the Church, whose head was Christ, and whose visible head was the vicar of Christ, the Roman pontiff" (*ibid.*, p. 194).

57 *Ibid.*, p. 203.

58 See Pamela Tudor-Craig, "Richard III's Triumphant Entry into York, August 29, 1483," in Rosemary Horrox (ed.), *Richard III and the North*, Studies in Regional and Local History 6 (Hull: Centre for Regional and Local History, 1986), pp. 108–16.

59 Tudor-Craig notes the intriguing fact that the body of Christ was symbolized in the fifteenth century by this other sacred "head," that of the Baptist, as explicitly stated in the York service book of the gild of Corpus Christi: "Caput Johannis in disco: signat corpus Christi: quo pascimur in sancto altari: Et quod ecclesie gentium in salutem ac remedium animarum" (*ibid.*, p. 113). Jonathan Hughes characterizes the staging of this entry as "Another indication of Richard's almost messianic conception of his kingship" (*The Religious Life of Richard III: Piety and Prayer in the North of England* [Phoenix Mill, etc., Gloucestershire: Sutton, 1997], p. 95).

60 Tudor–Craig, "Richard III's Triumphant Entry," p. 111. The symbolism culminated in a ceremony in York Minster, where Richard knelt on a prie-dieu by the font and recited the Pater noster. Tudor-Craig points out the significance of the fact that this entry took place on the Feast of the Decollation of St. John the Baptist.

61 "… es aussi tost que le roy entra dedens la ville ilz lui mirent ung gran ciel d'azur sur la teste … et le porterent sur lui les IIII eschevins tout en la fourme et maniere c'on fait à nostre Seigneur à la Feste-Dieu, et plus, car chascun criot: Nouel! par où il passoit." Quoted in Robert Withington, *English Pageantry: An Historical Outline*, 2 vols. (New York: Benjamin Blom, 1918; repr. 1963 by Harvard University Press), vol. I, p. 135. Original also quoted in Kipling, *Enter the King*, p. 179.

62 Lawrence M. Bryant, *The King and the City in the Parisian Royal Entry Ceremony: Politics, Ritual, and Art in the Renaissance* (Geneva: Droz, 1986), pp. 101–3, and the same author's "Configurations of the Community in Late Medieval Spectacles: Paris and London during the Dual Monarchy," in Barbara A. Hanawalt and Kathryn L. Beyerson (eds.), *City and Spectacle in Medieval Europe* (Minneapolis and London: University of Minnesota Press, 1994), pp. 3–33, particularly pp. 14–15. Gordon Kipling adds the important point that use of the canopy thus became a jealously guarded privilege, one refused to all but the king (see Kipling, *Enter the King*, p. 27).

63 On the general custom of chanting "Nowell, Nowell" at French royal entries see Kipling, *Enter the King*, p. 28. Kipling adds the important point that the first Sunday of Advent was the day appointed, in the Sarum and Gallican rites, for the reading of Matthew's account of Christ's entry into Jerusalem (*ibid.*, p. 85).

64 Craig Wright, *Music and Ceremonial at Notre Dame of Paris 500–1550* (Cambridge University Press, 1989), p. 208.

65 As explained, in the case of the entry of Louis XI in 1461, by Georges Chastellain, *Traité par form d'allégorie mystique sur l'entrée du Roy Louys en nouveau règne*, in *Oeuvres de Georges Chastellain*, ed. Kervyn de Lettenhove, vol. VII (Brussels: Académie Royale de Belgique, 1865), p. 6. See Bryant, *The King and the City*, pp. 132–3, and Kipling, *Enter the King*, p. 73.

66 See Richard Rastall, "Music for a Royal Entry, 1474," *Musical Times* 118 (1977), 463–4. See also Withington, *English Pageantry*, vol. I, p. 153.

67 Kipling, *Enter the King*, pp. 20–7 and *passim*.

68 *Ibid.*, pp. 23, 28.

69 Bernard Guenée and Françoise Lehoux, *Les Entrées Royales Françaises de 1328 à 1515* (Paris: Centre National de la Recherche Scientifique, 1968), p. 247.

70 Kipling, *Enter the King*, p. 100 and Bryant, *The King and the City*, p. 181.

71 Kipling, *Enter the King*, pp. 36, 37. The continuation of the latter passage, of interest for its extra musical detail, is omitted by Kipling but transcribed in Arthur W. Reed, "The Beginnings of the English Sacred and Secular Romantic Drama," paper read before the Shakespeare Association on Friday, February 29, 1920 (www.archive.org/stream/beginningsofeng100reeduoft/beginningsofeng100reeduoft_djvu.txt): "wt shalmys and Organs wt most swetyst musyke that cowed be devysede."

72 Withington, *English Pageantry*, vol. I, p. 159.

73 Sydney Anglo, *Spectacle, Pageantry, and Early Tudor Policy* (2nd edn., Oxford and New York: Oxford University Press, 1997), pp. 21–8, and Kipling, *Enter the King*, pp. 134–9. Kipling notes that "In the streets of the Yorkist capital, [Henry] is crowned King by his former enemies and manifests himself to these once-rebellious citizens as the messianic king chosen by God to rule all the people of England" (*ibid.*, p. 139).

74 In the words of the verse account ascribed to Lydgate:

An Antelope and a Lyon stondyng hym by
Above hem seynt George oure lady knyght
Benedictus thei gan synge
Qui venit in nomine domini goddes knyght
Gracia dei with yow doth sprynge.

A contemporary prose chronicle observed the same scene: "on the turrettes stonding a lyon and a antilope with many angeles syngyng *Benedictus qui venit in nomine domini*. And so rode he forth in to london." Both are quoted in Margaret Bent, "Sources of the Old Hall Music," *Proceedings of the Royal Musical Association* 94 (1967–8), 23.

75 *Ibid.*, 22–6. The pieces are Damett: *Salvatoris mater pia / O Georgi Deo care / Benedictus Marie filius qui ve-* (ff. 89v–90r); Cooke: *Alma proles regia / Christi miles inclite / Ab inimicis nostris defende nos Christe* (ff. 90v–1r); and Sturgeon: *Salve mater Domini / Salve templum gratie / -it in nomine Domini* (ff. 91v–2r).

76 The motet by Damett proceeds through the music for "Benedictus Marie Filius qui ven-" while the Sturgeon picks up again up with "-it in nomine Domini."

77 Bukofzer, *Studies*, p. 70.

78 Bent herself noted, in light of Bukofzer's remark, that "After the *Sanctus* was one of the places prescribed for polyphony, and these motets are flanked by first-layer *Sanctus* settings" ("Sources of the Old Hall Music," 25).

79 Kipling, *Enter the King*, p. 169.

80 *Ibid.*, pp. 147–51.

81 See S. B. Chrimes, *English Constitutional Ideas in the Fifteenth Century* (Cambridge University Press, 1936), p. 180. Also discussed in Kantorowicz, *The King's Two Bodies*, p. 225.

82 S. B. Chrimes (ed. and transl.), *Sir John Fortescue: De Laudibus Legum Anglie* (Cambridge University Press, 1949), p. 31; original Latin facing page 30. See also the discussion in Kantorowicz, *The King's Two Bodies*, pp. 223–4.

83 *Ibid.*, pp. 227–8.

84 Quoted in *ibid.*, p. 228. Kantorowicz notes the telling use to which the metaphor was put in the Henrician struggle over control of the English church. Thus, he notes, "It now served Henry VIII to incorporate the *Anglicana Ecclesia*, so to speak, the genuine *corpus mysticum* of his 'empire,' into the *corpus politicum* of England, of which he as king was the head." From the opposite perspective he notes the incredulity at the turning of events as expressed, for example, in 1533 in the following terms by Richard Sampson: "Quis nescit totum regnum unum esse politicum corpus, singulos homines eiusdem corporis membra esse? Ubi nam est huius corporis caput? Estne aliud quam rex?" By now, he suggests, things had come to a point at which "all Englishmen were incorporated in the king, and … the king's personal acts and deeds were those of a body politic absorbed by its monarchical head."

85 *Ibid.*, pp. 215–18 .

86 Giesey, "The French Estates," p. 157.

87 Bryant, *The King and the City*, pp. 135–6.

88 Jean Masselin, *Journal des États Généraux de France, Tenus à Tours en 1484*, transl. A Bernier (Paris: Imprimerie Royale, 1835), pp. 601–2.

89 Kipling, *Enter the King*, p. 46; see the relevant passage from a rhymed chronicle of the event in Guenée and Lehoux, *Les Entrées Royales Françaises*, p. 114.

90 Giesey, "The French Estates," pp. 166–9, which gives the original Latin of Terre Rouge's comment as follows: "[Quintum (in quod fidelitas consitit) est] quod membrum quodlibet polyticum, sive mysticum tenetur adherere, et sequi voluntatem sui domini, sive capitis mystici illi totaliter se informando" (*Contra Rebelles Suorum Regum* [Lyon: Constantine Fradin, 1526], Tract. III, Art. 3, concl. v. "Caput mysticum influit esse in quolibet suorum membrorum," Tract. III, Art. 3, concl. ii [both quoted on p. 166]).

91 www.newadvent.org/summa. "… sicut dicit Augustinus, super Ioan., *si praepositi Ecclesiae pastores sunt, quomodo unus pastor est, nisi quia sunt illi omnes unius membra pastoris?* Et similiter alii possunt dici fundamenta et capita, inquantum sunt unius capitis et fundamenti membra" (*Summa theologica*, III, Q. 8, article 6). (www.ccel.org/ccel/aquinas/summa.FP.html.)

Chapter 5 Sounding armor: the sacred meaning of *L'homme armé*

1 See the discussion later in this chapter.

2 Craig Wright, *The Maze and the Warrior* (Cambridge, MA and London: Harvard University Press, 2001), chapters 6 and 7, pp. 159–205.

3 A direct linking of Christ with the *L'homme armé* song can be seen in its contrapuntal intertwining, in a combinative song by Basiron, with *D'ung aultre amer* (see the discussion in Chapter 3, p. 52).

4 "Induite vos arma Dei ut possitis stare adversus insidias diaboli. Quia non est nobis conluctatio adversus carnem et sanguinem sed adversus principes et potestates adversus mundi rectores tenebrarum harum contra spiritualia nequitiae in caelestibus. Propterea accipite armaturam Dei ut possitis resistere in dei malo et omnibus perfectis stare. State ergo succincti lumbos vestros in veritate et induti loricam iustitiae et calciati pedes in praeparatione evangelii pacis. In omnibus sumentes scutum fidei in quo possitis omnia tela nequissimi ignea extinguere. Et galeam salutis adsumite et gladium spiritus quod est verbum Dei" (Ephesians 6: 11–17). Translation from *The New Oxford Annotated Bible* (New Revised Standard Version) (New York: Oxford University Press, 1991), New Testament, p. 278. Paul's own sources, presumably the Old Testament Book of Isaiah and/or the apocryphal Wisdom of Solomon, are suggestive, since in both cases the armed man is God himself: "vidit Dominus et malum apparuit in oculis eius quia non est iudicium … Indutus est iustitia ut lorica et galea salutis in capite eius indutus est vestimentis ultionis et opertus est quasi pallio zeli" (Isaiah 59: 15, 17). "Accipiet armaturum zelus illius et armabit creaturam ad ultionem inimicorum. Induet pro lorice iustitiam et accipiet pro galea iudicium certum; sumet scutum inexpugnabilem aequitatem, acuet autem duram iram in lanceam …" (Wisdom of Solomon 5: 18–21). Paul also draws on the same imagery in his second epistle to the Corinthians (10: 3–4; see the quotation from Durandus below) and his first to the Thessalonians (5: 8), where the breastplate and helmet are presented in analogy to the three theological virtues.

5 For a discussion of some late-antique and medieval adaptations of Paul's words, used in reference both to Christ and to his Christian soldiers as "armed men," see Wright, *The Maze*, pp. 169–74.

6 See e.g. Psalms: "res principium sapientiae timor Domini" (Psalm 111: 10); Proverbs: "timor Domini principium scientiae" (Proverbs 1: 7); "tunc intelleges timorem Domini et scientiam Dei invenies" (Proverbs 2: 5); "in timore Domini fiducia fortitudinis et filiis eius erit spes" (Proverbs 14: 26); "timor Domini fons vitae ut declinet a ruina mortis" (Proverbs 14: 27).

7 See his discussion of the individual vestments, Chapters 2–17 (Guillelmus Durandus, *Guillelmi Duranti Rationale divinorum officiorum*, ed. A. Davril and T. M. Thibodeau, Corpus Christianorum, continuatio mediaevalis CXL, CXL A, CXL B, 3 vols. [Turnhout: Brepols, 1995, 1998, 2000], vol. 1 [CXL], pp. 184–224).

8 "Itaque sacerdos christi armis armatus de altari vel vestiario ad populum gradiens ad locum scilicet confessionis ibique peccata sua devote confitendo et pro se sibi commissis sine astantibus deum devote orando. Et cogitat christum

derisorie corona spinea coronatum sicque foras ad populum iudeorum deductum et de variis excessibus durissime accusatum et finaliter ut sic ad mortem usque iniuste dividicatus est" (Balthasar de Porta, *Tractatus de misteriis missae* [Augsburg: Johannes Froschauer, 1501], fol. A v^v). According to the early-fifteenth-century *Officii misse sacrique canonis expositio* of Nikolaus Stör, "hec indumenta quorundam armorum dei et xpi representant insignia. Superhumerale representat cooptorium quo iudei faciem xpi velaverunt." (He goes on to reiterate the same equations between Passion garments and vestments detailed by Durandus.) Franz dates the treatise 1412, and lists three prints before 1500, in addition to a large number of manuscript copies (see Adolph Franz, *Die Messe im deutschen Mittelalter* [Herder: Freiburg im Breisgau, 1902; repr. Darmstadt: Wissenschaftliche Buchgesellschaft, 1963], pp. 527–30). I used the edn., c.1476, of the Printer of Henricus Ariminensis, Strasbourg. For the late-fifteenth-century Franciscan Stephan Brulefer, mindfulness of the vestments as the "arma passionis" took precedence over their embodiment of the virtues expected of a priest (see Franz, *Die Messe*, pp. 602–3). See also the summary discussion in Franz, *ibid.*, pp. 734–5.

9 See the detailed analysis of Durandus's sources in Guillelmus Durandus, *Guillelmi Duranti Rationale divinorum officiorum*,. ed. A. Davril and T. M. Thibodeau, Corpus Christianorum, continuatio mediaevalis CXL, CXL A, CXL B, 3 vols. (Turnhout: Brepols, 1995, 1998, 2000), vol. 3 (CXL B), pp. 248–69.

10 This is the ultimate source of Christ's appellation "savior." Thus the Hebrew/Aramaic Yeshu/Yeshua/Joshua, which embodies the meaning of "saving" (he saves, he will save, God saves), finds its New Testament reflection in Matthew 1: 21: "call his name Joshua/Jesus, for he will save his people from their sins." The same etymology is revealed in Sirach 46: 1 where praise for the Old Testament Joshua is revealed to be explicitly revealed in "his name," since he excelled "in the saving of God's elect people."

11 See Bruce M. Metzger and Roland E. Murphy (eds.), *The New Oxford Annotated Bible* (New York: Oxford University Press, 1989), Old Testament, p. 276.

12 David's frequently cited role as an archetype of Christ is underscored by the notion, as postulated by Matthew and Luke, that the two were linked by direct genealogy as members of the royal dynasty of Judah, and by the reference to Christ as "son of David." In Matthew's genealogy (Matthew 1: 1–17), Jesus is a royal descendant of Abraham and David, indeed a new David. Luke, whose lineage differs, traces Jesus's ancestors back to Adam, presumably to cast Jesus as the fulfillment of the history not only of Israel, but of the world, through his redemption of original sin (Luke 3: 23–38). See Bruce M. Metzger, "Genealogies," in Bruce M. Metzger and Michael D. Coogan (eds.), *The Oxford Companion to the Bible* (New York and Oxford: Oxford University Press, 1993), pp. 244–5.

13 "Pulsatur ... ut ... pellantur hostiles exercitus et omnes insidie inimici ..." "Sciendum autem est quod campane ... significant tubas argenteas quibus in ueteri lege populus ad sacrificandum acciebatur ... Quemadmodum enim

uigiles in castris tubis, sic et Ecclesiarum ministri campanarum sonitu se excitant, ut contra insidiantem dyabolum pernoctent." "Ceterum campane in processionibus pulsantur ut demones timentes fugiant … Timent enim auditis tubis Ecclesie militantis, scilicet campanis, sicut aliquis tyrannus timet audiens in terra sua tubas alicuius potentis regis inimici sui." *Rationale Divinorum Officiorum*, Book 1, Chapters 2, 3, 14; see Guillelmus Durandus, *Guillelmi Duranti*, vol. I (CXL), I–IV, pp. 52–3, 56–7. Available in English translation in Guillelmus Durandus, *The Symbolism of Churches and Church Ornaments: A Translation of the First Book of the Rationale Divinorum Officiorum Written by William Durandus, Sometime Bishop of Mende*, ed. John Mason Neale and Benjamin Webb, 3rd edn. (London: Gibbings and Co., 1906), pp. 67–8, 75.

14 *De sacro altaris mysterio libri sex*, Book II, Chapter XXVIII; original in Appendix 1 of this book, text 2.

15 See the discussion of manuscript copies and redactions in Guillelmus Durandus, *Guillelmi Duranti*, vol. 3 (CXL B: Books VII-VIII, *Praefatio, Indices*), pp. 195–207, 229–35, and the list of sources on pp. 211–17.

16 By comparison, the same period saw nineteen editions of Augustine's *De civitate Dei* and sixteen of Caesar's *De bello gallico*. For these details see James F. White, "Durandus and the Interpretation of Christian Worship," in George H. Shriver (ed.), *Contemporary Reflections on the Medieval Christian Tradition: Essays in Honor of Ray C. Petry* (Durham, NC: Duke University Press, 1974), pp. 49–50. For pre-1500 editions of Durandus see Kommission für den Gesamtkatalog der Wiegendrucke (eds.), *Gesamtkatalog der Wiegendrucke* (Leipzig: K. W. Hiersemann, 1925–), vol. VII (1938), pp. 727–51. A complete listing, with classifications and chronology, of all editions of Durandus from 1459 to 1859 can be found in Michel Albaric, "Les Éditions imprimées du *Rationale divinorum officiorum* de Guillaume Durand de Mende," and Bertrand Guyot, "Essai de Classement des Éditions du *Rationale*," in Pierre-Marie Gy, OP (ed.), *Guillaume Durand, Évêque de Mende (v. 1230–1296): Canoniste, liturgiste et homme politique* (Paris: Éditions du Centre national de la recherche scientifique, 1992), pp. 183–200 and 201–5, respectively. Cyrille Vogel, *Medieval Liturgy: An Introduction to the Sources* (Washington: Pastoral, 1981), pp. 15–16 and Richard Pfaff, *Medieval Latin Liturgy: A Select Bibliography* (Toronto: University of Toronto Press, 1982), p. 58 list modern editions and translations before Davril and Thibodeau.

17 See the observations on this point by Franz, *Die Messe*, p. 482, and Joseph Braun, *Die liturgische Gewandung im Occident und Orient: nach Ursprung und Entwicklung, Verwendung und Symbolik* (Freiburg im Breisgau: Herder, 1907), pp. 704, 726.

18 Braun, *Die liturgische Gewandung*, p. 705.

19 Franz, *Die Messe*, p. 423.

20 See for example the sermon, for the twenty-first Sunday after Trinity, by the thirteenth-century Chancellor of the University of Paris and Bishop of

Cambrai, Gaiardus de Laon (Paris, Nat. lat. 15953 f.51r–51v and Paris, Nat. lat. 15383 f. 278r–f. 278v), and the early-sixteenth-century manual for priests *Speculum curatorum* by Artur Fillon (Paris: J. Parvo, 1503, ff. 7v–8r). Both draw the same multilayered parallels between the priestly vestments, Christ's accoutrements during his Passion, and actual items of armor.

21 See Rudolf Hirsch, "Surgant's List of Recommended Books for Preachers (1502–3)," *Renaissance Quarterly* 20 (1967), 198–210. Surgant's manual itself ran to no fewer than 10 editions between 1503 and 1520, and was listed by the *Statuta synodalia* of the diocese of Basel in October 1503 as among only 12 books "with which priests should be familiar" (*ibid.*, 200).

22 See Don Harrán, *In Defense of Music: The Case for Music as Argued by a Singer and Scholar of the Late Fifteenth Century* (Lincoln and London: University of Nebraska Press, 1989), p. 22. My thanks to Bonnie Blackburn for this reference.

23 Appendix 1, texts 6 and 7 offer two examples: text 6 gives the relevant quotation from Ephesians as framed, following Innocent III, in the 1476 *Officij misse sacrique canonis expositio* of Nikolaus Stör; text 7, describing the vestments as armor and the priest as Christ's "champioun," is from Lydgate's *Vertue of the Masse*. On the wide circulation of such texts and their perceived importance to the proper instruction of the clergy see also Miri Rubin, *Corpus Christi: The Eucharist in Late Medieval Culture* (Cambridge University Press, 1991), pp. 83–98.

24 Galigaen makes clear that his abridgement and simplification of Durandus is aimed "ad utilitatem simplicium sacerdotum" (see the discussion and list of sources in Guillelmus Durandus, *Guillelmi Duranti*, vol. III [CXL B], pp. 224–8).

25 See the beautiful summary of this situation in Franz, *Die Messe*, pp. 738–9.

26 See Braun, *Die liturgische Gewandung*, pp. 710–27.

27 See, for example, the vesting prayers in *The Saint Andrew Daily Missal* (Bruges: Abbey of St. Andrew; and St. Paul, MN: E. M. Lohmann, 1958), pp. 783–4. I am grateful to James Farge for directing me to this source. The equation of the amice with a helmet, deriving from the ancient custom of placing it first on the head before (after donning the chasuble) lowering it onto the shoulders, is still indicated in the St. Andrew Missal. For other, earlier echoes of Paul's sacred armory see Wright, *The Maze*, pp. 169–74.

28 Thus, according to her principal source, Giovanni Rucellai, "in the city of Cologne in Germany [he is unspecific about which church or churches in that city fostered the practice], Masses are said on certain days of the year with the priest who says it armed with all arms" (Flynn Warmington, "The Ceremony of the Armed Man: The Sword, the Altar, and the *L'homme armé* Masses," in Paula Higgins [ed.], *Antoine Busnoys: Method, Meaning, and Context in Late Medieval Music* [Oxford and New York: Oxford University Press, 1996], p. 121). Similarly, Warmington cites an anonymous chronicle of 1340 to the effect that Christmas Matins in the patriarchate of Aquileia was celebrated by

the patriarch "in armor as well as sacred vestments, assisted by a Benedictine abbot wearing a cuirass." A 1433 lectionary has the rubric "Here follows the Gospel said at Mass on the day of the Epiphany, having a drawn sword with which the helmeted deacon, escorting the priest and escorted by the subdeacon, proceeds to the altar." A similar, apparently more elaborate, permutation has survived to modern times in Cividale del Friuli, another town in the former patriarchate (*ibid.*, pp. 105–7).

29 Rucellai comments "in certain places I have seen put on the altar while the priest says the Mass a helmet of iron with a bishop's mitre on it" (*ibid.*, p. 121). In another example from Cahors, southern France, "the bishop, in exercise of his temporal title of baron and count of the city, traditionally placed an array of arms and armor beside the altar for pontifical Masses: 'helmet, sword, burning fuse, gauntlets, or iron gloves, as well as boots and spurs.'" According to Warmington's source, Gaetano Moroni's *Dizionario di erudizione storico-ecclesiastico da S. Pietro sino ai nostri giorni...*, 103 vols. in 53 (Venice, 1840–61), "Cahors," vi, 225, such practices were generally exercised by sovereign bishops and abbots (*ibid.*, pp. 107–8).

30 *Ibid.*, pp. 97–100. The implied parallel, noted by Warmington, between the emperor and Augustus, seen as a prophet because his peaceful reign was chosen by God for the birth of Christ, is significant, and will be expanded on below.

31 *Ibid.*, pp. 103–4. The custom was imitated, Warmington notes, by future English monarchs as far as James II in the late seventeenth century.

32 See *ibid.*, p. 96, and the literature cited there.

33 Michel Andrieu (ed.), *Le pontifical Romain au moyen-âge*, vol. 3: *Le Pontifical de Guillaume Durand* (Vatican City: Biblioteca Apostolica Vaticana, 1940), pp. 669–77.

34 See Warmington, "The Ceremony," 104, and Joseph Jungmann, *The Mass of the Roman Rite: Its Origins and Development* (translation, by Francis A. Brunner, of *Missarum Solemnia*), 2 vols. (Westminster, MD: Christian Classics, 1986), vol. I, p. 449. Jungmann cites a mid-eighteenth-century source testifying that the practice was still current at that time. The same medieval custom is noted by the seventeenth-century cardinal Johannes Bona: "Nunc milites Religiosi & equestris ordinis viri, ensi manum admovent, vel educunt de vagina, cum recitatur Evangelium, ut eo gestu testentur se paratos esse, pro Evangelii defensione viriliter pugnare & sanguinem effundere" *Rerum liturgicarum libri duo* (Cologne: Joan. Wilhelmum Friessem Juniorem, 1674); I have used the reading of the *Opera Omnia* (Antwerp: Schipperus, 1677 [?]), p. 532. My thanks to Philip Weller for supplying me with this.

35 Ernst H. Kantorowicz, *Laudes Regiae: A Study in Liturgical Acclamations and Mediaeval Ruler Worship* (Berkeley and Los Angeles: University of California Press, 1946), p. 31 (for more on this chant and its connotations see below).

36 See Marc Dykmans (ed.), *Le Pontifical Romain revisé au XVe siècle* (Vatican City: Biblioteca Apostolica Vaticana, 1985), p. 8.

37 *Ibid.*, pp. 15, 23–4.

38 *Pontificale Romanum Clementis VIII Pont. Max. Iussu Restitutum Atque Editum Romae, MDXCV.* Comparison between the original print of 1595 and a print of 1769 (Venice: Typographia Balleoniana) revealed that, though newly set, the latter is almost entirely identical both in text and illustration.

39 See for example the quotation from Innocent III, above.

40 Described in Franz, *Die Messe*, p. 101; see also Edmund A. Bowles, "Were Musical Instruments Used in the Liturgical Service during the Middle Ages?" *Galpin Society Journal* 10 (1957), 52.

41 Kantorowicz, *Laudes Regiae*, pp. 13–64.

42 *Ibid.*, p. 1. In a similar connection, Kantorowicz comments on the "extraordinary space ... granted, in the Gallic and Frankish sacramentaries, to the liturgical hallowing of weapons, standards, army, and ruler" (*ibid.*, p. 30).

43 *Ibid.*, p. 3.

44 *Ibid.*, pp. 81–2.

45 "The king's day of exaltation was to coincide with the days of the exaltation of the Lord in order to make, by this coincidence, the terrestrial kingship appear all the more transparent against the background of the kingship of Christ. This tendency, however, also had a retroactive effect: the commemoration of the Lord's days of exaltation was to recall the most solemn celebration in a king's life, his coronation" (*ibid.*, p. 92).

46 Kantorowicz emphasizes that such entries cast the entering anointed monarch as a type of Christ, with the city in question becoming another Jerusalem (*ibid.*, pp. 71–6).

47 *Ibid.*, pp. 85–146.

48 *Ibid.*, pp. 136–46 and Marc Bloch's classic study *The Royal Touch: Sacred Monarchy and Scrofula in England and France*, translated by J. E. Anderson (London: Routledge and Kegan Paul, 1973 [first published in French in 1924]), p. 116.

49 The privilege of being anointed was bestowed periodically on royal houses until well into the fourteenth century (see Kantorowicz, *Laudes Regiae*, p. 162, and Bloch, *The Royal Touch*, p. 337).

50 Bloch, *The Royal Touch*, p. 116.

51 Ironically this claim received its sanction from none other than Innocent III. Innocent's bull *Per Venerabilem*, with its key clause affirming that "the king has no superior in the temporal realm," was issued in an attempt to enlist the support of Philip Augustus against imperial assertions of universal power. See Carra Ferguson O'Meara, *Monarchy and Consent: The Coronation Book of Charles V of France* (London/Turnhout: Harvey Miller, 2001), pp. 38, 46–7. O'Meara cites as her source Jacques Krynen, *L'empire du roi: Idées et croyances politiques en France, XIIIe–XVe siècle* (Paris: Gallimard, 1993).

52 O'Meara, *Monarchy and Consent*, pp. 63–4, 116, and Bloch, *The Royal Touch*, p. 119.

53 Of the twenty-eight illuminated images illustrating the coronation of Charles V in 1364, the sword features in all but the first four (see O'Meara, *Monarchy and Consent*, plates, and the discussion on pp. 293–306).

54 O'Meara, *Monarchy and Consent*, p. 62. On the unique status of the French king and the rationale behind his unique assumption of the title *Rex Christianissimus* see also *ibid.*, pp. 113–19.

55 See Bloch, *The Royal Touch*, pp. 82 and 323.

56 On the distinctions between the precise, modern definition of this disease and its likely more diffuse medieval applications see *ibid.*, pp. 11–12.

57 This claim, which seems to have originated independently in Norman England and Capetian France in the eleventh century, persisted until the eighteenth, breathing its last gasp with, respectively, the Stuart dynasty and the fall of the *ancien regime* (see *ibid.*, pp. 11–27, 214–28).

58 *Ibid.*, p. 53.

59 See the edition in Jean Molinet, *Les faictz et dictz de Jean Molinet*, ed. Noël Dupire, 3 vols. (Paris: Société des anciens textes Français, 1936, 1937, 1939), vol. II, p. 617.

60 Kantorowicz, *Laudes Regiae*, p. 11.

61 Anmon Linder, *Raising Arms: Liturgy in the Struggle to Liberate Jerusalem in the Late Middle Ages* (Turnhout: Brepols, 2003).

62 *Ibid.*, pp. 1–3.

63 The most widespread of these is the so-called "Clementine set" promulgated, in bulls of 1308 and 1309, by Clement V, to be inserted into every Mass. Linder notes that with this move, "The pope practically converted all Masses into Holy Land Masses." The Mass circulated widely up until the early sixteenth century and became a permanent fixture as a votive Mass. It ultimately became the only official "anti-pagan" Mass, a status it maintained until it was renamed by Vatican II in 1961 as the *Missa pro defensione Ecclesiae* (*ibid.*, pp. 120 and 137).

64 *Ibid.*, p. 178.

65 The earliest such Mass to be written was apparently that composed by Bernard, Bishop of Kotor, in 1453–4, which circulated in German-speaking territories in the later fifteenth century (*ibid.*, p. 186).

66 *Ibid.*, Chapter 2. E.g. Linder's Mass no. 30, found in fifteenth- and early-sixteenth-century copies from Cambrai, Noyon, Rheims, and no. 31, from Poitiers (pp. 248–51). The closeness of the particularly bellicose no. 30 to the 1456 *Missa contra Turcos* of Calixtus III makes it a particularly suggestive forum for *L'homme armé* Masses.

67 *Ibid.*, pp. 187, 189, 222–3. The Turkish occupation of Otranto on 21 August 1480 sent shudders through Christendom. Planned as the first step in a conquest of Italy, it delivered an uncompromising message: some 12,000 inhabitants of the town were slaughtered, including its entire clergy, with the archbishop

being apparently quartered. Rome was thrown into convulsions, with the pope and other senior clerics attributing the crisis to God's judgment on an Italy wallowing in iniquity and infighting. On this and its liturgical responses, see Penny J. Cole, "Cambridge, Fitzwilliam Museum, MS McClean 51, Pope Sixtus IV and the Fall of Otranto (August 1480)," in Jacqueline Brown and William P. Stoneman (eds.), *A Distinct Voice: Medieval Studies in Honor of Leonard E. Boyle* (Notre Dame: University of Notre Dame Press, 1997), pp. 103–20.

68 Advances of Sixtus's reign included the considerable augmentation of the papal choir, in which the pope took a personal interest of a kind not hitherto documented in the papacy. See for instance Adalbert Roth, "Liturgical (and Paraliturgical) Music in the Papal Chapel towards the End of the Fifteenth Century," in Richard Sherr (ed.), *Papal Music and Musicians in Late Medieval and Renaissance Rome* (Oxford University Press, 1998), pp. 124–37, and Christopher Reynolds, *Papal Patronage and the Music of St. Peter's, 1380–1513* (Berkeley: University of California Press, 1995), pp. 49–53. On the manuscripts Cappella Sistina 14 and 51, which are documented in the Sistine Chapel from the reign of Sixtus's successor, Innocent VIII, and their contents see Adalbert Roth, *Studien zum frühen Repertoire der päpstlichen Kapelle unter dem Pontificat Sixtus' IV (1471–1484): Die Chorbücher 14 und 51 des Fondo Cappella Sistina der Biblioteca Apostolica Vaticana* (Vatican City: Bibloteca Apostolica Vaticana, 1991).

69 Roth has also proposed a link between the *L'homme armé* corpus of Cappella Sistina 14 and the Turkish menace (*ibid.*, pp. 356–7). He places this in the context of an alliance forged earlier in the 1470s between Sixtus and Ferrante I, King of Naples, and proposes that the two choirbooks comprise an anthology of works current at the Neapolitan court and assembled there as a gift to the pope in the first half of 1474 (*ibid.*, pp. 328–88). By contrast, Flynn Warmington has made a case that the two manuscripts were copied in Venice and illuminated in the workshop of the Master of the Pliny of Pico della Mirandola and associated ateliers. She dates the sources to *circa* 1480–1 on the basis of close similarities between miniatures and floral decoration in the Cappella Sistina sources and the work of the Pico Master in other sources datable to these two years (Warmington, "*Abeo semper Fortuna regressum*: Evidence for the Venetian Origin of the Manuscripts Cappella Sistina 14 and 51," paper read at the 22nd Conference on Medieval and Renaissance Music, Glasgow, 10 July 1994, private discussion on June 22, 2006, and e-mail communication of July 26, 2006).

70 Such durability would relate, as Linder notes in connection with war liturgy, "to their universal applicability rather than their obsolete specificity" (*Raising Arms*, p. 123).

71 For more on this Mass, see below. Michael was the primary focus of the Holy Angels Mass incorporated as one of a Holy Land sequence of three votive

Masses with Holy Land clamor that was instituted to promote a crusade to Armenia and Cyprus by John XXII in 1322 (*ibid.*, pp. 100–02).

72 *Ibid.*, p. 187; text on p. 239.

73 *Ibid.*, p. 185; text on p. 207. In this context it is worth noting the self-stylization, inherited from Frankish forebears (see above), of the French king as a "novus David," the leader of a new tribe of Israel, a conceit that seems to have had a particular vogue in the later fifteenth and early sixteenth century (see Patrick Macey, "Josquin's 'Misericordias Domini' and Louis XI," *Early Music* 19 (1991), 175–6).

74 *Ibid.*, pp. xvi, 119, 178, 247. See also the depiction of the two facets of this battle in Linder's cover illustration, from the late thirteenth-century Psalter of St. Louis, in which the Israelites are depicted as crusaders. Color plates 1 and 2 (pp. 13–14), from the same source, likewise depict the Israelites respectively in the siege and destruction of Jericho dressed in contemporary military garb. (See the discussion of these images in *ibid.*, pp. 80–1.)

75 *Ibid.*, p. 97.

76 For text and translation see Barbara Haggh, communication, *Journal of the American Musicological Society* 40 (1987), 139–40.

77 Wright, *The Maze*, p. 185.

78 For what follows I am indebted to Marie Tanner, *The Last Descendant of Aeneas* (New Haven and London: Yale University Press, 1993).

79 Laurenz Lütteken, "Ritual und Krise: Die neapolitanischen 'L'homme armé'-Zyklen und die Semantik der Cantus firmus-Messe," in Hermann Danuser and Tobias Plebuch (eds.), *Musik als Text: Bericht über den Internationalen Kongreß der Gesellschaft für Musikforschung Freiburg im Breisgau 1993* (Kassel: Bärenreiter, 1998), p. 210.

80 Wright, *The Maze*, p. 185.

81 On Dante see particularly the classic study by Nancy Lenkeith, *Dante and the Legend of Rome* (London: Warburg Institute, 1952).

82 In Tanner's words, "The adaptation of the Aeneid to political realities was endemic to the myth, for Vergil had shaped his artistry to glorify Augustus" (Tanner, *The Last Descendant*, p. 31).

83 *Ibid.*, p. 98 (Philip the Good; also p. 277 on Edward de Dynter); pp. 93–8 (the Emperor Charles IV).

84 Philip's well-known sense of personal connection with the figure of Jason is attested, *inter alia*, by the many tapestries and tableaux featured in his court rooms, ceremonies and entertainments, and in the number of Troy-related books in his library. Gert Pinkernell notes in this connection the contrast between the 1420 book inventory after the death of Duke John the Fearless, which lists only one manuscript concerning the Trojan legends, and that on Philip's death, by which time the number had risen to seventeen (see Pinkernell's introduction to Raoul Lefèvre, *L'Histoire de Jason* (Frankfurt: Athenäum, 1971), p. 99.

85 See Tanner, *The Last Descendant*, pp. 146–53. This conflation of pagan and Christian lambs, and the prophesies they embodied, is clarified by the treatise on the Golden Fleece by the chancellor of the Order Guillaume Fillastre: "When Juno, our first mother, chased her children from heaven for their sin, they embarked on this world of tribulations. Some fall; others, fixed on the ram like Phrixus, arrive at Colchis to the Temple of Jupiter that is the Church Triumphant ... Jupiter sent us the ram of His Grace Jesus, the Lamb of God, who offered His sacrifice to the world ... covered in the golden fleece of our humanity" (quoted in *ibid.*, p. 150). The same conflation can be seen in the identification, since Carolingian times, of the constellation Aries, originally seen to signify the Golden Fleece, with the Lamb of God (see *ibid.*, p. 149). The link received lavish visual depiction at the meeting arranged by Charles the Bold with Frederick III, on October 7, 1473, at the Church of St. Maximian in Trier, as we learn from the *Libellus de magnificentia ducis Burgundiae*: "One side of the church was hung with rich gold and silver tapestries embroidered with the Passion of our Lord Christ Jesus; the other with the story of how Jason got the Golden Fleece in the Land of Colchis ..." The allegorical parallels continued with the banquet which followed Mass, in a room "hung with rich cloth of gold tapestries with the history of Gideon the regent of Israel ..." (quoted in Richard Vaughan, *Charles the Bold: The Last Valois Duke of Burgundy* [London: Longman, 1973], p. 146).

86 Tanner, *The Last Descendant*, pp. 17, 148. Thus, as Tanner says, "it is not surprising that this stellar beacon, which enfolded pagan and imperial as well as Christian concepts of the earth's first light and the perennial promise of the conquest over darkness should represent the objectives of the Order" (*ibid.*, p. 151).

87 This claim is credited to William Prizer by Alejandro Enrique Planchart, "Guillaume Du Fay's Benefices and His Relationship to the Court of Burgundy," *Early Music History* 8 (1988), 159–60, and Ronald Woodley, "Tinctoris's Italian Translation of the Golden Fleece Statutes: A Text and a (Possible) Context," *Early Music History* 8 (1988), 185–6; in fact no such direct claim is made in Prizer's article "Music and Ceremonial in the Low Countries: Philip the Fair and the Order of the Golden Fleece," *Early Music History* 5 (1985), 113–53, though Planchart ascribes it to Prizer's paper "The Order of the Golden Fleece and Music," read at the meeting of the American Musicological Society, Vancouver, 1985. See also Lütteken, "Ritual und Krise," p. 213. Barbara Haggh notes that the archives of the Order in Vienna provide no direct evidence for this, or indeed for any other specific use of surviving polyphony, but that need not preclude the possibility that the practice was followed ("The Archives of the Order of the Golden Fleece and Music," *Journal of the Royal Musical Association* 120 [1995], 36–7).

88 Lütteken, "Ritual und Krise," p. 211.

89 Lütteken describes the conceptual and musical summation of the series in Mass 6: "Erst am Ende des gesamten Zyklus der sechs Ordinarien erscheint

gleichsam gestalthaft der bewaffnete Ritter selbst, und er übertrifft ('sic undique pergit') ... so jenen Sänger, der ihn bisher nur beschrieben hat. Die Ankündigung des Zweikampfes mündet also im tatsächlichen Erscheinen des geharnischten Ritters quasi in personam, also des vollständigen 'L'homme-armé' Liedes" (*ibid.*, p. 212).

90 Quoted in Prizer, "Music and Ceremonial," 138, 139, with translation on pp. 146, 148. The clearly intended mutual reference between these two tapestry series is noted by Lütteken, "Ritual und Krise," p. 214.

91 Lütteken, "Ritual und Krise," p. 213. For Lütteken, this crisis is also reflected in a particular expansion, in the 1450s and 1460s, of Troy-related literature, a reaction, as he sees it, to the perceived parallel between the contemporary catastrophe and the fall of Troy.

92 See Michael Long, "*Arma virumque cano*: Echoes of a Golden Age," in Paula Higgins (ed.), *Antoine Busnoys: Method, Meaning and Context in Late Medieval Music* (Oxford and New York: Oxford University Press, 1996), p. 136. Tinctoris's remarks are found in the *Liber de arte contrapuncti* III, Chapter 6; see Johannes Tinctoris, *Liber de arte contrapuncti* (1477), ed. Albert Seay, in *Johannis Tinctoris opera theoretica*, Corpus scriptorum de musica, no. 22/2 (Rome: American Institute of Musicology, 1975), pp. 152–3.

93 The importance of the use of the trumpet as a call to arms is attested by Vegetius's *De re militari* (an antique treatise that enjoyed a strong revival in the Renaissance) a point made in connection with *L'homme armé* by Michael Long ("*Arma virumque cano*," p. 136).

94 Johannes Tinctoris, *Complexus effectuum musices*, translated, annotated and edited by J. Donald Cullington and Reinhard Strohm as "A Compendium of Music's Effects," in *On the Dignity and the Effects of Music*, Institute of Advanced Musical Studies Study Texts, no. 2 (London: King's College London, 1996), pp. 58–9.

95 The accompaniment of trumpets was traditionally viewed in the later Middle Ages to have been the province only of noble lords (see, for example, Théodore Gérold, "Les instruments de musique au moyen âge," *Revue des Cours et Conférences* 32 [1928–9], 463, who cites Virdung [1511] in corroboration of this view). In practice, though, attempts by royal houses to restrict the spread of their use lost ground, especially in the course of the fifteenth century, when they were used increasingly by lower ranks of nobility and in cities, many of which instituted trumpet bands (see Keith Polk, *German Instrumental Music of the Late Middle Ages: Players, Patrons and Performance Practice* [Cambridge University Press, 1992], p. 48).

96 In this connection it is worth noting the heavily repetitive and harmonically static passage that heralds Christ's coming at "Et iterum venturus est" of the Credo of Josquin's *Missa Pange lingua*. This passage was cited by Bernhard Meier as an instance of "imitatio tubarum" (trans. Ellen Beebe as: *The Modes of Classical Vocal Polyphony* [New York: Broude, 1988]; first published in German as *Die Tonarten der klassischen Vokalpolyphonie: nach den Quellen*

dargestellt [Utrecht: Oosthoek, Scheltema & Holkema, 1974], p. 412). Timothy
McKinney has pointed out the double textual association here: "not only the
heraldic trumpets that signal the arrival of an important personage, but
also the trumpet signaling the Day of Judgment referenced in the following
line: 'judicare vivos et mortuos' ('to judge the living and the dead')" ("Major
and Minor Sonorities and Harmonic Affect in Josquin's Sacred Polyphony,"
paper read at the international conference New Directions in Josquin
Scholarship, Princeton University, 29–31 October, 1999, pp. 7–8).

97 On the functions of the elevation bell see Chapter 8. The metaphorical
parallel between the bell and this function of the trumpet is made explicit in
the thirteenth-century statutes of Coventry quoted by Miri Rubin: "And we
therefore ordain that at the elevation, when it is finally raised up high, the bell
will first sound, to be like a gentle trumpet announcing the arrival of a judge,
indeed of the saviour" ("Unde precipimus quod in elevatione eucharistie
quando ultimo elevatur et magis in altum, tunc primo sonet campanella, que
sit modica tuba denuntians adventum judicis, immo salvatoris ..."), *Corpus
Christi*, p. 58.

98 On this practice see Bowles, "Musical Instruments," 52. See also David
Fallows, "Specific Information on the Ensembles for Composed Polyphony,
1400–1474," in Stanley Boorman (ed.), *Studies in the Performance of Late
Medieval Music* (Cambridge University Press, 1983), p. 127, which also cites,
among others, the Mézières and Manetti references (see below) and further
bibliography referring to them.

99 See Frank D'Accone, *The Civic Muse: Music and Musicians in Siena during the
Middle Ages and Renaissance* (Chicago and London: University of Chicago
Press, 1997), pp. 465–6. The practice was clearly still being followed by 1524,
when a decree notes "Et decreverunt quod tubicines qualibet mane, quando
elevatur Corpus Christi ad Cappellam Campo Fori, teneantur sonare, sub
pena eis imponendam per priorem una cum consiliarii[s] prioris." Cathedral
payments also record the presence of trumpeters at numerous feasts, and
even, according to a record of 1470, "at all feasts of the year in the duomo, as
is customary" (*ibid.*, p. 466). My thanks to Keith Polk for this reference.

100 See Rob C. Wegman, *Born for the Muses: the Life and Masses of Jacob Obrecht*
(Oxford University Press, 1994), pp. 51, 54.

101 As, for example, in the case of the German cornettist paid to play his "cornu"
at high Mass in St. Goedele, Brussels in 1496/7, possibly the same player who
played at high Mass at St. Rombout, Mechelen in 1501. See Barbara Haggh,
"Music, Liturgy and Ceremony in Brussels, 1350–1500," unpublished PhD
dissertation, 2 vols., University of Illinois at Urbana-Champaign, 1988, vol.
1, p. 219. A trumpeter, along with singers and organist, was employed as part
of the Savoy Chapel at least from 1449 to 1455 and probably (though earlier
accounts specifically for the chapel are lacking) from 1428 or before (see
Marie-Thérèse Bouquet, "La cappella musicale dei duchi di Savoie dal 1450 al

1500," *Rivista italiana di musicologia* 3 [1968], 251–2 and Alejandro Enrique Planchart's essays "Fifteenth-Century Masses: Notes on Performance and Chronology," *Studi Musicali* 10 [1981], 5–6, and "Parts with Words and Without Words: the Evidence for Multiple Texts in Fifteenth-century Masses," in Stanley Boorman (ed.), *Studies in the Performance of Late Medieval Music* [Cambridge University Press, 1983], pp. 229–30). Further in this connection, Rob Wegman has pointed out that cities in the Low Countries began in the 1510s to fund the performance of trumpeters in the Mass and the *Salve* service (see Haggh, "Golden Fleece," 12). He notes that this commenced in the Marian confraternity of Bergen op Zoom in 1518/19 (see Wegman, "Music and Musicians at the Guild of Our Lady in Bergen op Zoom, *c.*1470–1510," *Early Music History* 9 [1990], 217), and at s'Hertogenbosch and Antwerp a little later.

102 Philippe de Mézières, *Le songe du vieil pelerin*, ed. C.W. Coopland, 2 vols. (Cambridge University Press, 1969), vol. II, pp. 242–3; also quoted in André Pirro, *La musique à Paris sous le règne de Charles VI (1380–1422)* (2nd edn., Strasburg, Baden-Baden: Heitz, 1958), p. 14, and elsewhere.

103 A similar practice at the royal court of England is suggested by the inclusion of two silver trumpets among the jewels and plate in three inventories of the Chapel Royal from late in the reign of Edward I, and by the purchase in 1346 of two extremely expensive silver trumpets by the Black Prince (see Richard Rastall, "Minstrelsy, Church and Clergy in Medieval England," *Proceedings of the Royal Musical Association* 97 [1970–1], 92).

104 Translation from Craig Wright, "Dufay's *Nuper rosarum flores*, King Solomon's Temple, and the Veneration of the Virgin," *Journal of the American Musicological Society* 47 (1994), 430, which also provides the original text. For a detailed analysis and contextual study of Manetti's musical pronouncements see Sabine Žak, "Die Quellenwert von Giannozzo Manettis Oratio über die Domweihe von Florenz 1436 für die Musikgeschichte," *Die Musikforschung* 40 (1987), 2–32; on the elevation music see 14, 29–30.

105 Vladimir Federov, "Des Russes au concile de Florence, 1438–1439," in Wilfried Brennecke and Hans Haase (eds.), *Hans Albrecht in memoriam* (Kassel, Basel, London: Bärenreiter, 1962), p. 30. See also Žak, "Die Quellenwert," 21–2.

106 Manfred Schuler, "Die Musik in Konstanz während des Konzils 1414–1418," *Acta Musicologica* 38 (1966), 165. In this context it is worth noting that this is the only place in a sacred context in which Durandus advocates use of the organ: "Sane in hoc angelorum et hominum concentu quandoque organa concrepant, quod a David (I Par 15, 16) et Salomone (II Par 5, 12 s) introductum est, qui instituerunt ympnos in sacrificio Domini organis et aliis musicis instrumentis concrepari et laudes a populo conclamari" (Book IV, XXXIV, 10, quoted in Herbert Douteil, *Studien zu Durantis "Rationale divinorum officiorum" als kirchenmusikalischer Quelle* [Regensburg: Gustav Bosse, 1969], p. 178).

107 Durandus, *Guillelmi Duranti*, Book IV, XLI, 53, quoted in Douteil, *Studien*, p. 35.

108 See Wright, *The Maze*, pp. 178–84, to which this paragraph is indebted, for a detailed consideration of the symbolic meaning of this Mass.

109 That the link between St. Michael and *L'homme armé* may have been more broadly cultivated is suggested by a much later reference in the *Ordenung der gesenge der Wittembergischen Kirchen* of 1543/4. Here, among a number of polyphonic Masses stipulated for specific feasts on account of the thematic appropriateness of their musical models, a *Missa L'homme armé* by Josquin is assigned to September 29, the Feast of St. Michael. Copies of both Josquin's *L'homme armé* Masses survive in the Jena choirbooks used by the Castle Church of Wittenburg, in which the *Ordenung* was presumably followed. See Kathryn Ann Duffy, "The Jena Choirbooks: Music and Liturgy at the Castle Church in Wittenberg under Frederick the Wise, Elector of Saxony," unpublished PhD dissertation, University of Chicago, 1995, p. 263. My thanks to Barbara Haggh for drawing my attention to this reference.

110 For a detailed consideration of the medieval allegorical equation between Michael's victory and that of Christ, see François Avril, "Interprétations symboliques du combat de Saint-Michel et du dragon," in *Millénaire monastique du Mont Saint-Michel*, 5 vols. (Nogent-sur-Marne: Société Parisienne d'histoire et d'archéologie Normandes, 1967), vol. 3, pp. 39–52.

111 On this point see the discussion in Chapter 8.

112 The principal source here is the first reading at Matins: "R[esponsum]: Factum est silentium in caelo, cum committeret bellum draco cum Michaele Archangelo; *Audita est vox millia millium dicentium: Salus honor et virtus omnipotenti Deo. V[ersus]: Millia millium ministrabant ei, et decies centena millia assistebant ei" (conflated from passages in Revelation 5, 8, 12). See also the third and fifth antiphon, and versicle of lectio 4, of the second Nocturn of Matins: "Michael praepositus paradise, quem honorificant angelorum cives."

113 See previous note.

114 On the symbolic meanings of the widespread iconographical tradition whereby Michael and other angels are clothed in priestly vestments see Barbara G. Lane, *The Altar and the Altarpiece: Sacramental Themes in Early Netherlandish Painting* (London: Harper and Row, 1984) and Maurice B. McNamee, *Vested Angels: Eucharistic Allusions in Early Netherlandish Paintings* (Leuven: Peeters, 1998).

115 Lewis Lockwood has suggested that the Regis Mass may have been commissioned for the French royal court, since Michael was patron saint of France and particularly of the French army. Since, as he further notes, the court instigated (in imitation of the Burgundian Order of the Golden Fleece) an Order of St. Michael, its ceremonies may have provided the original setting for this cycle. See his "Aspects of the "L'homme armé" Tradition," *Proceedings of the Royal Musical Association* 100 (1973–4), 115.

Chapter 6 The profane made sacred: outside texts and music in the Mass

1   Recognizing the repeated, totemic use of certain preexistent pieces, Maniates notes that "standard *meloi* constitute a corpus of sacred and secular melodies which can be drawn upon for various musical purposes. Thus, *De tous biens plaine* and *Salve regina* may be introduced separately or combined in a new polyphonic complex whose text bears a symbolic relation to the original words of these melodies" (Maria Rika Maniates, "Combinative Techniques in Franco-Flemish Polyphony: A Study of Mannerism in Music from 1450–1530," unpublished PhD dissertation, Columbia University, 1965, p. 12; the same point is also elaborated on p. 185. See also Julie Cumming, "The Goddess Fortuna Revisited," *Current Musicology* 30 (1980), 7–23, which uses Maniates's views in its exploration of the meanings behind the widespread applications and recompositions of the chanson *Fortuna desperata*. Maniates sees the shift, in the later fifteenth century, away from stratified textures over a tenor cantus firmus and towards imitative polyphony as the pervasive structural model as a sign of the breakdown of earlier notions of an inextricable unity binding music to its original text ("Combinative Techniques," p. 240).

2   Long draws attention to the two-way process thereby elicited with reference to the use in Josquin's motet *Stabat mater* of Binchois's *Comme femme desconfortée*: "The despair of an unhappy woman on earth is not merely a symbol which 'stands for' the grief of the Virgin, but is a fragment of the mundane which reveals or reflects something greater than itself. In so doing, not only the *femme desconfortée*, but the chanson itself undergoes a process of 'sanctification'" (Michael Long, "Symbol and Ritual in Josquin's *Missa Di Dadi*," *Journal of the American Musicological Society* 42 [1989], 2).

3   Christopher Reynolds, "The Counterpoint of Allusion in Fifteenth-Century Masses," *Journal of the American Musicological Society* 45 (1992), 230–1; see also his *Papal Patronage and the Music of St. Peter's, 1380–1513* (Berkeley, Los Angeles and London: University of California Press, 1995), p. 253.

4   David Rothenberg, "Marian Feasts, Seasons, and Songs in Medieval Polyphony: Studies in Musical Symbolism," unpublished PhD dissertation, Yale University, 2004, p. 75.

5   For a general survey of these Masses from the second and third quarters of the fifteenth century see Alejandro Enrique Planchart, "Parts with Words and Parts without Words: The Evidence for Multiple Texts in Fifteenth-century Masses," in Stanley Boorman (ed.), *Studies in the Performance of Late Medieval Music* (Cambridge University Press, 1983), pp. 227–51. The most frequently discussed cases from this period are the two late cantus-firmus Masses – on *Ecce ancilla domini* and *Ave regina caelorum* – of Du Fay, and Regis's *Missa Ecce ancilla domini*. On the Du Fay Masses see, *inter alia*, Gareth Curtis, "Brussels, Bibliothèque Royale MS. 5557, and the Texting of Dufay's 'Ecce ancilla domini'

and 'Ave regina celorum' Masses," *Acta musicologica* 51 (1979), 73–86; Planchart "Parts with Words," 246; and Rob C. Wegman, "*Miserere supplicanti Dufay*: The Creation and Transmission of Guillaume Dufay's *Missa Ave regina celorum*," *Journal of Musicology* 13 (1995), 18–54. On the *Ecce ancilla domini* Masses of Du Fay and Regis see Planchart, "Parts with Words," 246; Edgar H. Sparks, *Cantus Firmus in Mass and Motet* (Berkeley and Los Angeles: University of California Press, 1963), pp. 183–8; M. Jennifer Bloxam, "A Survey of Late Medieval Service Books from the Low Countries: Implications for Sacred Polyphony, 1460–1520," unpublished PhD dissertation, Yale University, 1987, pp. 232–52; and Rothenberg, "Marian Feasts," pp. 121–36.

6 Discussion of this practice in Masses by Du Fay, Obrecht, La Rue, Pipelare, Champion and in a single anonymous cycle comprises part two of Bloxam, "A Survey." On cycles from this group see also her articles "Sacred Polyphony and Local Traditions of Liturgy and Plainsong: Reflections on Music by Jacob Obrecht," in Thomas Kelly (ed.), *Plainsong in the Age of Polyphony* (Cambridge University Press, 1992), pp. 140–77, and "In Praise of Spurious Saints: the *Missae Floruit egregiis* by Pipelare and La Rue," *Journal of the American Musicological Society* 44 (1991), 163–220. See for instance the discussion of the *Ecce ancilla domini* Masses of Du Fay and Regis in "A Survey," pp. 232–52. Bloxam's findings are reiterated and further discussed in Rothenberg, "Marian Feasts," pp. 121–36. Such dialogue extends from the general (such as that between the Virgin and annunciatory angel implied by the two chants quoted back to back in each movement of the Du Fay Mass) to the specific (as in the Credo of Regis's *Ecce ancilla domini* Mass, where the Mass text, "Et incarnatus est de Spiritu Sancto ex Maria Virgine et homo factus est," is glossed by two antiphons addressing, respectively, Gabriel's Annunciation to Mary and her response).

7 It bears comment, however, that verbal dialogue rooted – as in the case of the *Ecce ancilla domini* Masses – in chants that were universally familiar need not always have relied for its effect on the actual presence of the texts concerned. The example, discussed in Chapter 3, of apparent dialogue between the text of the Benedictus and that of a line of the song *Le serviteur* in an anonymous Mass in Trent 89, in which there is no evidence that the song text was to be sung, would seem to underscore this point.

8 As Sparks observed, noting the rather fluid approach of the *Ecce ancilla domini* Mass to the melodic specifics of its antecedents, "the aim may have been more to get a concentration of texts than of melodies, since the integrity of the latter is not always carefully maintained" (*Cantus Firmus*, pp. 184–5; on the same point see Bloxam, "A Survey," pp. 245–9). On Regis's *L'homme armé* Mass, see Chapter 5. Here the emphasis is even more clearly on the texts rather than the music of the five quoted chants for the Office of St. Michael, only two of which are quoted with their melodies at all (on the cantus firmus borrowings in this Mass see, *inter alia*, the discussion in Sparks, *Cantus Firmus*, pp. 182–3).

9 For consideration of various possibilities see also Planchart, "Parts with Words," p. 247.

10 See for instance the copy of Pierre de la Rue's Mass for St. Anthony Abbot that opens Verona, Biblioteca Capitolare 756 (ff. 1v–16r), where the tenor carries texting reassigning the Mass to St. Vincent. Here the text, "Agnosce, O Vincenti," is underlaid to its music in the tenor throughout the Kyrie before disappearing except for brief incipits at the beginnings of the following two movements.

11 Not all such examples are quite so clear-cut, however: a case in point is the anonymous *Missa Thomas cesus* in Rome, Biblioteca Apostolica Vaticana, San Pietro B 80 (ff. 166v–181r), where, following detailed cantus firmus texting in the tenor in the Kyrie I and Christe, the remainder of the Mass is characterized by a combination of fragments of the original text along with sparse reference to the words of the Mass. This situation may suggest that, as in the case of the reading of Du Fay's *Missa Ave regina caelorum* in the same source, this copy represents a bastardization of a work that originally carried the cantus firmus text throughout.

12 The two sources for the Regis *Missa Ecce ancilla domini* are Brussels, Koninklijke Bibliothek MS 5557, ff. 121v–136v and Rome, Biblioteca Apostolica Vaticana, Cappella Sistina, MS 14, ff. 87v–101r. Edition in Johannes Regis, *Johannis Regis Opera Omnia*, I, ed. Cornelis Lindenburg, *Corpus Mensurabilis Musicae* 9 (n.p.: American Institute of Musicology, 1956), pp. 25–61. Planchart has discussed what appears to be evidence of the same procedure in the copy, in the Chigi Codex, of Ockeghem's *Missa Ecce ancilla domini*, and in Masses in the middle Trent codices. Although only the first section of the Sanctus in the tenor of the Ockeghem Mass actually carries dual texting, the remainder of the copy, with its haphazard shifts between the texts of the Mass and that of the antecedent antiphon, strongly suggests descent from a copy whose tenor, like that of the Regis Mass, had dual texts throughout. Similar double tenor texting in the first part of the Gloria of Du Fay's *Missa Ecce ancilla domini* as copied in Cappella Sistina 14 (ff. 76v–87r) may likewise be a remnant of what was originally a more thoroughgoing application of the same procedure. Regarding the Trent examples, Planchart draws attention particularly to Johannes Wiser's copy, in Trent 90, of the anonymous *Missa Fuit homo*, where the tenor incipits of his Trent 93 model have been extended to include, alongside the Mass text, the entire text of the antecedent gradual for the Feast of St. John the Baptist ("Parts with Words," 250–1 and 247–9).

13 See Planchart, "Parts with Words," *passim*. Planchart proposes that textual quotation was a practice typical in north-western Europe, but that such texts were frequently ignored by scribes of copies – which are, of course, most of those that survive – made elsewhere (*ibid.* 251).

14 The parallel meanings articulated by the motet *Missus est Gabriel angelus*, and the Marian significance of its song quotation, are noted in Maniates, "Combinative Techniques," p. 190.

15 Rothenberg, "Marian Feasts," pp. 143–4 and 246–7. Rothenberg's reading of *Missus est Gabriel angelus* results in a rather bumpy progression from the first-person register of the French incipit to the simple narrative of the Gospel text; the progression from the shorter cue ("A une dame") in other sources, resulting in the more seamless "To a woman the angel Gabriel was sent …" makes clearer sense. But the possible confusion here between what may just be a label of identification and something more loaded with meaning serves only to highlight the danger, in such circumstances, of overinterpretation.

16 Alejandro Enrique Planchart, "Fifteenth-Century Masses: Notes on Performance and Chronology," *Studi musicali* 10 (1981), 7. A tantalizing clue, not mentioned by Planchart, may perhaps be contained in the instruction "dicitur ut prius," directly following the double bar at the end of this section; but whether this should be taken to indicate the (continued) singing of the text of the underlaid song text, or some quite distinct facet of performance, is unclear.

17 See the facsimile and discussion in Jaap van Benthem, "Was 'Une mousse de Biscaye' really appreciated by 'L'ami Baudichon?'" *Muziek & Wetenschap* 1 (1991), 175–6.

18 Trent 88, ff. 276v–284r. The text reads: "Ayo visto lo mappa mundi et la carta di navigare, ma Cicilia pure me pare la più bella de questo mundo" ("I have seen the the map of the world and the navigational chart, but Sicily seems to me the most beautiful in this world"). While the text receives a devotional adaptation in the lauda "Haggio visto il cieco mondo," which sets the same melody, the text as given in the Mass has no obvious devotional connotations. For consideration of the Mass and its model see Johannes Cornago, *Johannes Cornago: Complete Works*, ed. Rebecca Gerber, Recent Researches in the Music of the Middle Ages and Early Renaissance 15 (Madison: A-R Editions, 1984), pp. viii–xi, and Allan Atlas, *Music at the Aragonese Court of Naples* (Cambridge University Press, 1985), p. 63.

19 See the "etc." following the incipit, "Ayo visto lo mappa mundi" in the first section of the Gloria, and the suggestive spacing that separates the final word, "mundi," from the remainder of the same incipit in the underlay to the "Qui tollis." Thereafter, however, such indications peter out save for the last section of the Credo.

20 The song, a plea in Dutch for alms for poor prisoners ("Give to the poor prisoners, for the sake of God, so that God may rescue you from all peril"), relates directly to the quotation elsewhere in the Mass of the Advent antiphon – also used as a prayer for the dead – *O clavis David*, with its text asking Christ, the "key of David," to "release the soul, sitting in darkness and the shadow of death, from the chains of prison." In a rare case in which evidence survives associating an existing polyphonic piece with a specific foundation, Reinhard Strohm determined that the Mass was composed for a personal endowment for the soul of a wealthy Bruges furrier, Donaes de Moor. Besides its group

of cantus firmi begging for the advocacy of Donaes's patron saint after his death, the Mass, with its connected allusions to the redemptive value of giving alms to prisoners and the metaphorical prison of purgatory, apparently refers directly to its donor's alms-giving in life. Strohm determined that Donaes and his wife had founded an almshouse and donated alms to the inmates of the city prison. Like other examples already discussed, the Mass is noteworthy for quoting its borrowed materials is such a way as to imply dialogue both between themselves and with the text of the Mass: Strohm notes the juxtaposition, in the Credo, of the prevailing text dealing with Christ's passion and resurrection and the antiphon text quoted above that becomes, in context, a prayer that Donaes's captive soul may also be released from the bounds of death. At the same time, the quotation of one of the chants for St. Donatian in yet another voice asks his patron to "defend us through your perpetual intercession." See Reinhard Strohm, *Music in Late Medieval Bruges* (Oxford University Press, 2nd, rev. edn., 1990), pp. 146–7; see also Strohm's report on this matter in Jacob Obrecht, *Jacob Obrecht: Collected Works*, ed. Barton Hudson, New Obrecht Edition, vol. 3 (Utrecht: Vereniging voor Nederlandse Muziekgeschiedenis, 1984), pp. xiii–xv. For a detailed consideration of the Mass's cantus firmus usage see Bloxam, "A Survey," pp. 275–87.

21 The *Fault d'argent* melody has been traced in the Use of Sarum, for which it also functioned as the Introit for the Mass of Septuagesima Sunday (*Manuale ad usum percelebris ecclesie Sarisburiensis ... per Desiderium Maheu* (Paris: Desiderium Maheu, 1526), p. 117. Available through Early English Books Online (Chadwyck-Healey: http://eebo.chadwyck.com).

22 An effect heightened still further in the case of the Offertory, in John Milsom's interpretation, by tessitura and tonal conflict ("Sense and Sound in Richafort's Requiem," *Early Music* 30 [2002], 456).

23 This proposition may lend credence to Ronsard's claim that Richafort had been a pupil of Josquin (Johannes Richafort, *Johannes Richafort: Opera Omnia*, ed. Harry Elzinga, Corpus Mensurabilis Musicae 81 [Neuhausen-Stuttgart, American Institute of Musicology, 1979], p. ix). The works in question by Josquin are *Sic Deus dilexit*, *Christus mortuus* and, most crucially, the lamenting chanson *Nimphes, nappés*. The hypothesis is strengthened still further by Gombert's use of the same cantus firmus in his own lament for Josquin, *Musae jovis*, and by the enveloping, in *Nimphes, nappés* and the first two movements of the Requiem, of the canonic "circumdederunt" in closely similar counterpoint (the latter an observation of John Milsom: see his "Sense and Sound," 449–53). Milsom also points to other similarities between the Requiem and individual works by Josquin. This dedicatory intent for the Mass seems first to have been proposed by Gustave Reese (*Music in the Renaissance* [London: Dent, 1954], p. 336). For a discussion of Josquin's other motets based on *Circumdederunt me* see Maniates, "Combinative Techniques," pp. 169–71 and 206–10, and the literature cited there, and, most recently, John Milsom,

"*Circumdederunt*: 'a favourite cantus firmus of Josquin's'?" *Soundings* 9 (1982), 2–10. On the Mass see also Planchart, "Parts with Words," p. 251 and Johannes Richafort, *Johannes Richafort*, p. xvii.

24 Bologna Q15, ff. 33v–38r. The texts are as follows: Gloria: "Tu m'as asoté / monté su[s] la pance et riens n'a[s] fait" / "Resurrexit dominus, Alleluia, Et apparuit Petro, Alleluia"; Credo: "La villanella non è bella, se non la dominica" / "Dic Maria, quid fecisti, postquam Iesum amisisti, Matrem flentem sociavi, quam ad domum reportavi, et in terra me prostravi, et utrumque deploravi. O Maria noli flere iam surrexit Christus vere." Besseler refers to the Gloria text as a trope, although he was unable to trace its source; the Credo text comprises verses 11 and 13 of the Easter sequence *Surgit Christus cum trophaeo* (*Analecta hymnica* 54, p. 366) (see Heinrich Besseler, *Bourdon und Fauxbourdon* [Leipzig: Breitkopf und Härtel, 1950], pp. 212–13 and Guillaume Du Fay, *Guilelmi Dufay: Opera Omnia* IV: *Fragmenta Missarum*, ed. Heinrich Besseler, Corpus Mensurabilis Musicae I [Rome: American Institute of Musicology, 1962], pp. iii–iv, xv–xvi). While the source of the French song has not been identified, the Italian song is clearly one of those vestiges of popular traditions that from time to time pierce the surface of written Italian "art" music: William Prizer has identified the same words (albeit set to different music) in a *barzelletta* by Antonio Capriolo of Brescia in Petrucci's ninth book of *frottole* (1509) (see his "Frottola and the Unwritten Tradition," *Studi musicali* 15 [1986], 3–37).

25 See the discussion in Rothenberg, "Marian Feasts," pp. 195–6. The quotations seem redolent of the dance that characterized both secular celebration of the onset of Spring and the Eastertide dances of the clergy. In this connection Rothenberg cites also Christopher Page, *The Owl and the Nightingale: Musical Life and Ideas in France, 1100–1300* (London: Dent, 1989), pp. 110–33, and Craig Wright, *The Maze and the Warrior: Symbols in Architecture, Theology, and Music* (Cambridge, MA and London: Harvard University Press, 2001), pp. 129–58. The dialogic format of the sequence text in the Credo is reminiscent of the widespread tradition of liturgical dialogues and dramas on Easter Sunday, deriving from the sepulchre scene in Matthew 28: 1–10, Mark 16: 5–7 and Luke 24: 4–6 (see the discussion in Rothenberg, "Marian Feasts," pp. 182–7).

26 This linkage is examined at length in Rothenberg, "Marian Feasts," chapters 5–7. Rothenberg discusses the musical roots of this phenomenon in the thirteenth-century motet, where, in secular texts concerned with springtime, the season is even conventionally referred to as the "tens pascour" ("Easter time") (*ibid.*, pp. 175–8 and *passim*). In the same connection see also Sylvia Huot, *Allegorical Play in the Old French Motet: The Sacred and the Profane in Thirteenth-century Polyphony* (Stanford University Press, 1997).

27 The pieces are recorded on *Guillaume Dufay: Music for St. James the Greater*, The Binchois Consort, conducted by Andrew Kirkman, Hyperion (Helios) CDH55272.

28 Later examples include Rore's *Vivat felix Hercules secundus dux Ferrariae*, Jacquet of Mantua's *Ferdinandus Dux Calabrie* and Lupus's *Carolus Imperator Romanus Quintus*.

29 Lewis Lockwood, *Music in Renaissance Ferrara, 1400–1505* (Oxford University Press, 1984), pp. 247–9. Encouraged by Lockwood's suggestion, Alexander Blachly has performed the Mass in this manner with his group *Pomerium*.

30 This point is perceptively elaborated by Jennifer Bloxam. Bloxam has proposed that "historians of music ... seem to admit their hesitations about the chanson Mass by simply avoiding the question as to why composers chose to incorporate chansons into their Masses. Indeed, Wilhelm Ambros's mid-nineteenth-century formulation of the cyclic Mass as a genre that transcended its function and materials through the composers' creative genius made the question irrelevant. Ambros characterized the song material within Masses exclusively as thematic and contrapuntal fuel, the 'formula at the foundation' of the Mass, whose materials are, compositionally speaking, everywhere and nowhere." She cites the *Geschichte der Musik*, vol. III (Leipzig: Lueckart, 1868; 3rd edn., rev. Otto Kade, 1893), p. 46. Bloxam also cites Peter Wagner (*Geschichte der Messe: I Teil: Bis 1600* [Leipzig: Breitkopf und Härtel, 1913], p. 64) for evidence of the same tendency (Bloxam, "A Cultural Context for the Chanson Mass," in Honey Meconi [ed.], *Early Musical Borrowing* [New York: Routledge, 2003], p. 29). For a detailed consideration of the role of Ambros in the foundation of modern perceptions of the Mass, see above, Chapter 1.

    For the thirteenth century, Sylvia Huot considers the evidence for the performance of vernacular and bilingual motets in actual services to be tenuous. However, she notes that "From the repeated complaints and condemnations that issued from high ecclesiastical offices ... one can conclude that secular, irreverent, and overly ornamental songs of some sort were part of the celebration of saints' days and other feasts, with certain holidays – for example, the feasts of Saint Stephen and Holy Innocents – being characterized by particularly rowdy behavior" (*Allegorical Play*, pp. 8–9).

31 The literature on this topic is of course voluminous. Most pertinent for the purposes here, though, are Karl Weinmann, *Das Konzil von Trient und die Kirchenmusik* (Leipzig: Breitkopf und Härtel, 1919), Karl Gustav Fellerer, "Church Music and the Council of Trent," *Musical Quarterly* 39 (1953), 576–94, and the recent, and valuable, corrective perspective provided by Craig Monson, "The Council of Trent Revisited," *Journal of the American Musicological Society* 55 (2002), 1–38. Monson emphasizes the point of recent historiography (one that is supported by the pattern of proscriptions against the performance of secular music in church) that the Council was to a large extent the culmination of a long-running trend of Catholic reform, rather than simply the reaction to outside pressures characterized by the term "Counter-Reformation."

32 "Ab ecclesiis vero musicas eas, ubi sive organo sive cantu lascivum aut impurum aliquid misceatur." (Monson, "The Council of Trent," 11).

33 "Tollantur de Ecclesia, seu templis non solum cantus prophani, sed etiam cantus occultans literam, qualis est in figurata modulatione" (*ibid.*, 7).

34 "Quae [missae] vero rhythmis musicis atque organis agi solent, in iis nihil profanum, sed hymni tantum et divinae laudes intermisceantur ..." (*ibid.*, 9).

35 "Item animadvertendum, an species musicae, quae nunc invaluit in figuratis modulationibus, quae magis aures quam mentem recreat et ad lasciviam potius quam ad religionem excitandam comparata videtur, tollenda sit in missis, in quibus etiam profana saepe cantantur, ut illa *della caccia* et *la bataglia*" (*ibid.*, 8; also quoted in Fellerer, "Church Music," 582; Weinmann, *Das Konzil von Trient*, pp. 55–6, etc.).

36 Monson, "The Council of Trent," 8; also Lewis Lockwood (ed.), *Palestrina: Pope Marcellus Mass: An Authoritative Score*, Norton Critical Scores (New York: Norton, 1975), p. 17.

37 "They say, 'Oh what a fine Mass was sung in chapel!' And what is it, if you please? It is *L'homme armé*, or *Hercules Dux Ferrariae* or *Philomena*. What the devil has the Mass to do with the armed man, or with Philomena, or with the duke of Ferrara? What numbers, what intervals, what sounds, what motions of the spirit, of devotion, or piety can be gathered from them, and how can music agree with such subjects as the armed man or the duke of Ferrara?" (quoted in Lockwood, *Pope Marcellus Mass*, pp. 12–13).

38 For full text and citation see Appendix 2.

39 See Monson's discussion of the dismay voiced by delegates concerning the limited scope of the officially recommended reforms emerging from the Council's twenty-second session (Monson, "The Council of Trent," 12–13).

40 *Ibid.*, 12–19.

41 Quoted in Fellerer, "Church Music," 590 (from Schannat, vol. VII, 412; see Appendix 2 for full citation). See *ibid.*, 590–1 for a range of similar citations from late sixteenth-century synods and councils. See also Appendix 2 for additional examples from the Council of Rheims (1564) and from the *Constitutiones* of the Holy House of Loreto.

42 The works in question were "a mass by Pipelare on *L'homme armé*"; "an old mass by Robert Févin in the old book," which could be the *Missa Le villain jaloux*, preserved in a Sistine Chapel manuscript; "a mass by Compère ... in the fourth mode," very probably his *Missa L'homme armé*, likewise surviving in the Sistine collection; and "another [mass] called *La Castagnia*" (Monson, "The Council of Trent," 24, citing Richard Sherr, "From the Diary of a Sixteenth-century Papal Singer," *Current Musicology* 25 [1978], 83–98). Perhaps even more striking is the extreme age, by the 1560s, of these Masses, yet more proof to add to considerable evidence elsewhere that polyphonic Masses from the late fifteenth and early sixteenth centuries maintained their position in the repertory a great deal longer than was formerly thought.

43 The Masses in question are a *Missa En doleur et tristesse* and a *Missa Ultimi mei sospiri* (see Monson, "The Council of Trent," 25, citing information received from Richard Sherr).

44 See Appendix 2 for a range of examples.

45 Translation from Fellerer, "Church Music," 579. See Appendix 2 for full citation, full text and original Latin.

46 See Appendix 2 for original text. Quoted in Harry Peter Clive, "The Calvinist Attitude to Music and Its Literary Aspects and sources," *Bibiothèque d'Humanisme et Renaissance* 19 (1957), 94–5 (see Appendix 2 for full text). I am grateful to Rob Wegman for drawing my attention to this study.

47 *Ibid.*, 95.

48 See Appendix 2 for full citation and original text.

49 See Appendix 2 for full citation and original text. My thanks to Rob Wegman for this reference. See also the discussion in Hubert Guicharrousse, *Les Musiques de Luther* (Geneva: Labor et Fides, 1995), pp. 206–8.

50 See David Fallows, *A Catalogue of Polyphonic Songs, 1415–1480* (Oxford University Press, 1999), pp. 493–4 for a brief overview of the various versions of this piece, all constructed on related tenor melodies. Fallows notes that the instrumental piece in the Buxheim organ book is the earliest surviving version. See also Helmuth Osthoff's study "'Wohlauf, gut G'sell von hinnen!': ein Beispiel deutsch–französischer Liedgemeinschaft um 1500," *Jahrbuch für Volksliedforschung* 8 (1951), 128–36. On the basis of its close marriage of words and music and use of barform, Osthoff proposed that the song originated with the German text; on the other hand he allows that the German version may, like so many contemporary songs with German texts, be an adaptation of a song that started life in French. On the French version see Ottaviano Petrucci, *Ottaviano Petrucci: Canti B numero cinquanta*, ed. Helen Hewitt, Monuments of Renaissance Music 2 (University of Chicago Press, 1967), pp. 46–9 and Allan Atlas (ed.), *The Cappella Giulia Chansonnier (Rome, Biblioteca Apostolica Vaticana, C.G.XIII.27)*, 2 vols., Wissenschaftliche Abhandlungen/ Musicological Studies 27 (Brooklyn: Institute of Mediaeval Music, 1975–6), vol. I, pp. 222–6. Louise Litterick proposes that the piece began as a French monophonic song, which then spawned a wide range of monophonic and polyphonic versions, in French and German (see her "Chansons for Three and Four Voices," in Richard Sherr [ed.], *The Josquin Companion* [Oxford University Press, 2000], p. 355).

51 For this text and a rhymed translation of the German see Petrucci, *Canti B*, pp. 48–9; for the French in similar translation see *ibid.*, p. 47. The adaptation, presumably by Glarean, of Josquin's setting of the song to a sacred text, "O Jesu fili David," does present a message directly germane to the moment of the elevation: taken from Matthew, 15: 22, 26 and 27, the text tells the story of the Canaanite woman who begs Christ to "Have mercy on me, Lord, Son of David; my daughter is tormented by a demon," and of how Christ ultimately grants, on account of her faith, the fulfillment of her wishes. There is no evidence, however, that this version circulated separately from the *Dodecachordon*, or that it could have been known by whomever Karlstadt had heard performing. See Heinrich Glarean, *Heinrich Glarean: Dodecachordon*, ed. and trans. Clement Miller, Musicological Studies and Documents 6, 2 vols. (n.p.: American Institute of

Musicology, 1965), vol. II, p. 263, where Glarean states that the contrafactum is "taken from the German and French languages." Edition in *ibid.*, II, pp.434–6. For the original see *Glareanus, Henricus Loritus: Dodekachordon* (facsimile edn. Hildesheim and New York: Georg Olms, 1969), pp.354, 356–7. Another contrafactum, this time setting an otherwise unknown *Comment peut avoir joye* as a nine-voice *Caelorum decus Maria*, occurs in Verona, Società Accademica Filarmonica, MS 218 (c.1536) (see John Milsom, "Motets for Five or More Voices," in Sherr [ed.], *The Josquin Companion*, p. 309, and the literature cited there).

52 Atlas, *The Cappella Giulia Chansonnier*, vol. 1, p. 223 and Helmuth Osthoff, *Theatergesang und darstellende Musik* (Tutzing: H. Schneider, 1969), p. 85.

53 In possible support for the primacy of the Mass version, Fallows has recently proposed that Josquin's four-voice *Comment peut avoir joye*, with its two-voice canon at the octave, is derived from Isaac's Mass, presumably meaning the three-voice Mass section/song under discussion (David Fallows, "Afterword: Thoughts for the Future," in Sherr (ed.), *The Josquin Companion*, p. 574). A corollary to that position would seem to be that Isaac's song version may similarly have been fashioned from his Mass.

54 For a discussion and transcription of the satire's musical descriptions see Clive, "The Calvinist Attitude to Music," 95–7.

55 Attributed variously also to Théodore de Bèze or to Pierre Viret, the tract is ascribed in its source to the aptly named "M. Frangidelphe Escorche-Messes." On the issue of authorship see Frank Lestringant, "*L'Histoire de la Mappe-Monde papistique*," *Comptes rendus des séances de l'académie des inscriptions et belles-lettres* 3 (July–October 1998), pp. 699–730, especially pp. 708–9. Whatever its specific authorship, it was clearly, as Lestringant notes, "né au coeur de la communauté italienne en exil" (*ibid*, p. 703).

56 This is clearly a reference to the revered soprano Polissena Pecorina, the subject of Willaert's madrigal *Qual dolcezza giamai* and the dedicatee of the first edition of his *Musica nova*, the original manuscript of which she later owned. The reference is likely to the *Musica nova* itself, which in large part seems to have been written for her. See Martha Feldman, *City Culture and the Madrigal at Venice* (Berkeley and Los Angeles: University of California Press, 1995), p. 34, and the literature cited there. See also *ibid.*, pp. 34–5 for the text and translation of *Qual dolcezza giamai*, and for a case against the assumption – widespread in the twentieth century as in this text from the sixteenth – that Pecorina was a courtesan.

57 See Appendix 2 for full citation and original text.

58 For sources, editions, texts and translations see Appendix 3. I have been unable to trace the source of *D'elle vient l'amoureux pensement*.

59 See for example Pierre Laurens, *L'Abeille dans l'ambre: célébration de l'épigramme de l'époque alexandrine à la fin de la Renaissance* (Paris: Les Belles Lettres, 1989), pp. 487–8.

60 See above, note 2, and Chapter 3.

61 Fellerer, "Church Music," 585–6; from Martin Gerbert, *De cantu et musica sacra a prima ecclesiae aetate usque ad praesens tempus* (San Blasien: Typis San-Blasiensis, 1774; repr., ed. Othmar Wessely: Graz: Akademische Druck- und Verlagsanstalt, 1968), p. 222. See Appendix 2 for the original Latin.

62 Quoted, with translation, in Johan Huizinga, *The Autumn of the Middle Ages*, trans. Rodney J. Payton and Ulrich Mammitzsch (Chicago University Press, 1996), pp. 417–18. See Appendix 2 for the original.

63 My thanks to David Marsh for assistance with this translation. For an alternative translation see Fellerer, "Church Music," 585. For the original Latin see Karl Gustav Fellerer, "Agrippa von Nettesheim und die Musik," *Archiv für Musikwissenschaft* 16 (1959), 81. The original is given in Appendix 2.

64 My translation. See Appendix 2 for full citation and original Latin. The original is also quoted in Bloxam, "A Cultural Context," 34.

65 Monson, "The Council of Trent," 28–9 (my translation). See Appendix 2 for the original Latin.

66 My translation; the original is in Appendix 2. The Latin is quoted in Clive, "The Calvinist Attitude to Music," 99–100, from Johannes Mansi, *Sacrorum conciliorum nova et amplissima collectio*, 36 vols. (Florence, 1759–98), vol. XXXIII, 1270 (see Appendix 2 for a full citation).

67 See Clive, "The Calvinist Attitude to Music," 99; Fellerer, "Church Music," 578, 580; Gerbert, *De cantu et musica sacra*, p. 195. See Appendix 2 for the original, and for similar edicts concerning organ music from other councils and synods.

68 See Appendix 2 for the full text. Translation in Fellerer, "Church Music," 578.

69 My thanks to Rob Wegman for this reference. See Appendix 2 for the original text and citation.

70 Oxford, Bodleian Library MS Eng. th. C57, ff. 49v–50r. My thanks to Mary Carruthers and Larry Scanlon for their assistance with this passage.

71 I am grateful for the following two references to Rob Wegman. See Appendix 2 for full citations, texts and translations.

72 See Appendix 2 for the full citation and original text.

73 See Appendix 2 for the full citation and original text.

74 Translations from Craig Wright, *Music at the Court of Burgundy, 1364–1419: A Documentary History* (Henryville: Institute of Medieval Music, 1979), p. 146. For the original texts, see Georges Doutrepont, *Inventaire de la "librairie" de Philippe le Bon (1420)* (Brussels: Commission royale d'histoire, 1906), pp. 27–8 (also given in Appendix 2). Doutrepont equates the first of these items with an entry in the inventory of 1477 describing "Ung liure en parchemin ouquel sont plusieurs Motez à deschant pour dire en vne chapelle."

75 The former work, *Fortune mere a doulour / Ma dolour ne cesse pas / [Dolor meus]*, has survived anonymously in Cambrai, Bibliothèque Municipale,

MS B. 1328, Ivrea, Biblioteca Capitolare, MS 115, and Paris, Bibliothèque Nationale, Coll. De Picardie, MS 67. See the transcription in Frank Ll. Harrison (ed.) *Polyphonic Music of the Fourteenth Century*, vol. V (Monaco: Éditions de l'Oiseau-Lyre, 1968), p. 92.

76 For these entries see Jean Baptiste Joseph Barrois, *Bibliothèque protypographique, ou Librairies des fils du roi Jean, Charles V, Jean de Berri, Philippe de Bourgogne et les siens* (Paris, Strasbourg, London: Treuttel et Würtz, 1830), pp. 287–8. I am grateful to David Fiala for kindly sharing with me his direct transcription of the original source (Lille, Archives départementales du nord, B 3501, no. 123.744, ff. 31r–81v), which corrects Barrois in a few details. For originals see Appendix 2.

77 The Alleluia for the first Sunday of Advent.

78 Following service as a choirboy at the Cathedral of Chartres, Templeuve seems to have begun his service in the chapel, as a *sommelier*, as far back as 1384. He was premier chapelain from 1400 to 1404 and again from 1418 until his death in 1436 (Jeanne Marix, *Histoire de la Musique et des Musiciens de la Cour de Bourgogne sous le règne de Philippe le Bon* [Strasbourg: Heitz, 1939; repr. Geneva: Minkoff, 1972], pp. 132–4, 145, 168).

79 See Doutrepont, *Inventaire*, p. 28; Wright, *Burgundy*, pp. 147–8.

80 On the early history of the source see Wright, *Burgundy*, p. 148 and Margaret Bent, "A Note on the Dating of the Trémouïlle Manuscript," in Bryan Gillingham and Paul Merkley (eds.), *Beyond the Moon: Festschrift Luther Dittmer*, Musicological Studies 53 (Ottawa: Institute of Mediaeval Music, 1990), pp. 217–42.

81 See the complete inventory, including modern editions of surviving works, in Wright, *Burgundy*, pp. 149–57. See also the slightly revised list in Bent, "A Note," pp. 231–42.

82 See Wright, *Burgundy*, p. 157.

83 Cambrai 1328, Florence, Biblioteca Nazionale Centrale, Panciatichiano MS 26, and the Ivrea Codex. An anonymous ballade *Quiconques veult user joieuse* also survives in Turin, Biblioteca Nazionale MS J.II.9, ff. 107v–108r; modern edition in Willi Apel (ed.), *French Secular Compositions of the Fourteenth Century*, vol. III, Corpus Mensurabilis Musicae 53 (n.p.: American Institute of Musicology, 1972), p. 126. Late medieval echoes of the Creed are far from uncommon, the most widespread surely being the vernacular prayer *Quiconques veult estre bien conseillié* (the introductory prayer to the Seven Requests to the Savior) directed, in numerous books of hours, to the five wounds of Christ and/or the Last Judgment. See Michael Camille, *Master of Death: The Lifeless Art of Pierre Remiet, Illuminator* (New Haven: Yale University Press, 1996), pp. 228–9 (referring to British Library, MS Yates Thompson 45, f. 129v [not 124v as stated by Camille]); John Harthan, *The Book of Hours* (New York: Thomas Y. Crowell, 1977), pp. 83–4, 115–16 (referring to Fitzwilliam Museum, Cambridge, MS 62, f. 199r [Hours of Isabella Stuart, Duchess of Brittany]); and Paris, MS Lat. 9471 [Rohan Hours], f. 194r).

84 In this cross-registral reference it, like other contemporary songs, has much in common with the thirteenth-century motets and secular-sacred contrafacta discussed by Sylvia Huot. Many motets, Huot notes, feature "the allegorical technique of recasting a moment from sacred history or a passage from Scripture in the language and imagery of secular literature" (*Allegorical Play*, p. 11; on contrafacta see pp. 9, 62–6).

85 The link is underscored by the prayer of the celebrant after the tract: "Omnipotens sempiterne Deus, respice propitius ad devotionem populi renascentis, qui sicut cervus, aquarum expetit fontem: et concede propitius; ut fidei ipsius sitis, baptismatis mysterio, animam corpusque sanctificet. Per Dominum."

86 The situation here appears slightly complicated by the fact that ordinary Office psalmody uses St. Jerome's translation from the Greek Septuagint, beginning "Quemadmodum desiderat cervus ad fontes aquarum," rather than the version of the Roman Psalter, beginning "Sicut cervus," as used in this item. I am grateful to John Caldwell for detailed information on these practices.

87 Translation from *Expositions on the Book of Psalms. By Saint Augustine, Bishop of Hippo*, edited, with brief annotations, and condensed from the six volumes of the Oxford translation, by A. Cleveland Cox, from Philip Schaff (ed.), *A Select Library of the Nicene and Post-Nicene Fathers of the Christian Church* (8 vols., New York: Christian Literature Publishing Co., 1886). In *Early Church Fathers: Nicene and Post-Nicene Fathers Series I*, vol. 8. (www.ccel.org/ccel/ schaff/npnf108.htm).

   The original text is as follows: "… cuiusdam unitatis christianae esse vocem hanc: *Quemadmodum desiderat cervus ad fontes aquarum, sic desiderat anima mea ad te, Deus*. Et quidem non male intelligitur vox esse eorum qui, cum sint catechumeni, ad gratiam sancti lavacri festinant. Unde et solemniter cantatur hic psalmus, ut ita desiderent fontem remissionis peccatorum, *quemadmodum desiderat cervus ad fontes aquarum* … nondum esse satiatum tale desiderium: sed fortassis, si norunt ubi peregrinentur, et quo eis transeundum sit, etiam ardentius inflammantur … *Sitivit anima mea ad Deum vivum*. Quod dico: *Quemadmodum cervus desiderat ad fontes aquarum, ita desiderat anima ad te, Deus*, hoc dico: *Sitivi anima mea ad Deum vivum*. Quid sitivit? *Quando veniam et apparebo ante faciem Dei*. Hoc est quod sitio, venire et apparere. Sitio in peregrinatione, sitio in cursu: satiabor in adventu" (*Augustinus Hipponensis: Sancti Aurelii Augustini Hipponensis Episcopi Enarrationes in Psalmos*. Patrologia Latina 36, Col. 0464).

88 The work survives in the Ivrea Codex, ff. 7v–8r. See the transcription in Harrison, *Polyphonic Music*, vol. V, p. 36.

89 On this putative use of the Mass at Tournai see Jean Dumoulin, Michel Huglo, Philippe Mercier and Jaques Pycke (eds.), *La Messe de Tournai: une messe polyphonique en l'honneur de Notre Dame à la cathédrale de Tournai au XIVe siècle*, Publications d'histoire de l'art et d'archéologie a l'Université

Catholique de Louvain 64 (Tournai: Archives du Chapitre Cathédral de Tournai, etc., 1988), p. 21. See also Anne Walters Robertson, "Remembering the Annunciation in Medieval Polyphony," *Speculum* 70 (1995), 295–6, which proposes, on the grounds of its particular chant basis, a use of this piece, along perhaps with the other movements of the Tournai Mass, as part of a paraliturgical Annunciation drama at Tournai.

90 It has been plausibly suggested that this work was composed on the death of another admired lady, Machaut's patroness Bonne of Luxembourg. See Lawrence Earp, *Guillaume de Machaut: A Guide to Research* (New York: Garland, 1995), pp. 25–6, and Anne Walters Robertson, *Guillaume de Machaut and Reims: Context and Meaning in His Musical Works* (Cambridge University Press, 2002), pp. 184–5.

91 See for example Huot, *Allegorical Play*; Alice Clark, "*Concordare cum materia*: the Tenor in the Fourteenth-century Motet," unpublished PhD dissertation, Princeton University, 1996; and Jacques Boogaert, "Encompassing Past and Present: Quotations and their Function in Machaut's Motets," *Early Music History* 20 (2001), 1–86.

92 It should be noted that it is far from clear that Machaut could have known the latter work: the window between the time it was written (c.1334) and the time he compiled his motet series (probably in the 1340s) is discouragingly narrow (see Robertson, *Guillaume de Machaut*, p. 102 for these dates). While Robertson notes that the *Horologium* was "one of the most widely copied devotional writings of the later middle ages" (*ibid.*, pp. 96–7), moreover, she herself observes that most manuscripts date from the fifteenth century, with only "a few" bearing fourteenth-century dates (*ibid.*, p. 360, n. 95). This need not, of course, discount the notion that such ideas were, as she says, "in the air" (*ibid.*, p. 102).

93 *Ibid.*, pp. 92–6. The figure of Wisdom is also of course commonly linked with the Virgin. Such an equation begins already with the Annunciation, when, as bearer of the word ("logos") in the personified sense of John, I: 1–14, she is commonly presented reading from a book (either the Book of Isaiah, with its premonition of the Virgin birth ["Ecce virgo concipiet"] or, as often in fifteenth-century depictions, a book of hours). The link between the Virgin and Christ as embodiments of Wisdom is most obviously articulated in the standardized iconography of the *sedes sapientiae*, the image of Christ seated on the Virgin's lap, with both facing forward towards the viewer. The import here is of the Virgin as the source and transmitter of the Wisdom of Christ. On the association of Mary with the Old Testament figure of Wisdom and the use of the "Wisdom" books (Proverbs, Wisdom and Ecclesiasticus) as sources for Marian liturgy, see Rothenberg, "Marian Feasts," pp. 35–6, 50.

94 Robertson, *Guillaume de Machaut*, p. 104.

95 *Ibid.*, pp. 133, 152–4.

96 Christopher Page, *Discarding Images: Reflections on Music and Culture in Medieval France* (Oxford University Press, 1993), pp. 43–64. For a contrary

position see Margaret Bent, "Reflections on Christopher Page's Reflections," *Early Music* 21 (1993), 631–2; for Page's response see "A Reply to Margaret Bent," *Early Music* 22 (1994), 130–1. See also Huot, *Allegorical Play*, pp. 202–3.

97 Christopher Page, "Johannes de Grocheio on Secular Music: A Corrected Text and a New Translation," *Plainsong and Medieval Music* 2 (1993), 36; also in Page, *Discarding Images*, 81. On the equation of *clericus* with *litteratus* see also Stephen J. P. Van Dijk and Joan Hazelden Walker, *The Origins of the Modern Roman Liturgy: The Liturgy of the Papal Court and the Franciscan Order in the Thirteenth Century* (London: Darton, Longman and Todd, 1960), pp. 38–9. Speaking of the later Middle Ages, they note that "At first, the term *clericus* had been synonymous with *litteratus* and *psalteratus*, that of *laicus* with *illiteratus* and *idiota*. By the end of the twelfth century the days when these terms reflected reality were gone. Although they were still used indiscriminately for some time, the 'cleric' became more and more distinguished from the 'laic' by his ecclesiastical status without regard to his literacy. In fact, many clerics, secular and religious, were unlettered."

98 Page's remarks come in the context of a discussion of Bakhtin's *Rabelais and His World*: "Bakhtin's book conveys the tone of much medieval festivity. The concept of holiday in the fullest sense is vital to his argument: a feast-day of the church's year may also coincide with a fair, marked not merely by the official celebrations of the liturgy but also by 'unoffocial' disguisings, dances (involving mock crownings), shows, songs, and more besides: all that is carnivalesque" (Page, *Discarding Images*, p. 50). As Page notes elsewhere, the congruence is frequently also one of place, with caroling in celebration of important religious feasts, particularly those of saints of local significance, occurring in churchyards and other holy places (Page, *The Owl and the Nightingale* [London: Dent, 1989], p. 125). It seems clear, for example from the prohibition of the Council of Avignon in 1209, that such festivities were not unknown also in church: "It is our edict that in churches on saints' eves there shall be no dance-mimers, no obscene movements and no round-dances; nor shall love-songs be sung there, nor dance-songs …" (see John Stevens, *Words and Music in the Middle Ages* [Cambridge University Press, 1986], p. 162).

99 Page notes that "Many of the monophonic songs which are quoted in motets may have been songs for caroles, the public dances that were a conspicuous feature of festive life in northern France during the thirteenth century and which may have mediated between the marketplace realities of festivity and the more sheltered milieu of the motet" (*Discarding Images*, p. 52; see also the general discussion on pp. 50–64).

100 Translation from Robertson, *Guillaume de Machaut*, which also gives the following transcription: "Nam melodias hoquetis intersecant, discantibus lubricant, triplis et motetis vulgaribus nonnunquam inculcant adeo … Hoc ideo dudum nos et fratres nostri correctione indigere percepimus; hoc relegare, immo prorsus abiicere, et ab eadem ecclesia Dei profligare efficacius

properamus. Quocirca ... districte praecipimus, ut nullus deinceps talia vel his similia in dictis officiis, praesertim horis canonicis, vel quum missarum solennia celebrantur, attentare presumat" (pp. 284–5).

101   Page, *Discarding Images*, p. 57, which also gives the following transcription: "Similiter dicimus quod illicite sunt opere magistrorum organicorum qui scurrilia et effeminata proponunt iuvenibus et rudibus ad effeminandos animos ipsorum, tamen locare possent operas suas in licitis cantibus in quibus servitur ecclesiis. Si autem prelatus lascivus lasciviis talibus cantatoribus det beneficia ut huiusmodi scurrilia et lascivia audiat in ecclesia sua, credo quod lepram symonie incurrit. Si tamen in aliqua sollemnitate pro consuetudine terre decantent aliqui in organis, dummodo scurriles notule non admisceantur, tolerari possunt." See also Page's citation of the 1261 visitation records of Odon Rigaud, *ibid.*, pp. 58–9.

102   "Item: we admonish that all priests may not permit vagabonds and other wandering scholars or goliards to sing verses on *Sanctus* and *Agnus Dei*, or other things, in Masses or in the divine Offices, because by these things the priest in the Canon is very greatly hindered, and those hearing are enticed into sin." Discussed in Joseph Jungmann, *The Mass of the Roman Rite: Its Origins and Development* (translation, by Francis A. Brunner, of *Missarum Solemnia*), 2 vols. (Westminster, MD: Christian Classics, 1986), vol. I, p. 125. Text in Mansi, vol. XXIII, p. 33 (see Appendix 2 for full citation).

103   Harrison further suggests that the organ, likewise located on the screen, would have collaborated with the singers in playing the liturgical tenor, a practice "developed in the secular churches of Paris and northern France and adopted by English secular cathedrals. and some of the larger abbeys." (Frank Ll. Harrison, *Music in Late Medieval Britain* [London: Routledge and Kegan Paul, 1958], pp. 207–8. See also *ibid.*, pp. 126–8).

104   See the discussion of use of this metaphor in the motets in Robertson, *Guillaume de Machaut*, p. 112.

105   Huot, *Allegorical Play*, pp. 65, 72–84.

106   There could be no more eloquent testimony to this than that of Robertson's primary witness, Suso's *Horologium sapientiae*, and the words of its protagonist Disciple. Thus, Suso notes, "Whenever [the Disciple] heard love songs or suchlike, he would turn all these about and apply them to his Wisdom, whom he loved with the most pure love of his heart, so that they encouraged his love for her to grow" (Robertson, *Guillaume de Machaut*, p. 186). For the original see p. 377: "quandocumque audivit cantilenas amorosas vel similia, quod haec omnia ad suam, quam diligebat, sapientiam purissimo cordis affectu tamquam amoris ipsius incitamenta retorquebat."

107   See, *inter alia*, Michael Camille, *Image on the Edge: The Margins of Medieval Art* (Cambridge, MA: Harvard University Press, 1992), *passim*; Huot, *Allegorical Play*, pp. 12–13; Kevin Brownlee, "Machaut's Motet 15 and the *Roman de la Rose*: The Literary Context of *Amours qui a le pouoir / Faus*

samblant m'a deceü / Vidi dominum," *Early Music History* 10 (1991), 4–5 and the literature cited there; and Page, *Discarding Images*, pp. 46–52.

108 "Diese Manuskriptform, die das erste Drittel des 15. Jahrhunderts beherrscht, bezeichnen wir als gemischte Quarthandschrift. Sie macht anschaulich, daß zwischen den verschiedenen Bezirken ein enger Austausch bestand. Nicht nur die Formen der geselligen Musik wurden für die Kirche benutzt, sondern auch die innere Haltung beim Musizieren war ähnlich. Sie führte zur geschilderten Aufzeichnungsweise, weil man offenbar nicht das Bedürfnis empfand, hier zu trennen, was im Leben eine Einheit bildete." See Besseler, *Bourdon und Fauxbourdon* (Leipzig: Breitkopf und Härtel, 1950), p. 140.

109 This was recognized some twenty years ago by Barbara Haggh; see her "Music, Liturgy and Ceremony in Brussels, 1350–1500," 2 vols., unpublished PhD dissertation, University of Illinois at Urbana-Champaign, 1988, vol. I, pp. 523–4.

Chapter 7 The shape of the Mass

1 P. A. Le Carou, *L'office divin chez les frères mineurs au xiiie siècle: son origine – sa destinée* (Paris: P. Lethielleux, 1928), p. 216.

2 See Miri Rubin, *Corpus Christi: The Eucharist in Late Medieval Culture* (Cambridge University Press, 1991), p. 34: "In tracing the design of the eucharist and the mass, one reaches a point in the late thirteenth century when all was said and done – not intellectually but in terms of the construction of a pastoral edifice, one which was conveyed through the guide-books, the synodal legislation, the sermons, and *exempla*, collected in the thirteenth century as never before."

3 As J. C. Payen has noted, "L'histoire de la pénitence au moyen-âge, est associée à celle de l'eucharistie" ("La Pénitence dans le contexte culturel des xiie et xiiie siècles," *Revue des sciences philosophiques et théologiques* 61 (1977), 44; quoted in Rubin, *Corpus Christi*, p. 85).

4 For more on this see Chapter 8.

5 In an exceptionally early example, prayers to be uttered by worshippers during the elevation of the host are advocated by the great thirteenth-century bishop of Paris Maurice de Sully ("De expositione ... mauricii ep[iscop]i parisiensis," Bourges, Bibliothèque Municipale, MS 116 [105], unpublished). Private eucharistic prayers for the same purpose from the fourteenth century on are cited in André Wilmart, *Auteurs spirituels et textes dévots du moyen âge Latin: études d'histoire littéraire* (Paris: Études Augustiniennes, 1971). A number of examples cited by Wilmart from a large compendium of devotional texts copied, apparently in or around Reichenau, about the end of the fourteenth century appear under such headings as "Oracio bona in eleuacione corporis Christi" and "In eleuacione," testifying to the devotional response of worshippers to the visual stimulus of the elevated host (*ibid.,*

pp. 367–74; see also, on the wide circulation of elevation prayers in books of hours and diverse other collections, pp. 377–80). My thanks to Michel Huglo for drawing my attention to these sources. See also Barbara H. Haggh, "Music, Liturgy and Ceremony in Brussels, 1350–1500," 2 vols., unpublished PhD dissertation, University of Illinois at Urbana-Champaign, 1988, vol. 1, p. 515. A coincident acceleration from the fourteenth century on, as Jacques Le Goff and others have noticed, can be traced in personal consciousness of purgatory (see his *The Birth of Purgatory* [English edition, translated by Arthur Goldhammer, University of Chicago Press, 1981], p. 356).

6 In terms of church building, this is nowhere truer than in England, where the extent of rebuilding and elaboration of churches was unprecedented. See Christopher Robinson, "'Excellent, New and Uniforme': Perpendicular Architecture *c*.1400–1547," in Richard Marks and Paul Williamson (eds.), *Gothic: Art for England 1400–1547* (London: V&A Publications, 2003), pp. 98–119, at p. 113. Similarly A. H. Thompson noted that "There is no period at which money was lavished so freely on English parish churches as in the fifteenth century … In church after church … the stone-mason provided the framework for the exhibition of the full powers of artists and craftsmen in wood-carving and stained glass, in painting and in tomb-making" (*The English Clergy and their Organisation in the Later Middle Ages* [Oxford University Press, 1947], p. 128). See also Eamon Duffy, *The Stripping of the Altars* (New Haven and London: Yale University Press, 1992), p. 132. To these physical ornaments Thompson might have added their sonic elaborations. Such efflorescence in building, decoration and musical adornment was succeeded by a corresponding decline in the post-Reformation period (see Robinson, "'Excellent, New and Uniforme,'"and Duffy, *The Stripping of the Altars*. On gilds see above, Chapter 4).

7 Haggh, "Music, Liturgy and Ceremony in Brussels," vol. I, pp. 115–16 and 519.

8 *Ibid.*, pp. 518–19.

9 Thus the Charter states: "And because we receive all monks coming from other monasteries into ours, and they in like manner receive ours, it seems proper to us, that all our monasteries should have the same usages in chanting, and the same books for the divine office day and night and the celebration of the holy sacrifice of the Mass, as we have in the New Monastery (Cîteaux); that there may be no discord in our daily actions, but that we may all live together in the bond of charity under one rule, and in the practice of the same observances" (quoted in Archdale A. King, *Liturgies of the Religious Orders* [London, New York and Toronto: Longmans, Green and Co., 1955], p. 68).

10 David Hiley, *Western Plainchant: A Handbook* (Oxford University Press, 1993), pp. 609–11.

11 Similar edicts regarding uniformity were promulgated by the Carthusians, at their first general chapter meeting in 1132, and by the Premonstratensians in 1130, and both similarly emphasized simplicity and aversion to liturgical

expansion. See King, *Liturgies of the Religious Orders*, pp. 18, 32–3, 37 (Carthusians); and 166–9, 172–3, 183 (Premonstratensians).

12 The standard study remains William R. Bonniwell, *A History of the Dominican Liturgy, 1215–1945* (New York: Joseph F. Wagner, 1945). On this point see particularly pp. 24–5.

13 *Ibid.*, pp. 76–7.

14 See Stephen J. P. Van Dijk and and Joan Hazelden Walker, *The Origins of the Modern Roman Liturgy* (Westminster, MD: Newman Press; London: Darton, Longman and Todd, 1960), pp. 187–201.

15 See for example Bonniwell, *A History of the Dominican Liturgy*, pp. 75–6.

16 Dom Pierre Salmon notes that the consolidation of Office materials into a single breviary was greatly facilitated by a shift in the technique of writing, from the Caroline minuscule of the eleventh and twelfth centuries, with its large format and paucity of abbreviations, to the new gothic minuscule, fine and delineated and rich in abbreviations (*L'office divin au moyen âge: Histoire de la formation du bréviare du IXe au XVIe siècle*, Lex Orandi 43 [Paris: Cerf, 1967], p. 160). Along similar lines, Van Dijk and Walker note the tiny script and small space allotted to the staves that facilitated the single-volume Franciscan noted choir breviary (*The Origins*, p. 221).

17 *Ibid.*, pp. 301–12.

18 On earlier diversity in liturgical practice see *ibid.*, p. 248. On the approval of this shift to greater brevity by Salimbene and others, and the objections of Ralph of Tongres, see *ibid.*, pp. 1–3. For further detail see *ibid.*, pp. 21, 25, 57.

19 See *ibid.*, pp. 265, 399–401. Pierre Salmon makes the important point that the papacy never stipulated the adoption of the curial liturgy, and made no attempt to proscribe local observations. Such stipulation would probably in any case have been superfluous: its spread was clearly supported by widespread consciousness, as attested and supported by Mass commentators, of the status of the curial liturgy as "totius christianae religionis caput et origo," and a similarly widespread desire to adopt it (Salmon, *L'office divin*, pp. 169–70).

20 Hiley, *Western Plainchant*, p. 595 and Van Dijk and Walker, *The Origins*, pp. 398–411.

21 Van Dijk and Walker, *The Origins*, p. 312.

22 No demonstration of the demand for such flexibility could be clearer than Haymo's own addition, in his ordinal, of no fewer than thirty votive Masses to the thirty-two that had already been available in the Franciscan Regula missal (*ibid.*, pp. 240, 308). See Van Dijk's edition in Stephen J. P. Van Dijk (ed.), *Sources of the Modern Roman Liturgy*, 2 vols. (Leiden: E. J. Brill, 1963), vol. 2, pp. 318–27.

23 Van Dijk and Walker, *The Origins*, pp. 293, 61.

24 Again, this seems to have been the achievement of the Franciscans: c.f. *ibid.*, p. 332: "it was through the Franciscan gradual of 1251 that the *francigena nota* superseded for ever the ancient *nota romana* [the "Beneventan" chant

notation] and thus became the accepted notation in Roman chant books."
See "The Preface to the Franciscan Gradual": "In primis iniungitur fratribus,
ut de cetero, tam in gradualibus quam antiphonariis nocturnis et aliis,
faciant notam quadratam et quatuor lineas, omnes rubeas sive nigras," in
Van Dijk, *Sources*, vol. 2, p. 361. See the discussion of this in Van Dijk and
Walker, *The Origins*, pp. 329–33. The instructions are also quoted in Michel
Huglo, "Notated Performance Practices in Parisian Chant Manuscripts of the
Thirteenth Century," in Thomas Forrest Kelly (ed.), *Plainsong in the Age of
Polyphony* (Cambridge University Press, 1992), p. 43, where they are directly
compared with the similar prescriptions of the Dominicans. Huglo here offers
a detailed consideration of the codification of this notation in the late twelfth
and thirteenth centuries and its importance in the early history of the notation
of polyphony (see *ibid.*, pp. 32–44).

25 See Hiley, *Western Plainchant*, p. 595.

26 Readability was enhanced also by the four-line stave which was also now
drawn in ink rather than using the old dry-point method (see Van Dijk and
Walker, *The Origins*, p. 331).

27 Huglo, "Notated Performance Practices," pp. 32–44. See also his *Les livres
de chant liturgique*, Typologie des sources du moyen âge occidental, 52
(Turnhout: Brepols, 1988), pp. 50, 76–7, 92–4, 119–20.

28 This is not, of course, to diminish the importance of the role of memory in
liturgical singing from this time forth, a faculty which, as Anna Maria Busse
Berger has traced brilliantly in a recent book, was exercised, during the age of
polyphony, in newly propitious ways (see her *Medieval Music and the Art of
Memory* [Berkeley: University of California Press, 2005]).

29 Credos, being much smaller in number, were typically copied separately.

30 On organization by "cycles" see Bruno Stäblein, "Messe, A. Die lat. Messe,"
in Friedrich Blume (ed.), *Die Musik in Geschichte und Gegenwart*, 17 vols.
(Kassel, London and New York: Bärenreiter, 1949–86) vol. 9, col. 154; on the
example mentioned see *ibid.*, col. 154. Michel Huglo notes the arrangement of
Masses by mode in the similarly early Missal of Saugnac (Langres, Séminaire,
MS. 126 [312]). See his *Les Tonaires: Inventaire, Analyse, Comparaison*
(Paris: Société Française de Musicologie, 1971), p. 110. He also points out the
highly suggestive report by Jacques de Liège that some of his contemporaries
advocate performance of all the chants in any given Mass in the same mode,
or alternatively, that all chants in a Mass, proper and ordinary, should proceed
through the numeric order of the modes (*ibid.*, 127). See also the discussion in
Richard H. Hoppin, "Reflections on the Origin of the Cyclic Mass," in Albert
Linden (ed.), *Liber amicorum Charles van den Borren* (Antwerp: L. Anversois,
1964), pp. 85–91.

31 Van Dijk and Walker, *The Origins*, pp. 327–8.

32 Both points are emphasized by Olivier Guillou, "Sources musicales du *Kyriale*
Vatican," *Études Grégoriennes* 31 (2003), 38–9. See also Kurt von Fischer, "Neue

Quellen zum einstimmigen Ordinariumszyklus des 14. und 15. Jahrhunderts aus Italien," in Linden (ed.), *Liber amicorum Charles van den Borren*, pp. 60–8.

33 See for example Hoppin, "Reflections."

34 On this development see von Fischer, "Neue Quellen," p. 68.

35 In a pioneering study, Geoffrey Chew long ago recognized the importance of such liturgical grouping of Ordinary chants as a harbinger of the future, musical, linkage of polyphonic cycles. See Chew, "The Early Cyclic Mass as an Expression of Royal and Papal Supremacy," *Music and Letters* 53 (1972), 254–5.

36 See John Harper, *The Forms and Orders of the Western Liturgy from the Tenth to the Eighteenth Century* (Oxford University Press, 1991), p. 163.

37 Salmon, *L'office divin*, pp. 168, 166.

38 Sally Elizabeth Roper, *Medieval English Benedictine Liturgy: Studies in the Formation, Structure, and Content of the Monastic Votive Office, c. 950–1540* (New York and London: Garland, 1993), pp. 58–61.

39 *Ibid.*, pp. 68–9.

40 For these details see Van Dijk and Walker, *The Origins*, pp. 393–8 (Franciscans); King, *Liturgies of the Religious Orders*, pp. 108, 111, 112 (Cistercians); 174, 199 (Premonstratensians); Bonniwell, *A History*, pp. 145–6 (Dominicans).

41 Roper, *Medieval English Benedictine Liturgy*, pp. 57, 81, 92, 113.

42 *Ibid.*, pp. 144–7.

43 Haymo of Faversham, apparently following the practice of his native England, raised the level of solemnity of the octave of the Assumption so that all other feasts occurring during the octave were transferred after the octave day (August 22), a tradition that in turn entered papal observance before the end of the thirteenth century. In 1245, Innocent IV stipulated observance of the Octave of the Nativity of the Virgin, which was already widely observed in England and France, for the whole church. The Office of Our Lady of Snows was added to the curial round by Honorius III in the 1220s, with the Franciscans following suit in the later years of the century. See Van Dijk and Walker, *The Origins*, pp. 307–8, 370–8.

44 Roper, *Medieval English Benedictine Liturgy*, p. 136.

45 Chew pointed out the parallel between troping and cantus firmus usage in the context of the Ordinary ("The Early Cyclic Mass," p. 255).

46 See Van Dijk and Walker, "The Origins," p. 360. The decree stated that Christ's "body and blood are truly contained in the sacrament of the altar beneath the species of bread and wine, the bread having been transubstantiated into the body and the wine into the blood, by divine power" (Charles Zika, "Hosts, Processions and Pilgrimages: Controlling the Sacred in Fifteenth-century Germany," *Past and Present* 118 [1988], 38, after Giovan Domenico, Mansi, *Sacrorum conciliorum nova et amplissima collectio, cujus Johannes Dominicus Mansi et post ipsius mortem Florentius et Venetianus editores ab anno 1758 ad annum 1798 priores triginta unum tomos ediderunt, nunc autem continuata et*

absoluta, 53 vols. [Florence, 1759–98; repr. Paris: H. Welter, 1901–27], vol. 22, col. 982). The same council, significantly, also saw the stipulation of annual confession for all who would avoid damnation.

47 The statutes, which apparently date from the first decade of the thirteenth century, instruct priests to "keep [the host] in front of their chests while they say *hoc est corpus meum* and then they should elevate it so that it can be seen by all" ("quasi ante pectus detineant donec dixerint 'Hoc est corpus meum' et tunc elevent eam ita quod possit ab omnibus videri") (quotation and translation from Rubin, *Corpus Christi*, p. 55). On this and for a detailed consideration of the twelfth-century debate, which preceded the establishment of the doctrine, on the status and timing of the moment of transubstantiation see V. L. Kennedy, "The Moment of Consecration and the Elevation of the Host," *Medieval Studies* 6 (1944), 121–50. Michel Huglo informs me that the elevation is documented already in some Parisian missals of the twelfth century (private communication).

48 Stated in a Parisian decree issued by Peter of Nemours, Bishop of Paris, shortly after the Council. Also approved by Honorius III, who "insisted that the parish clergy should instruct the people to adore the host when it is lifted up at Mass" (see Van Dijk and Walker, *The Origins*, pp. 360–1).

Chapter 8 Counterpoint of images, counterpoint of sounds

1 While both bread and wine – body and blood – are consecrated, each was held, at least from the later thirteenth century, to contain the whole Christ (see Thomas Aquinas, *Summa theologiae*, Book III, Question 76, article 2; www.ccel. org/ccel/aquinas/summa.FP.html). The 1281 Lambeth Constitutions of John Peckham, Archbishop of Canterbury stress the same point in the instruction to the clergy to administer only the bread to the faithful at communion. (See Martin R. Dudley, "Sacramental Liturgies in the Middle Ages," in Thomas J. Hefferman and E. Ann Matter [eds.], *The Liturgy of the Medieval Church* [2nd edn., Kalamazoo, MI: Medieval Institute Publications, 2005], p. 205.) Peckham's charges are indicative also of the custom, beginning in the late thirteenth century, of reserving communication in both species to the clergy (see Marc Bloch, *The Royal Touch: Sacred Monarchy and Scrofula in England and France*, translated by J. E. Anderson [London: Routledge and Kegan Paul, 1973; first published in French in 1924], p. 119). Elevation of the chalice, though sporadic from the thirteenth century, became doctrinal only following the Council of Trent, one of the major arguments against it being the fact that, in contrast to the host, the wine held in the chalice was not visible to the people. (See Joseph Jungmann, *The Mass of the Roman Rite: Its Origins and Development* [translation, by Francis A. Brunner, of *Missarum Solemnia*], 2 vols. [Westminster, MD: Christian Classics, 1986], vol. II, pp. 207–8.) Of course the wine, and its specific relation to the blood from Christ's side wound, had its own broad complex of imagery.

Most obvious is surely the Mass of St. Gregory, in depictions of which (as in Plate 1, p. 103) blood from Christ's side is often shown literally pouring into the chalice; related to this is the widespread devotion to the side wound itself, which is sometimes depicted, usually supported by angels, within a chalice.

2 See for instance Johan Huizinga, *The Autumn of the Middle Ages*, trans. Rodney J. Payton and Ulrich Mammitzsch, (University of Chicago Press, 1996), p. 177; Eamon Duffy, *The Stripping of the Altars* (New Haven and London: Yale University Press, 1992), p. 100; Charles Zika, "Hosts, Processions and Pilgrimages in Fifteenth-century Germany," *Past and Present* 118 (1988), 31; Miri Rubin, *Corpus Christi: The Eucharist in Late Medieval Culture* (Cambridge University Press, 1991), p. 63.

3 John Bossy, "The Mass as a Social Institution," *Past and Present* 100 (1983), 47. Bossy notes that the commemoration of the dead became a consistent feature of public Masses only in the thirteenth century (*ibid.*, 36). The desired association with Christ's sacrifice was clarified by the bowing of the priest's head at the end of the Commemoration of the Dead, in remembrance of the death of the Savior (Jungmann, *The Mass*, vol. I, p. 117; see also vol. II, p. 240).

4 See Duffy, *The Stripping of the Altars*, pp. 117–18, 119–21, 210–11, and Peter Browe, *Die Verehrung der Eucharistie im Mittelalter* (Munich: Max Hueber, 1933; repr. Freiburg im Breisgau: Herder, 1967), pp. 53–4.

5 Bossy, "The Mass as a Social Institution," especially 32–4; see also Virginia Reinburg, "Liturgy and the Laity in Late Medieval and Reformation France," *Sixteenth Century Journal* 23 (1992), 531.

6 On the frequency of communion and legislation pertaining to it, see for instance Rubin, *Corpus Christi*, pp. 64–70.

7 Gazing on the consecrated host came itself to acquire a sacramental value. See *ibid.*, pp. 147–55, and particularly Charles Caspers, "The Western Church during the Late Middle Ages: *Augenkommunion* or Popular Mysticism?" in Charles Caspers, Gerard Lukken and Gerard Rouwhorst (eds.), *Bread of Heaven: Customs and Practices Surrounding Holy Communion* (Kampen: Kok Pharos, 1995), pp. 83–97. Caspers notes how the "spiritual communion" of gazing on the host came to be believed to carry similar benefits to actual communion, but it acquired a particular attractiveness because it lacked the risk – attendant on actual, physical communion – of receiving the host in a state of unworthiness, an act that carried serious implications for the welfare of one's soul. This explains the widespread reluctance to take physical communion, but it also explains the corresponding eagerness to gaze on the elevated host. On the same point see also Reinburg, "Liturgy and the Laity," 539–41.

8 Bossy, "The Mass as a Social Institution," 54. The quasi-sacramental value of the pax and reception, following Mass, of *pain bénit* have also been noted by Reinburg and others (see Reinburg, "Liturgy and the Laity," 539, 541, and her "Popular Prayers in Late Medieval and Reformation France," unpublished PhD dissertation, Princeton University, 1985, pp. 191, 205, 207–8).

9   On the various theories regarding the origin of the practice see Rubin, *Corpus Christi*, p. 55.

10 Jungmann, *The Mass*, vol. I, pp. 81–4.

11 *Ibid.*, vol. I, pp. 119–21; vol. II, pp. 206–12; Rubin, *Corpus Christi*, pp. 49–63; Duffy, *The Stripping of the Altars*, pp. 95–107.

12 On the relation of clerical power to control of the host, see Zika, "Hosts, Processions and Pilgrimages," 25–64, especially 30–7 and 59–64, and Rubin, *Corpus Christi*, e.g. pp. 13, 35.

13 On the role of the priest as Christ, and the reciprocal depiction in contemporary iconography of Christ, at the Last Supper, as officiating priest, see especially Barbara G. Lane, *The Altar and the Altarpiece: Sacramental Themes in Early Netherlandish Painting* (New York: Harper and Row, 1984), particularly pp. 107–36. See also Rubin, *Corpus Christi*, pp. 50, 205–6 and 300.

14 See for example Browe, *Die Verehrung*, p. 54.

15 For Cranmer's comments see for example Gregory Dix, *The Shape of the Liturgy* (London: Dacre, 1945), p. 620, and Duffy, *The Stripping of the Altars*, p. 98, which also quotes disapproving remarks of a similar nature from the early fifteenth century by the Lollard priest William Thorpe. For the same opprobrium as expressed in 1563 by Thomas Becon, see J. Wickham Legg (ed.), *Tracts on the Mass* (London: Henry Bradshaw Society, 1904), p. 235. In spite of widespread proscriptions, for many people attendance at Mass meant simply to go into church for the elevation and then to leave or, alternatively, to rush to wherever the next elevation was taking place: "They come when they hear the bells ring, enter, see the elevation; and when it's over, they leave, fleeing as if they'd seen the devil" (after Gottschalk Hollen, in *Sermones dominicales* [Hagenau, 1498, sermon 74], quoted in Zika, "Hosts, Processions and Pilgrimages," 31; also quoted in Adolph Franz, *Die Messe im deutschen Mittelalter* [Herder: Freiburg im Breisgau, 1902; repr. Darmstadt: Wissenschaftliche Buchgesellschaft, 1963], p. 18; Browe, *Die Verehrung*, p. 68; Edouard Dumoutet, *Le désir de voir l'hostie et les origines de la dévotion au saint-sacrement* [Paris: Gabriel Beauchesne, 1926], pp. 69–70). Clearly the problem was widespread: in emphasizing the importance of remaining to receive the pax board at the end of Mass, the anonymous *Les misteres de la saincte messe* (Lyon: Guillaume Le Roy, 1490) scolds that "Those who leave [Mass] as soon as they have seen the body of the Lord [the elevation] are like those who go to a wedding and depart as soon as they see the bride depart. He who departs before receiving the pax is like he who dines at a wedding and departs before taking leave of the host" (quoted in Reinburg, "Liturgy and the Laity," 539). It seems clear that the pax (by the late Middle Ages an object circulated to be kissed by the people as a token of community) along with the distribution of blessed bread, functioned at least partially to keep people at Mass until its end. See also Rubin, *Corpus Christi*, pp. 73–4.

16 On the spread of such devotions see Jungmann, *The Mass*, vol. I, pp. 121–3 and Zika, "Hosts, Processions and Pilgrimages," especially 32–7. It is noteworthy

that the Feast of Corpus Christi, introduced in Liège in the mid thirteenth century and formally instituted for the universal church by Urban IV in 1264, was not celebrated again in Rome until 1315, becoming widely established, along with its attendant processions, only during the course of the fourteenth century and into the fifteenth (see Zika, "Hosts, Processions and Pilgrimages," 37–9, and Mervyn James, "Ritual, Drama and Social Body in the Late Medieval English Town," *Past and Present* 98 [1983], 4). Zika notes a similar pattern with regard to other host venerations ("Hosts, Processions and Pilgrimages," *passim*). See also the dating of Corpus Christi devotions in Rubin, *Corpus Christi, passim* and particularly Chapter 4, pp. 213–87.

17 See Duffy, *The Stripping of the Altars*, p. 239 on the huge indulgences offered for reciting series of prayers before images of the Mass of St. Gregory, the classic narrative demonstration of the doctrine of transubstantiation.

18 Jungmann, *The Mass*, vol. I, p. 106.

19 Duffy, *The Stripping of the Altars*, p. 111.

20 See Bossy, "The Mass as a Social Institution," and Reinburg, "Liturgy and the Laity."

21 The bibliography on this topic is considerable. For a brief general introduction to choir screens and their functions see Elizabeth C. Parker, "Architecture as Liturgical Setting," in Heffernan and Matter (eds.), *The Liturgy of the Medieval Church*, pp. 270–4. For a useful general bibliography on the phenomenon in France, Germany, Italy, the Netherlands and England see Jacqueline E. Jung, "Seeing through Screens: The Gothic Choir Enclosure as Frame," in Sharon E. J. Gerstel (ed.), *Thresholds of the Sacred: Architectural, Art Historical, Liturgical, and Theological Perspectives on Religious Screens, East and West* (Dumbarton Oaks: Harvard University Press, 2006), p. 185. While the thirteenth and early fourteenth centuries comprised the great age of monumental screen building in cathedral, collegiate and conventual churches, screens in parish churches, though similarly dating back to the thirteenth century, seem more clearly to have come into vogue rather later. Referring to examples in parish churches in East Anglia and Devon, Duffy (*The Stripping of the Altars*, p. 157) notes that most were fairly recent at the time of the Reformation, a pattern that is borne out by surviving screens across the rest of the country. Jung detects a similar trend in Germany while, as Reinburg notes, many of the surviving French examples date from the sixteenth century (see Jung, "Beyond the Barrier: The Unifying Role of the Choir Screen in Gothic Churches," *The Art Bulletin* 82/4 (2000), 629, and Reinburg, "Popular Prayers," pp. 180, 250).

22 Reinburg offers a useful consideration of these circumstances in the context of a discussion of lay versus clerical experience of Mass ("Liturgy and the Laity," 527; "Popular Prayers," pp. 180–1).

23 Jung, "Beyond the Barrier," 624–5, and "Seeing through Screens," pp. 192–3.

24 A particularly elegant example can be seen in the delicate early-sixteenth-century *jubé* of St. Étienne du Mont, Paris, its sweeping stairways and gallery

picked out in the lightest tracery. Almost all the parish church screens constructed in fifteenth-century England are similarly characterized, at least above the dado level, by open tracery. The classic study, with lavish illustrations, remains Aymer Vallance, *Greater English Church Screens, Being Great Roods, Screenwork and Rood-Lofts in Cathedral, Monastic, and Collegiate Churches in England and* Wales (London and New York: Batsford, 1947). See also the discussion in Duffy, *The Stripping of the Altars*, pp. 110–13, 157–60, and the numerous screens illustrated in his plates. On the comparative openness of late screens see also Jung, "Seeing through Screens," p. 192.

25 A number of religious orders cultivated the convention – in a pattern of alternating revelation and concealment reminiscent of the display of reliquaries, monstrances and painted polyptychs – of facilitating outside access to the Real Presence by the opening and closing of the door. Thus the minutes of the 1261 general chapter meeting of the Carthusians instruct that the choir doors in the order's churches are to be closed throughout the Mass except during the elevation, when they are to be opened to permit lay adoration of the host (see Browe, *Die Verehrung*, p. 55; Jung, "Beyond the Barrier," 627 and 651). For the same instruction from the statutes of 1368, and for the similar dictum of the Celestines, see Browe, *Die Verehrung*, pp. 55–6 and Dumoutet, *Le désir de voir l'hostie*, p. 58. For the similar stipulation, in 1249, of the Dominicans, see R. A. Sundt, "*Mediocres domos et humiles habeant fratres nostri*: Dominican Legislation on Architecture and Architectural Decoration in the 13th Century," *Journal of the Society of Architectural Historians* 46 (1987), 406; quoted in Jung, "Seeing through Screens," p. 189.

26 See Jung, "Beyond the Barrier," 627–8 for a range of examples.

27 A series of examples from fourteenth- and fifteenth-century Germany bewail the crowding of the laity around the altar, to the extent even of hindering the progress of Mass (see Browe, *Die Verehrung*, p. 67 and Franz, *Die Messe*, p. 32). The same eagerness in England to get as close as possible to the host elicited a similar complaint by Caxton (see Duffy, *The Stripping of the Altars*, pp. 112–13).

28 Duffy, *The Stripping of the Altars*," p. 97.

29 See the discussion and literature cited in Reinburg, "Liturgy and the Laity," 532.

30 Duffy, *The Stripping of the Altars*," p. 132.

31 On Jesus altars see *ibid.*, pp. 113–16. This shift of emphasis in the fifteenth century towards lay devotion finds a revealing resonance, in English parish churches, also in patterns of architectural development. Peter Draper notes the coincidence between the most intensive period in the expansion and rebuilding of chancels and what he sees as the zenith in the church's institutional power in the thirteenth century. He compares this with later building efforts, which tended to be concentrated in the nave in programs of rebuilding financed by the laity. See his "Architecture and Liturgy," in Jonathan Alexander and

Paul Binski (eds.), *Age of Chivalry: Art in Plantagenet England, 1200–1400* (London: Weidenfeld and Nicolson, 1987), p. 88.

32 Reinburg emphasizes that the laity, while divorced from the verbal and intellectual content of the Mass, had an integral role to play as observers of and respondents to its greater "drama" from a broader, social viewpoint. That role, she argues, gains particular point through its close relation to the accustomed role of unquestioning fealty towards secular lords ("Liturgy and the Laity," *passim*). She develops this perspective at greater length in "Popular Prayers," pp. 178–209, where she traces the involvement of the late medieval laity throughout the process of Mass.

33 For exegesis of the sculptural reliefs on the screens of the cathedrals of Naumburg, Strasbourg, Mainz, Wechselburg, Amiens, and Chartres see Jung, "Beyond the Barrier," 634–50.

34 Discussion and quotation in *ibid.*, 632–4.

35 The parallel is underscored by the text on the bandarole above the officiating priest: "Hic Pa[n]is manu s[anc]ti sp[iritu]s for[m]at[us] i[n] vi[r]gi[n]e / Igne passio[n]is e[st] decoct[us] in cruce / A[m]bro[sius] i[n] li[bro] sac[ra]me[n] t[is]." See Paul Vandenbroeck, *Catalogus schilderijen 14e en 15e eeuw* (Antwerp: Koninklijk Museum voor Schone Kunsten Antwerpen, 1985), p. 155. My thanks to Griet Steyaert, who is currently restoring the panel, for this detail.

A similar configuration (showing some apparent debt to the van der Weyden example) of crucifixion and elevation, but with a much flatter perspective, occurs in the central panel, *Crucifixion in a Church*, of the triptych in the Convent of the Angels, Madrid by Vrancke van der Stockt. See Jung, "Seeing through Screens," pp. 203–5.

36 Such clarification was especially crucial in the Canon, its words forbidden to public access, where the proliferation of such gestures may in part have resulted from the desire to communicate key moments in the central action of the Mass to lay observers (on this point see Jungmann, *The Mass*, vol. II, pp. 143–4). On the reference of particular crosses to specific events in the Passion, and in particular the reference of the raising of the priest's arms at the elevation to the raising of Christ on the cross, see *ibid.*, vol. I., pp. 107, 112, 116; see also Rubin, *Corpus Christi*, p. 58.

37 Reinburg, "Liturgy and the Laity," Bossy, "The Mass as a Social Institution," Duffy, *The Stripping of the Altars*, pp. 91–130.

38 See Browe, *Die Verehrung*, p. 56. See also Jungmann (*The Mass*, vol. II, p. 109), who observes that this practice persisted in Rouen and other French cathedrals until at least 1700, and in Spain even into the nineteenth century (*ibid.*, p. 209). For English examples, at St. Peter Cheap in London and in York, see Duffy, *The Stripping of the Altars*, p. 96, and Wickham Legg, *Tracts on the Mass*, pp. 234–5. For another at the Cathedral of Chartres, see Browe, *Die Verehrung*, p. 56, which quotes this view as expressed by Jean de Moléon (*Voyages liturgiques en France* [Paris, 1718]): "il y a un petit rideau violet d'un pied ou environ en quarré

suspendu à une petite corde audessus de l'autel, comme à Orléans. Le diacre un peu avant la consecracion le fait venir au milieu de l'autel, afin (dit-on) que la s. hostie paroisse à ceux qui étant au bas du choeur, ne la pourroient voir … Je crois que [ce petit rideau] étoit plutôt pour représenter plus vivement au prêtre au tems de la consecration Jesus-Christ en croix" (discussed and quoted also in Dumoutet, *Le désir de voir l'hostie*, pp. 58–9 and elsewhere). The latter is also discussed in Wickham Legg, *Tracts on the Mass*, p. 235, which mentions the same custom at Laon and in Spanish churches.

39 See the testimony of de Moléon, above, and Reinburg, "Liturgy and the Laity," 533–7. Reinburg further draws attention to the many images of this moment in which the celebrant is depicted with an acolyte lifting the edge of his vestments so that their weight need not impede his lifting the wafer as high as possible.

40 See Browe, *Die Verehrung*, p. 56: "Caveat tamen ne fumus incensi sit talis aut tantus quod visum Sacramenti impediat vel aliunde offendat sacerdotem" (Carmelite ordinal of 1312). See also Dumoutet, *Le désir de voir l'hostie*, p. 58.

41 See Rubin, *Corpus Christi*, p. 62, who notes that the donor in question was inspired by a similar machine he had seen at King's Lynn. This was clearly a very literal response to the words of the Canon: "We humbly beseech you, almighty God, to bid [the bread and cup] be borne by the hands of your angel to your altar on high, in the sight of your divine majesty, that all of us who have received the most holy body and blood of your Son by partaking at this altar may be filled with all heavenly blessing and grace; through Christ our Lord" (see for instance "The Mass of the Roman Rite," in R. C. D. Jasper and G. J. Cuming, *Prayers of the Eucharist, Early and Reformed* [London: Collins, 1975], p. 108). As Pope Gregory the Great famously expressed it, "What right believing Christian can doubt that in the very hour of the sacrifice, at the words of the Priest, the heavens be opened, and the quires of Angels are present in that mystery of Jesus Christ; that high things are accomplished with low, and earthly joined to heavenly, and that one thing is made of visible and invisible" (from the *Dialogues*, 4: 58; cited in Parker, "Architecture as Liturgical Setting," p. 246).

42 Duffy, *The Stripping of the Altars*, pp. 96, 330. For further endowments of lighting see Rubin, *Corpus Christi*, pp. 60–2.

43 Duffy, *The Stripping of the Altars*, pp. 96, 122, 129, 330.

44 *Ibid.*, p. 111.

45 John Harper makes the important point that almost all the parts of Mass that were intended for public consumption were sung, with a subdivision between choral chants and texts intoned by the celebrant or an assisting cleric (see his *The Forms and Orders of the Western Liturgy from the Tenth to the Eighteenth Century* [Oxford University Press, 1991], pp. 114–15).

46 My thanks to Alexandra Buckle, who will report on this phenomenon particularly as it applies to the Beauchamp Chapel of St. Mary's, Warwick in her forthcoming Oxford doctoral dissertation, for drawing my attention to this

phenomenon. The noted authority on choir stalls Charles Tracy asserts that such trenches "occur under most sets of North European, including English, choir-stalls" (see his "The Choir-Stalls," in Charmian Woodfield [ed.], *The Church of Our Lady of Mount Carmel and Some Conventual Buildings at the Whitefriars, Coventry*, BAR British Series 389 [Oxford: Hadrian Books, 2005], p. 169).

47 See, *inter alia*, the famous example in the mid-fifteenth-century Parisian Book of Hours (British Library, MS Harley 2971), folio 109v, and that in the Christmas Mass depicted in the *Très riches heures du duc de Berry* (Chantilly, Museé Condé, MS 65), folio 158.

48 British Library, MS Egerton 2125, folio 117v. See the similar arrangement, with lecterns swivelled to face the altar at the elevation, in the miniature, by the Boucicaut Master and Workshop, in British Library, MS Add. 16997, folio 145 (reproduced, along with related images, in James W. McKinnon, "Representations of the Mass in Medieval and Renaissance Art," *Journal of the American Musicological Society* 31 [1978], 37). Clearly such an arrangement for polyphony would have been impossible in performance involving more than one to a part, or, crucially, boys, where requirements of space would have demanded a free-standing lectern.

49 See the discussion in Ronald Lewcock, Rijn Pirn with Jürgen Meyer, "Acoustics," *Grove Music Online. Oxford Music Online.* Accessed November 24, 2008; Kenneth Harrison, "Vitruvius and Acoustic Jars in England during the Middle Ages," Transactions of the Ancient Monuments Society 15 (1967–8), 49–58; and Charles Tracy, "Choir-stalls from the 14th-century Whitefriars Church in Coventry," *Journal of the British Archaeological Association* 90 (1997), 84–6.

50 Harrison, "Vitruvius," 51.

51 Lewcock et al., "Acoustics," and Tracy, "The Choir Stalls," p. 169, both of which also quote the Metz example.

52 See for example Johannes Burckard's *Ordo Missae* (1502) which, besides giving a detailed description of the gestures of the celebrant that are to be seen by the laity, draws a clear distinction between those of his words that are to be heard and those that "dici debent secrete: ita quod a circumstantibus seu interessentibus misse non audiuntur" (see Wickham Legg, *Tracts on the Mass*, pp. 137–8).

53 On proscriptions concerning access to the words of the Canon, and stories of dire things befalling those who transgressed, see Duffy, *The Stripping of the Altars*, p. 110 and Jungmann, *The Mass*, vol. II, p. 105.

54 Thomas F. Simmons (ed.), *The Lay Folks Mass Book, or The Manner of Hearing Mass*, Early English Text Society, Original Series, vol. 71 (London: Trübner, 1879; repr. London, New York, Toronto: Oxford University Press, 1968), p. 4.

55 Jung, "Seeing through Screens," pp. 196–9.

56 See note 41.

57 Cited in Duffy, *The Stripping of the Altars*, p. 119.

58 On this question of dating see Bryan D. Spinks, *The Sanctus in the Eucharistic Prayer* (Cambridge University Press, 1991), p. 93.

59 Baugois also specified that the bell be struck every Saturday and on the vigils of all Marian feasts while the *Salve* was being sung in the nave, seven times each day at Matins, and at the hour that his daily endowed Mass was begun in the Chapel of Sts. Julian and Basil, where he was buried (Saint-Omer, Bibliothèque Municipale, MS II. G. 473).

60 See Jungmann, *The Mass*, vol. II, pp. 209–10, 131. Only the large, cast bells hung in church towers or belfries were dignified with names such as that given by Baugois to his bell.

61 The inscription on the bell names its endower and founders: "Me Juliana vocavit, hinc Juliam, Ecclesiae Beati Audomari devote donavit egregius vir Magister Baugelius Beguini de Falcoberga oriundus, decretorum doctor hujus ecclesiae canonicus Conflatibus Gobelino Moer et Willelmo Carpet fusoribus. Anno Domini M CCCC LXXIIII." The bell, which was the "bourdon," or lowest-sounding, weighed in at 18,000 lb. and required no fewer than six men to swing it into sound. See Monique Ducrocq, *La Cathédrale de Saint-Omer: son symbolisme, ses grands dignitaires* (Saint-Omer: Cathédrale de Saint-Omer, 1997), p. 64.

62 As Browe colorfully expresses this moment, "Wenn die Glocke die hl. Weihehandlung ankündigte, so wirkte das wie ein Trompetenstoß, der die draußen Herumstehenden in die Kirche rief, die Lachenden und Schwätzenden zur Ruhe brachte, die Unandächtigen aufmerken ließ und die Blicke aller gebannt auf die Hostie lenkte" (*Die Verehrung*, p. 67). Browe quotes evidence to the effect that in many places people would while away the foregoing parts of Mass in the church graveyard. At the sound of the bell they would surge into the church and, having seen the host, just as quickly surge out again (*ibid.*, p. 68). Such considerations also lay behind the practice, documented by Browe, whereby priests would hold the host aloft for a long time (*ibid.*, p. 63). Indulgences were granted by the pope to anyone who, hearing such a bell, turned to worship the sacrament (see Jungmann, *The Mass*, vol. II, p. 210).

63 For various views on the date of the introduction of the Sanctus, which occurred at some point between the fourth and sixth century, see especially Paul F. Bradshaw, *The Search for the Origins of Christian Worship: Sources and Methods for the Study of Early Liturgy* (2nd edn., Oxford University Press, 2002), pp. 106, 111–12, 126–37, 139–43, 211–20, and the same author's *Eucharistic Origins* (Oxford University Press, 2004), pp. 147–52; see also Herbert Douteil, *Studien zu Durantis "Rationale divinorum officiorum" als kirchenmusikalischer Quelle* (Regensburg: Gustav Bosse, 1969), p. 179; Spinks, *The Sanctus*, pp. 95–6 and *passim*; Gregory Dix, *The Shape of the Liturgy* (London: Dacre, 1945), p. 165; Lucien Chavoutier, "Un Libellus Pseudo-Ambrosien sur le Saint-Esprit," *Sacris Erudiri* 11 (1960), 149. Whatever the fluctuations of its early history, the

mandatory presence of the Sanctus is indicated by the Council of Vaison (529) (see F. L. Cross and E. A. Livingstone [eds.], "Sanctus," *The Oxford Dictionary of the Christian Church* [3rd edn., Oxford and New York: Oxford University Press, 1997], p. 1452).

64 Isaiah 6: 3: "et clamabant alter ad alterum et dicebant sanctus sanctus sanctus Dominus exercituum plena est omnis terra gloria eius."

65 Jungmann, *The Mass*, vol. II, p. 134.

66 See *The Oxford Dictionary of the Christian Church*, p. 1452. The Benedictus seems already to have been current in Gaul by the sixth century, and customary in the Roman Mass by the seventh (Jungmann, *The Mass*, vol. II, p. 136 and Spinks, *The Sanctus*, p. 121).

67 See Matthew 21: 8–9: "Plurima autem turba straverunt vestimenta sua in via alii autem caedebant ramos de arboribus et sternebant in via. Turbae autem quae praecedebant et quae sequebantur clamabant dicentes osanna filio David benedictus qui venturus est in nomine Domini osanna in altissimis." Mark 11: 9–10: "osanna benedictus qui venit in nomine Domini. Benedictum quod venit regnum patris nostri David osanna in excelsis." John 12: 13: "Acceperunt ramos palmarum et processerunt obviam ei et clamabant osanna benedictus qui venit in nomine Domini rex Israhel." Luke 19: 37–8: "Et cum adpropinquaret iam ad descensum montis Oliveti coeperunt omnes turbae discentium gaudentes laudare Deum voce magna super omnibus quas viderant virtutibus dicentes benedictus qui venit rex in nomine Domini pax in caelo et gloria in excelsis." "Benedictus … domini" as used in the Gospels is itself drawn from Psalm 117: 26.

68 The urge for earthly voices to join in the perpetual heavenly praise described by Isaiah is made explicit by commentators as early as the first century: see the quotation from Clement of Rome in Jungmann, *The Mass*, vol. II, p. 132. The role of the Benedictus in effecting that union is widely attested in medieval Mass commentary. See for example Honorius Augustodunensis: "Hic hymnus partim ab angelis, partim ab hominibus concinitur, quia per Christum immolatum humanum genus angelis conjungitur, laus quippe angelorum est: *Sanctus, sanctus, sanctus, Dominus Deus Sabaoth. Pleni sunt coeli et terra gloria tua. Hosanna in excelsis.* Laus vero hominum est: *Benedictus qui venit in nomine Domine. Hosanna in excelsis.* In hoc cantu se signant, quia signum Christi cui contradicitur se recipere designant" (*Gemma Animae* Liber 1, cap. XLII. [Patrologia Latina vol. 172]). The nature of the composite origin of the text of the present-day Sanctus may explain why its point of internal division remained to some extent ambiguous even when, in the later Middle Ages, it became customary to conceive of it in terms of two symmetrical halves each ending with an Osanna. This ambiguity had, as we shall see, an impact on musical, including polyphonic, settings throughout the Middle Ages, and gave rise to equivocation concerning the coordination of the musical setting with the consecration.

69 See Jungmann, *The Mass*, vol. II. pp. 128–9; see also Amédée Gastoué, "Le Sanctus et le Benedictus," *Revue du chant Grégorien* 38 (1934), 35–6, for a sketch of early developments regarding the singing of the Sanctus.

70 See the discussion in Douteil, *Studien*, p. 178.

71 Jungmann, *The Mass*, vol. II, p. 131.

72 Like many similar developments this shift was surely gradual and piecemeal. The singing together of clergy and laity seems to have persisted in some places even as late as the twelfth century. Jungmann notes the reference to the practice for example in the *Gemma animae* of Honorius Augustodunensis (see Patrologia Latina vol. 172, p. 156 [Liber I, Cap. XLII]). For these details see Jungmann, *The Mass*, vol. II, pp. 128–30. Edward Foley notes that congregational performance of the Sanctus seems to have persisted longer in some places than that of any other part of the Ordinary. In his view – significantly for our purposes here – the end of congregational singing of the Sanctus was closely linked to the practice, accentuated increasingly from the late eighth century on, of its silent priestly recitation. The separation of the priest from the rest of the assembly meant that he no longer had to wait until the end of the Sanctus to begin the Canon, but could recite it while the Sanctus was sung by attending clerics or the schola (see Foley, "The Song of the Assembly in Medieval Eucharist," in Lizette Larson-Miller [ed.], *Medieval Liturgy: A Book of Essays* [New York: Garland, 1997], pp. 207–9).

73 Duffy, *The Stripping of the Altars*, p. 111. As he notes, "The phrase 'velum templi' was no idle one, since the veil was dramatically lowered at the mention of the rending of the veil of the Jerusalem temple, during the reading of the Gospel at masses on the ferial days." Duffy comments that by the end of the Middle Ages this practice was succumbing to pressure from the people to see the host.

74 See Kornelia Imesch-Oehry, *Die Kirchen der Franziskanerobservanten in der Lombardei, im Piemont und im Tessin und ihre "Lettnerwände": Architektur und Dekoration* (Essen: Die blaue Eule, 1991), pp. 96–9. See also Reiner Sörries, *Die Alpenländischer Fastentücher* (Klagenfurt: Universitätsverlag, 1988). As in England, later medieval Germany saw a development towards increasing visual access to the liturgical action: what had earlier been blanket coverings were steadily reduced to the status of symbolic hangings above the altar (see Imesch-Oehry, *Die Kirchen*, p. 97). In a French example of the same phenomenon, the chapter of the collegiate church of Saint-Omer, northern France paid in the year 1412/13 for "1. drap de quaresme a pendre dessus lautel" (Saint-Omer, Archives Municipales II. G. CF 18, f. 3v).

75 See Percy Dearmer, *The Parson's Handbook*, (6th, rev. edn., London and New York: H. Frowe, 1907), where this image is reproduced as Plate XVI; discussion on pp. 441, 450–2. See also Ronald Hutton, *Stations of the Sun: A History of the Ritual Year in Britain* (New York: Oxford University Press, 1996), pp. 170–2. My thanks to John Harper for these references.

76 Jungmann, *The Mass*, vol. II, pp. 104, 138.

77 *Ibid.*, pp. 139–40.

78 *Ibid.*, p. 140. For a detailed, and to some extent necessarily speculative, treatment of this process see Gastoué, "Le Sanctus et le Benedictus." Jungmann draws attention to an early instance of this cleavage in the ninth-century Sacramentary of Amiens: here, the instruction is given "Quando tractim canitur Sanctus, idem sacerdos cursim decantet"; the celebrant is then to proceed directly to the recitation of one of the *apologiae* that, in the early Middle Ages, marked the celebrant's preparation to be worthy of enacting the consecration (*The Mass*, vol. II, p. 129).

79 Gastoué notes that the text drawn from the Gospels (Osanna I to the end of the present-day Sanctus) seems originally to have been situated before the communion, only later assuming its position, in tandem with the rest of the Sanctus, around the time of the consecration ("Le Sanctus et le Benedictus," p. 16; see also pp. 167, 168).

80 See Jungmann, *The Mass*, vol. II, p. 137, and Gastoué, "Le Sanctus et le Benedictus," p. 164. Similarly Luther's wording, in calling for its continuation in his *Formula missae* of 1523, suggests a long-established procedure. Luther speaks of the same procedure being followed for the chalice, a practice that became definitively established only in the sixteenth century, though its history is almost as old as that of the elevation of the host: "Beim Gesang des Benediktus sollen das Brot und der Kelch wie bisher emporgehoben werden." He expresses the same sentiments in his "Deutsche Messe," adding that these actions work well with the German Sanctus: "Das auffheben wollen wir nicht abthun, sondern behalten, darumb, das es feyn mit dem deudschen Sanctus stymmet und bedeut, das Christus befolhen hat, seyn zu gedencken" (quoted in Browe, *Die Verehrung*, p. 39).

81 Malibu, California, Getty Museum, MS 34, folio 130r (formerly Bodleian Library MS Astor A. 5). A similar case is presented by New York, Morgan Library MS 800, folio 40r. Though the miniatures in this source are by Niccolò da Bologna, who signed the Crucifixion scene on folio 39v, the identical text hand and border decoration reveal that the manuscript must have been produced in the same Bolognese atelier. As in the Getty example, this page from c.1370 combines the words of the Canon (beginning at "Te igitur") with an initial depicting a celebrant, who is clearly uttering its words while holding the host that he is about to elevate, and a pair of clerics singing the Sanctus from an open book. For two further proposed examples of the same coincidence in sixteenth-century engravings see McKinnon, "Representations of the Mass," 45 and 46, which also (33) reproduces the two Bolognese miniatures.

82 Gastoué, "Le Sanctus et le Benedictus," 167 and Eugenio Costa, *Tropes et séquences dans le cadre de la vie liturgique au moyen-âge* (Rome: CLV, 1979), p. 53. See the many examples in Clemens Blume and Henry Marriott Bannister, *Analecta Hymnica Medii aevi* vol. 47 (Leipzig: Reisland, 1905).

83 Franz Xaver Haberl, "Das traditionelle Musikprogramm der sixtinischen Kapelle," *Kirchenmusikalisches Jahrbuch* XII (1897), 56. For the supposition that this practice was a much older one, see Peter Wagner, *Geschichte der Messe, I. Teil: Bis 1600* (Leipzig: Breitkopf und Härtel, 1913), p. 62.

84 While the evidence of later practices should clearly be interpreted with caution, just such a procedure, which may be suggestive of earlier tradition, is indicated by a directive in the *Ceremoniale episcoporum* that seems largely to have been observed from its publication in 1600 until the mid-twentieth-century reforms of the Second Vatican Council. This instructed that the singing of the first Osanna was to end around the time of the consecration and that, after a silence, the Benedictus was to follow it. The similar instruction, in the *Motu proprio* of Pius X (1903–14), that the celebrant should wait until the first Osanna had been completely sung before proceeding with the consecration gives an indication of the longevity of this procedure (see Gastoué, "Le Sanctus et le Benedictus," 163–4).

85 See Michael P. Long, "Symbol and Ritual in Josquin's *Missa Di Dadi*", *Journal of the American Musicological Society* 42 (1989), 6–7. The relevant passage from Biel is as follows: "Prima eius pars angelorum est; unde Isaiah 6, Seraphin clamabant sub excelso dei solio … Secunda eius pars est hominum, qui preibant comitabantur and sequebantur dominum in hierusalem loco sue oblationis et vespertini sacrificii se presentantem …" (Heiko A. Oberman and William J. Courtenay [eds.], *Gabrielis Biel: Canonis Misse Expositio*, 4 vols. [Wiesbaden: Franz Steiner, 1963], vol. II, p. 162).

86 Gastoué makes a strong case that precisely this division is embodied in the pattern of repetitions in the ferial chant XVIII, the most simple, and presumably the oldest, Sanctus chant in the Roman Rite. He notes that except for the special case of Sanctus XVI, in which he perceives a Byzantine legacy, the other, apparently later, chants situate the division before the Benedictus, each Osanna making a strong and frequently identical conclusion to what precedes it ("Le Sanctus et le Benedictus," 37–9).

87 A point made by Gastoué, *ibid.*, 167.

88 Many such instances can be seen in sources such as Old Hall and the early Trent Codices. Gastoué suggests that, since the time of the troped settings, separation of the Benedictus from what precedes it would have entailed the intoning of at least its opening word by the soloists, cantors or celebrant, just as they had, at various times, likewise intoned the first statement of the repeated first word of the Sanctus (*ibid.*, 36).

89 As Dumoutet noted, "Un jour vint où l'on sentit le besoin de chanter les prières qu'on avait jusqu'alors seulement murmurés" (*Le désir de voir l'hostie*, p. 61).

90 This prayer comprises the last two strophes of the Lauds hymn for Corpus Christi, *Verbum supernum*, itself also widely used as an elevation prayer.

91 See Dumoutet, *Le désir de voir l'hostie*, p. 60, plus discussion on pp. 60–2. See also Jungmann, *The Mass*, vol. II, p. 216; Gastoué, "Le Sanctus et le Benedictus," 164–5; and Long, "Symbol and Ritual," 6.

92 Thus the final "da robur, fer auxilium" gives way to "da pacem, serva lilium" (the latter referring to the *fleur de lis* of France).

93 "Quodque etiam omnibus sextis feriis perpetuis temporibus tempore decantationis 'Sanctus' in summa missa in elevacione immediate post 'Benedictus' cantor ... flexis genibus istam sollempnem antiphonam de venerabili sacramento videlicet 'O s. Convivium etc.' inchoare et chorus eandem ad finem decantare et ista antiphona finita ... versiculum una cum collecta de corpore Christi devote legere debeat" (quoted in Browe, *Die Verehrung*, p. 53, as a representative example of such foundations in late medieval Germany).

94 Both endowments are cited in Dumoutet, *Le désir de voir l'hostie*, pp. 61–2, which goes on to mention similar endowments for the singing of the *Ave verum corpus*.

95 "Item donne mil livres pour dire devant le grand autel chacun jour de lan a la grand messe. auprez dieu leur O salutaris hostia ou O sacrum convivium qui soit dit Devant ou tantost aprez le pater noster. devant agnus dei et ou cas que messeigneurs ne le voeullent permettre ici donne lesdits mil livres." There are two reasons for the supposition that the endowment by Rembert, who maintained an active interest in music throughout his career, was for polyphony: first the staggering sum – £1,000 in money of Artois, more than one eighth of his enormous estate at death – guaranteed for the purpose; and second the endowment of the same sum for the daily performance of the *Salve Regina* by – as we learn from the next entry in the account – "the singers and choirboys" (see Saint-Omer, Bibliothèque Municipale, MS II. G. 484, folio 4v). In fact, as the payments for its performance, entered annually in the fabric accounts, reveal, the performing forces for the *Salve* were no fewer than five male voices and (presumably the full complement of six) choirboys, plus an organist.

96 This supposition is supported by the various payments made at Saint-Omer in the mid-1490s for the copying of new Masses into the "grant livre de discant au coeur." See my article "La musique à la collégiale à la fin du moyen âge," in Nicolette Delanne-Logié and Yves-Marie Hilaire (eds.), *La cathédrale de Saint-Omer: 800 ans de mémoire vive* (Paris: Centre National de la Recherche Scientifique, 2000), p. 136. I will discuss these records in detail in a forthcoming study of music at the collegiate church of St. Omer in the later Middle Ages.

97 This point is underscored by a similar foundation discussed by Barbara Haggh: in his testament of 1486, Philippe Siron, first chaplain of the dukes of Burgundy from 1465 to 1482, endowed funds for the singing by the canons of *O salutaris hostia* at the elevation of High Mass at St. Goedele, Brussels, on unspecified major feast days. See Haggh, "Music, Liturgy and Ceremony in Brussels, 1350–1500," 2 vols., unpublished PhD dissertation, University of Illinois at Urbana-Champaign, 1988, vol. I, p. 174.

98 Gastoué notes that more recent custom was to place the elevation motet, if there was to be one, after the Benedictus (like Rembert's) rather than before it ("Le Sanctus et le Benedictus," 39). Jungmann notes a Roman edict of 1894 to the same effect (*The Mass*, vol. II, p. 217).

99 See Gastoué, "Le Sanctus et le Benedictus," 166–7, which cites a large number of fourteenth- and fifteenth-century chant sources for this composite text, as well as the similar, but this time polyphonic, interpolation of the conductus *Divinum mysterium semper declaratur* in the earlier, predominantly thirteenth-century, Las Huelgas Manuscript (Burgos, Monasterio de Las Huelgas, Codex IX).

100 Ff. 24v-5r and 22v respectively. The texts are as follows: "Ecce panis angelorum/ factus cibus viatorum / vere panis filiorum / non mittendus canibus" (Tenor I: "Sanctus," Osanna); "Bone pas[tor] panis vere / ihu nostri miserere / tu nos pascis [*recte* pasce] nos tuere" (Tenor II: Osanna); the contra part in the Osanna carries the text of "O salutaris hostia." The fact that these extra texts were clearly added later does not alter the general point: the hand appears to be the same and certainly attests to contemporary practice in the Chapel of the "Heilige Stede," built on the site of the Miracle of the Wonderworking Host of Amsterdam, where the codex was in use for many years. See Bernard Huys, "An Unknown Alamire-Choirbook ('Occo Codex') Recently Acquired by the Royal Library of Belgium: A New Source for the History of Music in Amsterdam," *Tijdshrift van de Vereniging voor Nederlandse Muziekgeschiedenis* 42 (1974), 1–19; and Bernard Huys (ed.), *Occo Codex (Brussels, Royal Library Albert I, MS. 1V.922): Facsimile Edition* (Buren, The Netherlands: Vereniging voor Nederlandse Muziekge-schiedenis, 1979).

101 Long, "Symbol and Ritual," 12.

102 My thanks to Rob Wegman for pointing this out to me. See his *Born for the Muses: The Life and Masses of Jacob Obrecht* (Oxford University Press, 1994), pp. 118 and 271.

103 The relationship of the cycles in these sources, which were all compiled for Milan Cathedral, to the local Ambrosian Use remains ambiguous, though the Ambrosian practice of the Canon and the Sanctus are in any case in accordance with those of the Use of Rome. On the issue of the relationship of the Masses in these volumes to the Ambrosian Rite see Howard Mayer Brown, Introduction to *Milan, Archivio della Veneranda Fabbrica del Duomo, Sezione Musicale, Librone 1* (olim 2269) Renaissance Music in Facsimile: Sources Central to the Music of the Late Fifteenth and Sixteenth Centuries, vol. 12a (New York and London: Garland, 1987), p. vi.

104 Compère's *Missa Galeazescha* in Milan 2267 specifies the intended location of each motet, including, on ff. 131v-2r, following *O Maria in supremo* "Loco Sanctus," an *Adoramus te Christe* "Ad elevationem." Similarly the same composer's Mass *sostituita da 8 mottetti* in Milan 2269 juxtaposes a *Salve salvator mundi* "Loco Sanctus" with an *Adoramus te Christe* "ad elevationem" (ff. 166v–8r).

105 Clarifying still further the relative position of the "Verbum caro" setting, the following "Memento salutis auctor" is designated "post elevationem."

106 On the elevation associations of this motet see Long, "Symbol and Ritual," 5 and Jeremy Noble, "The Function of Josquin's Motets," *Tijdschrift van de Vereniging voor Nederlandse Muziekgeschiedenis* 35 (1985), 12. See also the discussion above, Chapter 3.

107 For the contents of this paragraph see the magisterial study of Franz, of which the summary in *Die Messe*, pp. 729–40, gives a useful overview. See also Jungmann, *The Mass*, vol. I, pp. 107–18.

108 On the use of primers and books of hours during Mass, see for example Reinburg, "Popular Prayers," pp. 221–39, and Duffy, *The Stripping of the Altars*, pp. 209–32.

109 For more on the proscription of lay access to the words of the Canon and its effects on Mass exegesis see Franz, *Die Messe*, pp. 628–34.

110 For Durandus the entire Mass is permeated by the presence of Christ, and by the events of his life and death. On this point see Douteil, *Studien*, pp. 39–40. In Durandus's own words: "Porro misse officium tam provida reperitur ordinatione dispositum, ut que per Christum et in Christum ex quo de celo descendit, usque dum in celum ascendit, gesta sunt, magna ex parte contineat et ea tam verbis quam signis admirabili quadam specie representat." (IV 1, 11.12). See *Guillelmi Duranti Rationale divinorum officiorum*, ed. A. Davril and T. M. Thibodeau, Corpus Christianorum, continuatio mediaevalis CXL, CXL A, CXL B, 3 vols. (Turnhout: Brepols, 1995, 1998, 2000), vol. I, p. 242.

111 On the former see Franz, *Die Messe*, pp. 704–6, 735; also discussed in Jungmann, *The Mass*, vol. I, p. 115. On the latter see Duffy, *The Stripping of the Altars*, p. 119. For the full text see Wickham Legg, *Tracts on the Mass*, p. 19.

112 See Bossy, "The Mass as a Social Institution."

113 Jungmann's wording (*The Mass*, vol. I, p. 122). See the discussion and extensive quotation of the original in Franz, *Die Messe*, pp. 486–90. Liebenegg's position is clearly stated at the outset of his consideration of Mass: "Missa sacramento seruit specialiter isti, Cuius ad ornatum patres hanc constituerunt" (*ibid.*, p. 488).

114 Jungmann, *The Mass*, vol. I, p. 122.

115 Bossy, "The Mass as a Social Institution," 54. For Honorius's allegorical interpretation of the communal affirmation symbolized by the conclusion of Mass see Chapter 5.

116 On the St. Donatian endowment see Reinhard Strohm, "Music in Late Medieval Bruges" (Oxford University Press, 2nd rev. edn., 1990), pp. 146–7. On the similar link between the same composer's Mass for St. Martin and an endowment by his musician colleague Pierre Basin see *ibid.*, pp. 40–1.

117 On this point see Duffy, *The Stripping of the Altars*, p. 114.

118 See above, note 39.

119 Donaes's *Lamentation Triptych*, by the Master of the St. Lucy Legend, is preserved in the Thyssen-Bornemisza Collection, Madrid. See the description

and reproductions in Colin T. Eisler, *Early Netherlandish Painting: The Thyssen-Bornemisza Collection* (London: P. Wilson for Sotheby's Publications, 1989), pp. 116–23, 273. See also M. Jennifer Bloxam, website on the St. Donatian Mass (http://obrechtmass.com/home.php).

Last Things

1 Eamon Duffy, *The Stripping of the Altars: Traditional Religion in England 1400–1580* (New Haven and London: Yale University Press, 1992), p. 92.

2 Bernhard Meier supports his observations by reference to Vicentino, Zarlino and Pontio, the first theorists, beginning in the mid sixteenth century, to discuss the affective associations of major and minor intervals familiar to modern practice. See his *The Modes of Classical Vocal Polyphony* (translation by Ellen Beebe of *Die Tonarten der klassischen Vokalpolyphonie*) (New York: Broude Brothers, 1988), pp. 407–9.

3 Thus Meier invokes "the principle of raising something intrinsically normal to something special, used in the service of word expression, by setting it aside and reserving it" (*ibid.*, p. 415).

4 *Ibid.*, p. 421.

5 Timothy McKinney, "Major and Minor Sonorities and Harmonic Affect in Josquin's Sacred Polyphony," paper presented at the International Conference: New Directions in Josquin Scholarship," Princeton University, October 29, 1999, pp. 1–2, 16–7.

6 For instance McKinney draws attention to the dolefulness seen by Glarean in emphasis on *mi*, which coincides with the recitation point of the lamentation tone. Similarly the C that accompanies the word "excelsis" takes its effect from pushing beyond the top note, B♭, of the lamentation tone. The presence of Phrygian cadences at key points in the text setting makes the same point. (McKinney, "Major and Minor Sonorities," pp. 14–15.)

7 As McKinney notes, "Any present-day interpretation of Glarean's comments must take into account the fact that what was 'apparent' to Glarean's audience might not be as recognizable to a present observer, and that what might seem obvious about the music to a present observer might have been completely foreign to the way Glarean and his audience perceived and thought about music" (*ibid.*, p. 6).

8 See Meier, *Modes*; Patrick Macey, "Josquin and Musical Rhetoric: *Miserere mei, Deus* and other Motets," in Richard Sherr (ed.), *The Josquin Companion* (Oxford University Press, 2000), pp. 485–530.

9 These signifiers of lamentation include use of low tessitura, narrow compass concentrated on small intervals, long note-values cast in "funereal" long-short-short patterns, and, particularly, fauxbourdon-like passages using parallel perfect intervals. Discussions of such procedures are many and varied. See for example Meier, *Modes*; Patrick Macey, "An Expressive Detail in

Josquin's *Nimphes, nappées*," *Early Music* 31 (2003), 400–12; Fritz Feldmann, "Untersuchungen zum Wort-Ton Verhältnis in den Gloria-Credo Sätzen von Dufay bis Josquin," *Musica Disciplina* 8 (1954), 141–71.

10 As McKinney notes, "The difference between hearing in Josquin's day and hearing now lies in the audience's horizons of expectation, in the particular set of associations each audience carries as part of their cultural baggage" ("Major and Minor Sonorities," p. 6.) Though a truism, the observation expressed here will need to be kept sharply in focus if significant progress is to be made in this endeavor.

11 Bonnie J. Blackburn, "Masses on Popular Songs and on Syllables," in Richard Sherr (ed.), *The Josquin Companion*, pp. 60–1.

12 Francisco Salinas, *De musica libri septem* (Salamanca, 1577, pp. 288–9; translation from Robert Stevenson, "Josquin in the Music of Spain and Portugal," in Edward E. Lowinsky and Bonnie J. Blackburn [eds.], *Josquin des Prez: Proceedings of the International Josquin Festival-Conference* [London: Oxford University Press, 1976], pp. 236–7).

13 See this and the associated discussion in Chapter 3.

14 As Anmon Linder has noted in the context of the "War Masses" discussed in Chapter 5, "Contemporary performers had no difficulty in perceiving … topicality … through generic rubrics and contents; they could grasp the link between the sign and the signified easily and almost unconsciously, because these links formed part of their common intellectual heritage. But no modern historian is equipped with these sensitive, almost congenital, antennae; we admit our inability to penetrate the specific meaning(s) of [certain] Masses" (Linder, *Raising Arms: Liturgy in the Struggle to Liberate Jerusalem in the Late Middle Ages* [Turnhout, Brepols, 2003], pp. 292).

Bibliography

Primary sources (pre-eighteenth century)

Ambrose, St., *Sancti Ambrosii Mediolanensis De Fide Ad Gratianum Augusti Libri Quinque*, 181, Patrologia Latina, vol. 16 (Patrologia Latina: The Full Text Database [Chadwyck Healy]).

Selected Works and Letters. Early Church Fathers: Nicene and Post-Nicene Fathers Series II, vol. 10: *Dogmatic Treatises, Ethical Works, and Sermons: Exposition of the Christian Faith*, and *Two Books Concerning Repentence* (www.ccel.org/ccel/schaff/npnf210.toc.html).

Analecta hymnica medii aevi, Guido Maria Dreves and Clemens Blume (eds.), with Henry M. Bannister, 55 vols. (Leipzig: Fues et al., 1886–1922) (abbreviated as Analecta hymnica). Reprinted Frankfurt am Main: Minerva, 1961; indices Bern: Francke, 1978.

Andrieu, Michel (ed.), *Le Pontifical Romain au moyen-âge*, vol. 2: *Le Pontifical de la curie Romaine au XIIIe siècle* (Vatican City: Biblioteca Apostolica Vaticana, 1940).

Le Pontifical Romain au moyen-âge, vol. 3: *Le Pontifical de Guillaume Durand* (Vatican City: Biblioteca Apostolica Vaticana, 1940).

Antoninus, St., *Summa theologica*, 4 vols. (Graz: Akademische Druck- und Verlagsanstalt, 1959).

Aquinas, St. Thomas, *Summa Theologica*, Corpus Thomisticum (www.corpusthomisticum.org/iopera.html).

Summa Theologica, English translation, Christian Classics Ethereal Library (www.ccel.org/ccel/aquinas/summa.html).

Augustine, St., *On Christian Doctrine* (*De doctrina christiana*), English translation from Philip Schaff (ed.), *A Select Library of the Nicene and Post-Nicene Fathers of the Christian Church*, 8 vols. (New York: Christian Literature Publishing Co., 1886) (http://ccat.sas.upenn.edu/jod/augustine.html).

Expositions on the Book of Psalms. By Saint Augustine, Bishop of Hippo, translated, edited, with brief annotations, and condensed from the six volumes of the Oxford translation, by A. Cleveland Cox, from Philip Schaff (ed.), *A Select Library of the Nicene and Post-Nicene Fathers of the Christian Church* (8 vols., New York: Christian Literature Publishing Co., 1886). In *Early Church Fathers: Nicene and Post-Nicene Fathers Series I*, vol. 8 (www.ccel.org/ccel/schaff/npnf108.html).

Sancti Aurelii Augustini Hipponensis Episcopi Enarrationes in Psalmos, Patrologia Latina, vol. 36 (Patrologia Latina: The Full Text Database [Chadwyck Healy]).

Augustodunensis, Honorius, *Honorii Augustodunensis Operum Pars Tertia Liturgica* (Patrologia Latina, vol. 172). *Honorius Augustodunensis: Gemma Animae sive De divinis officiis et antiquo ritu missarum, deque horis canonicis et totius annis solemnitatibus* (Bibl. Patr. XX, p. 1046, ex edit. Melchioris Lotteri, Lipsiensis urbis typographi, anno 1514 data) (Patrologia Latina: The Full Text Database [Chadwyck Healy]).

Beleth, Johannes, *Johannis Beleth Summa de ecclesiasticis officiis,* ed. Herbert Douteil, 2 vols., Corpus Christianorum, Continuatio Mediaevalis 41–41A (Turnhout: Brepols, 1976).

Biel, Gabriel, *Gabrielis Biel: Canonis Misse Expositio,* ed. Heiko A. Oberman and William J. Courtenay, 4 vols. (Wiesbaden: Franz Steiner, 1963).

Bona, Johannes, *Rerum liturgicarum libri duo* (Cologne: Joan. Wilhelmum Friessem Juniorem, 1674).

Chastellain, Georges, *Traité par form d'allégorie mystique sur l'entrée du Roy Louys en nouveau règne,* in Kervyn de Lettenhove (ed.), *Oeuvres de Georges Chastellain,* vol. VII (Brussels: Académie Royale de Belgique, 1865).

Chomel, Vital, "Droit de patronage et pratique religieuse dans l'archevêché de Narbonne au début du XVe siècle," *Bibliothèque de l'école des chartes,* 115 (1957), 58–137.

Durandus, Guillelmus, *The Symbolism of Churches and Church Ornaments: A Translation of the First Book of the Rationale Divinorum Officiorum Written by William Durandus, Sometime Bishop of Mende,* ed. and trans. John Mason Neale and Benjamin Webb, 3rd edn. (London: Gibbings and Co., 1906).

  Guillelmi Duranti Rationale divinorum officiorum, ed. A. Davril and T. M. Thibodeau, Corpus Christianorum, continuatio mediaevalis CXL, CXL A, CXL B, 3 vols. (Turnhout: Brepols, 1995, 1998, 2000).

Dykmans, Marc (ed.), *Le Pontifical Romain revisé au XVe siècle* (Vatican City: Biblioteca Apostolica Vaticana, 1985).

Gaffurius, Franchinus, *Practica musice Franchini Gafori Laudensis* (Milan: Ioannes Petrus de Lomatio, 1496; repr. New York: Broude Brothers, 1979).

Gerbert, Martin, *De cantu et musica sacra a prima ecclesiae aetate usque ad praesens tempus,* 2 vols. (San Blasien: Typis San-Blasiensis, 1774; repr., ed. Othmar Wessely, Graz: Akademische Druck- und Verlagsanstalt, 1968).

Glarean, Heinrich, *Heinrich Glarean: Dodecachordon,* ed. and trans. Clement Miller, Musicological Studies and Documents 6, 2 vols. (n.p.: American Institute of Musicology, 1965).

  Glareanus, Henricus Loritus: Dodekachordon (Basel: H. Petri, 1547; facsimile edition, Hildesheim and New York: Georg Olms, 1969).

Gümpel, Karl-Werner, *Die Musiktraktate Conrads von Zabern,* Akademie der Wissenschaften und der Literatur: Abhandlungen der geistes- und sozialwissenschaftlichen Klasse Jahrgang 1956, No. 4 (Wiesbaden: Franz Steiner, 1956).

Innocent III, *Opera Omnia Innocentii III* (Patrologia Latina, vol. 217). *Innocentii III Romani Pontificis Operum Pars Altera: Sermones, Opuscula. II. Opuscula: Innocentius III Romani Pontificis Mysteriorum Evangelicae Legis et Sacramenti Eucharistiae Libri Sex* (Edit. Opp. Innocentii III, Colon., 1575, in-folio.) (*De sacro altaris mysterio libri sex.*) (*Patrologia latina: The Full Text Database* [Chadwyck Healy]).

Lefèvre, Raoul, *L'Histoire de Jason*, ed. Gert Pinkernell (Frankfurt: Athenäum, 1971).

Luther, Martin, *Luthers Werke: Schriften, 35. Band, Lieder, Haupttext: [Die Lieder Luthers] IV. Certe. 2. Die Gesangbuchvorreden. 4.* Die Vorrede zu der Sammlung der Begräbnis Lieder (1542) (from http://luther.chadwyck.com/english/frames/werke/fulltext).

Mansi, Giovan Domenico, *Sacrorum conciliorum nova et amplissima collectio, cujus Joannes Dominicus Mansi et post ipsius mortem Florentinus et Venetianus editores ab anno 1758 ad annum 1798 priores triginta unum tomos ediderunt, nunc autem continuata et absoluta*, 53 vols. (Florence, 1759–98; repr. Paris: H. Welter, 1901–27).

Manuale ad usum percelebris ecclesie Sarisburiensis ... per Desiderium Maheu (Paris: Desiderium Maheu, 1526). (Available through *Early English Books Online* [Chadwyck-Healey: http://eebo.chadwyck.com]).

Masselin, Jean, *Journal des États Généraux de France, Tenus a Tours en 1484,* trans. A. Bernier (Paris: Imprimerie Royale, 1835).

Mézières, Philippe de, *Le songe du vieil pelerin*, 2 vols., ed. C. W. Coopland (Cambridge University Press, 1969).

Molinet, Jean, *Les faictz et dictz de Jean Molinet*, 3 vols., ed. Noël Dupire, (Paris: Société des anciens textes Français, 1936, 1937, 1939).

Patrologiae cursus completus, series latina, 221 vols., ed. Jacques-Paul Migne (Paris: Migne, etc., 1844–65) (abbreviated as Patrologia Latina). Electronically available as Patrologia latina: The Full Text Database (Chadwyck Healy).

Pontificale Romanum Clementis VIII Pont. Max. Iussu Restitutum Atque Editum Romae, MDXCV (Rome: Parasoli, 1595).

Porta, Balthasar de, *Tractatus de misteriis missae* (Augsburg: Johannes Froschauer, 1501).

Pseudo-Dionysius: The Complete Works, ed. Colm Luibheid and Paul Rorem (Mahwah, NJ: Paulist Press, 1987).

Sabisch, Alfred (ed.), *Acta Capituli Wratislaviensis 1500–1562: Die Sitzungsprotokolle des Breslauer Domkapitels in der ersten Hälfte des 16. Jahrhunderts, Erster Band, 1500–1516*, Erster Halbband 1500–1513 (Cologne and Vienna: Böhlau, 1972).

Schannat, Johann Friedrich, *Concilia Germaniae*, 11 vols. (Cologne: Simon, 1759–90; repr. Aalen: Scientia, 1970–96).

Sicard of Cremona, *Opera Omnia Sicardi* (Patrologia Latina, vol. 213), *Sicardus Cremonensis, Sicardi Cremonensis Episcopi Mitrale seu de Officiis Ecclesiasticis Summa* (Nunc primum in lucem prodit juxta apographum quod asservatur in bibliotheca comitis de l'Escalopier) (Patrologia Latina: The Full Text Database [Chadwyck Healy]).

Simmons, Thomas F. (ed.), *The Lay Folks' Mass Book, or The Manner of Hearing Mass*, Early English Text Society, Original Series, vol. 71 (London: Trübner, 1879; repr. London, New York, Toronto: Oxford University Press, 1968).

(?) Stör, Nikolaus, *Officij misse sacrique canonis expositio* (Strasbourg: Printer of Henricus Ariminensis, c.1476).

Suso, Heinrich, *Wisdom's Watch upon the Hours* [*Horologium Sapientiae*], trans. Edmund Colledge, The Fathers of the Church, Medieval Continuation 4 (Washingon, DC: Catholic University of America Press, 1994).

Tinctoris, Johannes, *Tinctoris: Dictionary of Musical Terms*, trans. and ed. Carl Parrish (New York: Free Press of Glencoe, 1963).

   Liber de arte contrapuncti (1477), ed. Albert Seay, in *Johannis Tinctoris opera theoretica*, Corpus scriptorum de musica, no. 22/2 (Rome: American Institute of Musicology, 1975).

Tinctoris, *Complexus effectuum musices*, translated, annotated and edited by J. Donald Cullington and Reinhard Strohm as "A Compendium of Music's Effects," in *On the Dignity and the Effects of Music*, Institute of Advanced Musical Studies Study Texts, no. 2 (London: King's College London, 1996), pp. 51–80.

(?) Trento, Jean-Baptiste, *Histoire de la Mappe-Monde papistique, en laquelle est declairé tout ce qui est contenu & pourtraict en la grande Table, ou Carte de la Mappe-Monde: Composée par M. Frangidelphe Escorche-Messes* (Luce Nouvelle: Brifaud Chasse-diables, 1567).

Vogel, Cyrille and Reinhard Elze (eds.), *Le Pontifical Romano-Germanique du dixième siècle*, 2 vols. (Vatican City: Biblioteca Apostolica Vaticana, 1963).

Wickham Legg, J., (ed.), *Tracts on the Mass* (London: Henry Bradshaw Society, 1904).

Wordsworth, C. (ed.), *Horae Eboracenses: The Prymer or Hours of the Blessed Virgin Mary, According to the Use of the Illustrious Church of York*, Surtees Society 132 (Durham and London: Quaritch, 1919).

Primary sources (eighteenth–nineteenth centuries)

Ambros, August Wilhelm, *Geschichte der Musik,* vol. II (Leipzig: Leuckart, 1864; 3rd edn., rev. Heinrich Riemann, 1891).

   Geschichte der Musik, vol. III (Leipzig: Leuckart, 1868; 3rd edn., rev. Otto Kade, 1893).

Baini, Giuseppe, *Memorie storico-critiche della vita e delle opere di Giovanni Pierluigi da Palestrina*, 2 vols. (Rome: Società tipografica, 1828; repr., Hildesheim: Georg Olms, 1966).

Brendel, Franz, *Geschichte der Musik* (Leipzig: Heinrich Matthes [F. C. Schilde], 1851).

Burney, Charles, *A General History of Music, From the Earliest Ages to the Present Period* (London: Printed for the Author, 2nd edn., 1789; repr., London: G. T. Foulis, 1935).

Dommer, Arrey von, *Handbuch der Musik-Geschichte* (Leipzig: Grunow, 1868).

Forkel, Johann Nicolaus, *Allgemeine Geschichte der Musik*, vol. II (Leipzig: Schwickertschen, 1801; repr. Graz: Akademische Druck- und Verlagsanstalt, 1967).

Hegel, G. W. F., *Vorlesungen über die Philosophie der Geschichte,* in *Sämtliche Werke,* vol. XI, ed. H. Glockner (Stuttgart: F. Frommann, 1928).

   Aesthetics: Lectures on Fine Art, 2 vols., trans. and ed. T. M. Knox (Oxford University Press, 1975).

Kiesewetter, Raphael Georg, *Geschichte der europäisch-abendländischen oder unserer heutigen Musik* (Leipzig: Breitkopf und Härtel, 1834); transl. by Robert Müller, as *History of the Modern Music of Western Europe, from the First Century of the Christian Era to the Present Day* (London: T. C. Tenby, 1848).

Schilling, Gustav, *Geschichte der heutigen oder modernen Musik. In ihrem Zusammenhange mit der allgemeinen Welt- und Völkergeschichte dargestellt* (Karlsruhe: C. T. Groos, 1841).

Musical editions

Apel, Willi (ed.), *French Secular Compositions of the Fourteenth Century,* vol. 3, Corpus Mensurabilis Musicae 53 ([Rome]: American Institute of Musicology, 1972).

Atlas, Allan (ed.), *The Cappella Giulia Chansonnier (Rome, Biblioteca Apostolica Vaticana, C.G.XIII.27),* 2 vols., Wissenschaftliche Abhandlungen/Musicological Studies 27 (Brooklyn: Institute of Mediaeval Music, 1975–6).

Brown, Howard Mayer (ed.), *A Florentine Chansonnier from the Time of Lorenzo the Magnificent: Florence, Biblioteca Nazionale Centrale MS Banco Rari 229,* Monuments of Renaissance Music 7, 2 vols. (Chicago University Press, 1983).

   Milan, Archivio della Veneranda Fabbrica del Duomo, Sezione Musicale, Librone 1 (olim 2269), Renaissance Music in Facsimile: Sources Central to the Music of the Late Fifteenth and Sixteenth Centuries, vol. 12a (New York and London: Garland, 1987).

Cornago, Johannes, *Johannes Cornago: Complete Works,* ed. Rebecca Gerber, Recent Researches in the Music of the Middle Ages and Early Renaissance 15 (Madison: A-R Editions, 1984).

Du Fay, Guillaume, *Guglielmi Dufay: Opera Omnia II: Missarum Pars Prior,* ed. Heinrich Besseler, Corpus Mensurabilis Musicae 1 (Rome: American Institute of Musicology, 1960).

   Guilielmi Dufay: Opera Omnia IV: Fragmenta missarum, ed. Heinrich Besseler, Corpus Mensurabilis Musicae I (Rome: American Institute of Musicology, 1962).

Des Prez, Josquin, *Werken van Josquin des Près, Motetten* i: 7, no. 24, ed. Albert Smijers (Amsterdam and Leipzig: Vereniging voor Nederlandse Muziekgeschiedenis, 1924).

   The Collected Works of Josquin des Prez, vol. 7: *Masses Based on Secular Polyphonic Songs,* ed. Thomas Noblitt (Utrecht: Koninklijke Vereniging voor Nederlandse Muziekgeschiedenis, 1997).

A Josquin Anthology: 12 Motets, ed. Ross Duffin (Oxford University Press, 1999).

Festa, Costanzo, *Costanzo Festa Opera Omnia*, vol. VII: *Madrigali*, ed. Albert Seay, Corpus Mensurabilis Musicae 25 (Neuhausen-Stuttgart: American Institute of Musicology, 1977).

Harrison, Frank Ll. (ed.), *Polyphonic Music of the Fourteenth Century*, vol. V (Monaco: Éditions de l'Oiseau-Lyre, 1968).

Hughes, Andrew and Margaret Bent (eds.), *The Old Hall Manuscript*, Corpus Mensurabilis Musicae 46, 3 vols. ([Rome]: American Institute of Musicology, 1969–73).

Huys, Bernard (ed.), *Occo Codex (Brussels, Royal Library Albert I, MS. IV.922): Facsimile Edition* (Buren, The Netherlands: Vereniging der Nederlandse Muziekgeschiedenis, 1979).

Kellman, Herbert (ed.), *Vatican City, Biblioteca Apostolica Vaticana, MS Chigi VIII.234* (New York and London: Garland, 1987).

Martini, Johannes, *Johannes Martini: Masses: Part 1: Masses without Known Polyphonic Models*, ed. Murray Steib and Elaine Moohan (Madison: A-R Editions, 1999).

Obrecht, Jacob, *Jacob Obrecht: Collected Works,* ed. Barton Hudson, New Obrecht Edition, vol. 3 (Utrecht: Vereniging voor Nederlandse Muziekgeschiedenis, 1984).

Ockeghem, Johannes, *Johannes Ockeghem: Masses and Mass Sections III: Masses based on secular settings, fascicle 1: Missa Primi toni Presumably by Johannes Touront, Missa Quinti Toni*, ed. Jaap van Benthem (Utrecht: Koninklijke Vereniging voor Nederlandse Muziekgeschiedenis, 2004).

Palestrina: Pope Marcellus Mass: An Authoritative Score, ed. Lewis Lockwood, Norton Critical Scores (New York: Norton, 1975).

Petrucci, Ottaviano, *Ottaviano Petrucci: Canti B numero cinquanta*, ed. Helen Hewitt, Monuments of Renaissance Music 2 (University of Chicago Press, 1967).

Regis, Johannes, *Johannis Regis Opera Omnia* I, ed. Cornelis Lindenburg, Corpus Mensurabilis Musicae 9 (n.p.: American Institute of Musicology, 1956).

Richafort, Jean, *Johannes Richafort: Opera Omnia*, ed. Harry Elzinga, Corpus Mensurabilis Musicae 81 (Neuhausen-Stuttgart: American Institute of Musicology, 1979).

Rore, Cipriano de, *Cipriani Rore Opera Omnia* II: *Madrigalia 5 vocum*, ed. Bernhard Meier, Corpus Mensurabilis Musicae 14 (n.p.: American Institute of Musicology, 1963).

Taruskin, Richard (ed.), *J'ay pris amours: Twenty-Eight Settings in Two, Three, and Four Parts*, Ogni Sorte Editions, RS 5 (Miami: Ogni Sorte, 1982).

Willaert, Adrian *Adriani Willaert: Opera Omnia vol. XIII: Musica Nova, 1559: Madrigalia*, ed. Hermann Zenck and Walter Gerstenberg, Corpus Mensurabilis Musicae 3 (n.p.: American Institute of Musicology, 1966).

Adriani Willaert: Opera Omnia vol. XIV: Madrigali e Canzoni Villanesche, ed. Helga Meier, Corpus Mensurabilis Musicae 3 (Neuhausen-Stuttgart: American Institute of Musicology, 1977).

Secondary literature

Albaric, Michel, "Les Éditions imprimées du *Rationale divinorum officiorum* de Guillaume Durand de Mende," in Pierre-Marie Gy, OP (ed.), *Guillaume Durand, Évêque de Mende (v. 1230–1296): Canoniste, liturgiste et homme politique* (Paris: Éditions du Centre National de la Recherche Scientifique, 1992), pp. 183–200.

Anglo, Sydney, *Spectacle, Pageantry, and Early Tudor Policy* (2nd edn., Oxford and New York: Oxford University Press, 1997).

Atlas, Allan, *Music at the Aragonese Court of Naples* (Cambridge University Press, 1985).

Avril, François, "Interprétations symboliques du combat de Saint-Michel et du dragon," in *Millénaire monastique du Mont Saint-Michel*, 5 vols. (Nogent-sur-Marne: Société Parisienne d'histoire et d'archéologie Normandes, 1967), vol. 3, pp. 39–52.

Barrois, Jean Baptiste Joseph, *Bibliothèque protypographique, ou Librairies des fils du roi Jean: Charles V, Jean de Berri, Philippe de Bourgogne et les siens* (Paris, Strasbourg, London: Treuttel et Würtz, 1830).

Bent, Margaret, "Sources of the Old Hall Music," *Proceedings of the Royal Musical Association* 94 (1967–8), 19–35.

   "A Contemporary Perception of Early Fifteenth-Century Style: Bologna Q15 as a Document of Scribal Editorial Initiative," *Musica Disciplina* 12 (1987), 183–97.

   "A Note on the Dating of the Trémouïlle Manuscript," in Bryan Gillingham and Paul Merkley (eds.), *Beyond the Moon: Festschrift Luther Dittmer* (Ottawa: Institute of Medieval Music, 1990), pp. 217–42.

   "The Late-Medieval Motet," in Tess Knighton and David Fallows (eds.), *A Companion to Medieval and Renaissance Music* (London: Dent, 1992), pp. 114–19.

   "Reflections on Christopher Page's Reflections," *Early Music* 21 (1993), 631–2.

Bent, Margaret and Ian Bent, "Dufay, Dunstable, Plummer: A New Source," *Journal of the American Musicological Society* 22 (1969), 394–434.

Benthem, Jaap van, "Was 'Une mousse de Biscaye' really appreciated by 'L'ami Baudichon'?" *Muziek & Wetenschap* 1 (1991), 175–94.

Berger, Anna Maria, *Medieval Music and the Art of Memory* (Berkeley: University of California Press, 2005).

Besseler, Heinrich, *Bourdon und Fauxbourdon* (Leipzig: Breitkopf und Härtel, 1950).

Bloch, Marc, *The Royal Touch: Sacred Monarchy and Scrofula in England and France*, trans. J. E. Anderson (London: Routledge and Kegan Paul, 1973 [first published in French in 1924]).

Bloxam, M. Jennifer, "A Survey of Late Medieval Service Books from the Low Countries: Implications for Sacred Polyphony, 1460–1520," unpublished PhD dissertation, Yale University, 1987.

   "In Praise of Spurious Saints: The *Missae Floruit Egregiis* by Pipelare and La Rue," *Journal of the American Musicological Society* 44 (1991), 163–220.

"Sacred Polyphony and Local Traditions of Liturgy and Plainsong: Reflections on Music by Jacob Obrecht," in Thomas Forrest Kelly (ed.), *Plainsong in the Age of Polyphony* (Cambridge and New York: Cambridge University Press, 1992), pp. 140–77.

"Obrecht as Exegete: Reading *Factor Orbis* as a Christmas Sermon," in Dolores Pesce (ed.), *Hearing the Motet: Essays on the Motet of the Middle Ages and Renaissance* (New York: Oxford University Press, 1997), pp. 169–92.

"Masses on Polyphonic Songs," in Richard Sherr (ed.), *The Josquin Companion* (Oxford University Press, 2000), pp. 151–209.

"A Cultural Context for the Chanson Mass," in Honey Meconi (ed.), *Early Musical Borrowing* (New York: Routledge, 2003), pp. 7–35.

Blume, Friedrich, *Renaissance and Baroque Music: A Comprehensive Survey*, trans. and ed. M. D. Herter Norton (London: Faber and Faber, 1969).

Bonniwell, William R., *A History of the Dominican Liturgy, 1215–1945* (New York: Joseph F. Wagner, 1945).

Boogaert, Jacques, "Encompassing Past and Present: Quotations and their Function in Machaut's Motets," *Early Music History* 20 (2001), 1–86.

Bossy, John, "The Mass as a Social Institution," *Past and Present* 100 (1983), 29–61.

Bouquet, Marie-Thérèse, "La cappella musicale dei duchi di Savoia dal 1450 al 1500," *Rivista Italiana di Musicologia* 3 (1968), 233–85.

Bowles, Edmund A., "Were Musical Instruments Used in the Liturgical Service during the Middle Ages?" *Galpin Society Journal* 10 (1957), 40–56.

Bradshaw, Paul F., *The Search for the Origins of Christian Worship: Sources and Methods for the Study of Early Liturgy* (2nd edn., Oxford University Press. 2002).

Eucharistic Origins (Oxford University Press, 2004).

Braun, Joseph, *Die liturgische Gewandung im Occident und Orient: nach Ursprung und Entwicklung, Verwendung und Symbolik* (Freiburg im Breisgau: Herder, 1907).

Brothers, Thomas, "Vestiges of the Isorhythmic Tradition in Mass and Motet, ca. 1450–1475," *Journal of the American Musicological Society* 44 (1991), 1–56.

Browe, Peter, *Die Verehrung der Eucharistie im Mittelalter* (Munich: Max Hueber, 1933; repr. Freiburg im Breisgau: Herder, 1967).

Brown, Howard Mayer, "Music and Ritual at Charles the Bold's Court: The Function of Liturgical Music by Busnoys and His Contemporaries," in Paula Higgins (ed.), *Antoine Busnoys: Method, Meaning, and Context in Late Medieval Music* (Oxford University Press, 1999), pp. 53–70.

Brownlee, Kevin, "Machaut's Motet 15 and the *Roman de la Rose*: The Literary Context of *Amours qui a le pouoir/ Faus samblant m'a deceü/ Vidi dominum*," *Early Music History* 10 (1991), 1–14.

Bryant, Lawrence M., *The King and the City in the Parisian Royal Entry Ceremony: Politics, Ritual, and Art in the Renaissance* (Geneva: Droz, 1986).

"Configurations of the Community in Late Medieval Spectacles: Paris and London during the Dual Monarchy," in Barbara A. Hanawalt and Kathryn

L. Beyerson (eds.), *City and Spectacle in Medieval Europe* (Minneapolis and London: University of Minnesota Press, 1994), pp. 3–33.

Bukofzer, Manfred, *Studies in Medieval and Renaissance Music* (New York: Norton, 1950), pp. 217–310.

"*Caput Redivivum*: A New Source for Dufay's *Missa Caput*," *Journal of the American Musicological Society* 4 (1951), 97–110.

"English Church Music of the Fifteenth Century," in Anselm Hughes and Gerald Abraham (eds.), *The New Oxford History of Music*, vol. III (London: Oxford University Press, 1960), pp. 165–213.

Camille, Michael, *Image on the Edge: The Margins of Medieval Art* (Cambridge, MA: Harvard University Press, 1992).

Master of Death: The Lifeless Art of Pierre Remiet, Illuminator (New Haven: Yale University Press, 1996).

Carmen Gómez Muntané, Maria del, *La Música en la casa real Catalano-Aragonesa durante los años 1336–1432*, 2 vols. (Barcelona: Antoni Bosch, 1977).

Caspers, Charles, "The Western Church during the Late Middle Ages: *Augenkommunion* or Popular Mysticism?" in Charles Caspers, Gerard Lukken and Gerard Rouwhorst (eds.), *Bread of Heaven: Customs and Practices Surrounding Holy Communion* (Kampen: Kok Pharos, 1995), pp. 83–97.

The Catholic Encyclopedia, 16 vols., ed. Charles Herbermann, etc. (New York, R. Appleton, c.1907–14). Available online at www.newadvent.org/cathen/.

Chavoutier, Lucien, "Un Libellus Pseudo-Ambrosien sur le Saint-Esprit," *Sacris Erudiri* 11 (1960), 136–92.

Chew, Geoffrey, "The Early Cyclic Mass as an Expression of Royal and Papal Supremacy," *Music and Letters* 53 (1972), 254–69.

Chiffoleau, Jacques, *La comptabilité de l'au-delà: les hommes, la mort et la religion dans la région d'Avignon à la fin du Moyen Âge (vers 1320–vers 1480)* (Rome: École française de Rome, 1980).

Chrimes, S. B., *English Constitutional Ideas in the Fifteenth Century* (Cambridge University Press, 1936).

(ed. and transl.), *Sir John Fortescue: De Laudibus Legum Anglie* (Cambridge University Press, 1949).

Clark, Alice V., "*Concordare cum Materia*: The Tenor in the Fourteenth-century Motet," unpublished PhD dissertation, Princeton University, 1996.

Clive, Harry Peter, "The Calvinist Attitude to Music, and Its Literary Aspects and Sources," *Bibiothèque d'Humanisme et Renaissance* 19 (1957), 80–102, 295–319; 20 (1958), 79–107.

Cohn, Richard and Douglas Dempster, "Hierarchical Unity, Plural Unities: Toward a Reconciliation," in Katherine Bergeron and Philip V. Bohlman (eds.), *Disciplining Music: Musicology and Its Canons* (Chicago and London: Chicago University Press, 1992), pp. 156–81.

Cole, Penny J., "Cambridge, Fitzwilliam Museum, MS McClean 51, Pope Sixtus IV and the Fall of Otranto (August 1480)," in Jacqueline Brown and William P.

Stoneman (eds.), *A Distinct Voice: Medieval Studies in Honor of Leonard E. Boyle* (Notre Dame: University of Notre Dame Press, 1997), pp. 103–20.

Costa, Eugenio, *Tropes et séquences dans le cadre de la vie liturgique au moyen-âge* (Rome: CLV, 1979).

Cross, F. L. and E. A. Livingstone (eds.), *The Oxford Dictionary of the Christian Church* (3rd edn., Oxford and New York: Oxford University Press, 1997).

Cumming, Julie, "The Goddess Fortuna Revisited," *Current Musicology* 30 (1980), 7–23.

Curtis, Gareth, "Brussels, Bibliothèque Royale MS. 5557, and the Texting of Dufay's 'Ecce ancilla domini' and 'Ave regina celorum' Masses," *Acta musicologica* 51 (1979), 73–86.

D'Accone, Frank, *The Civic Muse: Music and Musicians in Siena during the Middle Ages and Renaissance* (Chicago and London: University of Chicago Press, 1997).

Dammann, Rolf, "Geschichte der Begriffsbestimmung Motette," *Archiv für Musikwissenschaft* 16 (1959), 337–77.

Dearmer, Percy, *The Parson's Handbook*, 6th, rev. edn., London and New York: H. Frowe, 1907).

Dewitte, Alfons, "Boek- en bibliotheekwezen in de Brugse Sint-Donaaskerk XIIIe–XVe eeuw," in Jean Luc Meulemeester (ed.), *Sint-Donaas en de voormalige Brugse Katedraal* (Bruges: Jong Kristen Onthaal voor Toerisme, 1978), pp. 61–95.

Dix, Gregory, *The Shape of the Liturgy* (London: Dacre, 1945).

Douteil, Herbert, *Studien zu Durantis "Rationale divinorum officiorum" als kirchenmusikalischer Quelle* (Regensburg: Gustav Bosse, 1969).

Doutrepont, Georges, *Inventaire de la "librairie" de Philippe le Bon (1420)* (Brussels: Commission royale d'histoire, 1906).

Draper, Peter, "Architecture and Liturgy," in Jonathan Alexander and Paul Binski (eds.), *Age of Chivalry: Art in Plantagenet England, 1200–1400* (London: Weidenfeld and Nicolson, 1987), pp. 216–31; notes on pp. 257–8.

Droz, Eugénie and Arthur Piaget (eds.), *Le Jardin de plaisance et fleur de rethorique*, 2 vols., Société des anciens textes français, 59 (Paris: Firmin-Didot, 1910 [facsimile] and 1925 [commentary]).

Dudley, Martin R., "Sacramental Liturgies in the Middle Ages," in Thomas J. Hefferman and E. Ann Matter (eds.), *The Liturgy of the Medieval Church* (2nd edn., Kalamazoo, MI: Medieval Institute Publications, 2005), pp. 193–218.

Duffy, Eamon, *The Stripping of the Altars* (New Haven and London: Yale University Press, 1992).

Duffy, Kathryn Ann, "The Jena Choirbooks: Music and Liturgy at the Castle Church in Wittenberg under Frederick the Wise, Elector of Saxony," 2 vols., unpublished PhD dissertation, University of Chicago, 1995.

Dumoulin, Jean, Michel Huglo, Philippe Mercier and Jaques Pycke (eds.), *La Messe de Tournai: une messe polyphonique en l'honneur de Notre Dame à la cathédrale de Tournai au XIVe siècle*, Publications d'histoire de l'art et d'archéologie à l'Université Catholique de Louvain 64 (Tournai: Archives du Chapitre Cathédral de Tournai, and Louvain-la-Neuve: Université Catholique de Louvain, 1988).

Dumoutet, Édouard, *Le désir de voir l'hostie et les origines de la dévotion au saint-sacrement* (Paris: Gabriel Beauchesne, 1926).

Eagleton, Terry, *The Ideology of the Aesthetic* (Oxford: Blackwell, 1990).

Earp, Lawrence, *Guillaume de Machaut: A Guide to Research* (New York: Garland, 1995).

Erviti, Manuel, "The Motet as an Expression of Sociocultural Value circa 1500," unpublished PhD dissertation, University of Illinois at Urbana-Champaign, 1997.

Fallows, David, "Specific Information on the Ensembles for Composed Polyphony, 1400–1474," in Stanley Boorman (ed.), *Studies in the Performance of Late Medieval Music* (Cambridge University Press, 1983), pp. 109–59.

Dufay (2nd, rev. edn., London: Dent, 1987).

A Catalogue of Polyphonic Songs, 1415–1480 (Oxford University Press, 1999).

"Afterword: Thoughts for the Future," in Richard Sherr (ed.), *The Josquin Companion* (Oxford University Press, 2000), pp. 569–78.

Federov, Vladimir, "Des Russes au concile de Florence, 1438–1439," in Wilfried Brennecke and Hans Haase (eds.), *Hans Albrecht in memoriam* (Kassel, Basel, and London: Bärenreiter, 1962), pp. 27–33.

Feldman, Martha, *City Culture and the Madrigal at Venice* (Berkeley and Los Angeles: University of California Press, 1995).

Fellerer, Karl Gustav, "Church Music and the Council of Trent," *Musical Quarterly* 39 (1953), 576–94.

"Agrippa von Nettesheim und die Musik," *Archiv für Musikwissenschaft* 16 (1959), 77–86.

Fischer, Kurt von, "Neue Quellen zum Einstimmigen Ordinariumszyklus des 14. und 15. Jahrhunderts aus Italien," in Albert Linden (ed.), *Liber Amicorum Charles van den Borren* (Antwerp: Lloyd Anversois, 1964), pp. 60–8.

Foley, Edward, "The Song of the Assembly in Medieval Eucharist," in Lizette Larson-Miller (ed.), *Medieval Liturgy: A Book of Essays* (New York: Garland, 1997), pp. 203–34.

Franz, Adolph, *Die Messe im deutschen Mittelalter* (Freiburg im Breisgau: Herder, 1902; repr. Darmstadt: Wissenschaftliche Buchgesellschaft, 1963).

Fulton, Rachel, "'Quae est ista quae ascendit sicut aurora consurgens?': The Song of Songs as the *Historia* for the Office of the Assumption," *Mediaeval Studies* 60 (1998), 55–122.

Gallagher, Sean, "Models of Varietas: Studies in Style and Attribution in the Motets of Johannes Regis and His Contemporaries," unpublished PhD dissertation, Harvard University, 1998.

Gastoué, Amédée, "Le Sanctus et le Benedictus," *Revue du chant Grégorien* 38 (1934), 163–8; 39 (1935), 12–17, 35–9.

Gérold, Théodore, "Les instruments de musique au moyen âge," *Revue des Cours et Conférences* 32 (1928–9).

Giesey, Ralph E., "The French Estates and the Corpus Mysticum Regni," in *Album Helen Maud Cam* (Louvain and Paris: University of Louvain/Éditions Béatrice-Nauwelaerts, 1960), pp. 155–71.

Gombrich, Ernst, "In Search of Cultural History," in his *Ideals and Idols: Essays on Values in History and in Art* (London: Phaidon, 1979; originally published 1969), pp. 25–59.

Gottlieb, Louis, "The Cyclic Masses of Trent 89," 2 vols., unpublished PhD dissertation, University of California at Berkeley, 1958.

Guenée, Bernard, and Françoise Lehoux, *Les Entrées Royales Françaises de 1328 à 1515* (Paris: Centre National de la Recherche Scientifique, 1968).

Guicharrousse, Hubert, *Les Musiques de Luther* (Geneva: Labor et Fides, 1995).

Guillou, Olivier, "Histoire et sources musicales du *Kyriale* Vatican," *Études Grégoriennes* 31 (2003), 25–43.

Gustavson, Royston, "Hans Ott, Hieronymus Formschneider, and the *Novum et insigne opus musicum (Nuremberg, 1537–1538)*," unpublished PhD dissertation, 2 vols., University of Melbourne, 1999.

Guyot, Bertrand, "Essai de Classement des Éditions du *Rationale*," in Pierre-Marie Gy, OP (ed.), *Guillaume Durand, Évêque de Mende (v. 1230–1296): Canoniste, liturgiste et homme politique* (Paris: Éditions du Centre national de la recherche scientifique, 1992), pp. 201–5.

Haar, James, "A Sixteenth-Century Attempt at Music Criticism," *Journal of the American Musicological Society* 36 (1983), 191–209.

Haberl, Franz X., "Wilhelm du Fay. Monographische Studie über dessen Leben und Werke," *Vierteljahrschrift der Musikwissenschaft* I (1885), 397–530.

    "Das traditionelle Musikprogramm der sixtinischen Kapelle nach den Aufzeichnungen von Andrea Adami da Bolsena," *Kirchenmusikalisches Jahrbuch* XII (1897), 36–58.

Haggh, Barbara H., "Music, Liturgy and Ceremony in Brussels, 1350–1500," 2 vols., unpublished PhD dissertation, University of Illinois at Urbana-Champaign, 1988.

    "The Archives of the Order of the Golden Fleece and Music," *Journal of the Royal Musical Association* 120 (1995), 1–43.

Hamm, Charles and Herbert Kellman (eds.), *Census Catalog of Manuscript Sources of Polyphonic Music 1400–1550*, vol. III ([n.p.]: Hänssler, American Institute of Musicology, 1984).

Harper, John, *The Forms and Orders of the Western Liturgy from the Tenth to the Eighteenth Century* (Oxford University Press, 1991).

Harrán, Don, *In Defense of Music: The Case for Music as Argued by a Singer and Scholar of the Late Fifteenth Century* (Lincoln and London: University of Nebraska Press, 1989).

Harrison, Frank Ll., *Music in Late Medieval Britain* (London: Routledge and Kegan Paul, 1958).

Harrison, Kenneth, "Vitruvius and Acoustic Jars in England during the Middle Ages," *Transactions of the Ancient Monuments Society* 15 (1967–8), 49–58.

Harthan, John, *The Book of Hours* (New York: Thomas Y. Crowell, 1977).

Hegar, Elisabeth, *Die Anfänge der neueren Musikgeschichtsschreibung um 1770 bei Gerbert, Burney und Hawkins* (Strasbourg: Heitz, 1933; repr. Baden-Baden: Valentin Koerner, 1974).

Higgins, Paula, "Antoine Busnois and Musical Culture in Late Fifteenth-Century France and Burgundy," unpublished PhD dissertation, Princeton University, 1987.

Hiley, David, *Western Plainchant: A Handbook* (Oxford University Press, 1993).

Hirsch, Rudolf, "Surgant's List of Recommended Books for Preachers (1502–3)," *Renaissance Quarterly* 20 (1967), 198–210.

Hoppin, Richard H. "Reflections on the Origin of the Cyclic Mass," in Albert Linden (ed.), *Liber amicorum Charles van den Borren* (Antwerp: Lloyd Anversois, 1964), pp. 85–91.

Houdoy, Jules, *Histoire artistique de la cathédrale de Cambrai*, Mémoires de la Société des sciences, de l'agriculture et des arts de Lille, 4th series, vol. VII (Lille: L. Danel, 1880; repr. Geneva: Slatkine, 1972).

Hughes, Jonathan, *The Religious Life of Richard III: Piety and Prayer in the North of England* (Phoenix Mill, Gloucestershire: Sutton, 1997).

Huglo, Michel, *Les Tonaires: Inventaire, Analyse, Comparaison* (Paris: Société Française de Musicologie, 1971).

  Les livres de chant liturgique, Typologie des sources du moyen âge occidental, 52 (Turnhout: Brepols, 1988).

  "Notated Performance Practices in Parisian Chant Manuscripts of the Thirteenth Century," in Thomas Forrest Kelly (ed.), *Plainsong in the Age of Polyphony* (Cambridge University Press, 1992), pp. 32–44.

Huizinga, Johan, *The Autumn of the Middle Ages*, trans. Rodney J. Payton and Ulrich Mammitzsch (University of Chicago Press, 1996).

Huot, Sylvia, *Allegorical Play in the Old French Motet: The Sacred and the Profane in Thirteenth-Century Polyphony* (Stanford University Press, 1997).

Hutton, Ronald, *Stations of the Sun: A History of the Ritual Year in Britain* (New York: Oxford University Press, 1996).

Huys, Bernard, "An Unknown Alamire-Choirbook ('Occo Codex') Recently Acquired by the Royal Library of Belgium. A New Source for the History of Music in Amsterdam," *Tijdshrift van de Vereniging voor Nederlandse Muziekgeschiedenis* 42 (1974), 1–19.

Imesch-Oehry, Kornelia, *Die Kirchen der Franziskanerobservanten in der Lombardei, im Piemont und im Tessin und ihre "Lettnerwände": Architektur und Dekoration* (Essen: Die blaue Eule, 1991).

James, Mervyn, "Ritual, Drama and Social Body in the Late Medieval English Town," *Past and Present* 98 (1983), 3–29.

Jasper, R. C. D. and G. J. Cuming, *Prayers of the Eucharist, Early and Reformed* (London: Collins, 1975).

Jung, Jacqueline E., "Beyond the Barrier: The Unifying Role of the Choir Screen in Gothic Churches," *The Art Bulletin* 82 (2000), 622–57.

"Seeing through Screens: The Gothic Choir Enclosure as Frame," in Sharon E. J. Gerstel (ed.), *Thresholds of the Sacred: Architectural, Art Historical, Liturgical, and Theological Perspectives on Religious Screens, East and West* (Dumbarton Oaks: Harvard University Press, 2006), pp. 184–213.

Jungmann, Joseph, *The Mass of the Roman Rite: Its Origins and Development* (translation, by Francis A. Brunner, of *Missarum Solemnia*), 2 vols. (Westminster, MD: Christian Classics, 1986).

Kantorowicz, Ernst H., *Laudes Regiae: A Study in Liturgical Acclamations and Mediaeval Ruler Worship* (Berkeley and Los Angeles: University of California Press, 1946).

The King's Two Bodies: A Study in Mediaeval Political Theology (Princeton University Press, 1957).

Kellman, Herbert, "Josquin and the Courts of the Netherlands and France," in Edward E. Lowinsky and Bonnie J. Blackburn (eds.), *Josquin des Prez: Proceedings of the International Josquin Festival–Conference* (London, New York, Toronto: Oxford University Press, 1976), pp. 181–216.

Kemp, Wolfgang, *The Narratives of Gothic Stained Glass,* transl. Caroline Dobson Salzwedel (Cambridge University Press, 1997); first published in German as *Sermo Corporeus: Die Erzählung der mittelalterlichen Glasfenster* (Munich: Schirmer/Mosel, 1987).

Kennedy, V. L., "The Moment of Consecration and the Elevation of the Host," *Medieval Studies* 6 (1944), 121–50.

King, Archdale A., *Liturgies of the Religious Orders* (London, New York and Toronto: Longmans, Green and Co., 1955).

Kipling, Gordon, " 'He That Saw It Would Not Believe It': Anne Boleyn's Royal Entry into London," in Alexandra F. Johnson and Wim Hüsken (eds.), *Civic Ritual and Drama* (Amsterdam and Atlanta, GA: Rodopi, 1997), pp. 39–79.

Enter the King: Theatre, Liturgy, and Ritual in the Medieval Civic Triumph (Oxford University Press, 1998).

Kirkman, Andrew, *The Three-voice Mass in the Later Fifteenth and Early Sixteenth Centuries* (London and New York: Garland, 1995).

"Innovation, Stylistic Patterns and the Writing of History: The Case of Bedyngham's Mass *Deuil angouisseux*," in Peter Wright and Marco Gozzi (eds.), *I Codici Musicali Trentini: Nuove scoperte e nuovi orientamenti della ricerca* (Trento: Provincia autonoma di Trento, 1996), pp. 149–75.

"Musical Life at the Collegiate Church of Saint-Omer, Northern France, in the Fifteenth Century," *Humanas (Revista do Instituto de Filosofia e Ciências Humanas da Universidade do Rio Grande do Sul)*, 21/1, pt. 2 (1998), 315–29.

"From Humanism to Enlightenment: Reinventing Josquin," *Journal of Musicology* 17 (1999), pp. 441–58.

"Quinti toni in Context: Currents in Three-voice Mass Writing in the Later Fifteenth Century," in Philippe Vendrix (ed.), *Johannes Ockeghem: Actes du*

Xle Colloque international d'études humanistes (Paris: Klincksieck, 1999), pp. 481–98.

"La musique à la collégiale à la fin du moyen âge," in Nicolette Delanne-Logié and Yves-Marie Hilaire (eds.), *La cathédrale de Saint-Omer: 800 ans de mémoire vive* (Paris: Centre National de la Recherche Scientifique, 2000), pp. 133–8.

"'Under Such Heavy Chains': The Discovery and Evaluation of Late Medieval Music before Ambros," *Nineteenth Century Music* 24 (2000), 89–112.

"The invention of the Cyclic Mass," *Journal of the American Musicological Society*, 54/1 (Spring, 2001), 1–47.

"Personal Endowment: The Economic Engine of the 'Cyclic' Mass?" in Bruno Bouckaert (ed.), *Yearbook of the Alamire Foundation* 7 (2008), 71–81.

Kisby, Fiona, "Music and Musicians of Early Tudor Westminster," *Early Music* 23 (1995), 223–40.

Kommission für den Gesamtkatalog der Wiegendrucke (eds.), *Gesamtkatalog der Wiegendrucke* (Leipzig: K. W. Hiersemann, 1925–).

Kreitner, Kenneth, "Music in the Corpus Christi Procession of Barcelona," *Early Music History* 14 (1995), 153–204.

Krummacher, Friedhelm, "Wissenschaftsgeschichte und Werkrezeption: Die 'alten Niederländer' im 19. Jahrhundert," in Hermann Danuser and Friedhelm Krummacher (eds.), *Rezeptionsästhetik und Rezeptionsgeschichte in der Musikwissenschaft* (Laaber: Laaber Verlag, c1991), pp. 205–22.

Lane, Barbara G., *The Altar and the Altarpiece: Sacramental Themes in Early Netherlandish Painting* (New York: Harper and Row, 1984).

Laurens, Pierre, *L'Abeille dans l'ambre: Célébration de l'épigramme de l'époque alex-andrine à la fin de la Renaissance* (Paris: Les Belles Lettres, 1989).

Le Carou, P. Arsène, *L'office divin chez les frères mineurs au xiiie siècle: Son origine, sa destinée* (Paris: P. Lethielleux, 1928).

Leech-Wilkinson, Daniel, *Compositional Techniques in the Four-part Isorhythmic Motets of Philippe de Vitry and His Contemporaries*, 2 vols. (New York and London: Garland, 1989).

Machaut's Mass: An Introduction (Oxford University Press, 1990).

Le Goff, Jacques, *The Birth of Purgatory* (English edition, trans. Arthur Goldhammer, University of Chicago Press, 1981).

Lenkeith, Nancy, *Dante and the Legend of Rome* (London: Warburg Institute, 1952).

Lestringant, Frank, "L'Histoire de la Mappe-Monde papistique," *Comptes rendus des séances de l'Académie des inscriptions et belles-lettres* 3 (July–October 1998), 699–730.

Lewcock, Ronald, Rijn Pirn and Jürgen Meyer, "Acoustics," Grove Music Online. Oxford Music Online. 24 November 2008.

Linder, Anmon, *Raising Arms: Liturgy in the Struggle to Liberate Jerusalem in the Late Middle Ages* (Turnhout: Brepols, 2003).

Litterick, Louise, "Chansons for Three and Four Voices," in Richard Sherr (ed.), *The Josquin Companion* (Oxford University Press, 2000), pp. 335–91.

Lockwood, Lewis, "Aspects of the 'L'homme armé' Tradition," *Proceedings of the Royal Musical Association* 100 (1973–4), 97–122.

Music in Renaissance Ferrara (Oxford University Press, 1984).

Long, Michael P., "Symbol and Ritual in Josquin's *Missa di Dadi*," *Journal of the American Musicological Society* 42 (1989), 1–22.

"*Arma virumque cano*: Echoes of a Golden Age," in Paula Higgins (ed.), *Antoine Busnoys: Method, Meaning and Context in Late Medieval Music* (Oxford and New York: Oxford University Press, 1996), pp. 133–54.

Ložar, Paula (trans.), "The Prologue to the Ordinances of the York Corpus Christi Guild," *Allegorica* 1 (1976), 104–9,

Lütteken, Laurenz, "Ritual und Krise: Die neapolitanischen 'L'homme armé'-Zyklen und die Semantik der Cantus firmus-Messe," in Hermann Danuser and Tobias Plebuch (eds.), *Musik als Text: Bericht über den Internationalen Kongreß der Gesellschaft für Musikforschung Freiburg im Breisgau 1993* (Kassel: Bärenreiter, 1998), pp. 207–18.

Macey, Patrick, "Josquin's 'Little' Ave Maria: A Misplaced Motet from the *Vultum tuum* Cycle?" *Tijdschrift van de Vereniging voor Nederlandse Muziekgeschiedenis* 29 (1989), 38–53.

"Josquin's 'Misericordias Domini' and Louis XI," *Early Music* 19 (1991), 163–77.

"Josquin as Classic: *Qui habitat*, *Memor esto*, and Two Imitations Unmasked," *Journal of the Royal Musical Association* 118 (1993), 1–43.

"An Expressive Detail in Josquin's *Nimphes, nappés*," *Early Music* 31 (2003), 401–11.

Maniates, Maria Rika, "Combinative Techniques in Franco-Flemish Polyphony: A Study of Mannerism in Music from 1450–1530," unpublished PhD dissertation, Columbia University, 1965.

Marix, Jeanne, *Histoire de la Musique et des Musiciens de la Cour de Bourgogne sous le règne de Philippe le Bon* (Strasbourg: Heitz, 1939; repr. Geneva: Minkoff, 1972).

Mateer, David and Elizabeth New, "'In Nomine Jesu': Robert Fayrfax and the Guild of the Holy Name in St. Paul's Cathedral," *Music and Letters* 81 (2000), 507–19.

McKinney, Timothy, "Major and Minor Sonorities and Harmonic Affect in Josquin's Sacred Polyphony," paper read at the International Conference: New Directions in Josquin Scholarship, Princeton University, October 29, 1999.

McKinnon, James W., "Representations of the Mass in Medieval and Renaissance Art," *Journal of the American Musicological Society* 31 (1978), 21–52.

McNamee, Maurice B., *Vested Angels: Eucharistic Allusions in Early Netherlandish Paintings* (Leuven: Peeters, 1998).

Meconi, Honey, "Art-song Reworkings: An Overview," *Journal of the Royal Musical Association* 119 (1994), 1–42.

Meier, Bernhard, *The Modes of Classical Vocal Polyphony*, trans. Ellen Beebe (New York: Broude, 1988); first published in German as *Die Tonarten der klassischen Vokalpolyphonie: nach den Quellen dargestellt* (Utrecht : Oosthoek, Scheltema & Holkema, 1974).

Metzger, Bruce M. and Michael D. Coogan, (eds.), *The Oxford Companion to the Bible* (New York and Oxford: Oxford University Press, 1993).

Milsom, John, "*Circumdederunt*: 'A Favourite Cantus Firmus of Josquin's'?" *Soundings* 9 (1982), 2–10.

"Motets for Five or More Voices," in Richard Sherr (ed.), *The Josquin Companion*, (Oxford University Press, 2000), pp. 281–320.

"Sense and Sound in Richafort's Requiem," *Early Music* 30 (2002), 447–63.

Mitchell, Robert J., "The Paleography and Repertory of Trent Codices 89 and 91, together with Analyses and Editions of Six Mass Cycles by Franco-Flemish Composers from Trent Codex 89," unpublished PhD dissertation, University of Exeter, 1989.

Monson, Craig, "The Council of Trent Revisited," *Journal of the American Musicological Society* 55 (2002), 1–38.

Naegele, Philipp Otto, "August Wilhelm Ambros: His Historical and Critical Thought," unpublished PhD dissertation, Princeton University, 1954.

Noble, Jeremy, "The Function of Josquin's Motets," *Tijdschrift van de Vereniging voor Nederlandse Muziekgeschiedenis* 35 (1985), 9–22.

O' Meara, Carra Ferguson, *Monarchy and Consent: The Coronation Book of Charles V of France* (London/Turnhout: Harvey Miller, 2001).

Osthoff, Helmuth, "'Wohlauf, gut G'sell von hinnen!': ein Beispiel deutsch-französischer Liedgemeinschaft um 1500," *Jahrbuch für Volksliedforschung* 8 (1951), 128–36.

Theatergesang und darstellende Musik (Tutzing: H. Schneider, 1969).

Owens, Jessie Ann, "Music Historiography and the Definition of 'Renaissance,'" *Notes* 47 (1990), 305–30.

Page, Christopher, *The Owl and the Nightingale: Musical Life and Ideas in France, 1100–1300* (London: Dent, 1989).

Discarding Images: Reflections on Music and Culture in Medieval France (Oxford: Oxford University Press, 1993).

"Johannes de Grocheio on Secular Music," *Plainsong and Medieval Music* 2 (1993), 17–41.

"A Reply to Margaret Bent," *Early Music* 22 (1994), 130–1.

Parker, Elizabeth C., "Architecture as Liturgical Setting," in Thomas J. Heffernan and E. Ann Matter (eds.), *The Liturgy of the Medieval Church* (2nd edn., Kalamazoo, MI: Medieval Institute Publications, 2005), pp. 270–4.

Peverada, Enrico, *Vita musicale nella chiesa Ferrarese del quattrocento* (Ferrara: Capitolo Cattedrale, 1991).

Pfaff, Richard, *New Liturgical Feasts in Later Medieval England* (Oxford University Press, 1970).

Medieval Latin Liturgy: A Select Bibliography (Toronto: University of Toronto Press, 1982).

Pirro, André, *La musique à Paris sous le règne de Charles VI (1380–1422)* (2nd edn., Strasbourg, Baden-Baden: Heitz, 1958).

Pirrotta, Nino, "Music and Cultural Tendencies in Fifteenth-century Italy," *Journal of the American Musicological Society* 19 (1966), 127–61.

Planchart, Alejandro Enrique, "Guillaume Dufay's Masses: Notes and Revisions," *Musical Quarterly* 58 (1972), 1–23.

"Fifteenth-century Masses: Notes on Performance and Chronology," *Studi musicali* 10 (1981), 3–29.

"Parts with Words and Parts without Words: The Evidence for Multiple Texts in Fifteenth-century Masses," in Stanley Boorman (ed.), *Studies in the Performance of Late Medieval Music* (Cambridge University Press, 1983), pp. 227–51.

"Guillaume Du Fay's Benefices and His Relationship to the Court of Burgundy," *Early Music History* 8 (1988), 117–71.

"Masses on Plainsong Cantus Firmi," in Richard Sherr (ed.), *The Josquin Companion* (Oxford University Press, 2000), pp. 89–150.

Polk, Keith, *German Instrumental Music of the Late Middle Ages: Players, Patrons and Performance Practice* (Cambridge University Press, 1992).

Prizer, William, "Music and Ceremonial in the Low Countries: Philip the Fair and the Order of the Golden Fleece," *Early Music History* 5 (1985), 113–53.

"The Order of the Golden Fleece and Music," paper read at the meeting of the American Musicological Society, Vancouver, 1985.

"Frottola and the Unwritten Tradition," *Studi musicali* 15 (1986), 3–37.

Rankin, Susan, "The Divine Truth of Scripture: Chant in the *Roman de Fauvel*," *Journal of the American Musicological Society* 47 (1994), 203–43.

Rastall, Richard, "Minstrelsy, Church and Clergy in Medieval England," *Proceedings of the Royal Musical Association* 97 (1970–1), 83–98.

"Music for a Royal Entry, 1474," *Musical Times* 118 (1977), 463–6.

Reese, Gustave, *Music in the Renaissance* (London: Dent, 1954).

Reinburg, Virginia, "Popular Prayers in Late Medieval and Reformation France," unpublished PhD dissertation, Princeton University, 1985.

"Liturgy and the Laity in Late Medieval and Reformation France," *Sixteenth Century Journal* 23 (1992), 526–47.

Reynolds, Christopher, "The Counterpoint of Allusion in Fifteenth-century Masses," *Journal of the American Musicological Society* 45 (1992), 228–60.

Papal Patronage and the Music of St. Peter's, 1380–1513 (Berkeley, Los Angeles and London: University of California Press, 1995).

Robertson, Anne Walters, "Remembering the Annunciation in Medieval Polyphony," *Speculum* 70 (1995), 275–304.

Guillaume de Machaut and Reims: Context and Meaning in His Musical Works (Cambridge University Press, 2002).

"The Savior, the Woman, and the Head of the Dragon in the *Caput* Masses and Motet," *Journal of the American Musicological Society* 59 (2006), 537–630.

Robinson, Christopher, " 'Excellent, New and Uniforme': Perpendicular Architecture *c.*1400–1547," in Richard Marks and Paul Williamson (eds.), *Gothic: Art for England 1400–1547* (London: V&A Publications, 2003), pp. 98–119.

Roper, Sally Elizabeth, "Medieval English Benedictine Liturgy: Studies in the Formation, Structure, and Content of the Monastic Votive Office, *c.* 950–1540," (New York and London: Garland, 1993).

Rorem, Paul, *Pseudo-Dionysius: A Commentary on the Texts and an Introduction to Their Influence* (New York and Oxford: Oxford University Press, 1993).

Rosenthal, Joel, *The Purchase of Paradise: Gift Giving and the Aristocracy, 1307–1485* (London: Routledge and Kegan Paul / Toronto: University of Toronto Press, 1972).

Rosser, Gervase, "Going to the Fraternity Feast: Commensality and Social Relations in Late Medieval England," *Journal of British Studies* 33 (1994), 430–46.

Roth, Adalbert, *Studien zum frühen Repertoire der päpstlichen Kapelle unter dem Pontificat Sixtus' IV (1471–1484): Die Chorbücher 14 und 51 des Fondo Cappella Sistina der Biblioteca Apostolica Vaticana* (Vatican City: Biblioteca Apostolica Vaticana, 1991).

"Liturgical (and Paraliturgical) Music in the Papal Chapel towards the End of the Fifteenth Century," in Richard Sherr (ed.), *Papal Music and Musicians in Late Medieval and Renaissance Rome* (Oxford University Press, 1998), pp. 125–37.

Rothenberg, David, "Marian Feasts, Seasons, and Songs in Medieval Polyphony: Studies in Musical Symbolism," unpublished PhD dissertation, Yale University, 2004.

Rubin, Miri, *Corpus Christi: The Eucharist in Late Medieval Culture* (Cambridge University Press, 1991).

Sadie, Stanley, ed. *The New Grove Dictionary of Music and Musicians*, 2nd edn., 27 vols. (London: Macmillan, 2001).

The Saint Andrew Daily Missal (Bruges: Abbey of St. Andrew; and St. Paul, MN: E. M. Lohmann, 1958).

Salmon, Dom Pierre, *L'office divin au moyen âge: Histoire de la formation du bréviaire du IXe au XVIe siècle*, Lex Orandi 43 (Paris: Cerf, 1967).

Saunders, Suparmi, *The Dating of the Trent Codices from Their Watermarks, with a Study of the Local Liturgy of Trent in the Fifteenth Century* (New York and London: Garland, 1989).

Schrade, Leo, "The Mass of Toulouse," *Revue Belge de Musicologie* 8 (1954), 84–96.

"News on the Chant Cycle of the *Ordinarium Missae*," *Journal of the American Musicological Society* 8 (1955), 66–9.

"The Cycle of the Ordinarium Missae," in H. Anglès, et al. (eds.), *In Memoriam Jacques Handschin* (Strasburg: P. H. Heitz, 1962), pp. 87–96.

Schuler, Manfred, "Die Musik in Konstanz während des Konzils 1414–1418," *Acta Musicologica* 38 (1966), 150–68.

Sherr, Richard, "From the Diary of a Sixteenth-century Papal Singer," *Current Musicology* 25 (1978), 83–98.

Sörries, Reiner, *Die Alpenländischer Fastentücher* (Klagenfurt: Universitätsverlag, 1988).

Sparks, Edgar H., *Cantus Firmus in Mass and Motet* (Berkeley: University of California Press, 1963).

Spinks, Bryan D., *The Sanctus in the Eucharistic Prayer* (Cambridge University Press, 1991).

Stäblein, Bruno, *Messe, A. Die lat. Messe*, in Friedrich Blume (ed.), *Die Musik in Geschichte und Gegenwart*, 17 vols. (Kassel, London and New York: Bärenreiter, 1949–86), vol. 9, cols. 149–58.

Staehelin, Martin, "Beschreibungen und Beispiele musikalischer Formen in einem unbeachteten Traktat des frühen 15. Jahrhunderts," *Archiv für Musikwissenschaft* 31 (1974), 237–42.

Stenzl, Jürg, "'In das Reich der schönen Kunst ganz einzutreten, war ihm nicht beschieden': zur Josquin-Reception im 19. Jahrhundert," in Heinz-Klaus Metzger and Rainer Riehn (eds.), *Musik Konzepte 26/27: Josquin des Prés* (Munich: Johannesdruck Hans Pribil, 1982), pp. 85–101.

Stevens, John, *Words and Music in the Middle Ages* (Cambridge University Press, 1986).

Strohm, Reinhard, *Music in Late Medieval Bruges* (Oxford University Press, 2nd, rev. edn., 1990).

   The Rise of European Music (Cambridge and New York: Cambridge University Press, 1993).

   Mass Settings from the Lucca Choirbook, Early English Church Music 49 (London: Stainer and Bell, 2007).

   "John Hothby, the Lucca Codex – and Further Dragons' Heads?" *Acta Musicologica* 80 (2008), 59–66.

Stubblebine, James H., *Assisi and the Rise of Vernacular Art* (New York: Harper and Row, 1985).

Sundt, R. A., "*Mediocres domos et humiles habeant fratres nostri*: Dominican Legislation on Architecture and Architectural Decoration in the 13th Century," *Journal of the Society of Architectural Historians* 46 (1987), 394–407.

Tanner, Marie, *The Last Descendant of Aeneas* (New Haven and London: Yale University Press, 1993).

Thompson, A. H., *The English Clergy and Their Organisation in the Later Middle Ages* (Oxford University Press, 1947).

Tracy, Charles, "Choir-stalls from the 14th-Century Whitefriars Church in Coventry," *Journal of the British Archaeological Association* 90 (1997), 76–95.

   "The Choir-Stalls," in Charmian Woodfield (ed.), *The Church of Our Lady of Mount Carmel and Some Conventual Buildings at the Whitefriars, Coventry*, BAR British Series 389 (Oxford: Hadrian Books, 2005), pp. 166–83.

Tudor-Craig, Pamela, "Richard III's Triumphant Entry into York, August 29, 1483," in Rosemary Horrox (ed.), *Richard III and the North*, Studies in Regional and Local History 6 (Hull: Centre for Regional and Local History, 1986), pp. 108–16.

Vallance, Aymer, *Greater English Church Screens, Being Great Roods, Screenwork and Rood-Lofts in Cathedral, Monastic, and Collegiate Churches in England and Wales* (London and New York: Batsford, 1947).

Van Dijk, Stephen J. P. (ed.), *Sources of the Modern Roman Liturgy*, 2 vols. (Leiden: E. J. Brill, 1963).

Van Dijk, Stephen J. P. and Joan Hazelden Walker, *The Origins of the Modern Roman Liturgy: The Liturgy of the Papal Court and the Franciscan Order in the Thirteenth Century* (London: Darton, Longman and Todd, 1960).

Vaughan, Richard, *Charles the Bold: The Last Valois Duke of Burgundy* (London: Longman, 1973).

Vogel, Cyrille, *Medieval Liturgy: An Introduction to the Sources* (Washington: Pastoral, 1981).

Wagner, Peter, *Geschichte der Messe: I. Teil: Bis 1600* (Leipzig: Breitkopf und Härtel, 1913).

Walker, Thomas, "A Severed Head: Notes on a Lost English *Caput* Mass," paper read at the Thirty-Fifth Annual Meeting of the American Musicological Society, St Louis, Missouri, December 27–29, 1969.

Warmington, Flynn, "*Abeo semper Fortuna regressum*: Evidence for the Venetian Origin of the Manuscripts Cappella Sistina 14 and 51," paper read at the 22nd Conference on Medieval and Renaissance Music, Glasgow, 10 July 1994.

"The Ceremony of the Armed Man: The Sword, the Altar, and the *L'homme armé* Masses," in Paula Higgins (ed.), *Antoine Busnoys: Method, Meaning, and Context in Late Medieval Music* (Oxford and New York: Oxford University Press, 1996), pp. 89–130.

Weber, Horst, "Varietas, variatio / Variation, Variante," in Hans Heinrich Eggebrecht (ed.), *Handwörterbuch der musikalischen Terminologie*, 14. Auslieferung (Stuttgart: Franz Steiner, Winter 1986–7), 1–48.

Wegman, Rob C., "Music and Musicians at the Guild of Our Lady in Bergen op Zoom, *c.*1470–1510," *Early Music History* 9 (1990), 175–249.

"Petrus de Domarto's *Missa Spiritus almus* and the Early History of the Four-voice Mass in the Fifteenth Century," *Early Music History* 10 (1991), 235–303.

Born for the Muses: The Life and Masses of Jacob Obrecht (Oxford University Press, 1994).

"*Miserere supplicanti Dufay*: The Creation and Transmission of Guillaume Dufay's *Missa Ave regina celorum*," *Journal of Musicology* 13 (1995), 18–54.

Weinmann, Karl, *Das Konzil von Trient und die Kirchenmusik* (Leipzig: Breitkopf & Härtel, 1919).

Welter, Jean-Thiébaut, *L'Exemplum dans la littérature religieuse et didactique du moyen âge* (Paris and Toulouse: Occitania, 1927; repr. Geneva: Slatkine, 1973).

Wicks, Robert, "Hegel's Aesthetics: An Overview," in Frederick C. Beiser (ed.), *The Cambridge Companion to Hegel* (Cambridge University Press, 1993), pp. 358–77.

Williamson, Magnus, "Royal Image-making and Textual Interplay in Gilbert Banaster's *O Maria et Elizabeth*," *Early Music History* 19 (2000), 237–78.

Wilmart, André, *Auteurs spirituels et textes dévots du moyen âge Latin: études d'histoire littéraire* (Paris: Études Augustiniennes, 1971).

Withington, Robert, *English Pageantry: An Historical* Outline, 2 vols., (New York: Benjamin Blom, 1918; repr. Cambridge, MA: Harvard University Press, 1963.)

Woodley, Ronald, "Johannes Tinctoris: A Review of the Documentary Evidence," *Journal of the American Musicological Society* 34 (1981), 217–48.

"Tinctoris's Italian Translation of the Golden Fleece Statutes: A Text and a (Possible) Context," *Early Music History* 8 (1988), 173–244.

Wright, Craig, "Dufay at Cambrai: Discoveries and Revisions," *Journal of the American Musicological Society* 28 (1975), 175–229.

Music at the Court of Burgundy, 1364–1419: A Documentary History (Henryville: Institute of Medieval Music, 1979).

Music and Ceremonial at Notre Dame of Paris 500–1550 (Cambridge University Press, 1989).

"Dufay's *Nuper rosarum flores*, King Solomon's Temple, and the Veneration of the Virgin," *Journal of the American Musicological Society* 47 (1994), 395–441.

The Maze and the Warrior (Cambridge, MA and London: Harvard University Press, 2001).

Wright, Peter, "Johannes Wiser's Paper and the Copying of His Manuscripts," in Peter Wright (ed.), *I Codici Musicali Trentini: Nuove scoperte e nuovi orientamenti della ricerca* (Trento: Provincia autonoma di Trento, 1996), pp. 31–53.

"Watermarks and Musicology: The Genesis of Johannes Wiser's Collection," *Early Music History* 22 (2003), 247–332.

Žak, Sabine, "Die Quellenwert von Giannozzo Manettis Oratio über die Domweihe von Florenz 1436 für die Musikgeschichte," *Die Musikforschung* 40 (1987), 2–32.

Zika, Charles, "Hosts, Processions and Pilgrimages in Fifteenth-century Germany," *Past and Present* 118 (1988), 25–64

Index